AWS Glue Developer Guide

A catalogue record for this book is available from the Hong Kong Public Libraries.

Published in Hong Kong by Samurai Media Limited.

Email: info@samuraimedia.org

ISBN 9789888407699

Contents

What Is AWS Glue?   24
   When Should I Use AWS Glue? 24

AWS Glue: How It Works   25
   Serverless ETL Jobs Run in Isolation 25

AWS Glue Concepts   26
   AWS Glue Terminology 27
      AWS Glue Data Catalog 27
      Table 27
      Crawler 27
      Classifier 27
      Connection 27
      Database 27
      Job 27
      Script 27
      Transform 28
      Trigger 28
      Development endpoint 28
      Notebook server 28

AWS Glue Components   29
   AWS Glue Console 29
   AWS Glue Data Catalog 29
   AWS Glue Crawlers and Classifiers 29
   AWS Glue ETL Operations 30
   The AWS Glue Jobs System 30

Converting Semi-Structured Schemas to Relational Schemas   31

Getting Started Using AWS Glue   33

Setting up IAM Permissions for AWS Glue   34

Step 1: Create an IAM Policy for the AWS Glue Service   35

Step 2: Create an IAM Role for AWS Glue   38

Step 3: Attach a Policy to IAM Users That Access AWS Glue   39

Step 4: Create an IAM Policy for Notebooks   44

Step 5: Create an IAM Role for Notebooks   47

Setting Up DNS in Your VPC   48

Setting Up Your Environment to Access Data Stores   49

Amazon VPC Endpoints for Amazon S3   50

Setting Up a VPC to Connect to JDBC Data Stores   52

Setting Up Your Environment for Development Endpoints   54
   Setting Up Your Network for a Development Endpoint 54

Setting Up Amazon EC2 for a Notebook Server 55

AWS Glue Console Workflow Overview   57

Authentication and Access Control for AWS Glue   59
Authentication 59
Access Control 60

Overview of Managing Access Permissions to Your AWS Glue Resources   61
AWS Glue Resources and Operations 61
Understanding Resource Ownership 61
Managing Access to Resources 61
    Identity-Based Policies (IAM Policies) 62
    Resource-Based Policies 63
Specifying Policy Elements: Actions, Effects, and Principals 63
Specifying Conditions in a Policy 63

Using Identity-Based Policies (IAM Policies) for AWS Glue   64
Permissions Required to Use the AWS Glue Console 64
AWS Managed (Predefined) Policies for AWS Glue 65

AWS Glue API Permissions: Actions and Resources Reference   66
Related Topics 69

Populating the AWS Glue Data Catalog   70

Defining Tables in the AWS Glue Data Catalog   72
Table Partitions 72

Working with Tables on the AWS Glue Console   73
Adding Tables on the Console 73
Table Attributes 73
Viewing and Editing Table Details 74

Cataloging Tables with a Crawler   76
Defining a Crawler in the AWS Glue Data Catalog 76
Which Data Stores Can I Crawl? 76
Using Include and Exclude Patterns 77
What Happens When a Crawler Runs? 79
Are Amazon S3 Folders Created as Tables or Partitions? 80

Configuring a Crawler   81
Configuring a Crawler on the AWS Glue Console 81
Configuring a Crawler Using the API 81
How to Prevent the Crawler from Changing an Existing Schema 83

Scheduling an AWS Glue Crawler   84

Working with Crawlers on the AWS Glue Console   85
Viewing Crawler Results 85

Defining a Database in Your Data Catalog   87

Working with Databases on the AWS Glue Console   88

Adding Classifiers to a Crawler   89
When Do I Use a Classifier? 89

Custom Classifiers 89
Built-In Classifiers in AWS Glue 89
    Built-In CSV Classifier 91

Writing Custom Classifiers   92
Writing Grok Custom Classifiers 92
    Custom Classifier Values in AWS Glue 92
    AWS Glue Built-In Patterns 93
Writing XML Custom Classifiers 96
    Custom Classifier Values in AWS Glue 96
Writing JSON Custom Classifiers 96
    Custom Classifier Values in AWS Glue 97

Working with Classifiers on the AWS Glue Console   102

Adding a Connection to Your Data Store   103
When Is a Connection Used? 103
Defining a Connection in the AWS Glue Data Catalog 103
Connecting to a JDBC Data Store in a VPC 103
    Accessing VPC Data Using Elastic Network Interfaces 104
    Elastic Network Interface Properties 104

Working with Connections on the AWS Glue Console   106
Adding a JDBC Connection to a Data Store 106

Populating the Data Catalog Using AWS CloudFormation Templates   108
Sample AWS CloudFormation Template for an AWS Glue Database 109
Sample AWS CloudFormation Template for an AWS Glue Database, Table, and Partition 110
Sample AWS CloudFormation Template for an AWS Glue Classifier 113
Sample AWS CloudFormation Template for an AWS Glue Crawler for Amazon S3 113
Sample AWS CloudFormation Template for an AWS Glue Connection 115
Sample AWS CloudFormation Template for an AWS Glue Crawler for JDBC 116
Sample AWS CloudFormation Template for an AWS Glue Job for Amazon S3 to Amazon S3 118
Sample AWS CloudFormation Template for an AWS Glue Job for JDBC to Amazon S3 119
Sample AWS CloudFormation Template for an AWS Glue On-Demand Trigger 120
Sample AWS CloudFormation Template for an AWS Glue Scheduled Trigger 121
Sample AWS CloudFormation Template for an AWS Glue Conditional Trigger 122
Sample AWS CloudFormation Template for an AWS Glue Development Endpoint 123

Authoring Jobs in AWS Glue   125
Workflow Overview 125

Adding Jobs in AWS Glue   127
Defining Job Properties 127

Built-In Transforms   129

Working with Jobs on the AWS Glue Console   131
Viewing Job Details 131
    History 132
    Details 132
    Script 132

Editing Scripts in AWS Glue   134
Defining a Script 134

Working with Scripts on the AWS Glue Console   **135**
Script Editor 135

Providing Your Own Custom Scripts   **136**

Triggering Jobs in AWS Glue   **137**
Triggering Jobs Based on Schedules or Events 137
Defining Trigger Types 137

Working with Triggers on the AWS Glue Console   **138**
Adding and Editing Triggers 138

Using Development Endpoints for Developing Scripts   **139**
Managing Your Development Environment 139
How to Use a Development Endpoint 139
Accessing Your Development Endpoint 139

Tutorial Setup: Prerequisites for the Development Endpoint Tutorials   **141**
Crawling the Sample Data Used in the Tutorials 141
Creating a Development Endpoint for Amazon S3 Data 141
Creating an Amazon S3 Location to Use for Output 142
Creating a Development Endpoint with a VPC 142

Tutorial: Set Up a Local Apache Zeppelin Notebook to Test and Debug ETL Scripts   **144**
Installing an Apache Zeppelin Notebook 144
Initiating SSH Port Forwarding to Connect to Your DevEndpoint 144
Running a Simple Script Fragment in a Notebook Paragraph 145
Troubleshooting Your Local Notebook Connection 146

Tutorial: Set Up an Apache Zeppelin Notebook on Amazon EC2   **147**
Creating an Apache Zeppelin Notebook Server on an Amazon EC2 Instance 147
Connecting to Your Notebook Server on Amazon EC2 148
Running a Simple Script Fragment in a Notebook Paragraph 148

Tutorial: Use a REPL Shell with Your Development Endpoint   **150**

Tutorial: Set Up PyCharm Professional with a Development Endpoint   **152**
Connecting PyCharm Professional to a Development Endpoint 152
Deploying the Script to Your Development Endpoint 155
Starting the Debug Server on `localhost` and a Local Port 156
Initiating Port Forwarding 157
Running Your Script on the Development Endpoint 157

Working with Development Endpoints on the AWS Glue Console   **159**
Adding an Endpoint 159
Creating a Notebook Hosted on Amazon EC2 160

Running and Monitoring AWS Glue   **162**
Automated Monitoring Tools 163

Time-Based Schedules for Jobs and Crawlers   **164**
Cron Expressions 164

Job Bookmarks   **166**

Automating AWS Glue with CloudWatch Events   **167**

Logging AWS Glue Operations Using AWS CloudTrail   **168**

AWS Glue Information in CloudTrail 168

CloudTrail Log File Entries for AWS Glue 168

AWS Glue Troubleshooting   **171**

Gathering AWS Glue Troubleshooting Information   **172**

Troubleshooting Connection Issues in AWS Glue   **173**

Troubleshooting Errors in AWS Glue   **174**

Error: Resource Unavailable 174

Error: Could Not Find S3 Endpoint or NAT Gateway for subnetId in VPC 174

Error: Inbound Rule in Security Group Required 174

Error: Outbound Rule in Security Group Required 174

Error: Custom DNS Resolution Failures 174

Error: Job run failed because the role passed should be given assume role permissions for the AWS

     Glue Service 175

Error: DescribeVpcEndpoints Action Is Unauthorized. Unable to Validate VPC ID vpc-id 175

Error: DescribeRouteTables Action Is Unauthorized. Unable to Validate Subnet Id: subnet-id in VPC

     id: vpc-id 175

Error: Failed to Call ec2:DescribeSubnets 175

Error: Failed to Call ec2:DescribeSecurityGroups 175

Error: Could Not Find Subnet for AZ 175

Error: Job Run Exception for Connection List with Multiple Subnet or AZ 175

Error: Job Run Exception When Writing to a JDBC Target 176

Error: Amazon S3 Timeout 176

Error: Amazon S3 Access Denied 176

Error: Amazon S3 Access Key ID Does Not Exist 176

Error: Job run fails when accessing Amazon S3 with an `s3a://` URI 177

Error: No Private DNS for Network Interface Found 178

Error: Development Endpoint Provisioning Failed 178

Error: Notebook Server CREATE_FAILED 178

Error: Local Notebook Fails to Start 179

Error: Notebook Usage Errors 179

Error: Running Crawler Failed 179

Error: Upgrading Athena Data Catalog 179

AWS Glue Limits   **180**

Programming ETL Scripts   **181**

General Information about Programming AWS Glue ETL Scripts   **182**

Special Parameters Used by AWS Glue   **183**

Connection Types and Options for ETL Output in AWS Glue   **184**

"connectionType": "s3" 184

"connectionType": "parquet" 185

"connectionType": "orc" 185

JDBC connectionType values 185

Format Options for ETL Output in AWS Glue   **186**

format="avro" 186

format="csv" 186

format="ion" 186

format="grokLog" 186
format="json" 187
format="orc" 187
format="parquet" 187
format="xml" 187

Managing Partitions for ETL Output in AWS Glue   **188**
Pre-Filtering Using Pushdown Predicates 188
Writing Partitions 189

Reading Input Files in Larger Groups   **190**

Program AWS Glue ETL Scripts in Python   **191**
Using Python with AWS Glue 191
AWS Glue PySpark Extensions 191
AWS Glue PySpark Transforms 191

Setting Up to Use Python with AWS Glue   **192**

Calling AWS Glue APIs in Python   **193**
AWS Glue API Names in Python 193
Passing and Accessing Python Parameters in AWS Glue 193
Example: Create and Run a Job 194

Using Python Libraries with AWS Glue   **195**
Zipping Libraries for Inclusion 195
Loading Python Libraries in a Development Endpoint 195
Using Python Libraries in a Job or JobRun 196

AWS Glue Python Code Samples   **197**

Code Example: Joining and Relationalizing Data   **198**
Step 1: Crawl the Data in the Amazon S3 Bucket 198
Step 2: Add Boilerplate Script to the Development Endpoint Notebook 198
Step 3: Examine the Schemas in the Data Catalog 199
Step 4: Filter the Data 200
Step 5: Put It All Together 202
Step 6: Write the Data to Relational Databases 203
Conclusion 206

Code Example: Data Preparation Using ResolveChoice, Lambda, and ApplyMapping   **207**
Step 1: Crawl the Data in the Amazon S3 Bucket 207
Step 2: Add Boilerplate Script to the Development Endpoint Notebook 207
Step 3: Compare Different Schema Parsings 208
Step 4: Map the Data and Use Apache Spark Lambda Functions 210
Step 5: Write the Data to Apache Parquet 212

AWS Glue PySpark Extensions Reference   **213**

Accessing Parameters Using getResolvedOptions   **214**

PySpark Extension Types   **215**
DataType 215
AtomicType and Simple Derivatives 215
DecimalType(AtomicType) 216
EnumType(AtomicType) 216

Collection Types 216
ArrayType(DataType) 216
ChoiceType(DataType) 216
MapType(DataType) 217
Field(Object) 217
StructType(DataType) 217
EntityType(DataType) 217
Other Types 217
DataSource(object) 218
DataSink(object) 218

DynamicFrame Class   **219**
— Construction — 219
__init__ 219
fromDF 219
toDF 220
— Information — 220
count 220
schema 220
printSchema 220
show 220
— Transforms — 220
apply_mapping 221
drop_fields 221
filter 221
join 222
map 222
relationalize 222
rename_field 223
resolveChoice 223
select_fields 224
spigot 224
split_fields 225
split_rows 225
unbox 225
unnest 226
write 226
— Errors — 227
assertErrorThreshold 227
errorsAsDynamicFrame 227
errorsCount 227
stageErrorsCount 227

DynamicFrameCollection Class   **228**
__init__ 228
keys 228
values 228
select 228
map 228
flatmap 228

DynamicFrameWriter Class   **229**
Methods 229
__init__ 229
from_options 229

  from_catalog 229
  from_jdbc_conf 230

DynamicFrameReader Class   **231**
 — Methods — 231
 ___init___ 231
 from_rdd 231
 from_options 231
 from_catalog 232

GlueContext Class   **233**
 Creating 233
 ___init___ 233
 getSource 233
 create_dynamic_frame_from_rdd 233
 create_dynamic_frame_from_catalog 234
 create_dynamic_frame_from_options 234
 Writing 234
 getSink 234
 write_dynamic_frame_from_options 235
 write_from_options 235
 write_dynamic_frame_from_catalog 236
 write_dynamic_frame_from_jdbc_conf 236
 write_from_jdbc_conf 236

AWS Glue PySpark Transforms Reference   **237**

GlueTransform Base Class   **238**
 Methods 238
 apply(cls, *args, **kwargs) 238
 name(cls) 238
 describeArgs(cls) 238
 describeReturn(cls) 238
 describeTransform(cls) 239
 describeErrors(cls) 239
 describe(cls) 239

ApplyMapping Class   **240**
 Methods 240
 ___call___(frame, mappings, transformation_ctx = "", info = "", stageThreshold = 0, totalThreshold
  = 0) 240
 apply(cls, *args, **kwargs) 240
 name(cls) 240
 describeArgs(cls) 240
 describeReturn(cls) 240
 describeTransform(cls) 241
 describeErrors(cls) 241
 describe(cls) 241

DropFields Class   **242**
 Methods 242
 ___call___(frame, paths, transformation_ctx = "", info = "", stageThreshold = 0, totalThreshold = 0) 242
 apply(cls, *args, **kwargs) 242
 name(cls) 242
 describeArgs(cls) 242

describeReturn(cls) 242
describeTransform(cls) 243
describeErrors(cls) 243
describe(cls) 243

DropNullFields Class   **244**
Methods 244
___call___(frame, transformation_ctx = "", info = "", stageThreshold = 0, totalThreshold = 0) . . . 244
apply(cls, *args, **kwargs) 244
name(cls) 244
describeArgs(cls) 244
describeReturn(cls) 244
describeTransform(cls) 245
describeErrors(cls) 245
describe(cls) 245

ErrorsAsDynamicFrame Class   **246**
Methods 246
___call___(frame) 246
apply(cls, *args, **kwargs) 246
name(cls) 246
describeArgs(cls) 246
describeReturn(cls) 246
describeTransform(cls) 246
describeErrors(cls) 246
describe(cls) 247

Filter Class   **248**
Methods 248
___call___(frame, f, transformation_ctx="", info="", stageThreshold=0, totalThreshold=0)) 248
apply(cls, *args, **kwargs) 248
name(cls) 248
describeArgs(cls) 248
describeReturn(cls) 249
describeTransform(cls) 249
describeErrors(cls) 249
describe(cls) 249
AWS Glue Python Example 249

FlatMap Class   **251**
Methods 251
___call___(dfc, BaseTransform, frame_name, transformation_ctx = "", **base_kwargs) 251
apply(cls, *args, **kwargs) 251
name(cls) 251
describeArgs(cls) 251
describeReturn(cls) 251
describeTransform(cls) 251
describeErrors(cls) 252
describe(cls) 252

Join Class   **253**
Methods 253
___call___(frame1, frame2, keys1, keys2, transformation_ctx = "") 253
apply(cls, *args, **kwargs) 253
name(cls) 253

describeArgs(cls) 253
describeReturn(cls) 253
describeTransform(cls) 253
describeErrors(cls) 254
describe(cls) 254

Map Class **255**
Methods 255
___call___(frame, f, transformation_ctx="", info="", stageThreshold=0, totalThreshold=0) 255
apply(cls, *args, **kwargs) 255
name(cls) 255
describeArgs(cls) 256
describeReturn(cls) 256
describeTransform(cls) 256
describeErrors(cls) 256
describe(cls) 256
AWS Glue Python Example 256

MapToCollection Class **259**
Methods 259
___call___(dfc, BaseTransform, frame_name, transformation_ctx = "", **base_kwargs) 259
apply(cls, *args, **kwargs) 259
name(cls) 259
describeArgs(cls) 259
describeReturn(cls) 259
describeTransform(cls) 259
describeErrors(cls) 260
describe(cls) 260

Relationalize Class **261**
Methods 261
___call___(frame, staging_path=None, name='roottable', options=None, transformation_ctx = "",
info = "", stageThreshold = 0, totalThreshold = 0) 261
apply(cls, *args, **kwargs) 261
name(cls) 261
describeArgs(cls) 261
describeReturn(cls) 262
describeTransform(cls) 262
describeErrors(cls) 262
describe(cls) 262

RenameField Class **263**
Methods 263
___call___(frame, old_name, new_name, transformation_ctx = "", info = "", stageThreshold = 0,
totalThreshold = 0) 263
apply(cls, *args, **kwargs) 263
name(cls) 263
describeArgs(cls) 263
describeReturn(cls) 264
describeTransform(cls) 264
describeErrors(cls) 264
describe(cls) 264

ResolveChoice Class **265**
Methods 265

___call___(frame, specs = None, choice = "", transformation_ctx = "", info = "", stageThreshold = 0, totalThreshold = 0) 265
apply(cls, *args, **kwargs) 266
name(cls) 266
describeArgs(cls) 266
describeReturn(cls) 266
describeTransform(cls) 266
describeErrors(cls) 266
describe(cls) 266

SelectFields Class   **267**
Methods 267
___call___(frame, paths, transformation_ctx = "", info = "", stageThreshold = 0, totalThreshold = 0) 267
apply(cls, *args, **kwargs) 267
name(cls) 267
describeArgs(cls) 267
describeReturn(cls) 267
describeTransform(cls) 268
describeErrors(cls) 268
describe(cls) 268

SelectFromCollection Class   **269**
Methods 269
___call___(dfc, key, transformation_ctx = "") 269
apply(cls, *args, **kwargs) 269
name(cls) 269
describeArgs(cls) 269
describeReturn(cls) 269
describeTransform(cls) 269
describeErrors(cls) 269
describe(cls) 270

Spigot Class   **271**
Methods 271
___call___(frame, path, options, transformation_ctx = "") 271
apply(cls, *args, **kwargs) 271
name(cls) 271
describeArgs(cls) 271
describeReturn(cls) 271
describeTransform(cls) 271
describeErrors(cls) 272
describe(cls) 272

SplitFields Class   **273**
Methods 273
___call___(frame, paths, name1 = None, name2 = None, transformation_ctx = "", info = "", stageThreshold = 0, totalThreshold = 0) 273
apply(cls, *args, **kwargs) 273
name(cls) 273
describeArgs(cls) 273
describeReturn(cls) 274
describeTransform(cls) 274
describeErrors(cls) 274
describe(cls) 274

SplitRows Class   **275**

Methods 275

__call__(frame, comparison_dict, name1="frame1", name2="frame2", transformation_ctx = "",
     info = None, stageThreshold = 0, totalThreshold = 0) 275

apply(cls, *args, **kwargs) 275

name(cls) 275

describeArgs(cls) 275

describeReturn(cls) 276

describeTransform(cls) 276

describeErrors(cls) 276

describe(cls) 276

Unbox Class   **277**

Methods 277

__call__(frame, path, format, transformation_ctx = "", info="", stageThreshold=0, totalThresh-
     old=0, **options) 277

apply(cls, *args, **kwargs) 277

name(cls) 277

describeArgs(cls) 277

describeReturn(cls) 278

describeTransform(cls) 278

describeErrors(cls) 278

describe(cls) 278

UnnestFrame Class   **279**

Methods 279

__call__(frame, transformation_ctx = "", info="", stageThreshold=0, totalThreshold=0) 279

apply(cls, *args, **kwargs) 279

name(cls) 279

describeArgs(cls) 279

describeReturn(cls) 279

describeTransform(cls) 279

describeErrors(cls) 280

describe(cls) 280

Programming AWS Glue ETL Scripts in Scala   **281**

Using Scala to Program AWS Glue ETL Scripts   **285**

Testing a Scala ETL Program in a Zeppelin Notebook on a Development Endpoint 285

Testing a Scala ETL Program in a Scala REPL 285

APIs in the AWS Glue Scala Library   **286**

com.amazonaws.services.glue 286

com.amazonaws.services.glue.types 286

com.amazonaws.services.glue.util 286

MappingSpec 286

     MappingSpec Case Class 287

     MappingSpec Object 287

     val orderingByTarget 287

     def apply 287

     def apply 287

     def apply 288

AWS Glue Scala ChoiceOption APIs   **289**

ChoiceOption Trait 289

ChoiceOption Object 289
    def apply 289
case class ChoiceOptionWithResolver 289
case class MatchCatalogSchemaChoiceOption 289

Abstract DataSink Class   **289**
def writeDynamicFrame 290
def pyWriteDynamicFrame 290
def supportsFormat 290
def setFormat 290
def withFormat 290
def setAccumulableSize 290
def getOutputErrorRecordsAccumulable 290
def errorsAsDynamicFrame 290
DataSink Object 290
    def recordMetrics 291

AWS Glue Scala DataSource Trait   **291**

AWS Glue Scala DynamicFrame APIs   **292**

AWS Glue Scala DynamicFrame Class   **293**
val errorsCount 293
def applyMapping 293
def assertErrorThreshold 294
def count 295
def dropField 295
def dropFields 295
def dropNulls 295
def errorsAsDynamicFrame 295
def filter 295
def getName 296
def getNumPartitions 296
def getSchemaIfComputed 296
def isSchemaComputed 296
def javaToPython 296
def join 296
def map 297
def printSchema 297
def recomputeSchema 297
def relationalize 297
def renameField 298
def repartition 299
def resolveChoice 299
def schema 300
def selectField 300
def selectFields 300
def show 300
def spigot 301
def splitFields 301
def splitRows 301
def stageErrorsCount 302
def toDF 302
def unbox 302
def unnest 303

def withFrameSchema 304
def withName 304
def withTransformationContext 304

The DynamicFrame Object   **304**
def apply 304
def emptyDynamicFrame 304
def fromPythonRDD 305
def ignoreErrors 305
def inlineErrors 305
def newFrameWithErrors 305

AWS Glue Scala DynamicRecord Class   **305**
def addField 306
def dropField 306
def setError 306
def isError 306
def getError 306
def clearError 306
def write 307
def readFields 307
def clone 307
def schema 307
def getRoot 307
def toJson 307
def getFieldNode 307
def getField 307
def hashCode 307
def equals 307
DynamicRecord Object 308
def apply 308
RecordTraverser Trait 308

AWS Glue Scala GlueContext APIs   **308**
def getCatalogSink 309
def getCatalogSource 309
def getJDBCSink 309
def getSink 310
def getSinkWithFormat 310
def getSource 311
def getSourceWithFormat 311
def getSparkSession 312
def this 312
def this 312
def this 313

AWS Glue Scala ResolveSpec APIs   **314**
ResolveSpec Object 314
def 314
def 314
ResolveSpec Case Class 314
ResolveSpec def Methods 315

AWS Glue Scala ArrayNode APIs   **315**
ArrayNode Case Class 315

ArrayNode def Methods 315

AWS Glue Scala BinaryNode APIs   **315**
BinaryNode Case Class 316
    BinaryNode val Fields 316
    BinaryNode def Methods 316

AWS Glue Scala BooleanNode APIs   **316**
BooleanNode Case Class 316
    BooleanNode val Fields 316
    BooleanNode def Methods 316

AWS Glue Scala ByteNode APIs   **316**
ByteNode Case Class 316
    ByteNode val Fields 317
    ByteNode def Methods 317

AWS Glue Scala DateNode APIs   **317**
DateNode Case Class 317
    DateNode val Fields 317
    DateNode def Methods 317

AWS Glue Scala DecimalNode APIs   **317**
DecimalNode Case Class 317
    DecimalNode val Fields 317
    DecimalNode def Methods 318

AWS Glue Scala DoubleNode APIs   **318**
DoubleNode Case Class 318
    DoubleNode val Fields 318
    DoubleNode def Methods 318

AWS Glue Scala DynamicNode APIs   **318**
DynamicNode Class 318
    DynamicNode def Methods 318
DynamicNode Object 319
    DynamicNode def Methods 319

AWS Glue Scala FloatNode APIs   **319**
FloatNode Case Class 319
    FloatNode val Fields 319
    FloatNode def Methods 319

AWS Glue Scala IntegerNode APIs   **319**
IntegerNode Case Class 319
    IntegerNode val Fields 320
    IntegerNode def Methods 320

AWS Glue Scala LongNode APIs   **320**
LongNode Case Class 320
    LongNode val Fields 320
    LongNode def Methods 320

AWS Glue Scala MapLikeNode APIs   **320**
MapLikeNode Class 320
    MapLikeNode def Methods 320

AWS Glue Scala MapNode APIs   **321**
MapNode Case Class 321
    MapNode def Methods 321

AWS Glue Scala NullNode APIs   **321**
NullNode Class 322
NullNode Case Object 322

AWS Glue Scala ObjectNode APIs   **323**
ObjectNode Object 323
    ObjectNode def Methods 323
ObjectNode Case Class 323
    ObjectNode def Methods 323

AWS Glue Scala ScalarNode APIs   **323**
ScalarNode Class 324
    ScalarNode def Methods 324
ScalarNode Object 324
    ScalarNode def Methods 324

AWS Glue Scala ShortNode APIs   **324**
ShortNode Case Class 324
    ShortNode val Fields 325
    ShortNode def Methods 325

AWS Glue Scala StringNode APIs   **325**
StringNode Case Class 325
    StringNode val Fields 325
    StringNode def Methods 325

AWS Glue Scala TimestampNode APIs   **325**
TimestampNode Case Class 325
    TimestampNode val Fields 325
    TimestampNode def Methods 326

AWS Glue Scala GlueArgParser APIs   **326**
GlueArgParser Object 326
    GlueArgParser def Methods 326

AWS Glue Scala Job APIs   **326**
Job Object 326
    Job def Methods 326

AWS Glue API   **327**

Catalog API   **332**

Database API   **333**
Data Types 333
Database Structure 333
DatabaseInput Structure 333
Operations 334
CreateDatabase Action (Python: create_database) 334
UpdateDatabase Action (Python: update_database) 334
DeleteDatabase Action (Python: delete_database) 335
GetDatabase Action (Python: get_database) 335

GetDatabases Action (Python: get_databases) 336

Table API   **337**

    Data Types 337
    Table Structure 337
    TableInput Structure 338
    Column Structure 339
    StorageDescriptor Structure 339
    SerDeInfo Structure 340
    Order Structure 341
    SkewedInfo Structure 341
    TableVersion Structure 341
    TableError Structure 341
    TableVersionError Structure 342
    Operations 342
    CreateTable Action (Python: create_table) 342
    UpdateTable Action (Python: update_table) 343
    DeleteTable Action (Python: delete_table) 343
    BatchDeleteTable Action (Python: batch_delete_table) 344
    GetTable Action (Python: get_table) 345
    GetTables Action (Python: get_tables) 345
    GetTableVersion Action (Python: get_table_version) 346
    GetTableVersions Action (Python: get_table_versions) 347
    DeleteTableVersion Action (Python: delete_table_version) 348
    BatchDeleteTableVersion Action (Python: batch_delete_table_version) 348

Partition API   **350**

    Data Types 350
    Partition Structure 350
    PartitionInput Structure 351
    PartitionSpecWithSharedStorageDescriptor Structure 351
    PartitionListComposingSpec Structure 351
    PartitionSpecProxy Structure 351
    PartitionValueList Structure 352
    Segment Structure 352
    PartitionError Structure 352
    Operations 353
    CreatePartition Action (Python: create_partition) 353
    BatchCreatePartition Action (Python: batch_create_partition) 353
    UpdatePartition Action (Python: update_partition) 354
    DeletePartition Action (Python: delete_partition) 355
    BatchDeletePartition Action (Python: batch_delete_partition) 355
    GetPartition Action (Python: get_partition) 356
    GetPartitions Action (Python: get_partitions) 357
    BatchGetPartition Action (Python: batch_get_partition) 357

Connection API   **359**

    Data Types 359
    Connection Structure 359
    ConnectionInput Structure 360
    PhysicalConnectionRequirements Structure 360
    GetConnectionsFilter Structure 361
    Operations 361
    CreateConnection Action (Python: create_connection) 361
    DeleteConnection Action (Python: delete_connection) 362

GetConnection Action (Python: get_connection) 362
GetConnections Action (Python: get_connections) 363
UpdateConnection Action (Python: update_connection) 363
BatchDeleteConnection Action (Python: batch_delete_connection) 364

User-Defined Function API   365

Data Types 365
UserDefinedFunction Structure 365
UserDefinedFunctionInput Structure 365
Operations 366
CreateUserDefinedFunction Action (Python: create_user_defined_function) 366
UpdateUserDefinedFunction Action (Python: update_user_defined_function) 366
DeleteUserDefinedFunction Action (Python: delete_user_defined_function) 367
GetUserDefinedFunction Action (Python: get_user_defined_function) 368
GetUserDefinedFunctions Action (Python: get_user_defined_functions) 368

Importing an Athena Catalog to AWS Glue   370

Data Types 370
CatalogImportStatus Structure 370
Operations 370
ImportCatalogToGlue Action (Python: import_catalog_to_glue) 370
GetCatalogImportStatus Action (Python: get_catalog_import_status) 370

Crawlers and Classifiers API   372

Classifier API   373

Data Types 373
Classifier Structure 373
GrokClassifier Structure 373
XMLClassifier Structure 374
JsonClassifier Structure 374
CreateGrokClassifierRequest Structure 375
UpdateGrokClassifierRequest Structure 375
CreateXMLClassifierRequest Structure 376
UpdateXMLClassifierRequest Structure 376
CreateJsonClassifierRequest Structure 376
UpdateJsonClassifierRequest Structure 377
Operations 377
CreateClassifier Action (Python: create_classifier) 377
DeleteClassifier Action (Python: delete_classifier) 378
GetClassifier Action (Python: get_classifier) 378
GetClassifiers Action (Python: get_classifiers) 378
UpdateClassifier Action (Python: update_classifier) 379

Crawler API   380

Data Types 380
Crawler Structure 380
Schedule Structure 381
CrawlerTargets Structure 381
S3Target Structure 381
JdbcTarget Structure 382
CrawlerMetrics Structure 382
SchemaChangePolicy Structure 382
LastCrawlInfo Structure 383
Operations 383

    CreateCrawler Action (Python: create_crawler) 383
    DeleteCrawler Action (Python: delete_crawler) 384
    GetCrawler Action (Python: get_crawler) 385
    GetCrawlers Action (Python: get_crawlers) 385
    GetCrawlerMetrics Action (Python: get_crawler_metrics) 386
    UpdateCrawler Action (Python: update_crawler) 386
    StartCrawler Action (Python: start_crawler) 387
    StopCrawler Action (Python: stop_crawler) 387

Crawler Scheduler API   **389**
    Data Types 389
    Schedule Structure 389
    Operations 389
    UpdateCrawlerSchedule Action (Python: update_crawler_schedule) 389
    StartCrawlerSchedule Action (Python: start_crawler_schedule) 390
    StopCrawlerSchedule Action (Python: stop_crawler_schedule) 390

AWS Glue API for Autogenerating ETL Scripts   **391**
    Data Types 391
    CodeGenNode Structure 391
    CodeGenNodeArg Structure 391
    CodeGenEdge Structure 391
    Location Structure 392
    CatalogEntry Structure 392
    MappingEntry Structure 392
    Operations 393
    CreateScript Action (Python: create_script) 393
    GetDataflowGraph Action (Python: get_dataflow_graph) 393
    GetMapping Action (Python: get_mapping) 394
    GetPlan Action (Python: get_plan) 394

Jobs API   **396**

Jobs   **397**
    Data Types 397
    Job Structure 397
    ExecutionProperty Structure 398
    NotificationProperty Structure 398
    JobCommand Structure 398
    ConnectionsList Structure 399
    JobUpdate Structure 399
    Operations 400
    CreateJob Action (Python: create_job) 400
    UpdateJob Action (Python: update_job) 401
    GetJob Action (Python: get_job) 402
    GetJobs Action (Python: get_jobs) 402
    DeleteJob Action (Python: delete_job) 403

Job Runs   **404**
    Data Types 404
    JobRun Structure 404
    Predecessor Structure 405
    JobBookmarkEntry Structure 405
    BatchStopJobRunSuccessfulSubmission Structure 406
    BatchStopJobRunError Structure 406

Operations 406
StartJobRun Action (Python: start_job_run) 407
BatchStopJobRun Action (Python: batch_stop_job_run) 408
GetJobRun Action (Python: get_job_run) 408
GetJobRuns Action (Python: get_job_runs) 409
ResetJobBookmark Action (Python: reset_job_bookmark) 409

Triggers   **410**
Data Types 410
Trigger Structure 410
TriggerUpdate Structure 410
Predicate Structure 411
Condition Structure 411
Action Structure 411
Operations 412
CreateTrigger Action (Python: create_trigger) 412
StartTrigger Action (Python: start_trigger) 413
GetTrigger Action (Python: get_trigger) 413
GetTriggers Action (Python: get_triggers) 414
UpdateTrigger Action (Python: update_trigger) 414
StopTrigger Action (Python: stop_trigger) 415
DeleteTrigger Action (Python: delete_trigger) 415

AWS Glue Development Endpoints API   **417**
Data Types 417
DevEndpoint Structure 417
DevEndpointCustomLibraries Structure 418
Operations 418
CreateDevEndpoint Action (Python: create_dev_endpoint) 418
UpdateDevEndpoint Action (Python: update_dev_endpoint) 420
DeleteDevEndpoint Action (Python: delete_dev_endpoint) 421
GetDevEndpoint Action (Python: get_dev_endpoint) 421
GetDevEndpoints Action (Python: get_dev_endpoints) 421

Common Data Types   **423**
Tag Structure 423
DecimalNumber Structure 423
ErrorDetail Structure 423
PropertyPredicate Structure 423
ResourceUri Structure 424
String Patterns 424

Exceptions   **425**
AccessDeniedException Structure 425
AlreadyExistsException Structure 425
ConcurrentModificationException Structure 425
ConcurrentRunsExceededException Structure 425
CrawlerNotRunningException Structure 425
CrawlerRunningException Structure 426
CrawlerStoppingException Structure 426
EntityNotFoundException Structure 426
IdempotentParameterMismatchException Structure 426
InternalServiceException Structure 426
InvalidExecutionEngineException Structure 426
InvalidInputException Structure 427

InvalidTaskStatusTransitionException Structure 427
JobDefinitionErrorException Structure 427
JobRunInTerminalStateException Structure 427
JobRunInvalidStateTransitionException Structure 427
JobRunNotInTerminalStateException Structure 428
LateRunnerException Structure 428
NoScheduleException Structure 428
OperationTimeoutException Structure 428
ResourceNumberLimitExceededException Structure 428
SchedulerNotRunningException Structure 429
SchedulerRunningException Structure 429
SchedulerTransitioningException Structure 429
UnrecognizedRunnerException Structure 429
ValidationException Structure 429
VersionMismatchException Structure 429

Document History for AWS Glue   **430**

AWS Glossary   **431**

What Is AWS Glue?

AWS Glue is a fully managed ETL (extract, transform, and load) service that makes it simple and cost-effective to categorize your data, clean it, enrich it, and move it reliably between various data stores. AWS Glue consists of a central metadata repository known as the AWS Glue Data Catalog, an ETL engine that automatically generates Python or Scala code, and a flexible scheduler that handles dependency resolution, job monitoring, and retries. AWS Glue is serverless, so there's no infrastructure to set up or manage.

Use the AWS Glue console to discover data, transform it, and make it available for search and querying. The console calls the underlying services to orchestrate the work required to transform your data. You can also use the AWS Glue API operations to interface with AWS Glue services. Edit, debug, and test your Python or Scala Apache Spark ETL code using a familiar development environment.

For pricing information, see AWS Glue Pricing.

When Should I Use AWS Glue?

You can use AWS Glue to build a data warehouse to organize, cleanse, validate, and format data. You can transform and move AWS Cloud data into your data store. You can also load data from disparate sources into your data warehouse for regular reporting and analysis. By storing it in a data warehouse, you integrate information from different parts of your business and provide a common source of data for decision making.

AWS Glue simplifies many tasks when you are building a data warehouse:

- Discovers and catalogs metadata about your data stores into a central catalog. You can process semi-structured data, such as clickstream or process logs.
- Populates the AWS Glue Data Catalog with table definitions from scheduled crawler programs. Crawlers call classifier logic to infer the schema, format, and data types of your data. This metadata is stored as tables in the AWS Glue Data Catalog and used in the authoring process of your ETL jobs.
- Generates ETL scripts to transform, flatten, and enrich your data from source to target.
- Detects schema changes and adapts based on your preferences.
- Triggers your ETL jobs based on a schedule or event. You can initiate jobs automatically to move your data into your data warehouse. Triggers can be used to create a dependency flow between jobs.
- Gathers runtime metrics to monitor the activities of your data warehouse.
- Handles errors and retries automatically.
- Scales resources, as needed, to run your jobs.

You can use AWS Glue when you run serverless queries against your Amazon S3 data lake. AWS Glue can catalog your Amazon Simple Storage Service (Amazon S3) data, making it available for querying with Amazon Athena and Amazon Redshift Spectrum. With crawlers, your metadata stays in sync with the underlying data. Athena and Redshift Spectrum can directly query your Amazon S3 data lake using the AWS Glue Data Catalog. With AWS Glue, you access and analyze data through one unified interface without loading it into multiple data silos.

You can create event-driven ETL pipelines with AWS Glue. You can run your ETL jobs as soon as new data becomes available in Amazon S3 by invoking your AWS Glue ETL jobs from an AWS Lambda function. You can also register this new dataset in the AWS Glue Data Catalog as part of your ETL jobs.

You can use AWS Glue to understand your data assets. You can store your data using various AWS services and still maintain a unified view of your data using the AWS Glue Data Catalog. View the Data Catalog to quickly search and discover the datasets that you own, and maintain the relevant metadata in one central repository. The Data Catalog also serves as a drop-in replacement for your external Apache Hive Metastore.

AWS Glue: How It Works

AWS Glue uses other AWS services to orchestrate your ETL (extract, transform, and load) jobs to build a data warehouse. AWS Glue calls API operations to transform your data, create runtime logs, store your job logic, and create notifications to help you monitor your job runs. The AWS Glue console connects these services into a managed application, so you can focus on creating and monitoring your ETL work. The console performs administrative and job development operations on your behalf. You supply credentials and other properties to AWS Glue to access your data sources and write to your data warehouse.

AWS Glue takes care of provisioning and managing the resources that are required to run your workload. You don't need to create the infrastructure for an ETL tool because AWS Glue does it for you. When resources are required, to reduce startup time, AWS Glue uses an instance from its warm pool of instances to run your workload.

With AWS Glue, you create jobs using table definitions in your Data Catalog. Jobs consist of scripts that contain the programming logic that performs the transformation. You use triggers to initiate jobs either on a schedule or as a result of a specified event. You determine where your target data resides and which source data populates your target. With your input, AWS Glue generates the code that's required to transform your data from source to target. You can also provide scripts in the AWS Glue console or API to process your data.

Topics

- Serverless ETL Jobs Run in Isolation
- AWS Glue Concepts
- AWS Glue Components
- Converting Semi-Structured Schemas to Relational Schemas

Serverless ETL Jobs Run in Isolation

AWS Glue runs your ETL jobs in an Apache Spark serverless environment. AWS Glue runs these jobs on virtual resources that it provisions and manages in its own service account.

AWS Glue is designed to do the following:

- Segregate customer data.
- Protect customer data in transit and at rest.
- Access customer data only as needed in response to customer requests, using temporary, scoped-down credentials, or with a customer's consent to IAM roles in their account.

During provisioning of an ETL job, you provide input data sources and output data targets in your virtual private cloud (VPC). In addition, you provide the IAM role, VPC ID, subnet ID, and security group that are needed to access data sources and targets. For each tuple (customer account ID, IAM role, subnet ID, and security group), AWS Glue creates a new Spark environment that is isolated at the network and management level from all other Spark environments inside the AWS Glue service account.

AWS Glue creates elastic network interfaces in your subnet using private IP addresses. Spark jobs use these elastic network interfaces to access your data sources and data targets. Traffic in, out, and within the Spark environment is governed by your VPC and networking policies with one exception: Calls made to AWS Glue libraries can proxy traffic to AWS Glue API operations through the AWS Glue VPC. All AWS Glue API calls are logged; thus, data owners can audit API access by enabling AWS CloudTrail, which delivers audit logs to your account.

AWS Glue managed Spark environments that run your ETL jobs are protected with the same security practices followed by other AWS services. Those practices are listed in the **AWS Access** section of the Introduction to AWS Security Processes whitepaper.

AWS Glue Concepts

The following diagram shows the architecture of an AWS Glue environment.

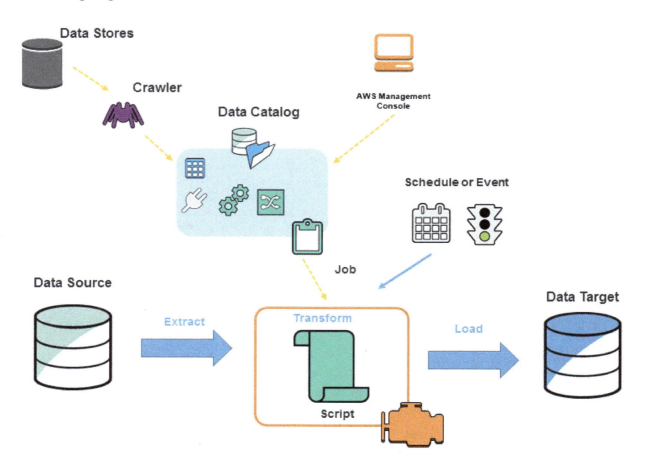

You define *jobs* in AWS Glue to accomplish the work that's required to extract, transform, and load (ETL) data from a data source to a data target. You typically perform the following actions:

- You define a *crawler* to populate your AWS Glue Data Catalog with metadata table definitions. You point your crawler at a data store, and the crawler creates table definitions in the Data Catalog.

  In addition to table definitions, the AWS Glue Data Catalog contains other metadata that is required to define ETL jobs. You use this metadata when you define a job to transform your data.

- AWS Glue can generate a script to transform your data. Or, you can provide the script in the AWS Glue console or API.

- You can run your job on demand, or you can set it up to start when a specified *trigger* occurs. The trigger can be a time-based schedule or an event.

  When your job runs, a script extracts data from your data source, transforms the data, and loads it to your data target. The script runs in an Apache Spark environment in AWS Glue.

Important
Tables and databases in AWS Glue are objects in the AWS Glue Data Catalog. They contain metadata; they don't contain data from a data store.

AWS Glue Terminology

AWS Glue relies on the interaction of several components to create and manage your data warehouse workflow.

AWS Glue Data Catalog

The persistent metadata store in AWS Glue. Each AWS account has one AWS Glue Data Catalog. It contains table definitions, job definitions, and other control information to manage your AWS Glue environment.

Table

The metadata definition that represents your data. Whether your data is in an Amazon Simple Storage Service (Amazon S3) file, an Amazon Relational Database Service (Amazon RDS) table, or another set of data, a table defines the schema of your data. A table in the AWS Glue Data Catalog consists of the names of columns, data type definitions, and other metadata about a base dataset. The schema of your data is represented in your AWS Glue table definition. The actual data remains in its original data store, whether it be in a file or a relational database table. AWS Glue catalogs your files and relational database tables in the AWS Glue Data Catalog. They are used as sources and targets when you create an ETL job.

Crawler

A program that connects to a data store (source or target), progresses through a prioritized list of classifiers to determine the schema for your data, and then creates metadata in the AWS Glue Data Catalog.

Classifier

Determines the schema of your data. AWS Glue provides classifiers for common file types, such as CSV, JSON, AVRO, XML, and others. It also provides classifiers for common relational database management systems using a JDBC connection. You can write your own classifier by using a grok pattern or by specifying a row tag in an XML document.

Connection

Contains the properties that are required to connect to your data store.

Database

A set of associated table definitions organized into a logical group in AWS Glue.

Job

The business logic that is required to perform ETL work. It is composed of a transformation script, data sources, and data targets. Job runs are initiated by triggers that can be scheduled or triggered by events.

Script

Code that extracts data from sources, transforms it, and loads it into targets. AWS Glue generates PySpark or Scala scripts. PySpark is a Python dialect for ETL programming.

Transform

The code logic that is used to manipulate your data into a different format.

Trigger

Initiates an ETL job. Triggers can be defined based on a scheduled time or an event.

Development endpoint

An environment that you can use to develop and test your AWS Glue scripts.

Notebook server

A web-based environment that you can use to run your PySpark statements. For more information, see Apache Zeppelin. You can set up a notebook server on a development endpoint to run PySpark statements with AWS Glue extensions.

AWS Glue Components

AWS Glue provides a console and API operations to set up and manage your extract, transform, and load (ETL) workload. You can use API operations through several language-specific SDKs and the AWS Command Line Interface (AWS CLI). For information about using the AWS CLI, see AWS CLI Command Reference.

AWS Glue uses the AWS Glue Data Catalog to store metadata about data sources, transforms, and targets. The Data Catalog is a drop-in replacement for the Apache Hive Metastore. The AWS Glue Jobs system provides a managed infrastructure for defining, scheduling, and running ETL operations on your data. For more information about the AWS Glue API, see AWS Glue API.

AWS Glue Console

You use the AWS Glue console to define and orchestrate your ETL workflow. The console calls several API operations in the AWS Glue Data Catalog and AWS Glue Jobs system to perform the following tasks:

- Define AWS Glue objects such as jobs, tables, crawlers, and connections.
- Schedule when crawlers run.
- Define events or schedules for job triggers.
- Search and filter lists of AWS Glue objects.
- Edit transformation scripts.

AWS Glue Data Catalog

The AWS Glue Data Catalog is your persistent metadata store. It is a managed service that lets you store, annotate, and share metadata in the AWS Cloud in the same way you would in an Apache Hive metastore.

Each AWS account has one AWS Glue Data Catalog. It provides a uniform repository where disparate systems can store and find metadata to keep track of data in data silos, and use that metadata to query and transform the data.

You can use AWS Identity and Access Management (IAM) policies to control access to the data sources managed by the AWS Glue Data Catalog. These policies allow different groups in your enterprise to safely publish data to the wider organization while protecting sensitive information. IAM policies let you clearly and consistently define which users have access to which data, regardless of its location.

The Data Catalog also provides comprehensive audit and governance capabilities, with schema change tracking, lineage of data, and data access controls. You can audit changes to data schemas and track the movement of data across systems, to ensure that data is not inappropriately modified or inadvertently shared.

For information about how to use the AWS Glue Data Catalog, see Populating the AWS Glue Data Catalog. For information about how to program using the Data Catalog API, see Catalog API.

AWS Glue Crawlers and Classifiers

AWS Glue also lets you set up crawlers that can scan data in all kinds of repositories, classify it, extract schema information from it, and store the metadata automatically in the AWS Glue Data Catalog. From there it can be used to guide ETL operations.

For information about how to set up crawlers and classifiers, see Cataloging Tables with a Crawler. For information about how to program crawlers and classifiers using the AWS Glue API, see Crawlers and Classifiers API.

AWS Glue ETL Operations

Using the metadata in the Data Catalog, AWS Glue can autogenerate Scala or PySpark (the Python API for Apache Spark) scripts with AWS Glue extensions that you can use and modify to perform various ETL operations. For example, you can extract, clean, and transform raw data, and then store the result in a different repository, where it can be queried and analyzed. Such a script might convert a CSV file into a relational form and save it in Amazon Redshift.

For more information about how to use AWS Glue ETL capabilities, see Programming ETL Scripts.

The AWS Glue Jobs System

The AWS Glue Jobs system provides managed infrastructure to orchestrate your ETL workflow. You can create jobs in AWS Glue that automate the scripts you use to extract, transform, and transfer data to different locations. Jobs can be scheduled and chained, or they can be triggered by events such as the arrival of new data.

For more information about using the AWS Glue Jobs system, see Running and Monitoring AWS Glue. For information about programming using the AWS Glue Jobs system API, see Jobs API.

Converting Semi-Structured Schemas to Relational Schemas

It's common to want to convert semi-structured data into relational tables. Conceptually, you are flattening a hierarchical schema to a relational schema. AWS Glue can perform this conversion for you on-the-fly.

Semi-structured data typically contains mark-up to identify entities within the data. It can have nested data structures with no fixed schema. For more information about semi-structured data, see Semi-structured data in Wikipedia.

Relational data is represented by tables that consist of rows and columns. Relationships between tables can be represented by a primary key (PK) to foreign key (FK) relationship. For more information, see Relational database in Wikipedia.

AWS Glue uses crawlers to infer schemas for semi-structured data. It then transforms the data to a relational schema using an ETL (extract, transform, and load) job. For example, you might want to parse JSON data from Amazon Simple Storage Service (Amazon S3) source files to Amazon Relational Database Service (Amazon RDS) tables. Understanding how AWS Glue handles the differences between schemas can help you understand the transformation process.

This diagram shows how AWS Glue transforms a semi-structured schema to a relational schema.

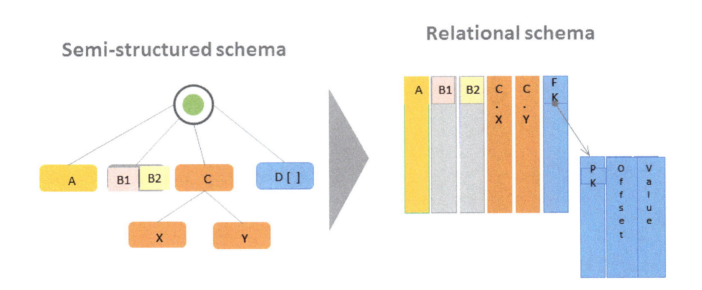

The diagram illustrates the following:

- Single value A converts directly to a relational column.
- The pair of values, B1 and B2, convert to two relational columns.
- Structure C, with children X and Y, converts to two relational columns.

- Array `D[]` converts to a relational column with a foreign key (FK) that points to another relational table. Along with a primary key (PK), the second relational table has columns that contain the offset and value of the items in the array.

Getting Started Using AWS Glue

The following sections provide an overview and walk you through setting up and using AWS Glue. For information about AWS Glue concepts and components, see AWS Glue: How It Works

Topics

- Setting up IAM Permissions for AWS Glue
- Setting Up DNS in Your VPC
- Setting Up Your Environment to Access Data Stores
- Setting Up Your Environment for Development Endpoints
- AWS Glue Console Workflow Overview

Setting up IAM Permissions for AWS Glue

You use AWS Identity and Access Management (IAM) to define policies and roles that are needed to access resources used by AWS Glue. The following steps lead you through the basic permissions that you need to set up your environment. Depending on your business needs, you might have to add or reduce access to your resources.

1. Create an IAM Policy for the AWS Glue Service: Create a service policy that allows access to AWS Glue resources.

2. Create an IAM Role for AWS Glue: Create an IAM role, and attach the AWS Glue service policy and a policy for your Amazon Simple Storage Service (Amazon S3) resources that are used by AWS Glue.

3. Attach a Policy to IAM Users That Access AWS Glue: Attach policies to any IAM user that signs in to the AWS Glue console.

4. Create an IAM Policy for Notebooks: Create a notebook server policy to use in the creation of notebook servers on development endpoints.

5. Create an IAM Role for Notebooks: Create an IAM role and attach the notebook server policy.

Step 1: Create an IAM Policy for the AWS Glue Service

For any operation that accesses data on another AWS resource, such as accessing your objects in Amazon S3, AWS Glue needs permission to access the resource on your behalf. You provide those permissions by using AWS Identity and Access Management (IAM).

Note
You can skip this step if you use the AWS managed policy **AWSGlueServiceRole**.

In this step, you create a policy that is similar to `AWSGlueServiceRole`. You can find the most current version of `AWSGlueServiceRole` on the IAM console.

To create an IAM policy for AWS Glue

This policy grants permission for some Amazon S3 actions to manage resources in your account that are needed by AWS Glue when it assumes the role using this policy. Some of the resources that are specified in this policy refer to default names that are used by AWS Glue for Amazon S3 buckets, Amazon S3 ETL scripts, CloudWatch Logs, and Amazon EC2 resources. For simplicity, AWS Glue writes some Amazon S3 objects into buckets in your account prefixed with `aws-glue-*` by default.

1. Sign in to the AWS Management Console and open the IAM console at https://console.aws.amazon.com/iam/.

2. In the left navigation pane, choose **Policies**.

3. Choose **Create Policy**.

4. On the **Create Policy** screen, navigate to a tab to edit JSON. Create a policy document with the following JSON statements, and then choose **Review policy**. **Note**
   Add any permissions needed for Amazon S3 resources. You might want to scope the resources section of your access policy to only those resources that are required.

```
1  {
2      "Version": "2012-10-17",
3      "Statement": [
4          {
5              "Effect": "Allow",
6              "Action": [
7                  "glue:*",
8                  "s3:GetBucketLocation",
9                  "s3:ListBucket",
10                 "s3:ListAllMyBuckets",
11                 "s3:GetBucketAcl",
12                 "ec2:DescribeVpcEndpoints",
13                 "ec2:DescribeRouteTables",
14                 "ec2:CreateNetworkInterface",
15                 "ec2:DeleteNetworkInterface",
16                 "ec2:DescribeNetworkInterfaces",
17                 "ec2:DescribeSecurityGroups",
18                 "ec2:DescribeSubnets",
19                 "ec2:DescribeVpcAttribute",
20                 "iam:ListRolePolicies",
21                 "iam:GetRole",
22                 "iam:GetRolePolicy"
23             ],
24             "Resource": [
25                 "*"
26             ]
```

```
27          },
28          {
29              "Effect": "Allow",
30              "Action": [
31                  "s3:CreateBucket"
32              ],
33              "Resource": [
34                  "arn:aws:s3:::aws-glue-*"
35              ]
36          },
37          {
38              "Effect": "Allow",
39              "Action": [
40                  "s3:GetObject",
41                  "s3:PutObject",
42                  "s3:DeleteObject"
43              ],
44              "Resource": [
45                  "arn:aws:s3:::aws-glue-*/*",
46                  "arn:aws:s3:::*/*aws-glue-*/*"
47              ]
48          },
49          {
50              "Effect": "Allow",
51              "Action": [
52                  "s3:GetObject"
53              ],
54              "Resource": [
55                  "arn:aws:s3:::crawler-public*",
56                  "arn:aws:s3:::aws-glue-*"
57              ]
58          },
59          {
60              "Effect": "Allow",
61              "Action": [
62                  "logs:CreateLogGroup",
63                  "logs:CreateLogStream",
64                  "logs:PutLogEvents"
65              ],
66              "Resource": [
67                  "arn:aws:logs:*:*:/aws-glue/*"
68              ]
69          },
70          {
71              "Effect": "Allow",
72              "Action": [
73                  "ec2:CreateTags",
74                  "ec2:DeleteTags"
75              ],
76              "Condition": {
77                  "ForAllValues:StringEquals": {
78                      "aws:TagKeys": [
79                          "aws-glue-service-resource"
80                      ]
```

```
81                }
82            },
83            "Resource": [
84                "arn:aws:ec2:*:*:network-interface/*",
85                "arn:aws:ec2:*:*:security-group/*",
86                "arn:aws:ec2:*:*:instance/*"
87            ]
88        }
89    ]
90 }
```

The following table describes the permissions granted by this policy.
[See the AWS documentation website for more details]

5. On the **Review Policy** screen, type your **Policy Name**, for example **GlueServiceRolePolicy**. Type an optional description, and when you're satisfied with the policy, then **Create policy**.

Step 2: Create an IAM Role for AWS Glue

You need to grant your IAM role permissions that AWS Glue can assume when calling other services on your behalf. This includes access to Amazon S3 for any sources, targets, scripts, and temporary directories that you use with AWS Glue. Permission is needed by crawlers, jobs, and development endpoints.

You provide those permissions by using AWS Identity and Access Management (IAM). Add a policy to the IAM role that you pass to AWS Glue.

**To create an IAM role for ** AWS Glue

1. Sign in to the AWS Management Console and open the IAM console at https://console.aws.amazon.com/iam/.

2. In the left navigation pane, choose **Roles**.

3. Choose **Create role**.

4. For role type, choose **AWS Service**, find and choose **Glue**, and choose **Next: Permissions**.

5. On the **Attach permissions policy** page, choose the policies that contain the required permissions; for example, the AWS managed policy **AWSGlueServiceRole** for general AWS Glue permissions and the AWS managed policy **AmazonS3FullAccess** for access to Amazon S3 resources. Then choose **Next: Review**. Note
Ensure that one of the policies in this role grants permissions to your Amazon S3 sources and targets. You might want to provide your own policy for access to specific Amazon S3 resources. Data sources require `s3:ListBucket` and `s3:GetObject` permissions. Data targets require `s3:ListBucket`, `s3:PutObject`, and `s3:DeleteObject` permissions. For more information about creating an Amazon S3 policy for your resources, see Specifying Resources in a Policy. For an example Amazon S3 policy, see Writing IAM Policies: How to Grant Access to an Amazon S3 Bucket.
If you plan to access Amazon S3 sources and targets that are encrypted with SSE-KMS, then attach a policy that allows AWS Glue crawlers, jobs, and development endpoints to decrypt the data. For more information, see Protecting Data Using Server-Side Encryption with AWS KMS-Managed Keys (SSE-KMS). The following is an example:

```
1  {
2      "Version":"2012-10-17",
3      "Statement":[
4          {
5              "Effect":"Allow",
6              "Action":[
7                  "kms:Decrypt"
8              ],
9              "Resource":[
10                 "arn:aws:kms:*:account-id-without-hyphens:key/key-id"
11             ]
12         }
13     ]
14 }
```

6. For **Role name**, type a name for your role; for example, **AWSGlueServiceRoleDefault**. Create the role with the name prefixed with the string **AWSGlueServiceRole** to allow the role to be passed from console users to the service. AWS Glue provided policies expect IAM service roles to begin with **AWSGlueServiceRole**. Otherwise, you must add a policy to allow your users the `iam:PassRole` permission for IAM roles to match your naming convention. Choose **Create Role**.

Step 3: Attach a Policy to IAM Users That Access AWS Glue

Any IAM user that signs in to the AWS Glue console or AWS Command Line Interface (AWS CLI) must have permissions to access specific resources. You provide those permissions by using AWS Identity and Access Management (IAM), through policies.

When you finish this step, your IAM user has the following policies attached:

- The AWS managed policy **AWSGlueConsoleFullAccess** or the custom policy **GlueConsoleAccessPolicy**
- **CloudWatchLogsReadOnlyAccess**
- **AWSCloudFormationReadOnlyAccess**
- **AmazonAthenaFullAccess**

To attach an inline policy and embed it in an IAM user

You can attach an AWS managed policy or an inline policy to an IAM user to access the AWS Glue console. Some of the resources specified in this policy refer to default names that are used by AWS Glue for Amazon S3 buckets, Amazon S3 ETL scripts, CloudWatch Logs, AWS CloudFormation, and Amazon EC2 resources. For simplicity, AWS Glue writes some Amazon S3 objects into buckets in your account prefixed with `aws-glue-*` by default. **Note**

You can skip this step if you use the AWS managed policy **AWSGlueConsoleFullAccess**. **Important**

AWS Glue needs permission to assume a role that is used to perform work on your behalf. **To accomplish this, you add the `iam:PassRole` permissions to your AWS Glue users.** This policy grants permission to roles that begin with `AWSGlueServiceRole` for AWS Glue service roles, and `AWSGlueServiceNotebookRole` for roles that are required when you create a notebook server. You can also create your own policy for `iam:PassRole` permissions that follows your naming convention.

In this step, you create a policy that is similar to `AWSGlueConsoleFullAccess`. You can find the most current version of `AWSGlueConsoleFullAccess` on the IAM console.

1. Sign in to the AWS Management Console and open the IAM console at https://console.aws.amazon.com/iam/.

2. In the navigation pane, choose **Users**.

3. In the list, choose the name of the user to embed a policy in.

4. Choose the **Permissions** tab and, if necessary, expand the **Inline Policies** section.

5. Choose the **Add Inline policy** link.

6. In the **Set Permissions** screen, choose **Custom Policy**, and then choose **Select** to open the policy editor.

7. Specify a name for the policy, for example **GlueConsoleAccessPolicy**. Create your policy document with the following statements:

```
1  {
2      "Version": "2012-10-17",
3      "Statement": [
4          {
5              "Effect": "Allow",
6              "Action": [
7                  "glue:*",
8                  "redshift:DescribeClusters",
9                  "redshift:DescribeClusterSubnetGroups",
10                 "iam:ListRoles",
11                 "iam:ListRolePolicies",
12                 "iam:GetRole",
```

```
13                    "iam:GetRolePolicy",
14                    "iam:ListAttachedRolePolicies",
15                    "ec2:DescribeSecurityGroups",
16                    "ec2:DescribeSubnets",
17                    "ec2:DescribeVpcs",
18                    "ec2:DescribeVpcEndpoints",
19                    "ec2:DescribeRouteTables",
20                    "ec2:DescribeVpcAttribute",
21                    "ec2:DescribeKeyPairs",
22                    "ec2:DescribeInstances",
23                    "rds:DescribeDBInstances",
24                    "s3:ListAllMyBuckets",
25                    "s3:ListBucket",
26                    "s3:GetBucketAcl",
27                    "s3:GetBucketLocation",
28                    "cloudformation:DescribeStacks",
29                    "cloudformation:GetTemplateSummary",
30                    "dynamodb:ListTables"
31                ],
32                "Resource": [
33                    "*"
34                ]
35            },
36            {
37                "Effect": "Allow",
38                "Action": [
39                    "s3:GetObject",
40                    "s3:PutObject"
41                ],
42                "Resource": [
43                    "arn:aws:s3:::aws-glue-*/*",
44                    "arn:aws:s3:::*/*aws-glue-*/*",
45                    "arn:aws:s3:::aws-glue-*"
46                ]
47            },
48            {
49                "Effect": "Allow",
50                "Action": [
51                    "s3:CreateBucket"
52                ],
53                "Resource": [
54                    "arn:aws:s3:::aws-glue-*"
55                ]
56            },
57            {
58                "Effect": "Allow",
59                "Action": [
60                    "logs:GetLogEvents"
61                ],
62                "Resource": [
63                    "arn:aws:logs:*:*:/aws-glue/*"
64                ]
65            },
66            {
```

```
67          "Effect": "Allow",
68          "Action": [
69              "cloudformation:CreateStack",
70              "cloudformation:DeleteStack"
71          ],
72          "Resource": "arn:aws:cloudformation:*:*:stack/aws-glue*/*"
73      },
74      {
75          "Effect": "Allow",
76          "Action": [
77              "ec2:RunInstances"
78          ],
79          "Resource": [
80              "arn:aws:ec2:*:*:instance/*",
81              "arn:aws:ec2:*:*:key-pair/*",
82              "arn:aws:ec2:*:*:image/*",
83              "arn:aws:ec2:*:*:security-group/*",
84              "arn:aws:ec2:*:*:network-interface/*",
85              "arn:aws:ec2:*:*:subnet/*",
86              "arn:aws:ec2:*:*:volume/*"
87          ]
88      },
89      {
90          "Effect": "Allow",
91          "Action": [
92              "ec2:TerminateInstances",
93              "ec2:CreateTags",
94              "ec2:DeleteTags"
95          ],
96          "Resource": [
97              "arn:aws:ec2:*:*:instance/*"
98          ],
99          "Condition": {
100             "StringLike": {
101                 "ec2:ResourceTag/aws:cloudformation:stack-id": "arn:aws:cloudformation
                        :*:*:stack/aws-glue-*/*"
102             },
103             "StringEquals": {
104                 "ec2:ResourceTag/aws:cloudformation:logical-id": "ZeppelinInstance"
105             }
106         }
107     },
108     {
109         "Action": [
110             "iam:PassRole"
111         ],
112         "Effect": "Allow",
113         "Resource": "arn:aws:iam::*:role/AWSGlueServiceRole*",
114         "Condition": {
115             "StringLike": {
116                 "iam:PassedToService": [
117                     "glue.amazonaws.com"
118                 ]
119             }
```

```
120              }
121          },
122          {
123              "Action": [
124                  "iam:PassRole"
125              ],
126              "Effect": "Allow",
127              "Resource": "arn:aws:iam::*:role/AWSGlueServiceNotebookRole*",
128              "Condition": {
129                  "StringLike": {
130                      "iam:PassedToService": [
131                          "ec2.amazonaws.com"
132                      ]
133                  }
134              }
135          },
136          {
137              "Action": [
138                  "iam:PassRole"
139              ],
140              "Effect": "Allow",
141              "Resource": [
142                  "arn:aws:iam::*:role/service-role/AWSGlueServiceRole*"
143              ],
144              "Condition": {
145                  "StringLike": {
146                      "iam:PassedToService": [
147                          "glue.amazonaws.com"
148                      ]
149                  }
150              }
151          }
152      ]
153 }
```

The following table describes the permissions granted by this policy.
[See the AWS documentation website for more details]

8. Choose **Validate Policy**, and ensure that no errors appear in a red box at the top of the screen. Correct any that are reported. **Note**
If **Use autoformatting** is selected, the policy is reformatted whenever you open a policy or choose **Validate Policy**.

9. When you are satisfied with the policy, choose **Apply Policy**.

To attach the AWSGlueConsoleFullAccess managed policy

You can attach the **AWSGlueConsoleFullAccess** policy to provide permissions that are required by the AWS Glue console user. **Note**
You can skip this step if you created your own policy for AWS Glue console access.

1. Sign in to the AWS Management Console and open the IAM console at https://console.aws.amazon.com/iam/.

2. In the navigation pane, choose **Policies**.

3. In the list of policies, select the check box next to the **AWSGlueConsoleFullAccess**. You can use the **Filter** menu and the search box to filter the list of policies.

4. Choose **Policy actions**, and then choose **Attach**.

5. Choose the user to attach the policy to. You can use the **Filter** menu and the search box to filter the list of principal entities. After choosing the user to attach the policy to, choose **Attach policy**.

To attach the CloudWatchLogsReadOnlyAccess managed policy

You can attach the **CloudWatchLogsReadOnlyAccess** policy to a user to view the logs created by AWS Glue on the CloudWatch Logs console.

1. Sign in to the AWS Management Console and open the IAM console at https://console.aws.amazon.com/iam/.

2. In the navigation pane, choose **Policies**.

3. In the list of policies, select the check box next to the **CloudWatchLogsReadOnlyAccess**. You can use the **Filter** menu and the search box to filter the list of policies.

4. Choose **Policy actions**, and then choose **Attach**.

5. Choose the user to attach the policy to. You can use the **Filter** menu and the search box to filter the list of principal entities. After choosing the user to attach the policy to, choose **Attach policy**.

To attach the AWSCloudFormationReadOnlyAccess managed policy

You can attach the **AWSCloudFormationReadOnlyAccess** policy to a user to view the AWS CloudFormation stacks used by AWS Glue on the AWS CloudFormation console.

1. Sign in to the AWS Management Console and open the IAM console at https://console.aws.amazon.com/iam/.

2. In the navigation pane, choose **Policies**.

3. In the list of policies, select the check box next to the **AWSCloudFormationReadOnlyAccess**. You can use the **Filter** menu and the search box to filter the list of policies.

4. Choose **Policy actions**, and then choose **Attach**.

5. Choose the user to attach the policy to. You can use the **Filter** menu and the search box to filter the list of principal entities. After choosing the user to attach the policy to, choose **Attach policy**.

To attach the AmazonAthenaFullAccess managed policy

You can attach the **AmazonAthenaFullAccess** policy to a user to view Amazon S3 data in the Athena console.

1. Sign in to the AWS Management Console and open the IAM console at https://console.aws.amazon.com/iam/.

2. In the navigation pane, choose **Policies**.

3. In the list of policies, select the check box next to the **AmazonAthenaFullAccess**. You can use the **Filter** menu and the search box to filter the list of policies.

4. Choose **Policy actions**, and then choose **Attach**.

5. Choose the user to attach the policy to. You can use the **Filter** menu and the search box to filter the list of principal entities. After choosing the user to attach the policy to, choose **Attach policy**.

Step 4: Create an IAM Policy for Notebooks

If you plan to use notebooks with development endpoints, you must specify permissions when you create the notebook server. You provide those permissions by using AWS Identity and Access Management (IAM).

This policy grants permission for some Amazon S3 actions to manage resources in your account that are needed by AWS Glue when it assumes the role using this policy. Some of the resources that are specified in this policy refer to default names used by AWS Glue for Amazon S3 buckets, Amazon S3 ETL scripts, and Amazon EC2 resources. For simplicity, AWS Glue defaults writing some Amazon S3 objects into buckets in your account prefixed with `aws-glue-*`.

Note
You can skip this step if you use the AWS managed policy **AWSGlueServiceNotebookRole**.

In this step, you create a policy that is similar to `AWSGlueServiceNotebookRole`. You can find the most current version of `AWSGlueServiceNotebookRole` on the IAM console.

To create an IAM policy for notebooks

1. Sign in to the AWS Management Console and open the IAM console at https://console.aws.amazon.com/iam/.

2. In the left navigation pane, choose **Policies**.

3. Choose **Create Policy**.

4. On the **Create Policy** screen, navigate to a tab to edit JSON. Create a policy document with the following JSON statements, and then choose **Review policy**.

```
1  {
2      "Version":"2012-10-17",
3      "Statement":[
4          {
5              "Effect":"Allow",
6              "Action":[
7                  "glue:CreateDatabase",
8                  "glue:CreatePartition",
9                  "glue:CreateTable",
10                 "glue:DeleteDatabase",
11                 "glue:DeletePartition",
12                 "glue:DeleteTable",
13                 "glue:GetDatabase",
14                 "glue:GetDatabases",
15                 "glue:GetPartition",
16                 "glue:GetPartitions",
17                 "glue:GetTable",
18                 "glue:GetTableVersions",
19                 "glue:GetTables",
20                 "glue:UpdateDatabase",
21                 "glue:UpdatePartition",
22                 "glue:UpdateTable",
23                 "glue:CreateBookmark",
24                 "glue:GetBookmark",
25                 "glue:UpdateBookmark",
26                 "glue:GetMetric",
27                 "glue:PutMetric",
28                 "glue:CreateConnection",
29                 "glue:CreateJob",
```

```
30        "glue:DeleteConnection",
31        "glue:DeleteJob",
32        "glue:GetConnection",
33        "glue:GetConnections",
34        "glue:GetDevEndpoint",
35        "glue:GetDevEndpoints",
36        "glue:GetJob",
37        "glue:GetJobs",
38        "glue:UpdateJob",
39        "glue:BatchDeleteConnection",
40        "glue:UpdateConnection",
41        "glue:GetUserDefinedFunction",
42        "glue:UpdateUserDefinedFunction",
43        "glue:GetUserDefinedFunctions",
44        "glue:DeleteUserDefinedFunction",
45        "glue:CreateUserDefinedFunction",
46        "glue:BatchGetPartition",
47        "glue:BatchDeletePartition",
48        "glue:BatchCreatePartition",
49        "glue:BatchDeleteTable",
50        "glue:UpdateDevEndpoint",
51        "s3:GetBucketLocation",
52        "s3:ListBucket",
53        "s3:ListAllMyBuckets",
54        "s3:GetBucketAcl"
55      ],
56      "Resource":[
57        "*"
58      ]
59    },
60    {
61      "Effect":"Allow",
62      "Action":[
63        "s3:GetObject"
64      ],
65      "Resource":[
66        "arn:aws:s3:::crawler-public*",
67        "arn:aws:s3:::aws-glue*"
68      ]
69    },
70    {
71      "Effect":"Allow",
72      "Action":[
73        "s3:PutObject",
74        "s3:DeleteObject"
75      ],
76      "Resource":[
77        "arn:aws:s3:::aws-glue*"
78      ]
79    },
80    {
81      "Effect":"Allow",
82      "Action":[
83        "ec2:CreateTags",
```

```
 84            "ec2:DeleteTags"
 85          ],
 86          "Condition":{
 87            "ForAllValues:StringEquals":{
 88              "aws:TagKeys":[
 89                "aws-glue-service-resource"
 90              ]
 91            }
 92          },
 93          "Resource":[
 94            "arn:aws:ec2:*:*:network-interface/*",
 95            "arn:aws:ec2:*:*:security-group/*",
 96            "arn:aws:ec2:*:*:instance/*"
 97          ]
 98        }
 99      ]
100  }
```

The following table describes the permissions granted by this policy.
[See the AWS documentation website for more details]

5. On the **Review Policy** screen, type your **Policy Name**, for example **GlueServiceNotebookPolicy-Default**. Type an optional description, and when you're satisfied with the policy, then **Create policy**.

Step 5: Create an IAM Role for Notebooks

If you plan to use notebooks with development endpoints, you need to grant the IAM role permissions. You provide those permissions by using AWS Identity and Access Management, through an IAM role.

Note
When you create an IAM role using the IAM console, the console creates an instance profile automatically and gives it the same name as the role to which it corresponds.

To create an IAM role for notebooks

1. Sign in to the AWS Management Console and open the IAM console at https://console.aws.amazon.com/iam/.

2. In the left navigation pane, choose **Roles**.

3. Choose **Create role**.

4. For role type, choose **AWS Service**, find and choose **EC2**, and choose the **EC2** use case, then choose **Next: Permissions**.

5. On the **Attach permissions policy** page, choose the policies that contain the required permissions; for example, **AWSGlueServiceNotebookRole** for general AWS Glue permissions and the AWS managed policy **AmazonS3FullAccess** for access to Amazon S3 resources. Then choose **Next: Review**. **Note** Ensure that one of the policies in this role grants permissions to your Amazon S3 sources and targets. Also confirm that your policy allows full access to the location where you store your notebook when you create a notebook server. You might want to provide your own policy for access to specific Amazon S3 resources. For more information about creating an Amazon S3 policy for your resources, see Specifying Resources in a Policy.
   If you plan to access Amazon S3 sources and targets that are encrypted with SSE-KMS, then attach a policy which allows notebooks to decrypt the data. For more information, see Protecting Data Using Server-Side Encryption with AWS KMS-Managed Keys (SSE-KMS). For example:

```
1  {
2      "Version":"2012-10-17",
3      "Statement":[
4          {
5              "Effect":"Allow",
6              "Action":[
7                  "kms:Decrypt"
8              ],
9              "Resource":[
10                 "arn:aws:kms:*:account-id-without-hyphens:key/key-id"
11             ]
12         }
13     ]
14 }
```

6. For **Role name**, type a name for your role. Create the role with the name prefixed with the string **AWSGlueServiceNotebookRole** to allow the role to be passed from console users to the notebook server. AWS Glue provided policies expect IAM service roles to begin with **AWSGlueServiceNotebookRole**. Otherwise you must add a policy to your users to allow the `iam:PassRole` permission for IAM roles to match your naming convention. For example, type **AWSGlueServiceNotebookRoleDefault**. Then choose **Create role**.

Setting Up DNS in Your VPC

Domain Name System (DNS) is a standard by which names used on the internet are resolved to their corresponding IP addresses. A DNS hostname uniquely names a computer and consists of a host name and a domain name. DNS servers resolve DNS hostnames to their corresponding IP addresses. When using a custom DNS for name resolution, both forward DNS lookup and reverse DNS lookup must be implemented.

To set up DNS in your VPC, ensure that DNS hostnames and DNS resolution are both enabled in your VPC. The VPC network attributes `enableDnsHostnames` and `enableDnsSupport` must be set to `true`. To view and modify these attributes, go to the VPC console at https://console.aws.amazon.com/vpc/.

For more information, see Using DNS with your VPC.

Note
If you are using Route 53, confirm that your configuration does not override DNS network attributes.

Setting Up Your Environment to Access Data Stores

To run your extract, transform, and load (ETL) jobs, AWS Glue must be able to access your data stores. If a job doesn't need to run in your virtual private cloud (VPC) subnet—for example, transforming data from Amazon S3 to Amazon S3—no additional configuration is needed.

If a job needs to run in your VPC subnet—for example, transforming data from a JDBC data store in a private subnet—AWS Glue sets up elastic network interfaces that enable your jobs to connect securely to other resources within your VPC. Each elastic network interface is assigned a private IP address from the IP address range within the subnet you specified. No public IP addresses are assigned. Security groups specified in the AWS Glue connection are applied on each of the elastic network interfaces. For more information, see Setting Up a VPC to Connect to JDBC Data Stores.

All JDBC data stores that are accessed by the job must be available from the VPC subnet. To access Amazon S3 from within your VPC, a VPC endpoint is required. If your job needs to access both VPC resources and the public internet, the VPC needs to have a Network Address Translation (NAT) gateway inside the VPC.

A job or development endpoint can only access one VPC (and subnet) at a time. If you need to access data stores in different VPCs, you have the following options:

- Use VPC peering to access the data stores. For more about VPC peering, see VPC Peering Basics
- Use an Amazon S3 bucket as an intermediary storage location. Split the work into two jobs, with the Amazon S3 output of job 1 as the input to job 2.

For JDBC data stores, you create a connection in AWS Glue with the necessary properties to connect to your data stores. For more information about the connection, see Adding a Connection to Your Data Store.

Note
Make sure you set up your DNS environment for AWS Glue. For more information, see Setting Up DNS in Your VPC.

Topics

- Amazon VPC Endpoints for Amazon S3
- Setting Up a VPC to Connect to JDBC Data Stores

Amazon VPC Endpoints for Amazon S3

For security reasons, many AWS customers run their applications within an Amazon Virtual Private Cloud environment (Amazon VPC). With Amazon VPC, you can launch Amazon EC2 instances into a virtual private cloud, which is logically isolated from other networks—including the public internet. With an Amazon VPC, you have control over its IP address range, subnets, routing tables, network gateways, and security settings.

Note

If you created your AWS account after 2013-12-04, you already have a default VPC in each AWS Region. You can immediately start using your default VPC without any additional configuration.
For more information, see Your Default VPC and Subnets in the Amazon VPC User Guide.

Many customers have legitimate privacy and security concerns about sending and receiving data across the public internet. Customers can address these concerns by using a virtual private network (VPN) to route all Amazon S3 network traffic through their own corporate network infrastructure. However, this approach can introduce bandwidth and availability challenges.

VPC endpoints for Amazon S3 can alleviate these challenges. A VPC endpoint for Amazon S3 enables AWS Glue to use a private IP addresses to access Amazon S3 with no exposure to the public internet. AWS Glue does not require public IP addresses, and you don't need an internet gateway, a NAT device, or a virtual private gateway in your VPC. You use endpoint policies to control access to Amazon S3. Traffic between your VPC and the AWS service does not leave the Amazon network.

When you create a VPC endpoint for Amazon S3, any requests to an Amazon S3 endpoint within the Region (for example, *s3.us-west-2.amazonaws.com*) are routed to a private Amazon S3 endpoint within the Amazon network. You don't need to modify your applications running on EC2 instances in your VPC—the endpoint name remains the same, but the route to Amazon S3 stays entirely within the Amazon network, and does not access the public internet.

For more information about VPC endpoints, see VPC Endpoints in the Amazon VPC User Guide.

The following diagram shows how AWS Glue can use a VPC endpoint to access Amazon S3.

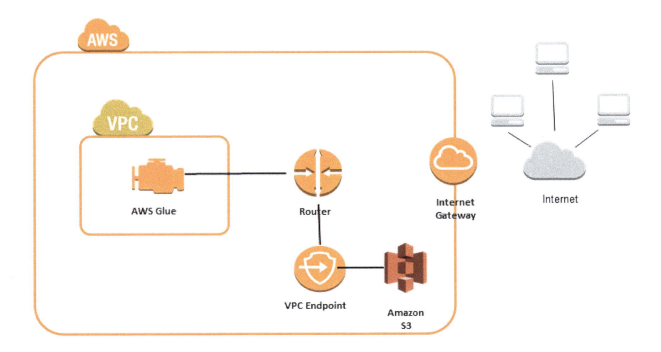

To set up access for Amazon S3

1. Sign in to the AWS Management Console and open the Amazon VPC console at https://console.aws.amazon.com/vpc/.

2. In the left navigation pane, choose **Endpoints**.

3. Choose **Create Endpoint**, and follow the steps to create an Amazon S3 endpoint in your VPC.

Setting Up a VPC to Connect to JDBC Data Stores

To enable AWS Glue components to communicate, you must set up access to your data stores, such as Amazon Redshift and Amazon RDS. To enable AWS Glue to communicate between its components, specify a security group with a self-referencing inbound rule for all TCP ports. By creating a self-referencing rule, you can restrict the source to the same security group in the VPC, and it's not open to all networks. The default security group for your VPC might already have a self-referencing inbound rule for ALL Traffic.

To set up access for Amazon Redshift data stores

1. Sign in to the AWS Management Console and open the Amazon Redshift console at https://console.aws.amazon.com/redshift/.

2. In the left navigation pane, choose **Clusters**.

3. Choose the cluster name that you want to access from AWS Glue.

4. In the **Cluster Properties** section, choose a security group in **VPC security groups** to allow AWS Glue to use. Record the name of the security group that you chose for future reference. Choosing the security group opens the Amazon EC2 console **Security Groups** list.

5. Choose the security group to modify and navigate to the **Inbound** tab.

6. Add a self-referencing rule to allow AWS Glue components to communicate. Specifically, add or confirm that there is a rule of **Type All TCP**, **Protocol** is TCP, **Port Range** includes all ports, and whose **Source** is the same security group name as the **Group ID**.

   The inbound rule looks similar to the following:

   _____

[See the AWS documentation website for more details]

For example:

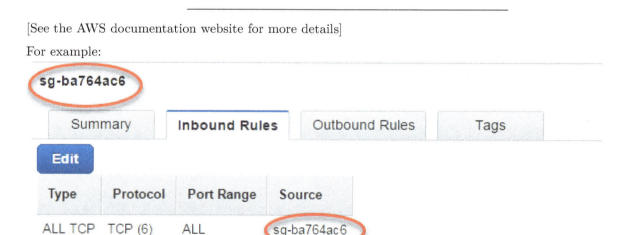

1. Add a rule for outbound traffic also. Either open outbound traffic to all ports, or create a self-referencing rule of **Type All TCP**, **Protocol** is TCP, **Port Range** includes all ports, and whose **Source** is the same security group name as the **Group ID**.

   The outbound rule looks similar to one of these rules:

   _____

[See the AWS documentation website for more details]

To set up access for Amazon RDS data stores

1. Sign in to the AWS Management Console and open the Amazon RDS console at https://console.aws.amazon.com/rds/.

2. In the left navigation pane, choose **Instances**.

3. Choose the Amazon RDS **Engine** and **DB Instance** name that you want to access from AWS Glue.

4. From **Instance Actions**, choose **See Details**. On the **Details** tab, find the **Security Groups** name you will access from AWS Glue. Record the name of the security group for future reference.

5. Choose the security group to open the Amazon EC2 console.

6. Confirm that your **Group ID** from Amazon RDS is chosen, then choose the **Inbound** tab.

7. Add a self-referencing rule to allow AWS Glue components to communicate. Specifically, add or confirm that there is a rule of **Type All TCP**, **Protocol** is TCP, **Port Range** includes all ports, and whose **Source** is the same security group name as the **Group ID**.

   The inbound rule looks similar to this:

   _____

[See the AWS documentation website for more details]

For example:

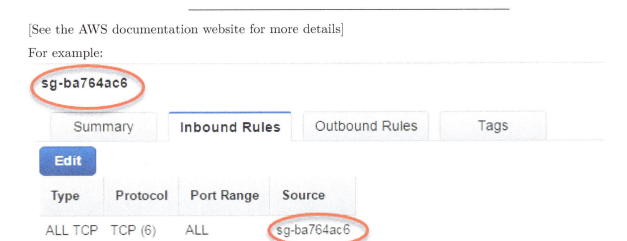

1. Add a rule to for outbound traffic also. Either open outbound traffic to all ports or create a self-referencing rule of **Type All TCP**, **Protocol** is TCP, **Port Range** includes all ports, and whose **Source** is the same security group name as the **Group ID**.

   The outbound rule looks similar to one of these rules:

   _____

[See the AWS documentation website for more details]

Setting Up Your Environment for Development Endpoints

To run your extract, transform, and load (ETL) scripts with AWS Glue, you sometimes develop and test your scripts using a development endpoint. When you set up a development endpoint, you specify a virtual private cloud (VPC), subnet, and security groups.

Note
Make sure you set up your DNS environment for AWS Glue. For more information, see Setting Up DNS in Your VPC.

Setting Up Your Network for a Development Endpoint

To enable AWS Glue to access required resources, add a row in your subnet route table to associate a prefix list for Amazon S3 to the VPC endpoint. A prefix list ID is required for creating an outbound security group rule that allows traffic from a VPC to access an AWS service through a VPC endpoint. To ease connecting to a notebook server that is associated with this development endpoint, from your local machine, add a row to the route table to add an internet gateway ID. For more information, see VPC Endpoints. Update the subnet routes table to be similar to the following table:

Destination	Target
10.0.0.0/16	local
pl-id for Amazon S3	vpce-id
0.0.0.0/0	igw-xxxx

To enable AWS Glue to communicate between its components, specify a security group with a self-referencing inbound rule for all TCP ports. By creating a self-referencing rule, you can restrict the source to the same security group in the VPC, and it's not open to all networks. The default security group for your VPC might already have a self-referencing inbound rule for ALL Traffic.

To set up a security group

1. Sign in to the AWS Management Console and open the Amazon EC2 console at https://console.aws.amazon.com/ec2/.

2. In the left navigation pane, choose **Security Groups**.

3. Either choose an existing security group from the list, or **Create Security Group** to use with the development endpoint.

4. In the security group pane, navigate to the **Inbound** tab.

5. Add a self-referencing rule to allow AWS Glue components to communicate. Specifically, add or confirm that there is a rule of **Type All TCP**, **Protocol** is TCP, **Port Range** includes all ports, and whose **Source** is the same security group name as the **Group ID**.

   The inbound rule looks similar to this:

[See the AWS documentation website for more details]

The following shows an example of a self-referencing inbound rule:

1. Add a rule to for outbound traffic also. Either open outbound traffic to all ports, or create a self-referencing rule of **Type All TCP**, **Protocol** is TCP, **Port Range** includes all ports, and whose **Source** is the same security group name as the **Group ID**.

   The outbound rule looks similar to one of these rules:

   _____

[See the AWS documentation website for more details]

Setting Up Amazon EC2 for a Notebook Server

With a development endpoint, you can create a notebook server to test your ETL scripts with Zeppelin notebooks. To enable communication to your notebook, specify a security group with inbound rules for both HTTPS (port 443) and SSH (port 22). Ensure that the rule's source is either 0.0.0.0/0 or the IP address of the machine that is connecting to the notebook.

Note
When using a custom DNS, ensure that the custom DNS server is able to do forward and reverse resolution for the entire subnet CIDR where the notebook server is launched.

To set up a security group

1. Sign in to the AWS Management Console and open the Amazon EC2 console at https://console.aws.amazon.com/ec2/.

2. In the left navigation pane, choose **Security Groups**.

3. Either choose an existing security group from the list, or **Create Security Group** to use with your notebook server. The security group that is associated with your development endpoint is also used to create your notebook server.

4. In the security group pane, navigate to the **Inbound** tab.

5. Add inbound rules similar to this:

   _____

[See the AWS documentation website for more details]

The following shows an example of the inbound rules for the security group:

Security Group: sg-19e1b768

| Description | **Inbound** | Outbound | Tags |

Edit

Type ⓘ	Protocol ⓘ	Port Range ⓘ	Source ⓘ
SSH	TCP	22	0.0.0.0/0
HTTPS	TCP	443	0.0.0.0/0

AWS Glue Console Workflow Overview

With AWS Glue, you store metadata in the AWS Glue Data Catalog. You use this metadata to orchestrate ETL jobs that transform data sources and load your data warehouse. The following steps describe the general workflow and some of the choices that you make when working with AWS Glue.

1. Populate the AWS Glue Data Catalog with table definitions.

   In the console, you can add a crawler to populate the AWS Glue Data Catalog. You can start the **Add crawler** wizard from the list of tables or the list of crawlers. You choose one or more data stores for your crawler to access. You can also create a schedule to determine the frequency of running your crawler.

   Optionally, you can provide a custom classifier that infers the schema of your data. You can create custom classifiers using a grok pattern. However, AWS Glue provides built-in classifiers that are automatically used by crawlers if a custom classifier does not recognize your data. When you define a crawler, you don't have to select a classifier. For more information about classifiers in AWS Glue, see Adding Classifiers to a Crawler.

   Crawling some types of data stores requires a connection that provides authentication and location information. If needed, you can create a connection that provides this required information in the AWS Glue console.

   The crawler reads your data store and creates data definitions and named tables in the AWS Glue Data Catalog. These tables are organized into a database of your choosing. You can also populate the Data Catalog with manually created tables. With this method, you provide the schema and other metadata to create table definitions in the Data Catalog. Because this method can be a bit tedious and error prone, it's often better to have a crawler create the table definitions.

   For more information about populating the AWS Glue Data Catalog with table definitions, see Defining Tables in the AWS Glue Data Catalog.

2. Define a job that describes the transformation of data from source to target.

   Generally, to create a job, you have to make the following choices:

   - Pick a table from the AWS Glue Data Catalog to be the source of the job. Your job uses this table definition to access your data store and interpret the format of your data.
   - Pick a table or location from the AWS Glue Data Catalog to be the target of the job. Your job uses this information to access your data store.
   - Tell AWS Glue to generate a PySpark script to transform your source to target. AWS Glue generates the code to call built-in transforms to convert data from its source schema to target schema format. These transforms perform operations such as copy data, rename columns, and filter data to transform data as necessary. You can modify this script in the AWS Glue console.

   For more information about defining jobs in AWS Glue, see Authoring Jobs in AWS Glue.

3. Run your job to transform your data.

   You can run your job on demand, or start it based on a one of these trigger types:

   - A trigger that is based on a cron schedule.
   - A trigger that is event-based; for example, the successful completion of another job can start an AWS Glue job.
   - A trigger that starts a job on demand.

   For more information about triggers in AWS Glue, see Triggering Jobs in AWS Glue.

4. Monitor your scheduled crawlers and triggered jobs.

   Use the AWS Glue console to view the following:

   - Job run details and errors.

- Crawler run details and errors.
- Any notifications about AWS Glue activities

For more information about monitoring your crawlers and jobs in AWS Glue, see Running and Monitoring AWS Glue.

Authentication and Access Control for AWS Glue

Access to AWS Glue requires credentials. Those credentials must have permissions to access AWS resources, such as an AWS Glue table or an Amazon Elastic Compute Cloud (Amazon EC2) instance. The following sections provide details on how you can use AWS Identity and Access Management (IAM) and AWS Glue to help secure access to your resources.

- Authentication
- Access Control

Authentication

You can access AWS as any of the following types of identities:

- **AWS account root user** – When you first create an AWS account, you begin with a single sign-in identity that has complete access to all AWS services and resources in the account. This identity is called the AWS account *root user* and is accessed by signing in with the email address and password that you used to create the account. We strongly recommend that you do not use the root user for your everyday tasks, even the administrative ones. Instead, adhere to the best practice of using the root user only to create your first IAM user. Then securely lock away the root user credentials and use them to perform only a few account and service management tasks.

- **IAM user** – An IAM user is an identity within your AWS account that has specific custom permissions (for example, permissions to create a table in AWS Glue). You can use an IAM user name and password to sign in to secure AWS webpages like the AWS Management Console, AWS Discussion Forums, or the AWS Support Center.

    In addition to a user name and password, you can also generate access keys for each user. You can use these keys when you access AWS services programmatically, either through one of the several SDKs or by using the AWS Command Line Interface (CLI). The SDK and CLI tools use the access keys to cryptographically sign your request. If you don't use AWS tools, you must sign the request yourself. AWS Glue supports *Signature Version 4*, a protocol for authenticating inbound API requests. For more information about authenticating requests, see Signature Version 4 Signing Process in the *AWS General Reference*.

- **IAM role** – An IAM role is an IAM identity that you can create in your account that has specific permissions. It is similar to an *IAM user*, but it is not associated with a specific person. An IAM role enables you to obtain temporary access keys that can be used to access AWS services and resources. IAM roles with temporary credentials are useful in the following situations:

    - **Federated user access** – Instead of creating an IAM user, you can use existing user identities from AWS Directory Service, your enterprise user directory, or a web identity provider. These are known as *federated users*. AWS assigns a role to a federated user when access is requested through an identity provider. For more information about federated users, see Federated Users and Roles in the *IAM User Guide*.

    - **AWS service access** – You can use an IAM role in your account to grant an AWS service permissions to access your account's resources. For example, you can create a role that allows Amazon Redshift to access an Amazon S3 bucket on your behalf and then load data from that bucket into an Amazon Redshift cluster. For more information, see Creating a Role to Delegate Permissions to an AWS Service in the *IAM User Guide*.

- **Applications running on Amazon EC2** – You can use an IAM role to manage temporary credentials for applications that are running on an EC2 instance and making AWS API requests. This is preferable to storing access keys within the EC2 instance. To assign an AWS role to an EC2 instance and make it available to all of its applications, you create an instance profile that is attached to the instance. An instance profile contains the role and enables programs that are running on the EC2 instance to get temporary credentials. For more information, see Using an IAM Role to Grant Permissions to Applications Running on Amazon EC2 Instances in the *IAM User Guide*.

Access Control

You can have valid credentials to authenticate your requests, but unless you have permissions you cannot create or access AWS Glue resources. For example, you must have permissions to create an AWS Glue table.

The following sections describe how to manage permissions for AWS Glue. We recommend that you read the overview first.

- Overview of Managing Access
- Using Identity-Based Policies (IAM Policies)
- AWS Glue API Permissions Reference

Overview of Managing Access Permissions to Your AWS Glue Resources

Every AWS resource is owned by an AWS account, and permissions to create or access a resource are governed by permissions policies. An account administrator can attach permissions policies to IAM identities (that is, users, groups, and roles), and some services (such as AWS Lambda) also support attaching permissions policies to resources.

Note

An *account administrator* (or administrator user) is a user with administrator privileges. For more information, see IAM Best Practices in the *IAM User Guide*.

When granting permissions, you decide who is getting the permissions, the resources they get permissions for, and the specific actions that you want to allow on those resources.

Topics

- AWS Glue Resources and Operations
- Understanding Resource Ownership
- Managing Access to Resources
- Specifying Policy Elements: Actions, Effects, and Principals
- Specifying Conditions in a Policy

AWS Glue Resources and Operations

AWS Glue provides a set of operations to work with AWS Glue resources. For a list of available operations, see AWS Glue AWS Glue API.

Understanding Resource Ownership

The AWS account owns the resources that are created in the account, regardless of who created the resources. Specifically, the resource owner is the AWS account of the principal entity (that is, the root account, an IAM user, or an IAM role) that authenticates the resource creation request. The following examples illustrate how this works:

- If you use the root account credentials of your AWS account to create a table, your AWS account is the owner of the resource (in AWS Glue, the resource is a table).
- If you create an IAM user in your AWS account and grant permissions to create a table to that user, the user can create a table. However, your AWS account, to which the user belongs, owns the table resource.
- If you create an IAM role in your AWS account with permissions to create a table, anyone who can assume the role can create a table. Your AWS account, to which the user belongs, owns the table resource.

Managing Access to Resources

A *permissions policy* describes who has access to what. The following section explains the available options for creating permissions policies.

Note

This section discusses using IAM in the context of AWS Glue. It doesn't provide detailed information about the IAM service. For complete IAM documentation, see What Is IAM? in the *IAM User Guide*. For information about IAM policy syntax and descriptions, see AWS IAM Policy Reference in the *IAM User Guide*.

Policies attached to an IAM identity are referred to as *identity-based* policies (IAM polices) and policies attached to a resource are referred to as *resource-based* policies. AWS Glue supports only identity-based policies (IAM policies).

Topics

- Identity-Based Policies (IAM Policies)
- Resource-Based Policies

Identity-Based Policies (IAM Policies)

You can attach policies to IAM identities. For example, you can do the following:

- **Attach a permissions policy to a user or a group in your account** – To grant a user permissions to create an AWS Glue resource, such as a table, you can attach a permissions policy to a user or group that the user belongs to.

- **Attach a permissions policy to a role (grant cross-account permissions)** – You can attach an identity-based permissions policy to an IAM role to grant cross-account permissions. For example, the administrator in account A can create a role to grant cross-account permissions to another AWS account (for example, account B) or an AWS service as follows:

  1. Account A administrator creates an IAM role and attaches a permissions policy to the role that grants permissions on resources in account A.

  2. Account A administrator attaches a trust policy to the role identifying account B as the principal who can assume the role.

  3. Account B administrator can then delegate permissions to assume the role to any users in account B. Doing this allows users in account B to create or access resources in account A. The principal in the trust policy can also be an AWS service principal if you want to grant an AWS service permissions to assume the role.

  For more information about using IAM to delegate permissions, see Access Management in the *IAM User Guide*.

The following is an example policy that grants permissions for one AWS Glue action (`glue:GetTables`). The wildcard character (*) in the `Resource` value means that you can use this action to obtain the names of all the tables in a database owned by the AWS account in the current AWS region.

```
1  {
2      "Version": "2012-10-17",
3      "Statement": [
4          {
5              "Sid": "GetTables",
6              "Effect": "Allow",
7              "Action": [
8                  "glue:GetTables"
9              ],
10             "Resource": "*"
11         }
12     ]
13 }
```

For more information about using identity-based policies with AWS Glue, see Using Identity-Based Policies (IAM Policies) for AWS Glue. For more information about users, groups, roles, and permissions, see Identities (Users, Groups, and Roles) in the *IAM User Guide*.

Resource-Based Policies

Other services, such as Amazon S3, also support resource-based permissions policies. For example, you can attach a policy to an S3 bucket to manage access permissions to that bucket. AWS Glue doesn't support resource-based policies.

Specifying Policy Elements: Actions, Effects, and Principals

For each AWS Glue resource, the service defines a set of API operations. To grant permissions for these API operations, AWS Glue defines a set of actions that you can specify in a policy. Some API operations can require permissions for more than one action in order to perform the API operation. For more information about resources and API operations, see AWS Glue Resources and Operations and AWS Glue AWS Glue API.

The following are the most basic policy elements:

- **Resource** – You use an Amazon Resource Name (ARN) to identify the resource that the policy applies to. For more information, see AWS Glue Resources and Operations.
- **Action** – You use action keywords to identify resource operations that you want to allow or deny. For example, you can use `create` to allow users to create a table.
- **Effect** – You specify the effect, either allow or deny, when the user requests the specific action. If you don't explicitly grant access to (allow) a resource, access is implicitly denied. You can also explicitly deny access to a resource, which you might do to make sure that a user cannot access it, even if a different policy grants access.
- **Principal** – In identity-based policies (IAM policies), the user that the policy is attached to is the implicit principal. For resource-based policies, you specify the user, account, service, or other entity that you want to receive permissions (applies to resource-based policies only). AWS Glue doesn't support resource-based policies.

To learn more about IAM policy syntax and descriptions, see AWS IAM Policy Reference in the *IAM User Guide*.

For a table showing all of the AWS Glue API operations and the resources that they apply to, see AWS Glue API Permissions: Actions and Resources Reference.

Specifying Conditions in a Policy

When you grant permissions, you can use the access policy language to specify the conditions when a policy should take effect. For example, you might want a policy to be applied only after a specific date. For more information about specifying conditions in a policy language, see Condition in the *IAM User Guide*.

To express conditions, you use predefined condition keys. There are AWS-wide condition keys and AWS Glue–specific keys that you can use as appropriate. For a complete list of AWS-wide keys, see Available Keys for Conditions in the *IAM User Guide*.

Using Identity-Based Policies (IAM Policies) for AWS Glue

This topic provides examples of identity-based policies that demonstrate how an account administrator can attach permissions policies to IAM identities (that is, users, groups, and roles) and thereby grant permissions to perform operations on AWS Glue resources.

Important

We recommend that you first review the introductory topics that explain the basic concepts and options available to manage access to your AWS Glue resources. For more information, see Overview of Managing Access Permissions to Your AWS Glue Resources.

The sections in this topic cover the following:

- Permissions Required to Use the AWS Glue Console
- AWS Managed (Predefined) Policies for AWS Glue

The following shows an example of a permissions policy for Amazon DynamoDB.

```
1  {
2      "Version": "2012-10-17",
3      "Statement": [
4          {
5              "Sid": "DescribeQueryScanBooksTable",
6              "Effect": "Allow",
7              "Action": [
8                  "dynamodb:DescribeTable",
9                  "dynamodb:Query",
10                 "dynamodb:Scan"
11             ],
12             "Resource": "arn:aws:dynamodb:us-west-2:account-id:table/Books"
13         }
14     ]
15 }
```

The policy has one statement that grants permissions for three DynamoDB actions (`dynamodb:DescribeTable`, `dynamodb:Query` and `dynamodb:Scan`) on a table in the `us-west-2` region, which is owned by the AWS account specified by `account-id`. The *Amazon Resource Name (ARN)* in the `Resource` value specifies the table to which the permissions apply.

Permissions Required to Use the AWS Glue Console

For a user to work with the AWS Glue console, that user must have a minimum set of permissions that allows the user to work with the AWS Glue resources for their AWS account. In addition to these AWS Glue permissions, the console requires permissions from the following services:

- Amazon CloudWatch Logs permissions to display logs.
- AWS Identity and Access Management permissions to list and pass roles.
- AWS CloudFormation permissions to work with stacks.
- Amazon Elastic Compute Cloud permissions to list VPCs, subnets, security groups, instances, and other objects.
- Amazon Simple Storage Service permissions to list buckets and objects. Also permission to retrieve and save scripts.
- Amazon Redshift permissions to work with clusters.
- Amazon Relational Database Service permissions to list instances.

For more information on the permissions that your users require to view and work with the AWS Glue console, see Step 3: Attach a Policy to IAM Users That Access AWS Glue.

If you create an IAM policy that is more restrictive than the minimum required permissions, the console won't function as intended for users with that IAM policy. To ensure that those users can still use the AWS Glue console, also attach the `AWSGlueConsoleFullAccess` managed policy to the user, as described in AWS Managed (Predefined) Policies for AWS Glue.

You don't need to allow minimum console permissions for users that are making calls only to the AWS CLI or the AWS Glue API.

AWS Managed (Predefined) Policies for AWS Glue

AWS addresses many common use cases by providing standalone IAM policies that are created and administered by AWS. These AWS managed policies grant necessary permissions for common use cases so that you can avoid having to investigate what permissions are needed. For more information, see AWS Managed Policies in the *IAM User Guide*.

The following AWS managed policies, which you can attach to users in your account, are specific to AWS Glue and are grouped by use case scenario:

- **AWSGlueConsoleFullAccess** – Grants full access to AWS Glue resources when using the AWS Management Console. If you follow the naming convention for resources specified in this policy, users have full console capabilities. This policy is typically attached to users of the AWS Glue console.
- **AWSGlueServiceRole** – Grants access to resources that various AWS Glue processes require to run on your behalf. These resources include AWS Glue, Amazon S3, IAM, CloudWatch Logs, and Amazon EC2. If you follow the naming convention for resources specified in this policy, AWS Glue processes have the required permissions. This policy is typically attached to roles specified when defining crawlers, jobs, and development endpoints.
- **AWSGlueServiceNotebookRole** – Grants access to resources required when creating a notebook server. These resources include AWS Glue, Amazon S3, and Amazon EC2. If you follow the naming convention for resources specified in this policy, AWS Glue processes have the required permissions. This policy is typically attached to roles specified when creating a notebook server on a development endpoint.

Note
You can review these permissions policies by signing in to the IAM console and searching for specific policies there.

You can also create your own custom IAM policies to allow permissions for AWS Glue actions and resources. You can attach these custom policies to the IAM users or groups that require those permissions.

AWS Glue API Permissions: Actions and Resources Reference

When you are setting up Access Control and writing a permissions policy that you can attach to an IAM identity (identity-based policies), you can use the following table as a reference. The table lists each AWS Glue API operation, the corresponding actions for which you can grant permissions to perform the action, and the AWS resource for which you can grant the permissions. You specify the actions in the policy's `Action` field, and you specify the resource value in the policy's `Resource` field.

You can use AWS-wide condition keys in your AWS Glue policies to express conditions. For a complete list of AWS-wide keys, see Available Keys in the *IAM User Guide*.

Note
To specify an action, use the `glue:` prefix followed by the API operation name (for example, `glue:GetTable`).

If you see an expand arrow () in the upper-right corner of the table, you can open the table in a new window. To close the window, choose the close button (**X**) in the lower-right corner.

AWS Glue API and Required Permissions for Actions

AWS Glue API Operations	Required Permissions (API Actions)	Resources
BatchCreatePartition Action (Python: batch_create_partition)	glue:BatchCreatePartition	*
BatchDeleteConnection Action (Python: batch_delete_connection)	glue:BatchDeleteConnection	*
BatchDeletePartition Action (Python: batch_delete_partition)	glue:BatchDeletePartition	*
BatchDeleteTable Action (Python: batch_delete_table)	glue:BatchDeleteTable	*
BatchGetPartition Action (Python: batch_get_partition)	glue:BatchGetPartition	*
BatchStopJobRun Action (Python: batch_stop_job_run)	glue:BatchStopJobRun	*
CreateClassifier Action (Python: create_classifier)	glue:CreateClassifier	*
CreateConnection Action (Python: create_connection)	glue:CreateConnection	*
CreateCrawler Action (Python: create_crawler)	glue:CreateCrawler	*
CreateDatabase Action (Python: create_database)	glue:CreateDatabase	*
CreateDevEndpoint Action (Python: create_dev_endpoint)	glue:CreateDevEndpoint	*
CreateJob Action (Python: create_job)	glue:CreateJob	*
CreatePartition Action (Python: create_partition)	glue:CreatePartition	*
CreateScript Action (Python: create_script)	glue:CreateScript	*

AWS Glue API Operations	Required Permissions (API Actions)	Resources
CreateTable Action (Python: create_table)	glue:CreateTable	*
CreateTrigger Action (Python: create_trigger)	glue:CreateTrigger	*
CreateUserDefinedFunction Action (Python: create_user_defined_function)	glue:CreateUserDefinedFunction	*
DeleteClassifier Action (Python: delete_classifier)	glue:DeleteClassifier	*
DeleteConnection Action (Python: delete_connection)	glue:DeleteConnection	*
DeleteCrawler Action (Python: delete_crawler)	glue:DeleteCrawler	*
DeleteDatabase Action (Python: delete_database)	glue:DeleteDatabase	*
DeleteDevEndpoint Action (Python: delete_dev_endpoint)	glue:DeleteDevEndpoint	*
DeleteJob Action (Python: delete_job)	glue:DeleteJob	*
DeletePartition Action (Python: delete_partition)	glue:DeletePartition	*
DeleteTable Action (Python: delete_table)	glue:DeleteTable	*
DeleteTrigger Action (Python: delete_trigger)	glue:DeleteTrigger	*
DeleteUserDefinedFunction Action (Python: delete_user_defined_function)	glue:DeleteUserDefinedFunction	*
GetCatalogImportStatus Action (Python: get_catalog_import_status)	glue:GetCatalogImportStatus	*
GetClassifier Action (Python: get_classifier)	glue:GetClassifier	*
GetClassifiers Action (Python: get_classifiers)	glue:GetClassifiers	*
GetConnection Action (Python: get_connection)	glue:GetConnection	*
GetConnections Action (Python: get_connections)	glue:GetConnections	*
GetCrawler Action (Python: get_crawler)	glue:GetCrawler	*
GetCrawlerMetrics Action (Python: get_crawler_metrics)	glue:GetCrawlerMetrics	*
GetCrawlers Action (Python: get_crawlers)	glue:GetCrawlers	*
GetDatabase Action (Python: get_database)	glue:GetDatabase	*
GetDatabases Action (Python: get_databases)	glue:GetDatabases	*

AWS Glue API Operations	Required Permissions (API Actions)	Resources
GetDataflowGraph Action (Python: get_dataflow_graph)	glue:GetDataflowGraph	*
GetDevEndpoint Action (Python: get_dev_endpoint)	glue:GetDevEndpoint	*
GetDevEndpoints Action (Python: get_dev_endpoints)	glue:GetDevEndpoints	*
GetJob Action (Python: get_job)	glue:GetJob	*
GetJobRun Action (Python: get_job_run)	glue:GetJobRun	*
GetJobRuns Action (Python: get_job_runs)	glue:GetJobRuns	*
GetJobs Action (Python: get_jobs)	glue:GetJobs	*
GetMapping Action (Python: get_mapping)	glue:GetMapping	*
GetPartition Action (Python: get_partition)	glue:GetPartition	*
GetPartitions Action (Python: get_partitions)	glue:GetPartitions	*
GetTable Action (Python: get_table)	glue:GetTable	*
GetTables Action (Python: get_tables)	glue:GetTables	*
GetTableVersions Action (Python: get_table_versions)	glue:GetTableVersions	*
GetTrigger Action (Python: get_trigger)	glue:GetTrigger	*
GetTriggers Action (Python: get_triggers)	glue:GetTriggers	*
GetUserDefinedFunction Action (Python: get_user_defined_function)	glue:GetUserDefinedFunction	*
GetUserDefinedFunctions Action (Python: get_user_defined_functions)	glue:GetUserDefinedFunctions	*
ImportCatalogToGlue Action (Python: import_catalog_to_glue)	glue:ImportCatalogToGlue	*
ResetJobBookmark Action (Python: reset_job_bookmark)	glue:ResetJobBookmark	*
StartCrawler Action (Python: start_crawler)	glue:StartCrawler	*
StartCrawlerSchedule Action (Python: start_crawler_schedule)	glue:StartCrawlerSchedule	*
StartJobRun Action (Python: start_job_run)	glue:StartJobRun	*
StartTrigger Action (Python: start_trigger)	glue:StartTrigger	*

AWS Glue API Operations	Required Permissions (API Actions)	Resources
StopCrawler Action (Python: stop_crawler)	glue:StopCrawler	*
StopCrawlerSchedule Action (Python: stop_crawler_schedule)	glue:StopCrawlerSchedule	*
StopTrigger Action (Python: stop_trigger)	glue:StopTrigger	*
UpdateClassifier Action (Python: update_classifier)	glue:UpdateClassifier	*
UpdateConnection Action (Python: update_connection)	glue:UpdateConnection	*
UpdateCrawler Action (Python: update_crawler)	glue:UpdateCrawler	*
UpdateCrawlerSchedule Action (Python: update_crawler_schedule)	glue:UpdateCrawlerSchedule	*
UpdateDatabase Action (Python: update_database)	glue:UpdateDatabase	*
UpdateDevEndpoint Action (Python: update_dev_endpoint)	glue:UpdateDevEndpoint	*
UpdateJob Action (Python: update_job)	glue:UpdateJob	*
UpdatePartition Action (Python: update_partition)	glue:UpdatePartition	*
UpdateTable Action (Python: update_table)	glue:UpdateTable	*
UpdateTrigger Action (Python: update_trigger)	glue:UpdateTrigger	*
UpdateUserDefinedFunction Action (Python: update_user_defined_function)	glue:UpdatateUserDefinedFunction	*

Related Topics

- Access Control

Populating the AWS Glue Data Catalog

The AWS Glue Data Catalog contains references to data that is used as sources and targets of your extract, transform, and load (ETL) jobs in AWS Glue. To create your data warehouse, you must catalog this data. The AWS Glue Data Catalog is an index to the location, schema, and runtime metrics of your data. You use the information in the Data Catalog to create and monitor your ETL jobs. Typically, you run a crawler to take inventory of the data in your data stores, but there are other ways to add metadata tables into your Data Catalog.

You can add table definitions to the AWS Glue Data Catalog in the following ways:

- Run a crawler that connects to one or more data stores, determines the data structures, and writes tables into the Data Catalog. You can run your crawler on a schedule. For more information, see Cataloging Tables with a Crawler.

- Use the AWS Glue console to create a table in the AWS Glue Data Catalog. For more information, see Working with Tables on the AWS Glue Console.

  Use the `CreateTable` operation in the AWS Glue API to create a table in the AWS Glue Data Catalog.

The following workflow diagram shows how AWS Glue crawlers interact with data stores and other elements to populate the Data Catalog.

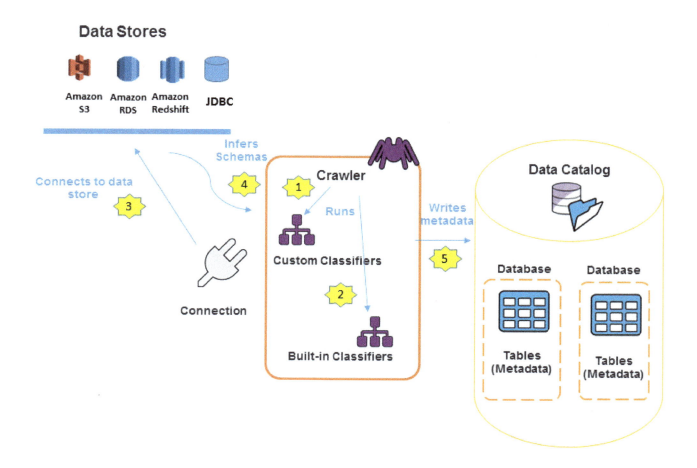

The following is the general workflow for how a crawler populates the AWS Glue Data Catalog:

1. A crawler runs any custom classifiers that you choose to infer the schema of your data. You provide the

code for custom classifiers, and they run in the order that you specify.

The first custom classifier to successfully recognize the structure of your data is used to create a schema. Custom classifiers lower in the list are skipped.

2. If no custom classifier matches your data's schema, built-in classifiers try to recognize your data's schema.

3. The crawler connects to the data store. Some data stores require connection properties for crawler access.

4. The inferred schema is created for your data.

5. The crawler writes metadata to the Data Catalog. A table definition contains metadata about the data in your data store. The table is written to a database, which is a container of tables in the Data Catalog. Attributes of a table include classification, which is a label created by the classifier that inferred the table schema.

Topics

- Defining Tables in the AWS Glue Data Catalog
- Cataloging Tables with a Crawler
- Defining a Database in Your Data Catalog
- Adding Classifiers to a Crawler
- Adding a Connection to Your Data Store
- Populating the Data Catalog Using AWS CloudFormation Templates

Defining Tables in the AWS Glue Data Catalog

When you define a table in AWS Glue, you also specify the value of a classification field that indicates the type and format of the data that's stored in that table. If a crawler creates the table, these classifications are determined by either a built-in classifier or a custom classifier. If you create a table manually in the console or by using an API, you specify the classification when you define the table. For more information about creating a table using the AWS Glue console, see Working with Tables on the AWS Glue Console.

When a crawler detects a change in table metadata, a new version of the table is created in the AWS Glue Data Catalog. You can compare current and past versions of a table.

The schema of the table contains its structure. You can also edit a schema to create a new version of the table.

The table's history is also maintained in the Data Catalog. This history includes metrics that are gathered when a data store is updated by an extract, transform, and load (ETL) job. You can find out the name of the job, when it ran, how many rows were added, and how long the job took to run. The version of the schema that was used by an ETL job is also kept in the history.

Table Partitions

An AWS Glue table definition of an Amazon Simple Storage Service (Amazon S3) folder can describe a partitioned table. For example, to improve query performance, a partitioned table might separate monthly data into different files using the name of the month as a key. In AWS Glue, table definitions include the partitioning key of a table. When AWS Glue evaluates the data in Amazon S3 folders to catalog a table, it determines whether an individual table or a partitioned table is added.

All the following conditions must be true for AWS Glue to create a partitioned table for an Amazon S3 folder:

- The schemas of the files are similar, as determined by AWS Glue.
- The data format of the files is the same.
- The compression format of the files is the same.

For example, you might own an Amazon S3 bucket named `my-app-bucket`, where you store both iOS and Android app sales data. The data is partitioned by year, month, and day. The data files for iOS and Android sales have the same schema, data format, and compression format. In the AWS Glue Data Catalog, the AWS Glue crawler creates one table definition with partitioning keys for year, month, and day.

The following Amazon S3 listing of `my-app-bucket` shows some of the partitions. The = symbol is used to assign partition key values.

```
1   my-app-bucket/Sales/year='2010'/month='feb'/day='1'/iOS.csv
2   my-app-bucket/Sales/year='2010'/month='feb'/day='1'/Android.csv
3   my-app-bucket/Sales/year='2010'/month='feb'/day='2'/iOS.csv
4   my-app-bucket/Sales/year='2010'/month='feb'/day='2'/Android.csv
5   ...
6   my-app-bucket/Sales/year='2017'/month='feb'/day='4'/iOS.csv
7   my-app-bucket/Sales/year='2017'/month='feb'/day='4'/Android.csv
```

Working with Tables on the AWS Glue Console

A table in the AWS Glue Data Catalog is the metadata definition that represents the data in a data store. You create tables when you run a crawler, or you can create a table manually in the AWS Glue console. The **Tables** list in the AWS Glue console displays values of your table's metadata. You use table definitions to specify sources and targets when you create ETL (extract, transform, and load) jobs.

To get started, sign in to the AWS Management Console and open the AWS Glue console at https://console.aws.amazon.com/glue/. Choose the **Tables** tab, and use the **Add tables** button to create tables either with a crawler or by manually typing attributes.

Adding Tables on the Console

To use a crawler to add tables, choose **Add tables, Add tables using a crawler**. Then follow the instructions in the **Add crawler** wizard. When the crawler runs, tables are added to the AWS Glue Data Catalog. For more information, see Cataloging Tables with a Crawler.

If you know the attributes that are required to create an Amazon Simple Storage Service (Amazon S3) table definition in your Data Catalog, you can create it with the table wizard. Choose **Add tables, Add table manually**, and follow the instructions in the **Add table** wizard.

When adding a table manually through the console, consider the following:

- If you plan to access the table from Amazon Athena, then provide a name with only alphanumeric and underscore characters. For more information, see Athena names.
- The location of your source data must be an Amazon S3 path.
- The data format of the data must match one of the listed formats in the wizard. The corresponding classification, SerDe, and other table properties are automatically populated based on the format chosen. You can define tables with the following formats:
  JSON
  JavaScript Object Notation.
  CSV
  Character separated values. You also specify the delimiter of either comma, pipe, semicolon, tab, or Ctrl-A.
  Parquet
  Apache Parquet columnar storage.
  Avro
  Apache Avro JSON binary format.
  XML
  Extensible Markup Language format. Specify the XML tag that defines a row in the data. Columns are defined within row tags.
- You can define a partition key for the table.
- Currently, partitioned tables that you create with the console cannot be used in ETL jobs.

Table Attributes

The following are some important attributes of your table:

Table name
The name is determined when the table is created, and you can't change it. You refer to a table name in many AWS Glue operations.

Database
The container object where your table resides. This object contains an organization of your tables that exists within the AWS Glue Data Catalog and might differ from an organization in your data store. When you delete a database, all tables contained in the database are also deleted from the Data Catalog.

Location

The pointer to the location of the data in a data store that this table definition represents.

Classification

A categorization value provided when the table was created. Typically, this is written when a crawler runs and specifies the format of the source data.

Last updated

The time and date (UTC) that this table was updated in the Data Catalog.

Date added

The time and date (UTC) that this table was added to the Data Catalog.

Description

The description of the table. You can write a description to help you understand the contents of the table.

Deprecated

If AWS Glue discovers that a table in the Data Catalog no longer exists in its original data store, it marks the table as deprecated in the data catalog. If you run a job that references a deprecated table, the job might fail. Edit jobs that reference deprecated tables to remove them as sources and targets. We recommend that you delete deprecated tables when they are no longer needed.

Connection

If AWS Glue requires a connection to your data store, the name of the connection is associated with the table.

Viewing and Editing Table Details

To see the details of an existing table, choose the table name in the list, and then choose **Action, View details**.

The table details include properties of your table and its schema. This view displays the schema of the table, including column names in the order defined for the table, data types, and key columns for partitions. If a column is a complex type, you can choose **View properties** to display details of the structure of that field, as shown in the following example:

```
1  {
2  "StorageDescriptor": {
3  "cols": {
4      "FieldSchema": [
5      {
6      "name": "primary-1",
7      "type": "CHAR",
8      "comment": ""
9      },
10     {
11     "name": "second ",
12     "type": "STRING",
13     "comment": ""
14     }
15     ]
16 },
17 "location": "s3://aws-logs-111122223333-us-east-1",
18 "inputFormat": "",
19 "outputFormat": "org.apache.hadoop.hive.ql.io.HiveIgnoreKeyTextOutputFormat",
20 "compressed": "false",
21 "numBuckets": "0",
22 "SerDeInfo": {
23     "name": "",
24     "serializationLib": "org.apache.hadoop.hive.serde2.OpenCSVSerde",
```

```
25      "parameters": {
26          "separatorChar": "|"
27      }
28 },
29 "bucketCols": [],
30 "sortCols": [],
31 "parameters": {},
32 "SkewedInfo": {},
33 "storedAsSubDirectories": "false"
34 },
35 "parameters": {
36 "classification": "csv"
37 }
38 }
```

For more information about the properties of a table, such as `StorageDescriptor`, see StorageDescriptor Structure.

To change the schema of a table, choose **Edit schema** to add and remove columns, change column names, and change data types.

To compare different versions of a table, including its schema, choose **Compare versions** to see a side-by-side comparison of two versions of the schema for a table.

To display the files that make up an Amazon S3 partition, choose **View partition**. For Amazon S3 tables, the **Key** column displays the partition keys that are used to partition the table in the source data store. Partitioning is a way to divide a table into related parts based on the values of a key column, such as date, location, or department. For more information about partitions, search the internet for information about "hive partitioning."

Note
To get step-by-step guidance for viewing the details of a table, see the **Explore table** tutorial in the console.

Cataloging Tables with a Crawler

You can use a crawler to populate the AWS Glue Data Catalog with tables. This is the primary method used by most AWS Glue users. You add a crawler within your Data Catalog to traverse your data stores. The output of the crawler consists of one or more metadata tables that are defined in your Data Catalog. Extract, transform, and load (ETL) jobs that you define in AWS Glue use these metadata tables as sources and targets.

Your crawler uses an AWS Identity and Access Management (IAM) role for permission to access your data stores and the Data Catalog. The role you pass to the crawler must have permission to access Amazon S3 paths that are crawled. Some data stores require additional authorization to establish a connection. For more information, see Adding a Connection to Your Data Store.

For more information about using the AWS Glue console to add a crawler, see Working with Crawlers on the AWS Glue Console.

Defining a Crawler in the AWS Glue Data Catalog

When you define a crawler, you choose one or more classifiers that evaluate the format of your data to infer a schema. When the crawler runs, the first classifier in your list to successfully recognize your data store is used to create a schema for your table. You can use built-in classifiers or define your own. AWS Glue provides built-in classifiers to infer schemas from common files with formats that include JSON, CSV, and Apache Avro. For the current list of built-in classifiers in AWS Glue, see Built-In Classifiers in AWS Glue .

Which Data Stores Can I Crawl?

A crawler can crawl both file-based and relational table-based data stores. Crawlers can crawl the following data stores:

- Amazon Simple Storage Service (Amazon S3)
- Amazon Redshift
- Amazon Relational Database Service (Amazon RDS)
  - Amazon Aurora
  - MariaDB
  - Microsoft SQL Server
  - MySQL
  - Oracle
  - PostgreSQL
- Publicly accessible databases
  - Amazon Aurora
  - MariaDB
  - Microsoft SQL Server
  - MySQL
  - Oracle
  - PostgreSQL

When you define an Amazon S3 data store to crawl, you can choose whether to crawl a path in your account or another account. The output of the crawler is one or more metadata tables defined in the AWS Glue Data Catalog. A table is created for one or more files found in your data store. If all the Amazon S3 files in a folder have the same schema, the crawler creates one table. Also, if the Amazon S3 object is partitioned, only one metadata table is created.

If the data store that is being crawled is a relational database, the output is also a set of metadata tables defined in the AWS Glue Data Catalog. When you crawl a relational database, you must provide authorization credentials for a connection to read objects in the database engine. Depending on the type of database engine, you can choose which objects are crawled, such as databases, schemas, and tables.

Using Include and Exclude Patterns

When evaluating what to include or exclude in a crawl, a crawler starts by evaluating the required include path. For every data store that you want to crawl, you must specify a single include path.

For Amazon S3 data stores, the syntax is `bucket-name/folder-name/file-name.ext`. To crawl all objects in a bucket, you specify just the bucket name in the include path.

For JDBC data stores, the syntax is either `database-name/schema-name/table-name` or `database-name/table-name`. The syntax depends on whether the database engine supports schemas within a database. For example, for database engines such as MySQL or Oracle, don't specify a `schema-name` in your include path. You can substitute the percent sign (%) for a schema or table in the include path to represent all schemas or all tables in a database. You cannot substitute the percent sign (%) for database in the include path.

A crawler connects to a JDBC data store using an AWS Glue connection that contains a JDBC URI connection string. The crawler only has access to objects in the database engine using the JDBC user name and password in the AWS Glue connection. *The crawler can only create tables that it can access through the JDBC connection.* After the crawler accesses the database engine with the JDBC URI, the include path is used to determine which tables in the database engine are created in the Data Catalog. For example, with MySQL, if you specify an include path of `MyDatabase/%`, then all tables within `MyDatabase` are created in the Data Catalog. When accessing Amazon Redshift, if you specify an include path of `MyDatabase/%`, then all tables within all schemas for database `MyDatabase` are created in the Data Catalog. If you specify an include path of `MyDatabase/MySchema/%`, then all tables in database `MyDatabase` and schema `MySchema` are created.

After you specify an include path, you can then exclude objects from the crawl that your include path would otherwise include by specifying one or more Unix-style `glob` exclude patterns.

AWS Glue supports the following kinds of `glob` patterns in the exclude pattern. These patterns are applied to your include path to determine which objects are excluded:

Exclude pattern	Description
*.csv	Matches an Amazon S3 path that represents an object name ending in .csv
.*	Matches all object names that contain a dot
.{csv,avro}	Matches object names ending with .csv or .avro
foo.?	Matches object names starting with foo. that are followed by a single character extension
/myfolder/*	Matches objects in one level of subfolder from myfolder, such as /myfolder/mysource
/myfolder/*/*	Matches objects in two levels of subfolders from myfolder, such as /myfolder/mysource/-data
/myfolder/**	Matches objects in all subfolders of myfolder, such as /myfolder/mysource/mydata and /myfolder/mysource/data
Market*	Matches tables in a JDBC database with names that begin with Market, such as Market_us and Market_fr

AWS Glue interprets `glob` exclude patterns as follows:

- The slash (/) character is the delimiter to separate Amazon S3 keys into a folder hierarchy.
- The asterisk (*) character matches zero or more characters of a name component without crossing folder boundaries.

- A double asterisk (**) matches zero or more characters crossing folder or schema boundaries.

- The question mark (?) character matches exactly one character of a name component.

- The backslash (\) character is used to escape characters that otherwise can be interpreted as special characters. The expression \\ matches a single backslash, and \{ matches a left brace.

- Brackets [ ] create a bracket expression that matches a single character of a name component out of a set of characters. For example, [abc] matches a, b, or c. The hyphen (-) can be used to specify a range, so [a-z] specifies a range that matches from a through z (inclusive). These forms can be mixed, so [abce-g] matches a, b, c, e, f, or g. If the character after the bracket ([) is an exclamation point (!), the bracket expression is negated. For example, [!a-c] matches any character except a, b, or c.

  Within a bracket expression, the *, ?, and \ characters match themselves. The hyphen (-) character matches itself if it is the first character within the brackets, or if it's the first character after the ! when you are negating.

- Braces ({ }) enclose a group of subpatterns, where the group matches if any subpattern in the group matches. A comma (,) character is used to separate the subpatterns. Groups cannot be nested.

- Leading period or dot characters in file names are treated as normal characters in match operations. For example, the * exclude pattern matches the file name .hidden.

Example of Amazon S3 Exclude Patterns

Each exclude pattern is evaluated against the include path. For example, suppose that you have the following Amazon S3 directory structure:

```
1  /mybucket/myfolder/
2      departments/
3          finance.json
4          market-us.json
5          market-emea.json
6          market-ap.json
7      employees/
8          hr.json
9          john.csv
10         jane.csv
11         juan.txt
```

Given the include path s3://mybucket/myfolder/, the following are some sample results for exclude patterns:

Exclude pattern	Results
departments/**	Excludes all files and folders below departments and includes the employees folder and its files
departments/market*	Excludes market-us.json, market-emea.json, and market-ap.json
.csv	Excludes all objects below myfolder that have a name ending with .csv
employees/*.csv	Excludes all .csv files in the employees folder

Example of Excluding a Subset of Amazon S3 Partitions

Suppose that your data is partitioned by day, so that each day in a year is in a separate Amazon S3 partition. For January 2015, there are 31 partitions. Now, to crawl data for only the first week of January, you must exclude all partitions except days 1 through 7:

```
1  2015/01/{[!0],0[8-9]}**, 2015/0[2-9]/**, 2015/1[0-2]/**
```

Take a look at the parts of this glob pattern. The first part, 2015/01/{[!0],0[8-9]}**, excludes all days that don't begin with a "0" in addition to day 08 and day 09 from month 01 in year 2015. Notice that "**" is used as the suffix to the day number pattern and crosses folder boundaries to lower-level folders. If "*" is used, lower folder levels are not excluded.

The second part, 2015/0[2-9]/**, excludes days in months 02 to 09, in year 2015.

The third part, 2015/1[0-2]/**, excludes days in months 10, 11, and 12, in year 2015.

Example of JDBC Exclude Patterns

Suppose that you are crawling a JDBC database with the following schema structure:

```
1 MyDatabase/MySchema/
2     HR_us
3     HR_fr
4     Employees_Table
5     Finance
6     Market_US_Table
7     Market_EMEA_Table
8     Market_AP_Table
```

Given the include path `MyDatabase/MySchema/%`, the following are some sample results for exclude patterns:

Exclude pattern	Results
HR*	Excludes the tables with names that begin with HR
Market_*	Excludes the tables with names that begin with Market_
_Table	Excludes all tables with names that end with _Table

What Happens When a Crawler Runs?

When a crawler runs, it takes the following actions to interrogate a data store:

- **Classifies data to determine the format, schema, and associated properties of the raw data** – You can configure the results of classification by creating a custom classifier.
- **Groups data into tables or partitions** ** – Data is grouped based on crawler heuristics.
- **Writes metadata to the Data Catalog** ** – You can configure how the crawler adds, updates, and deletes tables and partitions.

The metadata tables that a crawler creates are contained in a database when you define a crawler. If your crawler does not define a database, your tables are placed in the default database. In addition, each table has a classification column that is filled in by the classifier that first successfully recognized the data store.

The crawler can process both relational database and file data stores.

If the file that is crawled is compressed, the crawler must download it to process it. When a crawler runs it interrogates files to determine their format and compression type and writes these properties into the Data Catalog. Some file formats, for example parquet, enable you to compress parts of the file as it is written. For these files, the compressed data is an internal component of the file and AWS Glue does not populate the `compressionType` property when it writes tables into the Data Catalog. In contrast, if an **entire file** is compressed by a compression algorithm, for example gzip, then the `compressionType` property is populated when tables are written into the Data Catalog.

The crawler generates the names for the tables it creates. The names of the tables that are stored in the AWS Glue Data Catalog follow these rules:

- Only alphanumeric characters and underscore (_) are allowed.

- Any custom prefix cannot be longer than 64 characters.
- The maximum length of the name cannot be longer than 128 characters. The crawler truncates generated names to fit within the limit.
- If duplicate table names are encountered, the crawler adds a hash string suffix to the name.

If your crawler runs more than once, perhaps on a schedule, it looks for new or changed files or tables in your data store. The output of the crawler includes new tables found since a previous run.

Are Amazon S3 Folders Created as Tables or Partitions?

When an AWS Glue crawler scans Amazon S3 and detects multiple folders in a bucket, it determines the root of a table in the folder structure and which folders are partitions of a table. The name of the table is based on the Amazon S3 prefix or folder name. You provide an **Include path** that points to the folder level to crawl. When the majority of schemas at a folder level are similar, the crawler creates partitions of a table instead of two separate tables. To influence the crawler to create separate tables, add each table's root folder as a separate data store when you define the crawler.

For example, with the following Amazon S3 structure:

```
1  s3://bucket01/folder1/table1/partition1/file.txt
2  s3://bucket01/folder1/table1/partition2/file.txt
3  s3://bucket01/folder1/table1/partition3/file.txt
4  s3://bucket01/folder1/table2/partition4/file.txt
5  s3://bucket01/folder1/table2/partition5/file.txt
```

If the schemas for table1 and table2 are similar, and a single data store is defined in the crawler with **Include path** s3://bucket01/folder1/, the crawler creates a single table with two partition columns. One partition column contains table1 and table2, and a second partition column contains partition1 through partition5. To create two separate tables, define the crawler with two data stores. In this example, define the first **Include path** as s3://bucket01/folder1/table1/ and the second as s3://bucket01/folder1/table2.

Note
In Athena, each table corresponds to an Amazon S3 prefix with all the objects in it. If objects have different schemas, Athena does not recognize different objects within the same prefix as separate tables. This can happen if a crawler creates multiple tables from the same Amazon S3 prefix. This might lead to queries in Athena that return zero results. For Athena to properly recognize and query tables, create the crawler with a separate **Include path** for each different table schema in the Amazon S3 folder structure. For more information, see Best Practices When Using Athena with AWS Glue.

Configuring a Crawler

When a crawler runs, it might encounter changes to your data store that result in a schema or partition that is different from a previous crawl. You can use the AWS Management Console or the AWS Glue API to configure how your crawler processes certain types of changes.

Topics

- Configuring a Crawler on the AWS Glue Console
- Configuring a Crawler Using the API
- How to Prevent the Crawler from Changing an Existing Schema

Configuring a Crawler on the AWS Glue Console

When you define a crawler using the AWS Glue console, you have several options for configuring the behavior of your crawler. For more information about using the AWS Glue console to add a crawler, see Working with Crawlers on the AWS Glue Console.

When a crawler runs against a previously crawled data store, it might discover that a schema has changed or that some objects in the data store have been deleted. The crawler logs changes to a schema. New tables and partitions are always created regardless of the schema change policy.

To specify what the crawler does when it finds changes in the schema, you can choose one of the following actions on the console:

- **Update the table definition in the Data Catalog** – Add new columns, remove missing columns, and modify the definitions of existing columns in the AWS Glue Data Catalog. Remove any metadata that is not set by the crawler. This is the default setting.
- **Add new columns only** – For tables that map to an Amazon S3 data store, add new columns as they are discovered, but don't remove or change the type of existing columns in the Data Catalog. Choose this option when the current columns in the Data Catalog are correct and you don't want the crawler to remove or change the type of the existing columns. If a fundamental Amazon S3 table attribute changes, such as classification, compression type, or CSV delimiter, mark the table as deprecated. Maintain input format and output format as they exist in the Data Catalog. Update SerDe parameters only if the parameter is one that is set by the crawler. *For all other data stores, modify existing column definitions.*
- **Ignore the change and don't update the table in the Data Catalog**

A crawler might also discover new or changed partitions. By default, new partitions are added and existing partitions are updated if they have changed. In addition, you can set a crawler configuration option to **Update all new and existing partitions with metadata from the table** on the AWS Glue console. When this option is set, partitions inherit metadata properties—such as their classification, input format, output format, SerDe information, and schema—from their parent table. Any changes to these properties in a table are propagated to its partitions. When this configuration option is set on an existing crawler, existing partitions are updated to match the properties of their parent table the next time the crawler runs.

To specify what the crawler does when it finds a deleted object in the data store, choose one of the following actions:

- **Delete tables and partitions from the Data Catalog**
- **Ignore the change and don't update the table in the Data Catalog**
- **Mark the table as deprecated in the Data Catalog** – This is the default setting.

Configuring a Crawler Using the API

When you define a crawler using the AWS Glue API, you can choose from several fields to configure your crawler. The `SchemaChangePolicy` in the crawler API determines what the crawler does when it discovers a changed schema or a deleted object. The crawler logs schema changes as it runs.

When a crawler runs, new tables and partitions are always created regardless of the schema change policy. You can choose one of the following actions in the `UpdateBehavior` field in the `SchemaChangePolicy` structure to determine what the crawler does when it finds a changed table schema:

- `UPDATE_IN_DATABASE` – Update the table in the AWS Glue Data Catalog. Add new columns, remove missing columns, and modify the definitions of existing columns. Remove any metadata that is not set by the crawler.
- `LOG` – Ignore the changes, and don't update the table in the Data Catalog.

You can also override the `SchemaChangePolicy` structure using a JSON object supplied in the crawler API `Configuration` field. This JSON object can contain a key-value pair to set the policy to not update existing columns and only add new columns. For example, provide the following JSON object as a string:

```
1  {
2      "Version": 1.0,
3      "CrawlerOutput": {
4          "Tables": { "AddOrUpdateBehavior": "MergeNewColumns" }
5      }
6  }
```

This option corresponds to the **Add new columns only** option on the AWS Glue console. It overrides the `SchemaChangePolicy` structure for tables that result from crawling Amazon S3 data stores only. Choose this option if you want to maintain the metadata as it exists in the Data Catalog (the source of truth). New columns are added as they are encountered, including nested data types. But existing columns are not removed, and their type is not changed. If an Amazon S3 table attribute changes significantly, mark the table as deprecated, and log a warning that an incompatible attribute needs to be resolved.

When a crawler runs against a previously crawled data store, it might discover new or changed partitions. By default, new partitions are added and existing partitions are updated if they have changed. In addition, you can set a crawler configuration option to `InheritFromTable` (corresponding to the **Update all new and existing partitions with metadata from the table** option on the AWS Glue console). When this option is set, partitions inherit metadata properties from their parent table, such as their classification, input format, output format, SerDe information, and schema. Any property changes to the parent table are propagated to its partitions.

When this configuration option is set on an existing crawler, existing partitions are updated to match the properties of their parent table the next time the crawler runs. This behavior is set crawler API `Configuration` field. For example, provide the following JSON object as a string:

```
1  {
2      "Version": 1.0,
3      "CrawlerOutput": {
4          "Partitions": { "AddOrUpdateBehavior": "InheritFromTable" }
5      }
6  }
```

The crawler API `Configuration` field can set multiple configuration options. For example, to configure the crawler output for both partitions and tables, you can provide a string representation of the following JSON object:

```
1  {
2      "Version": 1.0,
3      "CrawlerOutput": {
4          "Partitions": { "AddOrUpdateBehavior": "InheritFromTable" },
5          "Tables": {"AddOrUpdateBehavior": "MergeNewColumns" }
6      }
7  }
```

You can choose one of the following actions to determine what the crawler does when it finds a deleted object in the data store. The `DeleteBehavior` field in the `SchemaChangePolicy` structure in the crawler API sets the behavior of the crawler when it discovers a deleted object.

- `DELETE_FROM_DATABASE` – Delete tables and partitions from the Data Catalog.
- `LOG` – Ignore the change and don't update the table in the Data Catalog.
- `DEPRECATE_IN_DATABASE` – Mark the table as deprecated in the Data Catalog. This is the default setting.

How to Prevent the Crawler from Changing an Existing Schema

If you don't want a crawler to overwrite updates you made to existing fields in an Amazon S3 table definition, choose the option on the console to **Add new columns only** or set the configuration option `MergeNewColumns`. This applies to tables and partitions, unless `Partitions.AddOrUpdateBehavior` is overridden to `InheritFromTable`.

If you don't want a table schema to change at all when a crawler runs, set the schema change policy to `LOG`. You can also set a configuration option that sets partition schemas to inherit from the table.

If you are configuring the crawler on the console, you can choose the following actions:

- **Ignore the change and don't update the table in the Data Catalog**
- **Update all new and existing partitions with metadata from the table**

When you configure the crawler using the API, set the following parameters:

- Set the `UpdateBehavior` field in `SchemaChangePolicy` structure to `LOG`.
- Set the `Configuration` field with a string representation of the following JSON object in the crawler API; for example:

```
1  {
2      "Version": 1.0,
3      "CrawlerOutput": {
4          "Partitions": { "AddOrUpdateBehavior": "InheritFromTable" }
5      }
6  }
```

Scheduling an AWS Glue Crawler

You can run an AWS Glue crawler on demand or on a regular schedule. Crawler schedules can be expressed in *cron* format. For more information, see cron in Wikipedia.

When you create a crawler based on a schedule, you can specify certain constraints, such as the frequency the crawler runs, which days of the week it runs, and at what time. These constraints are based on cron. When setting up a crawler schedule, you should consider the features and limitations of cron. For example, if you choose to run your crawler on day 31 each month, keep in mind that some months don't have 31 days.

For more information about using cron to schedule jobs and crawlers, see Time-Based Schedules for Jobs and Crawlers.

Working with Crawlers on the AWS Glue Console

A crawler accesses your data store, extracts metadata, and creates table definitions in the AWS Glue Data Catalog. The **Crawlers** tab in the AWS Glue console lists all the crawlers that you create. The list displays status and metrics from the last run of your crawler.

To add a crawler using the console:

1. Sign in to the AWS Management Console and open the AWS Glue console at https://console.aws.amazon.com/glue/. Choose the **Crawlers** tab.

2. Choose **Add crawler**, and follow the instructions in the **Add crawler** wizard. **Note**
   To get step-by-step guidance for adding a crawler, see the **Add crawler** tutorial link in the navigation pane on the AWS Glue console at https://console.aws.amazon.com/glue/. You can also use the **Add crawler** wizard to create and modify an IAM role that attaches a policy that includes permissions for your Amazon S3 data stores.

For Amazon S3 data stores, an exclude pattern is relative to the include path. For more information about glob patterns, see Which Data Stores Can I Crawl?.

When you crawl a JDBC data store, a connection is required. For more information, see Working with Connections on the AWS Glue Console. An exclude path is relative to the include path. For example, to exclude a table in your JDBC data store, type the table name in the exclude path.

Viewing Crawler Results

To view the results of a crawler, find the crawler name in the list and choose the **Logs** link. This link takes you to the CloudWatch Logs, where you can see details about which tables were created in the AWS Glue Data Catalog and any errors that were encountered. You can manage your log retention period in the CloudWatch console. The default log retention is `Never Expire`. For more information about how to change the retention period, see Change Log Data Retention in CloudWatch Logs.

To see details of a crawler, choose the crawler name in the list. Crawler details include the information you defined when you created the crawler with the **Add crawler** wizard. When a crawler run completes, choose the **Tables** tab to see the tables that were created by your crawler in the database you specified.

Note
The crawler assumes the permissions of the **IAM role** that you specify when you define it. This IAM role must have permissions to extract data from your data store and write to the Data Catalog. The AWS Glue console lists only IAM roles that have attached a trust policy for the AWS Glue principal service. From the console, you can also create an IAM role with an IAM policy to access Amazon S3 data stores accessed by the crawler. For more information about providing roles for AWS Glue, see Using Identity-Based Policies (IAM Policies).

The following are some important properties and metrics about the last run of a crawler:

Name
When you create a crawler, you must give it a unique name.

Schedule
You can choose to run your crawler on demand or choose a frequency with a schedule. For more information about scheduling a crawler, see Scheduling a Crawler.

Status
A crawler can be ready, starting, stopping, scheduled, or schedule paused. A running crawler progresses from starting to stopping. You can resume or pause a schedule attached to a crawler.

Logs
Links to any available logs from the last run of the crawler.

Last runtime

The amount of time it took the crawler to run when it last ran.

Median runtime

The median amount of time it took the crawler to run since it was created.

Tables updated

The number of tables in the AWS Glue Data Catalog that were updated by the latest run of the crawler.

Tables added

The number of tables that were added into the AWS Glue Data Catalog by the latest run of the crawler.

Defining a Database in Your Data Catalog

When you define a table in the AWS Glue Data Catalog, you add it to a database. A database is used to organize tables in AWS Glue. You can organize your tables using a crawler or using the AWS Glue console. A table can be in only one database at a time.

Your database can contain tables that define data from many different data stores. This data can include objects in Amazon Simple Storage Service (Amazon S3) and relational tables in Amazon Relational Database Service.

Note
When you delete a database, all the tables in the database are also deleted.

For more information about defining a database using the AWS Glue console, see Working with Databases on the AWS Glue Console.

Working with Databases on the AWS Glue Console

A database in the AWS Glue Data Catalog is a container that holds tables. You use databases to organize your tables into separate categories. Databases are created when you run a crawler or add a table manually. The database list in the AWS Glue console displays descriptions for all your databases.

To view the list of databases, sign in to the AWS Management Console and open the AWS Glue console at https://console.aws.amazon.com/glue/. Choose **Databases**, and then choose a database name in the list to view the details.

From the **Databases** tab in the AWS Glue console, you can add, edit, and delete databases:

- To create a new database, choose **Add database** and provide a name and description. For compatibility with other metadata stores, such as Apache Hive, the name is folded to lowercase characters. **Note** If you plan to access the database from Amazon Athena, then provide a name with only alphanumeric and underscore characters. For more information, see Athena names.
- To edit the description for a database, select the check box next to the database name and choose **Action**, **Edit database**.
- To delete a database, select the check box next to the database name and choose **Action**, **Delete database**.
- To display the list of tables contained in the database, select the check box next to the database name and choose **View tables**.

To change the database that a crawler writes to, you must change the crawler definition. For more information, see Cataloging Tables with a Crawler.

Adding Classifiers to a Crawler

A classifier reads the data in a data store. If it recognizes the format of the data, it generates a schema. The classifier also returns a certainty number to indicate how certain the format recognition was.

AWS Glue provides a set of built-in classifiers, but you can also create custom classifiers. AWS Glue invokes custom classifiers first, in the order that you specify in your crawler definition. Depending on the results that are returned from custom classifiers, AWS Glue might also invoke built-in classifiers. If a classifier returns `certainty=1.0` during processing, it indicates that it's 100 percent certain that it can create the correct schema. AWS Glue then uses the output of that classifier.

If no classifier returns `certainty=1.0`, AWS Glue uses the output of the classifier that has the highest certainty. If no classifier returns a certainty greater than `0.0`, AWS Glue returns the default classification string of `UNKNOWN`.

When Do I Use a Classifier?

You use classifiers when you crawl a data store to define metadata tables in the AWS Glue Data Catalog. You can set up your crawler with an ordered set of classifiers. When the crawler invokes a classifier, the classifier determines whether the data is recognized. If the classifier can't recognize the data or is not 100 percent certain, the crawler invokes the next classifier in the list to determine whether it can recognize the data.

For more information about creating a classifier using the AWS Glue console, see Working with Classifiers on the AWS Glue Console.

Custom Classifiers

The output of a classifier includes a string that indicates the file's classification or format (for example, `json`) and the schema of the file. For custom classifiers, you define the logic for creating the schema based on the type of classifier. Classifier types include defining schemas based on grok patterns, XML tags, and JSON paths.

If you change a classifier definition, any data that was previously crawled using the classifier is not reclassified. A crawler keeps track of previously crawled data. New data is classified with the updated classifier, which might result in an updated schema. If the schema of your data has evolved, update the classifier to account for any schema changes when your crawler runs. To reclassify data to correct an incorrect classifier, create a new crawler with the updated classifier.

For more information about creating custom classifiers in AWS Glue, see Writing Custom Classifiers.

Note
If your data format is recognized by one of the built-in classifiers, you don't need to create a custom classifier.

Built-In Classifiers in AWS Glue

AWS Glue provides built-in classifiers for various formats, including JSON, CSV, web logs, and many database systems.

If AWS Glue doesn't find a custom classifier that fits the input data format with 100 percent certainty, it invokes the built-in classifiers in the order shown in the following table. The built-in classifiers return a result to indicate whether the format matches (`certainty=1.0`) or does not match (`certainty=0.0`). The first classifier that has `certainty=1.0` provides the classification string and schema for a metadata table in your Data Catalog.

Classifier type	Classification string	Notes
Apache Avro	avro	Reads the beginning of the file to determine format.

Classifier type	Classification string	Notes
Apache ORC	orc	Reads the file metadata to determine format.
Apache Parquet	parquet	Reads the beginning of the file to determine format.
JSON	json	Reads the beginning of the file to determine format.
Binary JSON	bson	Reads the beginning of the file to determine format.
XML	xml	Reads the beginning of the file to determine format. AWS Glue determines the table schema based on XML tags in the document. For information about creating a custom XML classifier to specify rows in the document, see Writing XML Custom Classifiers.
Ion log	ion	Reads the beginning of the file to determine format.
Combined Apache log	combined_apache	Determines log formats through a grok pattern.
Apache log	apache	Determines log formats through a grok pattern.
Linux kernel log	linux_kernel	Determines log formats through a grok pattern.
Microsoft log	microsoft_log	Determines log formats through a grok pattern.
Ruby log	ruby_logger	Reads the beginning of the file to determine format.
Squid 3.x log	squid	Reads the beginning of the file to determine format.
Redis monitor log	redismonlog	Reads the beginning of the file to determine format.
Redis log	redislog	Reads the beginning of the file to determine format.
CSV	csv	Checks for the following delimiters: comma (,), pipe (|), tab (\t), semicolon (;), and Ctrl-A (\u0001). Ctrl-A is the Unicode control character for Start Of Heading.
Amazon Redshift	redshift	Uses JDBC connection to import metadata.
MySQL	mysql	Uses JDBC connection to import metadata.
PostgreSQL	postgresql	Uses JDBC connection to import metadata.
Oracle database	oracle	Uses JDBC connection to import metadata.
Microsoft SQL Server	sqlserver	Uses JDBC connection to import metadata.

Files in the following compressed formats can be classified:

- ZIP (as compression format, not as archive format)
- BZIP
- GZIP
- LZ4
- Snappy (as standard Snappy format, not as Hadoop native Snappy format)

Built-In CSV Classifier

The built-in CSV classifier parses CSV file contents to determine the schema for an AWS Glue table. This classifier checks for the following delimiters:

- Comma (,)

- Pipe (|)

- Tab (\t)

- Semicolon (;)

- Ctrl-A (\u0001)

    Ctrl-A is the Unicode control character for `Start Of Heading`.

To be classified as CSV, the table schema must have at least two columns and two rows of data. The CSV classifier uses a number of heuristics to determine whether a header is present in a given file. If the classifier can't determine a header from the first row of data, column headers are displayed as `col1`, `col2`, `col3`, and so on. The built-in CSV classifier determines whether to infer a header by evaluating the following characteristics of the file:

- Every column in a potential header parses as a STRING data type.
- Except for the last column, every column in a potential header has content that is fewer than 150 characters. To allow for a trailing delimiter, the last column can be empty throughout the file.
- Every column in a potential header must meet the AWS Glue `regex` requirements for a column name.
- The header row must be sufficiently different from the data rows. To determine this, one or more of the rows must parse as other than STRING type. If all columns are of type STRING, then the first row of data is not sufficiently different from subsequent rows to be used as the header.

Note
If the built-in CSV classifier does not create your AWS Glue table as you want, you might be able to use one of the following alternatives:
Change the column names in the Data Catalog, set the `SchemaChangePolicy` to LOG, and set the partition output configuration to `InheritFromTable` for future crawler runs. Create a custom grok classifier to parse the data and assign the columns that you want. The built-in CSV classifier creates tables referencing the `LazySimpleSerDe` as the serialization library, which is a good choice for type inference. However, if the CSV data contains quoted strings, edit the table definition and change the SerDe library to `OpenCSVSerDe`. Adjust any inferred types to STRING, set the `SchemaChangePolicy` to LOG, and set the partitions output configuration to `InheritFromTable` for future crawler runs. For more information about SerDe libraries, see SerDe Reference in the Amazon Athena User Guide.

Writing Custom Classifiers

You can provide a custom classifier to classify your data using a grok pattern or an XML tag in AWS Glue. A crawler calls a custom classifier. If the classifier recognizes the data, it returns the classification and schema of the data to the crawler. You might need to define a custom classifier if your data doesn't match any built-in classifiers, or if you want to customize the tables that are created by the crawler.

For more information about creating a classifier using the AWS Glue console, see Working with Classifiers on the AWS Glue Console.

AWS Glue runs custom classifiers before built-in classifiers, in the order you specify. When a crawler finds a classifier that matches the data, the classification string and schema are used in the definition of tables that are written to your AWS Glue Data Catalog.

Writing Grok Custom Classifiers

Grok is a tool that is used to parse textual data given a matching pattern. A grok pattern is a named set of regular expressions (regex) that are used to match data one line at a time. AWS Glue uses grok patterns to infer the schema of your data. When a grok pattern matches your data, AWS Glue uses the pattern to determine the structure of your data and map it into fields.

AWS Glue provides many built-in patterns, or you can define your own. You can create a grok pattern using built-in patterns and custom patterns in your custom classifier definition. You can tailor a grok pattern to classify custom text file formats.

The following is the basic syntax for the components of a grok pattern:

```
1 %{PATTERN:field-name}
```

Data that matches the named `PATTERN` is mapped to the `field-name` column in the schema, with a default data type of `string`. Optionally, the data type for the field can be cast to `byte, boolean, double, short, int, long, or float` in the resulting schema.

```
1 %{PATTERN:field-name:data-type}
```

For example, to cast a `num` field to an `int` data type, you can use this pattern:

```
1 %{NUMBER:num:int}
```

Patterns can be composed of other patterns. For example, you can have a pattern for a `SYSLOG` time stamp that is defined by patterns for month, day of the month, and time (for example, `Feb 1 06:25:43`). For this data, you might define the following pattern.

```
1 SYSLOGTIMESTAMP %{MONTH} +%{MONTHDAY} %{TIME}
```

Note
Grok patterns can process only one line at a time. Multiple-line patterns are not supported. Also, line breaks within a pattern are not supported.

Custom Classifier Values in AWS Glue

When you define a grok classifier, you supply the following values to AWS Glue to create the custom classifier.

Name
Name of the classifier.

Classification
The text string that is written to describe the format of the data that is classified; for example, `special-logs`.

Grok pattern

The set of patterns that are applied to the data store to determine whether there is a match. These patterns are from AWS Glue built-in patterns and any custom patterns you define.

The following is an example of a grok pattern:

```
1  %{TIMESTAMP_ISO8601:timestamp} \[%{MESSAGEPREFIX:message_prefix}\] %{CRAWLERLOGLEVEL:loglevel} :
     %{GREEDYDATA:message}
```

When the data matches TIMESTAMP_ISO8601, a schema column `timestamp` is created. The behavior is similar for the other named patterns in the example.

Custom patterns

Optional custom patterns that you define. These patterns are referenced by the grok pattern that classifies your data. You can reference these custom patterns in the grok pattern that is applied to your data. Each custom component pattern must be on a separate line. Regular expression (regex) syntax is used to define the pattern. The following is an example of using custom patterns:

```
1  CRAWLERLOGLEVEL (BENCHMARK|ERROR|WARN|INFO|TRACE)
2  MESSAGEPREFIX .*-.*-.*-.*-.*
```

The first custom named pattern, CRAWLERLOGLEVEL, is a match when the data matches one of the enumerated strings. The second custom pattern, MESSAGEPREFIX, tries to match a message prefix string.

AWS Glue keeps track of the creation time, last update time, and version of your classifier.

AWS Glue Built-In Patterns

AWS Glue provides many common patterns that you can use to build a custom classifier. You add a named pattern to the `grok pattern` in a classifier definition.

The following list consists of a line for each pattern. In each line, the pattern name is followed its definition. Regular expression (regex) syntax is used in defining the pattern.

```
1  #AWS Glue Built-in patterns
2  USERNAME [a-zA-Z0-9._-]+
3  USER %{USERNAME:UNWANTED}
4  INT (?:[+-]?(?:[0-9]+))
5  BASE10NUM (?<![0-9.+-])(?>[+-]?(?:(?:[0-9]+(?:\.[0-9]+)?)|(?:\.[0-9]+)))
6  NUMBER (?:%{BASE10NUM:UNWANTED})
7  BASE16NUM (?<![0-9A-Fa-f])(?:[+-]?(?:0x)?(?:[0-9A-Fa-f]+))
8  BASE16FLOAT \b(?<![0-9A-Fa-f.])(?:[+-]?(?:0x)?(?:(?:[0-9A-Fa-f]+(?:\.[0-9A-Fa-f]*)?)|(?:\.[0-9A
     -Fa-f]+)))\b
9  BOOLEAN (?i)(true|false)
10
11 POSINT \b(?:[1-9][0-9]*)\b
12 NONNEGINT \b(?:[0-9]+)\b
13 WORD \b\w+\b
14 NOTSPACE \S+
15 SPACE \s*
16 DATA .*?
17 GREEDYDATA .*
18 #QUOTEDSTRING (?:(?<!\\)(?:"(?:\\.|[^\\"])*"|(?:'(?:\\.|[^\\'])*')|(?:`(?:\\.|[^\\`])*`)))
19 QUOTEDSTRING (?>(?<!\\)(?>"(?>\\.|[^\\"]+)+"|""|(?>'(?>\\.|[^\\']+)+')|''|(?>`(?>\\.|[^\\`]+)
     +`)|``))
20 UUID [A-Fa-f0-9]{8}-(?:[A-Fa-f0-9]{4}-){3}[A-Fa-f0-9]{12}
21
22 # Networking
```

```
23  MAC (?:%{CISCOMAC:UNWANTED}|%{WINDOWSMAC:UNWANTED}|%{COMMONMAC:UNWANTED})
24  CISCOMAC (?:(?:[A-Fa-f0-9]{4}\.){2}[A-Fa-f0-9]{4})
25  WINDOWSMAC (?:(?:[A-Fa-f0-9]{2}-){5}[A-Fa-f0-9]{2})
26  COMMONMAC (?:(?:[A-Fa-f0-9]{2}:){5}[A-Fa-f0-9]{2})
27  IPV6 ((([0-9A-Fa-f]{1,4}:){7}([0-9A-Fa-f]{1,4}|:))|(([0-9A-Fa-f]{1,4}:){6}(:[0-9A-Fa-f
        ]{1,4}|((25[0-5]|2[0-4]\d|1\d\d|[1-9]?\d)(\.(25[0-5]|2[0-4]\d|1\d\d|[1-9]?\d)){3})|:))
        |(([0-9A-Fa-f]{1,4}:){5}(((:[0-9A-Fa-f]{1,4}){1,2})|:((25[0-5]|2[0-4]\d|1\d\d|[1-9]?\d)
        (\.(25[0-5]|2[0-4]\d|1\d\d|[1-9]?\d)){3})|:))|(([0-9A-Fa-f]{1,4}:){4}(((:[0-9A-Fa-f]{1,4})
        {1,3})|((:[0-9A-Fa-f]{1,4})?:((25[0-5]|2[0-4]\d|1\d\d|[1-9]?\d)(\.(25[0-5]|2[0-4]\d|1\d\d
        |[1-9]?\d)){3}))|:))|(([0-9A-Fa-f]{1,4}:){3}(((:[0-9A-Fa-f]{1,4}){1,4})|((:[0-9A-Fa-f
        ]{1,4}){0,2}:((25[0-5]|2[0-4]\d|1\d\d|[1-9]?\d)(\.(25[0-5]|2[0-4]\d|1\d\d|[1-9]?\d)){3}))
        |:))|(([0-9A-Fa-f]{1,4}:){2}(((:[0-9A-Fa-f]{1,4}){1,5})|((:[0-9A-Fa-f]{1,4})
        {0,3}:((25[0-5]|2[0-4]\d|1\d\d|[1-9]?\d)(\.(25[0-5]|2[0-4]\d|1\d\d|[1-9]?\d)){3}))|:))
        |(([0-9A-Fa-f]{1,4}:){1}(((:[0-9A-Fa-f]{1,4}){1,6})|((:[0-9A-Fa-f]{1,4})
        {0,4}:((25[0-5]|2[0-4]\d|1\d\d|[1-9]?\d)(\.(25[0-5]|2[0-4]\d|1\d\d|[1-9]?\d)){3}))|:))
        |(:(((:[0-9A-Fa-f]{1,4}){1,7})|((:[0-9A-Fa-f]{1,4}){0,5}:((25[0-5]|2[0-4]\d|1\d\d|[1-9]?\d)
        (\.(25[0-5]|2[0-4]\d|1\d\d|[1-9]?\d)){3}))|:)))(%.+)?
28  IPV4 (?<![0-9])(?:(?:25[0-5]|2[0-4][0-9]|[0-1]?[0-9]{1,2})
        [.](?:25[0-5]|2[0-4][0-9]|[0-1]?[0-9]{1,2})[.](?:25[0-5]|2[0-4][0-9]|[0-1]?[0-9]{1,2})
        [.](?:25[0-5]|2[0-4][0-9]|[0-1]?[0-9]{1,2}))(?![0-9])
29  IP (?:%{IPV6:UNWANTED}|%{IPV4:UNWANTED})
30  HOSTNAME \b(?:[0-9A-Za-z][0-9A-Za-z-_]{0,62})(?:\.(?:[0-9A-Za-z][0-9A-Za-z-_]{0,62}))*(\.?|\b)
31  HOST %{HOSTNAME:UNWANTED}
32  IPORHOST (?:%{HOSTNAME:UNWANTED}|%{IP:UNWANTED})
33  HOSTPORT (?:%{IPORHOST}:%{POSINT:PORT})
34
35  # paths
36  PATH (?:%{UNIXPATH}|%{WINPATH})
37  UNIXPATH (?>/(?>[\w_%!$@:.,~-]+|\\.)*)+
38  #UNIXPATH (?<![\w\/])(?:/[^\/\s?*]*)+
39  TTY (?:/dev/(pts|tty([pq])?)(\w+)?/?(?:[0-9]+))
40  WINPATH (?>[A-Za-z]+:|\\)(?:\\[^\\?*]*)+
41  URIPROTO [A-Za-z]+(\+[A-Za-z+]+)?
42  URIHOST %{IPORHOST}(?::%{POSINT:port})?
43  # uripath comes loosely from RFC1738, but mostly from what Firefox
44  # doesn't turn into %XX
45  URIPATH (?:/[A-Za-z0-9$.+!*'(){},~:;=@#%_\-]*)+
46  #URIPARAM \?(?:[A-Za-z0-9]+(?:=(?:[^&]*))?(?:&(?:[A-Za-z0-9]+(?:=(?:[^&]*))?)?)*)?
47  URIPARAM \?[A-Za-z0-9$.+!*'|(){},~@#%&/=:;_?\-\[\]]*
48  URIPATHPARAM %{URIPATH}(?:%{URIPARAM})?
49  URI %{URIPROTO}://(?:%{USER}(?::[^@]*)?@)?(?:%{URIHOST})?(?:%{URIPATHPARAM})?
50
51  # Months: January, Feb, 3, 03, 12, December
52  MONTH \b(?:Jan(?:uary)?|Feb(?:ruary)?|Mar(?:ch)?|Apr(?:il)?|May|Jun(?:e)?|Jul(?:y)?|Aug(?:ust)
        ?|Sep(?:tember)?|Oct(?:ober)?|Nov(?:ember)?|Dec(?:ember)?)\b
53  MONTHNUM (?:0?[1-9]|1[0-2])
54  MONTHNUM2 (?:0[1-9]|1[0-2])
55  MONTHDAY (?:(?:0[1-9])|(?:[12][0-9])|(?:3[01])|[1-9])
56
57  # Days: Monday, Tue, Thu, etc...
58  DAY (?:Mon(?:day)?|Tue(?:sday)?|Wed(?:nesday)?|Thu(?:rsday)?|Fri(?:day)?|Sat(?:urday)?|Sun(?:
        day)?)
59
60  # Years?
```

```
61  YEAR (?>\d\d){1,2}
62  # Time: HH:MM:SS
63  #TIME \d{2}:\d{2}(?::\d{2}(?:\.\d+)?)?
64  # TIME %{POSINT<24}:%{POSINT<60}(?::%{POSINT<60}(?:\.%{POSINT})?)?
65  HOUR (?:2[0123]|[01]?[0-9])
66  MINUTE (?:[0-5][0-9])
67  # '60' is a leap second in most time standards and thus is valid.
68  SECOND (?:(?:[0-5]?[0-9]|60)(?:[:.,][0-9]+)?)
69  TIME (?!<[0-9])%{HOUR}:%{MINUTE}(?::%{SECOND})(?![0-9])
70  # datestamp is YYYY/MM/DD-HH:MM:SS.UUUU (or something like it)
71  DATE_US %{MONTHNUM}[/-]%{MONTHDAY}[/-]%{YEAR}
72  DATE_EU %{MONTHDAY}[./-]%{MONTHNUM}[./-]%{YEAR}
73  DATESTAMP_US %{DATE_US}[- ]%{TIME}
74  DATESTAMP_EU %{DATE_EU}[- ]%{TIME}
75  ISO8601_TIMEZONE (?:Z|[+-]%{HOUR}(?::?%{MINUTE}))
76  ISO8601_SECOND (?:%{SECOND}|60)
77  TIMESTAMP_ISO8601 %{YEAR}-%{MONTHNUM}-%{MONTHDAY}[T ]%{HOUR}:?%{MINUTE}(?::?%{SECOND})?%{
        ISO8601_TIMEZONE}?
78  TZ (?:[PMCE][SD]T|UTC)
79  DATESTAMP_RFC822 %{DAY} %{MONTH} %{MONTHDAY} %{YEAR} %{TIME} %{TZ}
80  DATESTAMP_RFC2822 %{DAY}, %{MONTHDAY} %{MONTH} %{YEAR} %{TIME} %{ISO8601_TIMEZONE}
81  DATESTAMP_OTHER %{DAY} %{MONTH} %{MONTHDAY} %{TIME} %{TZ} %{YEAR}
82  DATESTAMP_EVENTLOG %{YEAR}%{MONTHNUM2}%{MONTHDAY}%{HOUR}%{MINUTE}%{SECOND}
83  CISCOTIMESTAMP %{MONTH} %{MONTHDAY} %{TIME}
84
85  # Syslog Dates: Month Day HH:MM:SS
86  SYSLOGTIMESTAMP %{MONTH} +%{MONTHDAY} %{TIME}
87  PROG (?:[\w._/%-]+)
88  SYSLOGPROG %{PROG:program}(?:\[%{POSINT:pid}\])?
89  SYSLOGHOST %{IPORHOST}
90  SYSLOGFACILITY <%{NONNEGINT:facility}.%{NONNEGINT:priority}>
91  HTTPDATE %{MONTHDAY}/%{MONTH}/%{YEAR}:%{TIME} %{INT}
92
93  # Shortcuts
94  QS %{QUOTEDSTRING:UNWANTED}
95
96  # Log formats
97  SYSLOGBASE %{SYSLOGTIMESTAMP:timestamp} (?:%{SYSLOGFACILITY} )?%{SYSLOGHOST:logsource} %{
        SYSLOGPROG}:
98
99  MESSAGESLOG %{SYSLOGBASE} %{DATA}
100
101 COMMONAPACHELOG %{IPORHOST:clientip} %{USER:ident} %{USER:auth} \[%{HTTPDATE:timestamp}\]
        "(?:%{WORD:verb} %{NOTSPACE:request}(?: HTTP/%{NUMBER:httpversion})?|%{DATA:rawrequest})"
        %{NUMBER:response} (?:%{Bytes:bytes=%{NUMBER}|-})
102 COMBINEDAPACHELOG %{COMMONAPACHELOG} %{QS:referrer} %{QS:agent}
103 COMMONAPACHELOG_DATATYPED %{IPORHOST:clientip} %{USER:ident;boolean} %{USER:auth} \[%{HTTPDATE:
        timestamp;date;dd/MMM/yyyy:HH:mm:ss Z}\] "(?:%{WORD:verb;string} %{NOTSPACE:request}(?:
        HTTP/%{NUMBER:httpversion;float})?|%{DATA:rawrequest})" %{NUMBER:response;int} (?:%{NUMBER:
        bytes;long}|-)
104
105
106 # Log Levels
107 LOGLEVEL ([A|a]lert|ALERT|[T|t]race|TRACE|[D|d]ebug|DEBUG|[N|n]otice|NOTICE|[I|i]nfo|INFO|[W|w]
```

95

```
arn?(?:ing)?|WARN?(?:ING)?|[E|e]rr?(?:or)?|ERR?(?:OR)?|[C|c]rit?(?:ical)?|CRIT?(?:ICAL)?|[F
|f]atal|FATAL|[S|s]evere|SEVERE|EMERG(?:ENCY)?|[Ee]merg(?:ency)?)
```

Writing XML Custom Classifiers

XML (Extensible Markup Language) defines the structure of a document with the use of tags in the file. With an XML custom classifier, you can specify the tag name used to define a row.

Custom Classifier Values in AWS Glue

When you define an XML classifier, you supply the following values to AWS Glue to create the classifier. The classification field of this classifier is set to xml.

Name
Name of the classifier.

Row tag
The XML tag name that defines a table row in the XML document, without angle brackets < >. The name must comply with XML rules for a tag.
The element containing the row data **cannot** be a self-closing empty element. For example, this empty element is **not** parsed by AWS Glue:

```
1          <row att1"="xx att2"="yy />
```

Empty elements can be written as follows:

```
1          <row att1"="xx att2"="yy> </row>
```

AWS Glue keeps track of the creation time, last update time, and version of your classifier.

For example, suppose you have the following XML file. To create an AWS Glue table that only contains columns for author and title, create a classifier in the AWS Glue console with **Row tag** as AnyCompany. Then add and run a crawler which uses this custom classifier.

```
1  <?xml version="1.0"?>
2  <catalog>
3     <book id="bk101">
4       <AnyCompany>
5         <author>Rivera, Martha</author>
6         <title>AnyCompany Developer Guide</title>
7       </AnyCompany>
8     </book>
9     <book id="bk102">
10      <AnyCompany>
11        <author>Stiles, John</author>
12        <title>Style Guide for AnyCompany</title>
13      </AnyCompany>
14    </book>
15 </catalog>
```

Writing JSON Custom Classifiers

JSON (JavaScript Object Notation) is a data-interchange format. It defines data structures with name-value pairs or an ordered list of values. With a JSON custom classifier, you can specify the JSON path to a data structure which is used to define the the schema for your table.

96

Custom Classifier Values in AWS Glue

When you define a JSON classifier, you supply the following values to AWS Glue to create the classifier. The classification field of this classifier is set to `json`.

Name
Name of the classifier.

JSON path
A JSON path that points to an object which is used to define a table schema. The JSON path can be written in dot notation or bracket notation. The following operators are supported:
[See the AWS documentation website for more details]

AWS Glue keeps track of the creation time, last update time, and version of your classifier.

Example of Using a JSON Classifier To Pull Records From an Array
Suppose your JSON data is an array of records. For example the first few lines of your file might look like:

```
1  [
2    {
3      "type": "constituency",
4      "id": "ocd-division\/country:us\/state:ak",
5      "name": "Alaska"
6    },
7    {
8      "type": "constituency",
9      "id": "ocd-division\/country:us\/state:al\/cd:1",
10     "name": "Alabama's 1st congressional district"
11   },
12   {
13     "type": "constituency",
14     "id": "ocd-division\/country:us\/state:al\/cd:2",
15     "name": "Alabama's 2nd congressional district"
16   },
17   {
18     "type": "constituency",
19     "id": "ocd-division\/country:us\/state:al\/cd:3",
20     "name": "Alabama's 3rd congressional district"
21   },
22   {
23     "type": "constituency",
24     "id": "ocd-division\/country:us\/state:al\/cd:4",
25     "name": "Alabama's 4th congressional district"
26   },
27   {
28     "type": "constituency",
29     "id": "ocd-division\/country:us\/state:al\/cd:5",
30     "name": "Alabama's 5th congressional district"
31   },
32   {
33     "type": "constituency",
34     "id": "ocd-division\/country:us\/state:al\/cd:6",
35     "name": "Alabama's 6th congressional district"
36   },
37   {
38     "type": "constituency",
39     "id": "ocd-division\/country:us\/state:al\/cd:7",
```

```
40        "name": "Alabama's 7th congressional district"
41   },
42   {
43        "type": "constituency",
44        "id": "ocd-division\/country:us\/state:ar\/cd:1",
45        "name": "Arkansas's 1st congressional district"
46   },
47   {
48        "type": "constituency",
49        "id": "ocd-division\/country:us\/state:ar\/cd:2",
50        "name": "Arkansas's 2nd congressional district"
51   },
52   {
53        "type": "constituency",
54        "id": "ocd-division\/country:us\/state:ar\/cd:3",
55        "name": "Arkansas's 3rd congressional district"
56   },
57   {
58        "type": "constituency",
59        "id": "ocd-division\/country:us\/state:ar\/cd:4",
60        "name": "Arkansas's 4th congressional district"
61   }
62 ]
```

When running a crawler using the built-in JSON classifier, the entire file is used to define the schema. Because you don't specify a JSON path, the crawler will treat the data as one object, that is, just an array. For example, the schema might look like:

```
1 root
2 |-- record: array
```

However, to create a schema that is based on each record in the JSON array, create a custom JSON classifier and specify the JSON path as $[*]. When you specify this JSON path, the classifier interrogates all 12 records in the array to determine the schema. The resulting schema contains separate fields for each object, similiar to this:

```
1 root
2 |-- type: string
3 |-- id: string
4 |-- name: string
```

Example of Using a JSON Classifier To Only Examine Parts Of a File

Suppose your JSON data follows the pattern of the example JSON file s3://awsglue-datasets/examples/us-legislators/all/areas.json drawn from http://everypolitician.org/. Example objects in the JSON file look like:

```
1 {
2   "type": "constituency",
3   "id": "ocd-division\/country:us\/state:ak",
4   "name": "Alaska"
5 }
6 {
7   "type": "constituency",
8   "identifiers": [
9     {
10       "scheme": "dmoz",
11       "identifier": "Regional\/North_America\/United_States\/Alaska\/"
```

```
12        },
13        {
14          "scheme": "freebase",
15          "identifier": "\/m\/0hjy"
16        },
17        {
18          "scheme": "fips",
19          "identifier": "US02"
20        },
21        {
22          "scheme": "quora",
23          "identifier": "Alaska-state"
24        },
25        {
26          "scheme": "britannica",
27          "identifier": "place\/Alaska"
28        },
29        {
30          "scheme": "wikidata",
31          "identifier": "Q797"
32        }
33      ],
34      "other_names": [
35        {
36          "lang": "en",
37          "note": "multilingual",
38          "name": "Alaska"
39        },
40        {
41          "lang": "fr",
42          "note": "multilingual",
43          "name": "Alaska"
44        },
45        {
46          "lang": "nov",
47          "note": "multilingual",
48          "name": "Alaska"
49        }
50      ],
51      "id": "ocd-division\/country:us\/state:ak",
52      "name": "Alaska"
53    }
```

When running a crawler using the built-in JSON classifier, the entire file is used to create the schema. You might end up with a schema like this:

```
1 root
2 |-- type: string
3 |-- id: string
4 |-- name: string
5 |-- identifiers: array
6 |      |-- element: struct
7 |      |      |-- scheme: string
8 |      |      |-- identifier: string
9 |-- other_names: array
```

```
10 |      |-- element: struct
11 |      |      |-- lang: string
12 |      |      |-- note: string
13 |      |      |-- name: string
```

However, to create a schema using just the "id" object, create a custom JSON classifier and specify the JSON path as $.id. Then the schema is based on only the "id" field:

```
1 root
2 |-- record: string
```

The first few lines of data extracted with this schema looks like this:

```
1  {"record": "ocd-division/country:us/state:ak"}
2  {"record": "ocd-division/country:us/state:al/cd:1"}
3  {"record": "ocd-division/country:us/state:al/cd:2"}
4  {"record": "ocd-division/country:us/state:al/cd:3"}
5  {"record": "ocd-division/country:us/state:al/cd:4"}
6  {"record": "ocd-division/country:us/state:al/cd:5"}
7  {"record": "ocd-division/country:us/state:al/cd:6"}
8  {"record": "ocd-division/country:us/state:al/cd:7"}
9  {"record": "ocd-division/country:us/state:ar/cd:1"}
10 {"record": "ocd-division/country:us/state:ar/cd:2"}
11 {"record": "ocd-division/country:us/state:ar/cd:3"}
12 {"record": "ocd-division/country:us/state:ar/cd:4"}
13 {"record": "ocd-division/country:us/state:as"}
14 {"record": "ocd-division/country:us/state:az/cd:1"}
15 {"record": "ocd-division/country:us/state:az/cd:2"}
16 {"record": "ocd-division/country:us/state:az/cd:3"}
17 {"record": "ocd-division/country:us/state:az/cd:4"}
18 {"record": "ocd-division/country:us/state:az/cd:5"}
19 {"record": "ocd-division/country:us/state:az/cd:6"}
20 {"record": "ocd-division/country:us/state:az/cd:7"}
```

To create a schema based on a deeply nested object, such as "identifier", in the JSON file, you can create a custom JSON classifier and specify the JSON path as $.identifiers[*].identifier. Although the schema is very simliar to the previous example, it is based on a different object in the JSON file. The schema looks like:

```
1 root
2 |-- record: string
```

Listing the first few lines of data from the table shows that the schema is based on the data in the "identifier" object:

```
1  {"record": "Regional/North_America/United_States/Alaska/"}
2  {"record": "/m/0hjy"}
3  {"record": "US02"}
4  {"record": "5879092"}
5  {"record": "4001016-8"}
6  {"record": "destination/alaska"}
7  {"record": "1116270"}
8  {"record": "139487266"}
9  {"record": "n79018447"}
10 {"record": "01490999-8dec-4129-8254-eef6e80fadc3"}
11 {"record": "Alaska-state"}
12 {"record": "place/Alaska"}
13 {"record": "Q797"}
```

```
14 {"record": "Regional/North_America/United_States/Alabama/"}
15 {"record": "/m/0gyh"}
16 {"record": "US01"}
17 {"record": "4829764"}
18 {"record": "4084839-5"}
19 {"record": "161950"}
20 {"record": "131885589"}
```

To create a table based on another deeply nested object, such as the "name" field in the "other_names" array in the JSON file, you can create a custom JSON classifier and specify the JSON path as $.other_names[*].name. Although the schema is very simliar to the previous example, it is based on a different object in the JSON file. The schema looks like:

```
1 root
2 |-- record: string
```

Listing the first few lines of data in the table shows that it is based on the data in the "name" object in the "other_names" array:

```
1 {"record": "Alaska"}
2 {"record": "Alaska"}
3 {"record": ""}
4 {"record": "Alaska"}
5 {"record": "Alaska"}
6 {"record": "Alaska"}
7 {"record": "Alaska"}
8 {"record": "Alaska"}
9 {"record": "Alaska"}
10 {"record": ""}
11 {"record": ""}
12 {"record": ""}
13 {"record": "Alaska"}
14 {"record": "Alyaska"}
15 {"record": "Alaska"}
16 {"record": "Alaska"}
17 {"record": " "}
18 {"record": ""}
19 {"record": "Alaska"}
20 {"record": ""}
```

Working with Classifiers on the AWS Glue Console

A classifier determines the schema of your data. You can write a custom classifier and point to it from AWS Glue. To see a list of all the classifiers that you have created, open the AWS Glue console at https://console.aws.amazon.com/glue/, and choose the **Classifiers** tab.

The list displays the following properties about each classifier:

Classifier
The classifier name. When you create a classifier you must provide a name for it.

Classification
The classification type of tables inferred by this classifier.

Last updated
The last time this classifier was updated.

From the **Classifiers** list in the AWS Glue console, you can add, edit, and delete classifiers. To see more details for a classifier, choose the classifier name in the list. Details include the information you defined when you created the classifier.

To add a classifier in the AWS Glue console, choose **Add classifier**. When you define a classifier, you supply values for the following:

Classifier name
Provide a unique name for your classifier.

Classification
For grok classifiers, describe the format or type of data that is classified or provide a custom label.

Grok pattern
For grok classifiers, this is used to parse your data into a structured schema. The grok pattern is composed of named patterns that describe the format of your data store. You write this grok pattern using the named built-in patterns provided by AWS Glue and custom patterns you write and include in the **Custom patterns** field. Although grok debugger results might not match the results from AWS Glue exactly, we suggest that you try your pattern using some sample data with a grok debugger. You can find grok debuggers on the web. The named built-in patterns provided by AWS Glue are generally compatible with grok patterns that are available on the web.
Build your grok pattern by iteratively adding named patterns and check your results in a debugger. This activity gives you confidence that when the AWS Glue crawler runs your grok pattern, your data can be parsed.

Custom patterns
For grok classifiers, these are optional building blocks for the **Grok pattern** that you write. When built-in patterns cannot parse your data, you might need to write a custom pattern. These custom patterns are defined in this field and referenced in the **Grok pattern** field. Each custom pattern is defined on a separate line. Just like the built-in patterns, it consists of a named pattern definition that uses regular expression (regex) syntax. For example, the following has the name `MESSAGEPREFIX` followed by a regular expression definition to apply to your data to determine whether it follows the pattern.

```
1 MESSAGEPREFIX .*-.*-.*-.*-.*
```

Row tag
For XML classifiers, this is the name of the XML tag that defines a table row in the XML document. Type the name without angle brackets < >. The name must comply with XML rules for a tag.

JSON path
For JSON classifiers, this is the JSON path to the object, array, or value that defines a row of the table being created. Type the name in either dot or bracket JSON syntax using AWS Glue supported operators. For more information, see the list of operators in Writing JSON Custom Classifiers

For more information, see Writing Custom Classifiers

Adding a Connection to Your Data Store

Connections are used by crawlers and jobs in AWS Glue to access certain types of data stores. For information about adding a connection using the AWS Glue console, see Working with Connections on the AWS Glue Console.

When Is a Connection Used?

If your data store requires one, the connection is used when you crawl a data store to catalog its metadata in the AWS Glue Data Catalog. The connection is also used by any job that uses the data store as a source or target.

Defining a Connection in the AWS Glue Data Catalog

Some types of data stores require additional connection information to access your data. This information might include an additional user name and password (different from your AWS credentials), or other information that is required to connect to the data store.

After AWS Glue connects to a JDBC data store, it must have permission from the data store to perform operations. The username you provide with the connection must have the required permissions or privileges. For example, a crawler requires SELECT privileges to retrieve metadata from a JDBC data store. Likewise, a job that writes to a JDBC target requires the necessary privileges to INSERT, UPDATE, and DELETE data into an existing table.

AWS Glue can connect to the following data stores by using the JDBC protocol:

- Amazon Redshift
- Amazon Relational Database Service
  - Amazon Aurora
  - MariaDB
  - Microsoft SQL Server
  - MySQL
  - Oracle
  - PostgreSQL
- Publicly accessible databases
  - Amazon Aurora
  - MariaDB
  - Microsoft SQL Server
  - MySQL
  - Oracle
  - PostgreSQL

A connection is not typically required for Amazon S3. However, to access Amazon S3 from within your virtual private cloud (VPC), an Amazon S3 VPC endpoint is required. For more information, see Amazon VPC Endpoints for Amazon S3.

In your connection information, you also must consider whether data is accessed through a VPC and then set up network parameters accordingly.

Connecting to a JDBC Data Store in a VPC

Typically, you create resources inside Amazon Virtual Private Cloud (Amazon VPC) so that they cannot be accessed over the public internet. By default, resources in a VPC can't be accessed from AWS Glue. To enable AWS Glue to access resources inside your VPC, you must provide additional VPC-specific configuration information that includes VPC subnet IDs and security group IDs. AWS Glue uses this information to set up elastic network interfaces that enable your function to connect securely to other resources in your private VPC.

Accessing VPC Data Using Elastic Network Interfaces

When AWS Glue connects to a JDBC data store in a VPC, AWS Glue creates an elastic network interface (with the prefix `Glue_`) in your account to access your VPC data. You can't delete this network interface as long as it's attached to AWS Glue. As part of creating the elastic network interface, AWS Glue associates one or more security groups to it. To enable AWS Glue to create the network interface, security groups that are associated with the resource must allow inbound access with a source rule. This rule contains a security group that is associated with the resource. This gives the elastic network interface access to your data store with the same security group.

To allow AWS Glue to communicate with its components, specify a security group with a self-referencing inbound rule for all TCP ports. By creating a self-referencing rule, you can restrict the source to the same security group in the VPC and not open it to all networks. The default security group for your VPC might already have a self-referencing inbound rule for `ALL Traffic`.

You can create rules in the Amazon VPC console. To update rule settings via the AWS Management Console, navigate to the VPC console (https://console.aws.amazon.com/vpc/), and select the appropriate security group. Specify the inbound rule for `ALL TCP` to have as its source the same security group name. For more information about security group rules, see Security Groups for Your VPC.

Each elastic network interface is assigned a private IP address from the IP address range in the subnets that you specify. The network interface is not assigned any public IP addresses. AWS Glue requires internet access (for example, to access AWS services that don't have VPC endpoints). You can configure a network address translation (NAT) instance inside your VPC, or you can use the Amazon VPC NAT gateway. For more information, see NAT Gateways in the *Amazon VPC User Guide*. You can't directly use an internet gateway attached to your VPC as a route in your subnet route table because that requires the network interface to have public IP addresses.

The VPC network attributes `enableDnsHostnames` and `enableDnsSupport` must be set to true. For more information, see Using DNS with your VPC.

Important
Don't put your data store in a public subnet or in a private subnet that doesn't have internet access. Instead, attach it only to private subnets that have internet access through a NAT instance or an Amazon VPC NAT gateway.

Elastic Network Interface Properties

To create the elastic network interface, you must supply the following properties:

VPC
The name of the VPC that contains your data store.

Subnet
The subnet in the VPC that contains your data store.

Security groups
The security groups that are associated with your data store. AWS Glue associates these security groups with the elastic network interface that is attached to your VPC subnet. To allow AWS Glue components to communicate and also prevent access from other networks, at least one chosen security group must specify a self-referencing inbound rule for all TCP ports.

For information about managing a VPC with Amazon Redshift, see Managing Clusters in an Amazon Virtual Private Cloud (VPC).

For information about managing a VPC with Amazon RDS, see Working with an Amazon RDS DB Instance in a VPC.

Working with Connections on the AWS Glue Console

A connection contains the properties that are needed to access your data store. To see a list of all the connections that you have created, open the AWS Glue console at https://console.aws.amazon.com/glue/, and choose the **Connections** tab.

The Connections list displays the following properties about each connection:

Name
When you create a connection, you give it a unique name.

Type
The data store type and the properties that are required for a successful connection. AWS Glue uses the JDBC protocol to access several types of data stores.

Date created
The date and time (UTC) that the connection was created.

Last updated
The date and time (UTC) that the connection was last updated.

Updated by
The user who created or last updated the connection.

From the **Connections** tab in the AWS Glue console, you can add, edit, and delete connections. To see more details for a connection, choose the connection name in the list. Details include the information you defined when you created the connection.

As a best practice, before you use a data store connection in an ETL job, choose **Test connection**. AWS Glue uses the parameters in your connection to confirm that it can access your data store and reports back any errors. Connections are required for Amazon Redshift, Amazon Relational Database Service (Amazon RDS), and JDBC data stores. For more information, see Connecting to a JDBC Data Store in a VPC.

Important
Currently, an ETL job can use only one JDBC connection. If you have multiple data stores in a job, they must be on the same subnet.

Adding a JDBC Connection to a Data Store

To add a connection in the AWS Glue console, choose **Add connection**. The wizard guides you through adding the properties that are required to create a JDBC connection to a data store. If you choose Amazon Redshift or Amazon RDS, AWS Glue tries to determine the underlying JDBC properties to create the connection.

When you define a connection, values for the following properties are required:

Connection name
Type a unique name for your connection.

Connection type
Choose either Amazon Redshift, Amazon RDS, or JDBC.

- If you choose Amazon Redshift, choose a **Cluster**, **Database name**, **Username**, and **Password** in your account to create a JDBC connection.
- If you choose Amazon RDS, choose an **Instance**, **Database name**, **Username**, and **Password** in your account to create a JDBC connection. The console also lists the supported database engine types.

JDBC URL
Type the URL for your JDBC data store. For most database engines, this field is in the following format.
`jdbc:protocol://host:port/db_name`
Depending on the database engine, a different JDBC URL format might be required. This format can have

slightly different use of the colon (:) and slash (/) or different keywords to specify databases.

For JDBC to connect to the data store, a `db_name` in the data store is required. The `db_name` is used to establish a network connection with the supplied `username` and `password`. When connected, AWS Glue can access other databases in the data store to run a crawler or run an ETL job.

The following JDBC URL examples show the syntax for several database engines.

- To connect to an Amazon Redshift cluster data store with a `dev` database:

  `jdbc:redshift://xxx.us-east-1.redshift.amazonaws.com:8192/dev`

- To connect to an Amazon RDS for MySQL data store with an `employee` database:

  `jdbc:mysql://xxx-cluster.cluster-xxx.us-east-1.rds.amazonaws.com:3306/employee`

- To connect to an Amazon RDS for PostgreSQL data store with an `employee` database:

  `jdbc:postgresql://xxx-cluster.cluster-xxx.us-east-1.rds.amazonaws.com:5432/employee`

- To connect to an Amazon RDS for Oracle data store with an `employee` service name:

  `jdbc:oracle:thin://@xxx-cluster.cluster-xxx.us-east-1.rds.amazonaws.com:1521/employee`

  The syntax for Amazon RDS for Oracle can follow the following patterns:

  - `jdbc:oracle:thin://@host:port/service_name`
  - `jdbc:oracle:thin://@host:port:SID`

- To connect to an Amazon RDS for Microsoft SQL Server data store with an `employee` database:

  `jdbc:sqlserver://xxx-cluster.cluster-xxx.us-east-1.rds.amazonaws.com:1433;database=employee`

  The syntax for Amazon RDS for SQL Server can follow the following patterns:

  - `jdbc:sqlserver://server_name:port;database=db_name`
  - `jdbc:sqlserver://server_name:port;databaseName=db_name`

Username

Provide a user name that has permission to access the JDBC data store.

Password

Type the password for the user name that has access permission to the JDBC data store.

VPC

Choose the name of the virtual private cloud (VPC) that contains your data store. The AWS Glue console lists all VPCs for the current region.

Subnet

Choose the subnet within the VPC that contains your data store. The AWS Glue console lists all subnets for the data store in your VPC.

Security groups

Choose the security groups that are associated with your data store. AWS Glue requires one or more security groups with an inbound source rule that allows AWS Glue to connect. The AWS Glue console lists all security groups that are granted inbound access to your VPC. AWS Glue associates these security groups with the elastic network interface that is attached to your VPC subnet.

Populating the Data Catalog Using AWS CloudFormation Templates

AWS CloudFormation is a service that can create many AWS resources. AWS Glue provides API operations to create objects in the AWS Glue Data Catalog. However, it might be more convenient to define and create AWS Glue objects and other related AWS resource objects in an AWS CloudFormation template file. Then you can automate the process of creating the objects.

AWS CloudFormation provides a simplified syntax—either JSON (JavaScript Object Notation) or YAML (YAML Ain't Markup Language)—to express the creation of AWS resources. You can use AWS CloudFormation templates to define Data Catalog objects such as databases, tables, partitions, crawlers, classifiers, and connections. You can also define ETL objects such as jobs, triggers, and development endpoints. You create a template that describes all the AWS resources you want, and AWS CloudFormation takes care of provisioning and configuring those resources for you.

For more information, see What Is AWS CloudFormation? and Working with AWS CloudFormation Templates in the *AWS CloudFormation User Guide.*

If you plan to use AWS CloudFormation templates that are compatible with AWS Glue, as an administrator, you must grant access to AWS CloudFormation and to the AWS services and actions on which it depends. To grant permissions to create AWS CloudFormation resources, attach the following policy to the IAM users that work with AWS CloudFormation:

```
1  {
2    "Version": "2012-10-17",
3    "Statement": [
4      {
5        "Effect": "Allow",
6        "Action": [
7          "cloudformation:*"
8        ],
9        "Resource": "*"
10     }
11   ]
12 }
```

The following table contains the actions that an AWS CloudFormation template can perform on your behalf. It includes links to information about the AWS resource types and their property types that you can add to an AWS CloudFormation template.

AWS Glue Resource	AWS CloudFormation Template	AWS Glue Samples
Classifier	AWS::Glue::Classifier	Grok classifier
Connection	AWS::Glue::Connection	MySQL connection
Crawler	AWS::Glue::Crawler	Amazon S3 crawler, MySQL crawler
Database	AWS::Glue::Database	Empty database, Database with tables
Development endpoint	AWS::Glue::DevEndpoint	Development endpoint
Job	AWS::Glue::Job	Amazon S3 job, JDBC job
Partition	AWS::Glue::Partition	Partitions of a table
Table	AWS::Glue::Table	Table in a database
Trigger	AWS::Glue::Trigger	On-demand trigger, Scheduled trigger, Conditional trigger

To get started, use the following sample templates and customize them with your own metadata. Then use the

AWS CloudFormation console to create an AWS CloudFormation stack to add objects to AWS Glue and any associated services. Many fields in an AWS Glue object are optional. These templates illustrate the fields that are required or are necessary for a working and functional AWS Glue object.

An AWS CloudFormation template can be in either JSON or YAML format. In these examples, YAML is used for easier readability. The examples contain comments (#) to describe the values that are defined in the templates.

AWS CloudFormation templates can include a **Parameters** section. This section can be changed in the sample text or when the YAML file is submitted to the AWS CloudFormation console to create a stack. The **Resources** section of the template contains the definition of AWS Glue and related objects. AWS CloudFormation template syntax definitions might contain properties that include more detailed property syntax. Not all properties might be required to create an AWS Glue object; these samples show example values for common properties to create an AWS Glue object.

Sample AWS CloudFormation Template for an AWS Glue Database

An AWS Glue database in the Data Catalog contains metadata tables. The database consists of very few properties and can be created in the Data Catalog with an AWS CloudFormation template. The following sample template is provided to get you started and to illustrate the use of AWS CloudFormation stacks with AWS Glue. The only resource created by the sample template is a database named cfn-mysampledatabase. You can change it by editing the text of the sample or changing the value on the AWS CloudFormation console when you submit the YAML.

The following shows example values for common properties to create an AWS Glue database. For more information about the AWS CloudFormation database template for AWS Glue, see AWS::Glue::Database.

```
1  ---
2  AWSTemplateFormatVersion: '2010-09-09'
3  # Sample CloudFormation template in YAML to demonstrate creating a database named
       mysampledatabase
4  # The metadata created in the Data Catalog points to the flights public S3 bucket
5  #
6  # Parameters section contains names that are substituted in the Resources section
7  # These parameters are the names the resources created in the Data Catalog
8  Parameters:
9    CFNDatabaseName:
10     Type: String
11     Default: cfn-mysampledatabse
12
13  # Resources section defines metadata for the Data Catalog
14  Resources:
15  # Create an AWS Glue database
16    CFNDatabaseFlights:
17      Type: AWS::Glue::Database
18      Properties:
19        # The database is created in the Data Catalog for your account
20        CatalogId: !Ref AWS::AccountId
21        DatabaseInput:
22          # The name of the database is defined in the Parameters section above
23          Name: !Ref CFNDatabaseName
24          Description: Database to hold tables for flights data
25          LocationUri: s3://crawler-public-us-east-1/flight/2016/csv/
26          #Parameters: Leave AWS database parameters blank
```

Sample AWS CloudFormation Template for an AWS Glue Database, Table, and Partition

An AWS Glue table contains the metadata that defines the structure and location of data that you want to process with your ETL scripts. Within a table, you can define partitions to parallelize the processing of your data. A partition is a chunk of data that you defined with a key. For example, using month as a key, all the data for January is contained in the same partition. In AWS Glue, databases can contain tables, and tables can contain partitions.

The following sample shows how to populate a database, a table, and partitions using an AWS CloudFormation template. The base data format is csv and delimited by a comma (,). Because a database must exist before it can contain a table, and a table must exist before partitions can be created, the template uses the DependsOn statement to define the dependency of these objects when they are created.

The values in this sample define a table that contains flight data from a publicly available Amazon S3 bucket. For illustration, only a few columns of the data and one partitioning key are defined. Four partitions are also defined in the Data Catalog. Some fields to describe the storage of the base data are also shown in the StorageDescriptor fields.

```
1  ---
2  AWSTemplateFormatVersion: '2010-09-09'
3  # Sample CloudFormation template in YAML to demonstrate creating a database, a table, and
        partitions
4  # The metadata created in the Data Catalog points to the flights public S3 bucket
5  #
6  # Parameters substituted in the Resources section
7  # These parameters are names of the resources created in the Data Catalog
8  Parameters:
9    CFNDatabaseName:
10     Type: String
11     Default: cfn-database-flights-1
12   CFNTableName1:
13     Type: String
14     Default: cfn-manual-table-flights-1
15 # Resources to create metadata in the Data Catalog
16 Resources:
17 ###
18 # Create an AWS Glue database
19   CFNDatabaseFlights:
20     Type: AWS::Glue::Database
21     Properties:
22       CatalogId: !Ref AWS::AccountId
23       DatabaseInput:
24         Name: !Ref CFNDatabaseName
25         Description: Database to hold tables for flights data
26 ###
27 # Create an AWS Glue table
28   CFNTableFlights:
29     # Creating the table waits for the database to be created
30     DependsOn: CFNDatabaseFlights
31     Type: AWS::Glue::Table
32     Properties:
33       CatalogId: !Ref AWS::AccountId
34       DatabaseName: !Ref CFNDatabaseName
35       TableInput:
36         Name: !Ref CFNTableName1
```

```
37        Description: Define the first few columns of the flights table
38        TableType: EXTERNAL_TABLE
39        Parameters: {
40    "classification": "csv"
41  }
42 #      ViewExpandedText: String
43        PartitionKeys:
44        # Data is partitioned by month
45        - Name: mon
46          Type: bigint
47        StorageDescriptor:
48          OutputFormat: org.apache.hadoop.hive.ql.io.HiveIgnoreKeyTextOutputFormat
49          Columns:
50          - Name: year
51            Type: bigint
52          - Name: quarter
53            Type: bigint
54          - Name: month
55            Type: bigint
56          - Name: day_of_month
57            Type: bigint
58          InputFormat: org.apache.hadoop.mapred.TextInputFormat
59          Location: s3://crawler-public-us-east-1/flight/2016/csv/
60          SerdeInfo:
61            Parameters:
62              field.delim: ","
63            SerializationLibrary: org.apache.hadoop.hive.serde2.lazy.LazySimpleSerDe
64 # Partition 1
65 # Create an AWS Glue partition
66    CFNPartitionMon1:
67      DependsOn: CFNTableFlights
68      Type: AWS::Glue::Partition
69      Properties:
70        CatalogId: !Ref AWS::AccountId
71        DatabaseName: !Ref CFNDatabaseName
72        TableName: !Ref CFNTableName1
73        PartitionInput:
74          Values:
75          - 1
76          StorageDescriptor:
77            OutputFormat: org.apache.hadoop.hive.ql.io.HiveIgnoreKeyTextOutputFormat
78            Columns:
79            - Name: mon
80              Type: bigint
81            InputFormat: org.apache.hadoop.mapred.TextInputFormat
82            Location: s3://crawler-public-us-east-1/flight/2016/csv/mon=1/
83            SerdeInfo:
84              Parameters:
85                field.delim: ","
86              SerializationLibrary: org.apache.hadoop.hive.serde2.lazy.LazySimpleSerDe
87 # Partition 2
88 # Create an AWS Glue partition
89    CFNPartitionMon2:
90      DependsOn: CFNTableFlights
```

```
91      Type: AWS::Glue::Partition
92      Properties:
93        CatalogId: !Ref AWS::AccountId
94        DatabaseName: !Ref CFNDatabaseName
95        TableName: !Ref CFNTableName1
96        PartitionInput:
97          Values:
98          - 2
99          StorageDescriptor:
100           OutputFormat: org.apache.hadoop.hive.ql.io.HiveIgnoreKeyTextOutputFormat
101           Columns:
102           - Name: mon
103             Type: bigint
104           InputFormat: org.apache.hadoop.mapred.TextInputFormat
105           Location: s3://crawler-public-us-east-1/flight/2016/csv/mon=2/
106           SerdeInfo:
107             Parameters:
108               field.delim: ","
109             SerializationLibrary: org.apache.hadoop.hive.serde2.lazy.LazySimpleSerDe
110 # Partition 3
111 # Create an AWS Glue partition
112   CFNPartitionMon3:
113     DependsOn: CFNTableFlights
114     Type: AWS::Glue::Partition
115     Properties:
116       CatalogId: !Ref AWS::AccountId
117       DatabaseName: !Ref CFNDatabaseName
118       TableName: !Ref CFNTableName1
119       PartitionInput:
120         Values:
121         - 3
122         StorageDescriptor:
123           OutputFormat: org.apache.hadoop.hive.ql.io.HiveIgnoreKeyTextOutputFormat
124           Columns:
125           - Name: mon
126             Type: bigint
127           InputFormat: org.apache.hadoop.mapred.TextInputFormat
128           Location: s3://crawler-public-us-east-1/flight/2016/csv/mon=3/
129           SerdeInfo:
130             Parameters:
131               field.delim: ","
132             SerializationLibrary: org.apache.hadoop.hive.serde2.lazy.LazySimpleSerDe
133 # Partition 4
134 # Create an AWS Glue partition
135   CFNPartitionMon4:
136     DependsOn: CFNTableFlights
137     Type: AWS::Glue::Partition
138     Properties:
139       CatalogId: !Ref AWS::AccountId
140       DatabaseName: !Ref CFNDatabaseName
141       TableName: !Ref CFNTableName1
142       PartitionInput:
143         Values:
144         - 4
```

```
145    StorageDescriptor:
146      OutputFormat: org.apache.hadoop.hive.ql.io.HiveIgnoreKeyTextOutputFormat
147      Columns:
148      - Name: mon
149        Type: bigint
150      InputFormat: org.apache.hadoop.mapred.TextInputFormat
151      Location: s3://crawler-public-us-east-1/flight/2016/csv/mon=4/
152      SerdeInfo:
153        Parameters:
154          field.delim: ","
155        SerializationLibrary: org.apache.hadoop.hive.serde2.lazy.LazySimpleSerDe
```

Sample AWS CloudFormation Template for an AWS Glue Classifier

An AWS Glue classifier determines the schema of your data. One type of custom classifier uses a grok pattern to match your data. If the pattern matches, then the custom classifier is used to create your table's schema and set the `classification` to the value set in the classifier definition.

This sample creates a classifier that creates a schema with one column named `message` and sets the classification to `greedy`.

```
1  ---
2  AWSTemplateFormatVersion: '2010-09-09'
3  # Sample CFN YAML to demonstrate creating a classifier
4  #
5  # Parameters section contains names that are substituted in the Resources section
6  # These parameters are the names the resources created in the Data Catalog
7  Parameters:
8  # The name of the classifier to be created
9    CFNClassifierName:
10     Type: String
11     Default: cfn-classifier-grok-one-column-1
12 #
13 #
14 # Resources section defines metadata for the Data Catalog
15 Resources:
16 # Create classifier that uses grok pattern to put all data in one column and classifies it as "
      greedy".
17   CFNClassifierFlights:
18     Type: AWS::Glue::Classifier
19     Properties:
20       GrokClassifier:
21         #Grok classifier that puts all data in one column
22         Name: !Ref CFNClassifierName
23         Classification: greedy
24         GrokPattern: "%{GREEDYDATA:message}"
25         #CustomPatterns: none
```

Sample AWS CloudFormation Template for an AWS Glue Crawler for Amazon S3

An AWS Glue crawler creates metadata tables in your Data Catalog that correspond to your data. You can then use these table definitions as sources and targets in your ETL jobs.

This sample creates a crawler, the required IAM role, and an AWS Glue database in the Data Catalog. When this crawler is run, it assumes the IAM role and creates a table in the database for the public flights data. The table is created with the prefix "cfn_sample_1_". The IAM role created by this template allows global permissions; you might want to create a custom role. No custom classifiers are defined by this classifier. AWS Glue built-in classifiers are used by default.

When you submit this sample to the AWS CloudFormation console, you must confirm that you want to create the IAM role.

```
1  ---
2  AWSTemplateFormatVersion: '2010-09-09'
3  # Sample CFN YAML to demonstrate creating a crawler
4  #
5  # Parameters section contains names that are substituted in the Resources section
6  # These parameters are the names the resources created in the Data Catalog
7  Parameters:
8  # The name of the crawler to be created
9    CFNCrawlerName:
10     Type: String
11     Default: cfn-crawler-flights-1
12   CFNDatabaseName:
13     Type: String
14     Default: cfn-database-flights-1
15   CFNTablePrefixName:
16     Type: String
17     Default: cfn_sample_1_
18 #
19 #
20 # Resources section defines metadata for the Data Catalog
21 Resources:
22 #Create IAM Role assumed by the crawler. For demonstration, this role is given all permissions.
23   CFNRoleFlights:
24     Type: AWS::IAM::Role
25     Properties:
26       AssumeRolePolicyDocument:
27         Version: "2012-10-17"
28         Statement:
29           -
30             Effect: "Allow"
31             Principal:
32               Service:
33                 - "glue.amazonaws.com"
34             Action:
35               - "sts:AssumeRole"
36       Path: "/"
37       Policies:
38         -
39           PolicyName: "root"
40           PolicyDocument:
41             Version: "2012-10-17"
42             Statement:
43               -
44                 Effect: "Allow"
45                 Action: "*"
46                 Resource: "*"
47 # Create a database to contain tables created by the crawler
```

```
48   CFNDatabaseFlights:
49     Type: AWS::Glue::Database
50     Properties:
51       CatalogId: !Ref AWS::AccountId
52       DatabaseInput:
53         Name: !Ref CFNDatabaseName
54         Description: "AWS Glue container to hold metadata tables for the flights crawler"
55  #Create a crawler to crawl the flights data on a public S3 bucket
56  CFNCrawlerFlights:
57     Type: AWS::Glue::Crawler
58     Properties:
59       Name: !Ref CFNCrawlerName
60       Role: !GetAtt CFNRoleFlights.Arn
61       #Classifiers: none, use the default classifier
62       Description: AWS Glue crawler to crawl flights data
63       #Schedule: none, use default run-on-demand
64       DatabaseName: !Ref CFNDatabaseName
65       Targets:
66         S3Targets:
67           # Public S3 bucket with the flights data
68           - Path: "s3://crawler-public-us-east-1/flight/2016/csv"
69       TablePrefix: !Ref CFNTablePrefixName
70       SchemaChangePolicy:
71         UpdateBehavior: "UPDATE_IN_DATABASE"
72         DeleteBehavior: "LOG"
```

Sample AWS CloudFormation Template for an AWS Glue Connection

An AWS Glue connection in the Data Catalog contains the JDBC and network information that is required to connect to a JDBC database. This information is used when you connect to a JDBC database to crawl or run ETL jobs.

This sample creates a connection to an Amazon RDS MySQL database named devdb. When this connection is used, an IAM role, database credentials, and network connection values must also be supplied. See the details of necessary fields in the template.

```
1  ---
2  AWSTemplateFormatVersion: '2010-09-09'
3  # Sample CFN YAML to demonstrate creating a connection
4  #
5  # Parameters section contains names that are substituted in the Resources section
6  # These parameters are the names the resources created in the Data Catalog
7  Parameters:
8  # The name of the connection to be created
9    CFNConnectionName:
10     Type: String
11     Default: cfn-connection-mysql-flights-1
12   CFNJDBCString:
13     Type: String
14     Default: "jdbc:mysql://xxx-mysql.yyyyyyyyyyyyyy.us-east-1.rds.amazonaws.com:3306/devdb"
15   CFNJDBCUser:
16     Type: String
17     Default: "master"
18   CFNJDBCPassword:
```

```
19      Type: String
20      Default: "12345678"
21      NoEcho: true
22  #
23  #
24  # Resources section defines metadata for the Data Catalog
25  Resources:
26    CFNConnectionMySQL:
27      Type: AWS::Glue::Connection
28      Properties:
29        CatalogId: !Ref AWS::AccountId
30        ConnectionInput:
31          Description: "Connect to MySQL database."
32          ConnectionType: "JDBC"
33          #MatchCriteria: none
34          PhysicalConnectionRequirements:
35            AvailabilityZone: "us-east-1d"
36            SecurityGroupIdList:
37            - "sg-7d52b812"
38            SubnetId: "subnet-84f326ee"
39          ConnectionProperties: {
40            "JDBC_CONNECTION_URL": !Ref CFNJDBCString,
41            "USERNAME": !Ref CFNJDBCUser,
42            "PASSWORD": !Ref CFNJDBCPassword
43          }
44          Name: !Ref CFNConnectionName
```

Sample AWS CloudFormation Template for an AWS Glue Crawler for JDBC

An AWS Glue crawler creates metadata tables in your Data Catalog that correspond to your data. You can then use these table definitions as sources and targets in your ETL jobs.

This sample creates a crawler, required IAM role, and an AWS Glue database in the Data Catalog. When this crawler is run, it assumes the IAM role and creates a table in the database for the public flights data that has been stored in a MySQL database. The table is created with the prefix "cfn_jdbc_1_". The IAM role created by this template allows global permissions; you might want to create a custom role. No custom classifiers can be defined for JDBC data. AWS Glue built-in classifiers are used by default.

When you submit this sample to the AWS CloudFormation console, you must confirm that you want to create the IAM role.

```
1  ---
2  AWSTemplateFormatVersion: '2010-09-09'
3  # Sample CFN YAML to demonstrate creating a crawler
4  #
5  # Parameters section contains names that are substituted in the Resources section
6  # These parameters are the names the resources created in the Data Catalog
7  Parameters:
8  # The name of the crawler to be created
9    CFNCrawlerName:
10     Type: String
11     Default: cfn-crawler-jdbc-flights-1
12 # The name of the database to be created to contain tables
13   CFNDatabaseName:
14     Type: String
```

```
15      Default: cfn-database-jdbc-flights-1
16  # The prefix for all tables crawled and created
17      CFNTablePrefixName:
18        Type: String
19        Default: cfn_jdbc_1_
20  # The name of the existing connection to the MySQL database
21      CFNConnectionName:
22        Type: String
23        Default: cfn-connection-mysql-flights-1
24  # The name of the JDBC path (database/schema/table) with wildcard (%) to crawl
25      CFNJDBCPath:
26        Type: String
27        Default: saldev/%
28  #
29  #
30  # Resources section defines metadata for the Data Catalog
31  Resources:
32  #Create IAM Role assumed by the crawler. For demonstration, this role is given all permissions.
33      CFNRoleFlights:
34        Type: AWS::IAM::Role
35        Properties:
36          AssumeRolePolicyDocument:
37            Version: "2012-10-17"
38            Statement:
39              -
40                Effect: "Allow"
41                Principal:
42                  Service:
43                    - "glue.amazonaws.com"
44                Action:
45                  - "sts:AssumeRole"
46          Path: "/"
47          Policies:
48            -
49              PolicyName: "root"
50              PolicyDocument:
51                Version: "2012-10-17"
52                Statement:
53                  -
54                    Effect: "Allow"
55                    Action: "*"
56                    Resource: "*"
57  # Create a database to contain tables created by the crawler
58      CFNDatabaseFlights:
59        Type: AWS::Glue::Database
60        Properties:
61          CatalogId: !Ref AWS::AccountId
62          DatabaseInput:
63            Name: !Ref CFNDatabaseName
64            Description: "AWS Glue container to hold metadata tables for the flights crawler"
65  #Create a crawler to crawl the flights data on a public S3 bucket
66      CFNCrawlerFlights:
67        Type: AWS::Glue::Crawler
68        Properties:
```

```
69    Name: !Ref CFNCrawlerName
70    Role: !GetAtt CFNRoleFlights.Arn
71    #Classifiers: none, use the default classifier
72    Description: AWS Glue crawler to crawl flights data
73    #Schedule: none, use default run-on-demand
74    DatabaseName: !Ref CFNDatabaseName
75    Targets:
76      JdbcTargets:
77        # JDBC MySQL database with the flights data
78        - ConnectionName: !Ref CFNConnectionName
79          Path: !Ref CFNJDBCPath
80        #Exclusions: none
81    TablePrefix: !Ref CFNTablePrefixName
82    SchemaChangePolicy:
83      UpdateBehavior: "UPDATE_IN_DATABASE"
84      DeleteBehavior: "LOG"
```

Sample AWS CloudFormation Template for an AWS Glue Job for Amazon S3 to Amazon S3

An AWS Glue job in the Data Catalog contains the parameter values that are required to run a script in AWS Glue.

This sample creates a job that reads flight data from an Amazon S3 bucket in csv format and writes it to an Amazon S3 Parquet file. The script that is run by this job must already exist. You can generate an ETL script for your environment with the AWS Glue console. When this job is run, an IAM role with the correct permissions must also be supplied.

Common parameter values are shown in the template. For example, AllocatedCapacity (DPUs) defaults to 5.

```
1  ---
2  AWSTemplateFormatVersion: '2010-09-09'
3  # Sample CFN YAML to demonstrate creating a job using the public flights S3 table in a public
     bucket
4  #
5  # Parameters section contains names that are substituted in the Resources section
6  # These parameters are the names the resources created in the Data Catalog
7  Parameters:
8  # The name of the job to be created
9    CFNJobName:
10     Type: String
11     Default: cfn-job-S3-to-S3-2
12 # The name of the IAM role that the job assumes. It must have access to data, script, temporary
     directory
13   CFNIAMRoleName:
14     Type: String
15     Default: AWSGlueServiceRoleGA
16 # The S3 path where the script for this job is located
17   CFNScriptLocation:
18     Type: String
19     Default: s3://aws-glue-scripts-123456789012-us-east-1/myid/sal-job-test2
20 #
21 #
22 # Resources section defines metadata for the Data Catalog
23 Resources:
```

```
24  # Create job to run script which accesses flightscsv table and write to S3 file as parquet.
25  # The script already exists and is called by this job
26  CFNJobFlights:
27    Type: AWS::Glue::Job
28    Properties:
29      Role: !Ref CFNIAMRoleName
30      #DefaultArguments: JSON object
31      # If script written in Scala, then set DefaultArguments={'--job-language'; 'scala', '--
             class': 'your scala class'}
32      #Connections:  No connection needed for S3 to S3 job
33      #  ConnectionsList
34      #MaxRetries: Double
35      Description: Job created with CloudFormation
36      #LogUri: String
37      Command:
38        Name: glueetl
39        ScriptLocation: !Ref CFNScriptLocation
40            # for access to directories use proper IAM role with permission to buckets and
                 folders that begin with "aws-glue-"
41            # script uses temp directory from job definition if required (temp directory not
                 used S3 to S3)
42            # script defines target for output as s3://aws-glue-target/sal
43      AllocatedCapacity: 5
44      ExecutionProperty:
45        MaxConcurrentRuns: 1
46      Name: !Ref CFNJobName
```

Sample AWS CloudFormation Template for an AWS Glue Job for JDBC to Amazon S3

An AWS Glue job in the Data Catalog contains the parameter values that are required to run a script in AWS Glue.

This sample creates a job that reads flight data from a MySQL JDBC database as defined by the connection named cfn-connection-mysql-flights-1 and writes it to an Amazon S3 Parquet file. The script that is run by this job must already exist. You can generate an ETL script for your environment with the AWS Glue console. When this job is run, an IAM role with the correct permissions must also be supplied.

Common parameter values are shown in the template. For example, AllocatedCapacity (DPUs) defaults to 5.

```
1  ---
2  AWSTemplateFormatVersion: '2010-09-09'
3  # Sample CFN YAML to demonstrate creating a job using a MySQL JDBC DB with the flights data to
        an S3 file
4  #
5  # Parameters section contains names that are substituted in the Resources section
6  # These parameters are the names the resources created in the Data Catalog
7  Parameters:
8  # The name of the job to be created
9    CFNJobName:
10     Type: String
11     Default: cfn-job-JDBC-to-S3-1
12  # The name of the IAM role that the job assumes. It must have access to data, script, temporary
        directory
13    CFNIAMRoleName:
```

```
14      Type: String
15      Default: AWSGlueServiceRoleGA
16 # The S3 path where the script for this job is located
17   CFNScriptLocation:
18      Type: String
19      Default: s3://aws-glue-scripts-827630067164-us-east-1/salinero/sal-job-dec4a
20 # The name of the connection used for JDBC data source
21   CFNConnectionName:
22      Type: String
23      Default: cfn-connection-mysql-flights-1
24 #
25 #
26 # Resources section defines metadata for the Data Catalog
27 Resources:
28 # Create job to run script which accesses JDBC flights table via a connection and write to S3
       file as parquet.
29 # The script already exists and is called by this job
30   CFNJobFlights:
31      Type: AWS::Glue::Job
32      Properties:
33        Role: !Ref CFNIAMRoleName
34        #DefaultArguments: JSON object
35        # For example, if required by script, set temporary directory as DefaultArguments={'--
             TempDir'; 's3://aws-glue-temporary-xyc/sal'}
36        Connections:
37          Connections:
38          - !Ref CFNConnectionName
39        #MaxRetries: Double
40        Description: Job created with CloudFormation using existing script
41        #LogUri: String
42        Command:
43          Name: glueetl
44          ScriptLocation: !Ref CFNScriptLocation
45              # for access to directories use proper IAM role with permission to buckets and
                   folders that begin with "aws-glue-"
46              # if required, script defines temp directory as argument TempDir and used in script
                   like redshift_tmp_dir = args["TempDir"]
47              # script defines target for output as s3://aws-glue-target/sal
48        AllocatedCapacity: 5
49        ExecutionProperty:
50          MaxConcurrentRuns: 1
51        Name: !Ref CFNJobName
```

Sample AWS CloudFormation Template for an AWS Glue On-Demand Trigger

An AWS Glue trigger in the Data Catalog contains the parameter values that are required to start a job run when the trigger fires. An on-demand trigger fires when you enable it.

This sample creates an on-demand trigger that starts one job named `cfn-job-S3-to-S3-1`.

```
1 ---
2 AWSTemplateFormatVersion: '2010-09-09'
3 # Sample CFN YAML to demonstrate creating an on-demand trigger
4 #
```

```
 5 # Parameters section contains names that are substituted in the Resources section
 6 # These parameters are the names the resources created in the Data Catalog
 7 Parameters:
 8   # The existing job to be started by this trigger
 9   CFNJobName:
10     Type: String
11     Default: cfn-job-S3-to-S3-1
12   # The name of the trigger to be created
13   CFNTriggerName:
14     Type: String
15     Default: cfn-trigger-ondemand-flights-1
16 #
17 # Resources section defines metadata for the Data Catalog
18 # Sample CFN YAML to demonstrate creating an on-demand trigger for a job
19 Resources:
20 # Create trigger to run an existing job (CFNJobName) on an on-demand schedule.
21   CFNTriggerSample:
22     Type: AWS::Glue::Trigger
23     Properties:
24       Name:
25         Ref: CFNTriggerName
26       Description: Trigger created with CloudFormation
27       Type: ON_DEMAND
28       Actions:
29         - JobName: !Ref CFNJobName
30         # Arguments: JSON object
31       #Schedule:
32       #Predicate:
```

Sample AWS CloudFormation Template for an AWS Glue Scheduled Trigger

An AWS Glue trigger in the Data Catalog contains the parameter values that are required to start a job run when the trigger fires. A scheduled trigger fires when it is enabled and the cron timer pops.

This sample creates a scheduled trigger that starts one job named `cfn-job-S3-to-S3-1`. The timer is a cron expression to run the job every 10 minutes on weekdays.

```
 1 ---
 2 AWSTemplateFormatVersion: '2010-09-09'
 3 # Sample CFN YAML to demonstrate creating a scheduled trigger
 4 #
 5 # Parameters section contains names that are substituted in the Resources section
 6 # These parameters are the names the resources created in the Data Catalog
 7 Parameters:
 8   # The existing job to be started by this trigger
 9   CFNJobName:
10     Type: String
11     Default: cfn-job-S3-to-S3-1
12   # The name of the trigger to be created
13   CFNTriggerName:
14     Type: String
15     Default: cfn-trigger-scheduled-flights-1
16 #
17 # Resources section defines metadata for the Data Catalog
```

```
18  # Sample CFN YAML to demonstrate creating a scheduled trigger for a job
19  #
20  Resources:
21  # Create trigger to run an existing job (CFNJobName) on a cron schedule.
22    TriggerSample1CFN:
23      Type: AWS::Glue::Trigger
24      Properties:
25        Name:
26          Ref: CFNTriggerName
27        Description: Trigger created with CloudFormation
28        Type: SCHEDULED
29        Actions:
30          - JobName: !Ref CFNJobName
31          # Arguments: JSON object
32        # # Run the trigger every 10 minutes on Monday to Friday
33        Schedule: cron(0/10 * ? * MON-FRI *)
34        #Predicate:
```

Sample AWS CloudFormation Template for an AWS Glue Conditional Trigger

An AWS Glue trigger in the Data Catalog contains the parameter values that are required to start a job run when the trigger fires. A conditional trigger fires when it is enabled and its conditions are met, such as a job completing successfully.

This sample creates a conditional trigger that starts one job named `cfn-job-S3-to-S3-1`. This job starts when the job named `cfn-job-S3-to-S3-2` completes successfully.

```
1  ---
2  AWSTemplateFormatVersion: '2010-09-09'
3  # Sample CFN YAML to demonstrate creating a conditional trigger for a job, which starts when
       another job completes
4  #
5  # Parameters section contains names that are substituted in the Resources section
6  # These parameters are the names the resources created in the Data Catalog
7  Parameters:
8    # The existing job to be started by this trigger
9    CFNJobName:
10     Type: String
11     Default: cfn-job-S3-to-S3-1
12   # The existing job that when it finishes causes trigger to fire
13   CFNJobName2:
14     Type: String
15     Default: cfn-job-S3-to-S3-2
16   # The name of the trigger to be created
17   CFNTriggerName:
18     Type: String
19     Default: cfn-trigger-conditional-1
20  #
21  Resources:
22  # Create trigger to run an existing job (CFNJobName) when another job completes (CFNJobName2).
23    CFNTriggerSample:
24      Type: AWS::Glue::Trigger
25      Properties:
26        Name:
```

```
27        Ref: CFNTriggerName
28      Description: Trigger created with CloudFormation
29      Type: CONDITIONAL
30      Actions:
31        - JobName: !Ref CFNJobName
32        # Arguments: JSON object
33      #Schedule: none
34      Predicate:
35        #Value for Logical is required if more than 1 job listed in Conditions
36        Logical: AND
37        Conditions:
38          - LogicalOperator: EQUALS
39            JobName: !Ref CFNJobName2
40            State: SUCCEEDED
```

Sample AWS CloudFormation Template for an AWS Glue Development Endpoint

An AWS Glue development endpoint is an environment that you can use to develop and test your AWS Glue scripts.

This sample creates a development endpoint with the minimal network parameter values required to successfully create it. For more information about the parameters that you need to set up a development endpoint, see Setting Up Your Environment for Development Endpoints.

You provide an existing IAM role ARN (Amazon Resource Name) to create the development endpoint. Supply a valid RSA public key and keep the corresponding private key available if you plan to create a notebook server on the development endpoint.

Note
For any notebook server that you create that is associated with a development endpoint, you manage it. Therefore, if you delete the development endpoint, to delete the notebook server, you must delete the AWS CloudFormation stack on the AWS CloudFormation console.

```
1  ---
2  AWSTemplateFormatVersion: '2010-09-09'
3  # Sample CFN YAML to demonstrate creating a development endpoint
4  #
5  # Parameters section contains names that are substituted in the Resources section
6  # These parameters are the names the resources created in the Data Catalog
7  Parameters:
8  # The name of the crawler to be created
9    CFNEndpointName:
10     Type: String
11     Default: cfn-devendpoint-1
12   CFNIAMRoleArn:
13     Type: String
14     Default: arn:aws:iam::123456789012/role/AWSGlueServiceRoleGA
15  #
16  #
17  # Resources section defines metadata for the Data Catalog
18  Resources:
19    CFNDevEndpoint:
20      Type: AWS::Glue::DevEndpoint
21      Properties:
22        EndpointName: !Ref CFNEndpointName
```

```
23    #ExtraJarsS3Path: String
24    #ExtraPythonLibsS3Path: String
25    NumberOfNodes: 5
26    PublicKey: ssh-rsa public.....key myuserid-key
27    RoleArn: !Ref CFNIAMRoleArn
28    SecurityGroupIds:
29      - sg-64986c0b
30    SubnetId: subnet-c67cccac
```

Authoring Jobs in AWS Glue

A *job* is the business logic that performs the extract, transform, and load (ETL) work in AWS Glue. When you start a job, AWS Glue runs a script that extracts data from sources, transforms the data, and loads it into targets. You can create jobs in the ETL section of the AWS Glue console. For more information, see Working with Jobs on the AWS Glue Console.

The following diagram summarizes the basic workflow and steps involved in authoring a job in AWS Glue:

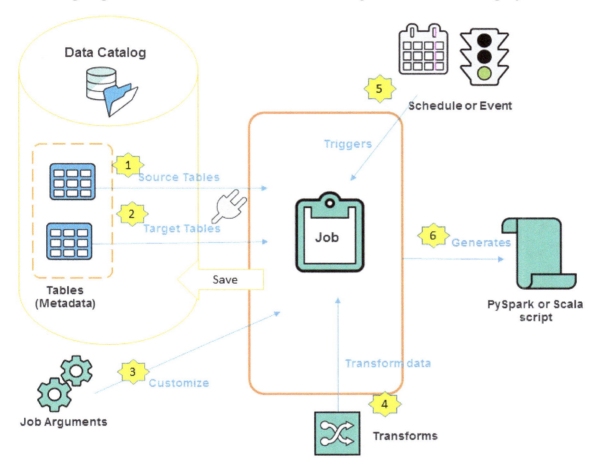

Topics

- Workflow Overview
- Adding Jobs in AWS Glue
- Editing Scripts in AWS Glue
- Triggering Jobs in AWS Glue
- Using Development Endpoints for Developing Scripts

Workflow Overview

When you author a job, you supply details about data sources, targets, and other information. The result is a generated Apache Spark API (PySpark) script. You can then store your job definition in the AWS Glue Data Catalog.

The following describes the overall process of authoring jobs in AWS Glue:

1. You choose the data sources for your job. The tables that represent your data source must already be defined in your Data Catalog. If the source requires a connection, the connection is also referenced in your job.

2. You choose the data targets of your job. The tables that represent the data target can be defined in your Data Catalog, or your job can create the target tables when it runs. You choose a target location when you author the job. If the target requires a connection, the connection is also referenced in your job.

3. You customize the job-processing environment by providing arguments for your job and generated script. For more information, see Adding Jobs in AWS Glue.

4. Initially, AWS Glue generates a script, but you can also edit your job to add transforms. For more information, see Built-In Transforms.

5. You specify how your job is invoked, either on demand, by a time-based schedule, or by an event. For more information, see Triggering Jobs in AWS Glue.

6. Based on your input, AWS Glue generates a PySpark or Scala script. You can tailor the script based on your business needs. For more information, see Editing Scripts in AWS Glue.

Adding Jobs in AWS Glue

A job consists of the business logic that performs extract, transform, and load (ETL) work in AWS Glue. You can monitor job runs to understand runtime metrics such as success, duration, and start time. The output of a job is your transformed data, written to a location that you specify.

Job runs can be initiated by triggers that start a job when they fire. A job contains a script that connects to your source data, processes your data using the script's logic, and then writes it out to your data target. Your job can have multiple data sources and multiple data targets. You can use scripts that are generated by AWS Glue to transform data, or you can provide your own. The AWS Glue code generator can automatically create an Apache Spark API (PySpark) script given a source schema and target location or schema. You can use this script as a starting point and edit it to meet your goals.

AWS Glue can write output files in several data formats, including JSON, CSV, ORC (Optimized Row Columnar), Apache Parquet, and Apache Avro. For some data formats, common compression formats can be written.

Defining Job Properties

When you define your job in the AWS Glue console, you provide the following information to control the AWS Glue runtime environment:

IAM role
Specify the IAM role that is used for authorization to resources used to run the job and access data stores. For more information about permissions for running jobs in AWS Glue, see Overview of Managing Access Permissions to Your AWS Glue Resources.

Generated or custom script
The code in the ETL script defines your job's procedural logic. The script can be coded in Python or Scala. You can choose whether the script that the job runs is generated by AWS Glue or provided by you. You provide the script name and location in Amazon Simple Storage Service (Amazon S3). Confirm that there isn't a file with the same name as the script directory in the path. To learn more about using scripts, see Editing Scripts in AWS Glue.

Scala class name
If the script is coded in Scala, a class name must be provided. The default class name for AWS Glue generated scripts is **GlueApp**.

Temporary directory
Provide the location of a working directory in Amazon S3 where temporary intermediate results are written when AWS Glue runs the script. Confirm that there isn't a file with the same name as the temporary directory in the path. This directory is used when AWS Glue reads and writes to Amazon Redshift and by certain AWS Glue transforms.

Job bookmark
Specify how AWS Glue processes state information when the job runs. You can have it remember previously processed data, update state information, or ignore state information.

Server-side encryption
If you select this option, when the ETL job writes to Amazon S3, the data is encrypted at rest using SSE-S3 encryption. Both your Amazon S3 data target and any data that is written to an Amazon S3 temporary directory is encrypted. For more information, see Protecting Data Using Server-Side Encryption with Amazon S3-Managed Encryption Keys (SSE-S3).

Script libraries
If your script requires it, you can specify locations for the following:

- Python library path
- Dependent jars path

- Referenced files path You can define the comma-separated Amazon S3 paths for these libraries when you define a job. You can override these paths when you run the job. For more information, see Providing Your Own Custom Scripts.

Concurrent DPUs per job run
A data processing unit (DPU) is a relative measure of processing power that is used by a job. Choose an integer from 2 to 100. The default is 10. A single DPU provides processing capacity that consists of 4 vCPUs compute and 16 GB of memory.

Max concurrency
Sets the maximum number of concurrent runs that are allowed for this job. The default is 1. An error is returned when this threshold is reached. The maximum value you can specify is controlled by a service limit. For example, if a previous run of a job is still running when a new instance is started, you might want to return an error to prevent two instances of the same job from running concurrently.

Job timeout
Sets the maximum execution time in minutes. The default is 2880 minutes. If this limit is greater than the execution time, the job run state changes to "TIMEOUT".

Delay notification threshold
Sets the threshold (in minutes) before a delay notification is sent. You can set this threshold to send notifications when a `RUNNING`, `STARTING`, or `STOPPING` job run takes more than an expected number of minutes.

Number of retries
Specify the number of times, from 0 to 10, that AWS Glue should automatically restart the job if it fails.

Job parameters
A set of key-value pairs that are passed as named parameters to the script invoked by the job. These are default values that are used when the script is run, but you can override them at run time. The key name is prefixed with `--`, for example `--myKey` and the value is `value-for-myKey`.

```
1  '--myKey' : 'value-for-myKey'
```

For more examples, see Python parameters in Passing and Accessing Python Parameters in AWS Glue.

Target path
For Amazon S3 target locations, provide the location of a directory in Amazon S3 where your output is written when AWS Glue runs the script. Confirm that there isn't a file with the same name as the target path directory in the path.

For more information about adding a job using the AWS Glue console, see Working with Jobs on the AWS Glue Console.

Built-In Transforms

AWS Glue provides a set of built-in transforms that you can use to process your data. You can call these transforms from your ETL script. Your data passes from transform to transform in a data structure called a *DynamicFrame*, which is an extension to an Apache Spark SQL `DataFrame`. The `DynamicFrame` contains your data, and you reference its schema to process your data. For more information about these transforms, see AWS Glue PySpark Transforms Reference.

AWS Glue provides the following built-in transforms:

ApplyMapping
Maps source columns and data types from a `DynamicFrame` to target columns and data types in a returned `DynamicFrame`. You specify the mapping argument, which is a list of tuples that contain source column, source type, target column, and target type.

DropFields
Removes a field from a `DynamicFrame`. The output `DynamicFrame` contains fewer fields than the input. You specify which fields to remove using the `paths` argument. The `paths` argument points to a field in the schema tree structure using dot notation. For example, to remove field B, which is a child of field A in the tree, type **A.B** for the path.

DropNullFields
Removes null fields from a `DynamicFrame`. The output `DynamicFrame` does not contain fields of the null type in the schema.

Filter
Selects records from a `DynamicFrame` and returns a filtered `DynamicFrame`. You specify a function, such as a Lambda function, which determines whether a record is output (function returns true) or not (function returns false).

Join
Equijoin of two `DynamicFrames`. You specify the key fields in the schema of each frame to compare for equality. The output `DynamicFrame` contains rows where keys match.

Map
Applies a function to the records of a `DynamicFrame` and returns a transformed `DynamicFrame`. The supplied function is applied to each input record and transforms it to an output record. The map transform can add fields, delete fields, and perform lookups using an external API operation. If there is an exception, processing continues, and the record is marked as an error.

MapToCollection
Applies a transform to each `DynamicFrame` in a `DynamicFrameCollection`.

Relationalize
Converts a `DynamicFrame` to a relational (rows and columns) form. Based on the data's schema, this transform flattens nested structures and creates `DynamicFrames` from arrays structures. The output is a collection of `DynamicFrames` that can result in data written to multiple tables.

RenameField
Renames a field in a `DynamicFrame`. The output is a `DynamicFrame` with the specified field renamed. You provide the new name and the path in the schema to the field to be renamed.

ResolveChoice
Use `ResolveChoice` to specify how a column should be handled when it contains values of multiple types. You can choose to either cast the column to a single data type, discard one or more of the types, or retain all types in either separate columns or a structure. You can select a different resolution policy for each column or specify a global policy that is applied to all columns.

SelectFields
Selects fields from a `DynamicFrame` to keep. The output is a `DynamicFrame` with only the selected fields. You

provide the paths in the schema to the fields to keep.

SelectFromCollection

Selects one `DynamicFrame` from a collection of `DynamicFrames`. The output is the selected `DynamicFrame`. You provide an index to the `DynamicFrame` to select.

Spigot

Writes sample data from a `DynamicFrame`. Output is a JSON file in Amazon S3. You specify the Amazon S3 location and how to sample the `DynamicFrame`. Sampling can be a specified number of records from the beginning of the file or a probability factor used to pick records to write.

SplitFields

Splits fields into two `DynamicFrames`. Output is a collection of `DynamicFrames`: one with selected fields, and one with the remaining fields. You provide the paths in the schema to the selected fields.

SplitRows

Splits rows in a `DynamicFrame` based on a predicate. The output is a collection of two `DynamicFrames`: one with selected rows, and one with the remaining rows. You provide the comparison based on fields in the schema. For example, `A > 4`.

Unbox

Unboxes a string field from a `DynamicFrame`. The output is a `DynamicFrame` with the selected string field reformatted. The string field can be parsed and replaced with several fields. You provide a path in the schema for the string field to reformat and its current format type. For example, you might have a CSV file that has one field that is in JSON format `{"a": 3, "b": "foo", "c": 1.2}`. This transform can reformat the JSON into three fields: an `int`, a `string`, and a `double`.

Working with Jobs on the AWS Glue Console

A job in AWS Glue consists of the business logic that performs extract, transform, and load (ETL) work. You can create jobs in the **ETL** section of the AWS Glue console.

To view existing jobs, sign in to the AWS Management Console and open the AWS Glue console at https: //console.aws.amazon.com/glue/. Then choose the **Jobs** tab in AWS Glue. The **Jobs** list displays the location of the script that is associated with each job, when the job was last modified, and the current job bookmark option.

From the **Jobs** list, you can do the following:

- To start an existing job, choose **Action**, and then choose **Run job**.
- To stop a Running or Starting job, choose **Action**, and then choose **Stop job run**.
- To add triggers that start a job, choose **Action**, **Choose job triggers**.
- To modify an existing job, choose **Action**, and then choose **Edit job** or Delete.
- To change a script that is associated with a job, choose **Action**, **Edit script**.
- To reset the state information that AWS Glue stores about your job, choose **Action**, **Reset job bookmark**.
- To create a development endpoint with the properties of this job, choose **Action**, **Create development endpoint**.

To add a new job using the console

1. Open the AWS Glue console, and choose the **Jobs** tab.

2. Choose **Add job**, and follow the instructions in the **Add job** wizard.

   If you decide to have AWS Glue generate a script for your job, you must specify the job properties, data sources, and data targets, and verify the schema mapping of source columns to target columns. The generated script is a starting point for you to add code to perform your ETL work. Verify the code in the script and modify it to meet your business needs. **Note**
   To get step-by-step guidance for adding a job with a generated script, see the **Add job** tutorial in the console.
   [See the AWS documentation website for more details]

Note
The job assumes the permissions of the **IAM role** that you specify when you create it. This IAM role must have permission to extract data from your data store and write to your target. The AWS Glue console only lists IAM roles that have attached a trust policy for the AWS Glue principal service. For more information about providing roles for AWS Glue, see Using Identity-Based Policies (IAM Policies).

Important
Check Troubleshooting Errors in AWS Glue for known problems when a job runs.

To learn about the properties that are required for each job, see Defining Job Properties.

To get step-by-step guidance for adding a job with a generated script, see the **Add job** tutorial in the AWS Glue console.

Viewing Job Details

To see details of a job, select the job in the **Jobs** list and review the information on the following tabs:

- History
- Details
- Script

History

The **History** tab shows your job run history and how successful a job has been in the past. For each job, the run metrics include the following:

- **Run ID** is an identifier created by AWS Glue for each run of this job.

- **Retry attempt** shows the number of attempts for jobs that required AWS Glue to automatically retry.

- **Run status** shows the success of each run listed with the most recent run at the top. If a job is `Running` or `Starting`, you can choose the action icon in this column to stop it.

- **Error** shows the details of an error meesage if the run was not successful.

- **Logs** links to the logs written to `stdout` for this job run.

  The **Logs** link takes you to the CloudWatch Logs, where you can see all the details about the tables that were created in the AWS Glue Data Catalog and any errors that were encountered. You can manage your log retention period in the CloudWatch console. The default log retention is `Never Expire`. For more information about how to change the retention period, see Change Log Data Retention in CloudWatch Logs.

- **Error logs** links to the logs written to `stderr` for this job run.

  This link takes you to the CloudWatch Logs, where you can see details about any errors that were encountered. You can manage your log retention period in the CloudWatch console. The default log retention is `Never Expire`. For more information about how to change the retention period, see Change Log Data Retention in CloudWatch Logs.

- **Execution time** shows the length of time during which the job run consumed resources. The amount is calculated from when the job run starts consuming resources until it finishes.

- **Timeout** shows the maximum execution time during which this job run can consume resources before it stops and goes into timeout status.

- **Delay** shows the threshold before sending a job delay notification. When a job run execution time reaches this threshold, AWS Glue sends a notification ("Glue Job Run Status") to CloudWatch Events.

- **Triggered by** shows the trigger that fired to start this job run.

- **Start time** shows the date and time (local time) that the job started.

- **End time** shows the date and time (local time) that the job ended.

Details

The **Details** tab includes attributes of your job. It shows you the details about the job definition and also lists the triggers that can start this job. Each time one of the triggers in the list fires, the job is started. For the list of triggers, the details include the following:

- **Trigger name** shows the names of triggers that start this job when fired.
- **Trigger type** lists the type of trigger that starts this job.
- **Trigger status** displays whether the trigger is created, activated, or deactivated.
- **Trigger parameters** shows parameters that define when the trigger fires.
- **Jobs to trigger** shows the list of jobs that start when this trigger fires.

Script

The **Script** tab shows the script that runs when your job is started. You can invoke an **Edit script** view from this tab. For more information about the script editor in the AWS Glue console, see Working with Scripts on the AWS Glue Console. For information about the functions that are called in your script, see Program AWS Glue ETL Scripts in Python.

Editing Scripts in AWS Glue

A script contains the code that extracts data from sources, transforms it, and loads it into targets. AWS Glue runs a script when it starts a job.

AWS Glue ETL scripts can be coded in Python or Scala. Python scripts use a language that is an extension of the PySpark Python dialect for extract, transform, and load (ETL) jobs. The script contains *extended constructs* to deal with ETL transformations. When you automatically generate the source code logic for your job, a script is created. You can edit this script, or you can provide your own script to process your ETL work.

For information about defining and editing scripts using the AWS Glue console, see Working with Scripts on the AWS Glue Console.

Defining a Script

Given a source and target, AWS Glue can generate a script to transform the data. This proposed script is an initial version that fills in your sources and targets, and suggests transformations in PySpark. You can verify and modify the script to fit your business needs. Use the script editor in AWS Glue to add arguments that specify the source and target, and any other arguments that are required to run. Scripts are run by jobs, and jobs are started by triggers, which can be based on a schedule or an event. For more information about triggers, see Triggering Jobs in AWS Glue.

In the AWS Glue console, the script is represented as code. You can also view the script as a diagram that uses annotations (##) embedded in the script. These annotations describe the parameters, transform types, arguments, inputs, and other characteristics of the script that are used to generate a diagram in the AWS Glue console.

The diagram of the script shows the following:

- Source inputs to the script
- Transforms
- Target outputs written by the script

Scripts can contain the following annotations:

Annotation	Usage
@params	Parameters from the ETL job that the script requires.
@type	Type of node in the diagram, such as the transform type, data source, or data sink.
@args	Arguments passed to the node, except reference to input data.
@return	Variable returned from script.
@inputs	Data input to node.

To learn about the code constructs within a script, see Program AWS Glue ETL Scripts in Python.

Working with Scripts on the AWS Glue Console

A script contains the code that performs extract, transform, and load (ETL) work. You can provide your own script, or AWS Glue can generate a script with guidance from you. For information about creating your own scripts, see Providing Your Own Custom Scripts.

You can edit a script in the AWS Glue console. When you edit a script, you can add sources, targets, and transforms.

To edit a script

1. Sign in to the AWS Management Console and open the AWS Glue console at https://console.aws.amazon.com/glue/. Then choose the **Jobs** tab.

2. Choose a job in the list, and then choose **Action, Edit script** to open the script editor.

   You can also access the script editor from the job details page. Choose the **Script** tab, and then choose **Edit script**.

Script Editor

The AWS Glue script editor lets you insert, modify, and delete sources, targets, and transforms in your script. The script editor displays both the script and a diagram to help you visualize the flow of data.

To create a diagram for the script, choose **Generate diagram**. AWS Glue uses annotation lines in the script beginning with ## to render the diagram. To correctly represent your script in the diagram, you must keep the parameters in the annotations and the parameters in the Apache Spark code in sync.

The script editor lets you add code templates wherever your cursor is positioned in the script. At the top of the editor, choose from the following options:

- To add a source table to the script, choose **Source**.
- To add a target table to the script, choose **Target**.
- To add a target location to the script, choose **Target location**.
- To add a transform to the script, choose **Transform**. For information about the functions that are called in your script, see Program AWS Glue ETL Scripts in Python.
- To add a Spigot transform to the script, choose **Spigot**.

In the inserted code, modify the **parameters** in both the annotations and Apache Spark code. For example, if you add a **Spigot** transform, verify that the **path** is replaced in both the **@args** annotation line and the **output** code line.

The **Logs** tab shows the logs that are associated with your job as it runs. The most recent 1,000 lines are displayed.

The **Schema** tab shows the schema of the selected sources and targets, when available in the Data Catalog.

Providing Your Own Custom Scripts

Scripts perform the extract, transform, and load (ETL) work in AWS Glue. A script is created when you automatically generate the source code logic for a job. You can either edit this generated script, or you can provide your own custom script.

Important
Your custom script must be compatible with Apache Spark 2.2.1.

To provide your own custom script in AWS Glue, follow these general steps:

1. Sign in to the AWS Management Console and open the AWS Glue console at https://console.aws.amazon. com/glue/.

2. Choose the **Jobs** tab, and then choose **Add job** to start the **Add job** wizard.

3. In the **Job properties** screen, choose the **IAM role** that is required for your custom script to run. For more information, see Authentication and Access Control for AWS Glue.

4. Under **This job runs**, choose one of the following:

   - An existing script that you provide
   - A new script to be authored by you

5. Choose any connections that your script references. These objects are needed to connect to the necessary JDBC data stores.

   An elastic network interface is a virtual network interface that you can attach to an instance in a virtual private cloud (VPC). Choose the elastic network interface that is required to connect to the data store that's used in the script.

6. If your script requires additional libraries or files, you can specify them as follows:
   Python library path
   Comma-separated Amazon Simple Storage Service (Amazon S3) paths to Python libraries that are required by the script.
   Only pure Python libraries can be used. Libraries that rely on C extensions, such as the pandas Python Data Analysis Library, are not yet supported.
   Dependent jars path
   Comma-separated Amazon S3 paths to JAR files that are required by the script.
   Currently, only pure Java or Scala (2.11) libraries can be used.
   Referenced files path
   Comma-separated Amazon S3 paths to additional files (for example, configuration files) that are required by the script.

7. If you want, you can add a schedule to your job. To change a schedule, you must delete the existing schedule and add a new one.

For more information about adding jobs in AWS Glue, see Adding Jobs in AWS Glue.

For step-by-step guidance, see the **Add job** tutorial in the AWS Glue console.

Triggering Jobs in AWS Glue

You decide what triggers an extract, transform, and load (ETL) job to run in AWS Glue. The triggering condition can be based on a schedule (as defined by a cron expression) or on an event. You can also run a job on demand.

Triggering Jobs Based on Schedules or Events

When you create a trigger for a job based on a schedule, you can specify constraints, such as the frequency the job runs, which days of the week it runs, and at what time. These constraints are based on *cron*. When you're setting up a schedule for a trigger, you should consider the features and limitations of cron. For example, if you choose to run your crawler on day 31 each month, keep in mind that some months don't have 31 days. For more information about cron, see Time-Based Schedules for Jobs and Crawlers.

When you create a trigger based on an event, you specify events to watch that cause the trigger to fire, such as when another job succeeded. For a conditional trigger based on a *job events* trigger, you specify a list of jobs that cause a trigger to fire when any or all jobs satisfy the watched job events. In turn, when the trigger fires, it starts a run of any dependent jobs.

Defining Trigger Types

A trigger can be one of the following types:

Schedule
A time-based trigger based on cron.

Job events (conditional)
An event-based trigger that fires when a previous job or multiple jobs satisfy a list of conditions. You provide a list of job events to watch for when their run state changes to `succeeded`, `failed`, `stopped`, or `timeout`. This trigger waits to fire until any or all the conditions are satisfied.
Dependent jobs are only started if the job which completes was started by a trigger (not run ad-hoc). To create a job dependency chain, start the first job in the chain with a **schedule** or **on-demand** trigger.

On-demand
The trigger fires when you start it. As jobs complete, any triggers watching for completion are also fired and dependent jobs are started.

So that they are ready to fire as soon as they exist, you can set a flag to enable (activate) **schedule** and **job events (conditional)** triggers when they are created.

For more information about defining triggers using the AWS Glue console, see Working with Triggers on the AWS Glue Console.

Working with Triggers on the AWS Glue Console

A trigger controls when an ETL job runs in AWS Glue. To view your existing triggers, sign in to the AWS Management Console and open the AWS Glue console at https://console.aws.amazon.com/glue/. Then choose the **Triggers** tab.

The **Triggers** list displays properties for each trigger:

Trigger name
The unique name you gave the trigger when you created it.

Trigger type
Indicates whether the trigger is time-based (**Schedule**), event-based (**Job events**), or started by you (**On-demand**).

Trigger status
Indicates whether the trigger is **Enabled** or **ACTIVATED** and ready to invoke associated jobs when it fires. The trigger can also be **Disabled** or **DEACTIVATED** and paused so that it doesn't determine whether a job is invoked. A **CREATED** trigger exists, but does not factor into whether a job runs.

Trigger parameters
For **Schedule** triggers, this includes the details about the frequency and time to fire the trigger. For **Job events** triggers, it includes the list of jobs to watch that, depending on their run state, might fire the trigger. See the details of the trigger for the watch list of jobs with events.

Jobs to trigger
Lists the jobs associated with the trigger that are invoked when this trigger fires.

Adding and Editing Triggers

To edit, delete, or start a trigger, select the check box next to the trigger in the list, and then choose **Action**. Here you can also disable a trigger to prevent it from starting any associated jobs, or enable it to start associated jobs when it fires.

Choose a trigger in the list to view details for the trigger. Trigger details include the information you defined when you created the trigger.

To add a new trigger, choose **Add trigger**, and follow the instructions in the **Add trigger** wizard.

You provide the following properties:

Name
Give your trigger a unique name.

Trigger type
Specify one of the following:

- **Schedule:** The trigger fires at a specific time.
- **Job events:** The trigger fires when any or all jobs in the list match the selected job event. For the trigger to fire, the watched job must have been started by a trigger. For any job you choose, you can only watch one job event.
- **On-demand:** The trigger fires when it is started from the triggers list page. For **Schedule** and **Job events** trigger types, you can enable them when they are created.

Jobs to trigger
List of jobs that are started by this trigger.

For more information, see Triggering Jobs in AWS Glue.

Using Development Endpoints for Developing Scripts

AWS Glue can create an environment for you to iteratively develop and test your extract, transform, and load (ETL) scripts. You can develop your script in a notebook and point to an AWS Glue endpoint to test it. When you're satisfied with the results of your development process, you can create an ETL job that runs your script. With this process, you can add functions and debug your script in an interactive manner.

Note
Your Python scripts must target Python 2.7, because AWS Glue development endpoints do not support Python 3 yet.

Managing Your Development Environment

With AWS Glue, you can create, edit, and delete development endpoints. You provide configuration values to provision the development environments. These values tell AWS Glue how to set up the network so that you can access your development endpoint securely, and your endpoint can access your data stores. Then, create a notebook that connects to the development endpoint, and use your notebook to author and test your ETL script.

For more information about managing a development endpoint using the AWS Glue console, see Working with Development Endpoints on the AWS Glue Console.

How to Use a Development Endpoint

To use a development endpoint, you can follow this workflow.

1. Create an AWS Glue development endpoint through the console or API. This endpoint is launched in your virtual private cloud (VPC) with your defined security groups.

2. The console or API can poll the development endpoint until it is provisioned and ready for work. When it's ready, you can connect to the development endpoint to create and test AWS Glue scripts.

   - You can install an Apache Zeppelin notebook on your local machine, connect it to a development endpoint, and then develop on it using your browser.
   - You can create an Apache Zeppelin notebook server in its own Amazon EC2 instance in your account using the AWS Glue console, and then connect to it using your browser.
   - You can open a terminal window to connect directly to a development endpoint.
   - If you have the Professional edition of the JetBrains PyCharm Python IDE, you can connect it to a development endpoint and use it to develop interactively. PyCharm can then support remote breakpoints if you insert `pydevd` statements in your script.

3. When you finish debugging and testing on your development endpoint, you can delete it.

Accessing Your Development Endpoint

If your development endpoint has a **Public address**, then confirm it is reachable with the SSH private key for the development endpoint. For example:

```
1 ssh -i dev-endpoint-private-key.pem glue@public-address
```

If your development endpoint has a **Private address** and your VPC subnet is routable from the public internet and its security groups allow inbound access from your client, then you can follow these instructions to attach an **elastic IP** to a development endpoint, thereby allowing access from the internet.

1. On the AWS Glue console, navigate to the development endpoint details page. Record the **Private address** for use in the next step.

2. On the Amazon EC2 console, navigate to **Network and Security**, then choose **Network Interfaces**. Search for the **Private DNS (IPv4)** that corresponds to the **Private address** in the AWS Glue console development endpoint details page. You might need to modify which columns are displayed in your Amazon EC2 console. Note the **Network interface ID (ENI)** for this address. For example `eni-12345678`.

3. On the Amazon EC2 console, navigate to **Network and Security**, then choose **Elastic IPs**. Choose **Allocate new address**, then **Allocate** to allocate a new elastic IP.

4. On the **Elastic IPs** page, choose the newly allocated **Elastic IP**. Then choose **Actions, Associate address**.

5. On the **Associate address** page make the following choices:

   - For **Resource type**, choose **Network interface**.
   - In the **Network interface** field, type the **Network interface ID (ENI)** for the private address.
   - Choose **Associate**.

6. Confirm if the newly associated **Elastic IP** is reachable with the SSH private key associated with the development endpoint. For example:

```
1 ssh -i dev-endpoint-private-key.pem glue@elastic-ip
```

Tutorial Setup: Prerequisites for the Development Endpoint Tutorials

Development endpoints create an environment where you can interactively test and debug ETL scripts in various ways before you run them as AWS Glue jobs. The tutorials in this section show you how to do this using different IDEs. All of them assume that you have set up a development endpoint and crawled sample data to create tables in your AWS Glue Data Catalog using the steps in the following sections.

Note
Your Python scripts must target Python 2.7, because AWS Glue development endpoints do not support Python 3 yet.

Because you're using only Amazon Simple Storage Service (Amazon S3) data in some cases, and a mix of JDBC and Amazon S3 data in others, you will set up one development endpoint that is not in a virtual private cloud (VPC) and one that is.

Crawling the Sample Data Used in the Tutorials

The first step is to create a crawler that can crawl some sample data and record metadata about it in tables in your Data Catalog. The sample data that is used is drawn from http://everypolitician.org/ and has been modified slightly for purposes of the tutorials. It contains data in JSON format about United States legislators and the seats that they have held in the US House of Representatives and Senate.

1. Sign in to the AWS Management Console and open the AWS Glue console at https://console.aws.amazon.com/glue/.

   In the AWS Glue console, choose **Databases** in the navigation pane, and then choose **Add database**. Name the database `legislators`.

2. Choose **Crawlers**, and then choose **Add crawler**. Name the crawler `legislator_crawler`, assign it your AWS Glue role, and then choose **Next**.

3. Leave Amazon S3 as the data store. Under **Crawl data in**, choose **Specified path in another account**. Then in the **Include path** box, type `s3://awsglue-datasets/examples/us-legislators/all`. Choose **Next**, and then choose **Next** again to confirm that you don't want to add another data store. Then choose **Next** to confirm that this crawler will be run on demand.

4. For **Database**, choose the `legislators` database. Choose **Next**, and then choose **Finish** to complete the creation of the new crawler.

5. Choose **Crawlers** in the navigation pane again. Select the check box next to the new `legislator_crawler` crawler, and choose **Run crawler**.

6. Choose **Databases** in the navigation pane. Choose the `legislators` database, and then choose **Tables in legislators**. You should see six tables created by the crawler in your Data Catalog, containing metadata that the crawler retrieved.

Creating a Development Endpoint for Amazon S3 Data

The next thing to do is to create a development endpoint for Amazon S3 data. When you use a JDBC data source or target, the development endpoint must be created with a VPC. However, this isn't necessary in this tutorial if you are only accessing Amazon S3.

1. In the AWS Glue console, choose **Dev endpoints**. Choose **Add endpoint**.

2. Specify an endpoint name, such as **demo-endpoint**.

3. Choose an **IAM role** with permissions similar to the IAM role that you use to run AWS Glue ETL jobs. For more information, see Step 2: Create an IAM Role for AWS Glue. Choose **Next**.

4. In **Networking**, leave **Skip networking information** selected, and choose **Next**.

5. In **SSH Public Key**, enter a public key generated by an SSH key generator program (do not use an Amazon EC2 key pair). Save the corresponding private key to later connect to the development endpoint using SSH. Choose **Next**. **Note**
   When generating the key on Microsoft Windows, use a current version of PuTTYgen and paste the public key into the AWS Glue console from the PuTTYgen window. Generate an **RSA** key. Do not upload a file with the public key, instead use the key generated in the field **Public key for pasting into OpenSSH authorized_keys file**. The corresponding private key (.ppk) can be used in PuTTY to connect to the development endpoint. To connect to the development endpoint with SSH on Windows, convert the private key from .ppk format to OpenSSH .pem format using the PuTTYgen **Conversion** menu. For more information, see Connecting to Your Linux Instance from Windows Using PuTTY.

6. In **Review**, choose **Finish**. After the development endpoint is created, wait for its provisioning status to move to **READY**.

Creating an Amazon S3 Location to Use for Output

If you don't already have a bucket, follow the instructions in Create a Bucket to set one up in Amazon S3 where you can save output from sample ETL scripts.

Creating a Development Endpoint with a VPC

Although not required for this tutorial, a VPC development endpoint is needed if both Amazon S3 and JDBC data stores are accessed by your ETL statements. In this case, when you create a development endpoint you specify network properties of the virtual private cloud (Amazon VPC) that contains your JDBC data stores. Before you start, set up your environment as explained in Setting Up Your Environment for Development Endpoints.

1. In the AWS Glue console, choose **Dev endpoints** in the navigation pane. Then choose **Add endpoint**.

2. Specify an endpoint name, such as **vpc-demo-endpoint**.

3. Choose an **IAM role** with permissions similar to the IAM role that you use to run AWS Glue ETL jobs. For more information, see Step 2: Create an IAM Role for AWS Glue. Choose **Next**.

4. In **Networking**, specify an Amazon VPC, a subnet, and security groups. This information is used to create a development endpoint that can connect to your data resources securely. Consider the following suggestions when filling in the properties of your endpoint:

   - If you already set up a connection to your data stores, you can use the same connection to determine the Amazon VPC, subnet, and security groups for your endpoint. Otherwise, specify these parameters individually.

   - Ensure that your Amazon VPC has **Edit DNS hostnames** set to **yes**. This parameter can be set in the Amazon VPC console (https://console.aws.amazon.com/vpc/). For more information, see Setting Up DNS in Your VPC.

   - For this tutorial, ensure that the Amazon VPC you select has an Amazon S3 VPC endpoint. For information about how to create an Amazon S3 VPC endpoint, see Amazon VPC Endpoints for Amazon S3.

   - Choose a public subnet for your development endpoint. You can make a subnet a public subnet by adding a route to an internet gateway. For IPv4 traffic, create a route with **Destination** 0.0.0.0/0 and **Target** the internet gateway ID. Your subnet's route table should be associated with an

142

internet gateway, not a NAT gateway. This information can be set in the Amazon VPC console (https://console.aws.amazon.com/vpc/). For example:

For more information, see Route tables for Internet Gateways. For information about how to create an internet gateway, see Internet Gateways.

- Ensure that you choose a security group that has an inbound self-reference rule. This information can be set in the Amazon VPC console (https://console.aws.amazon.com/vpc/). For example:

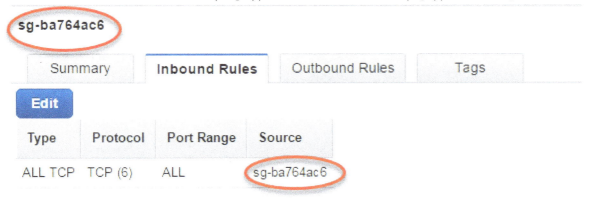

For more information about how to set up your subnet, see Setting Up Your Environment for Development Endpoints.

Choose **Next**.

5. In **SSH Public Key**, enter a public key generated by an SSH key generator program (do not use an Amazon EC2 key pair). Save the corresponding private key to later connect to the development endpoint using SSH. Choose **Next**. **Note**
When generating the key on Microsoft Windows, use a current version of PuTTYgen and paste the public key into the AWS Glue console from the PuTTYgen window. Generate an **RSA** key. Do not upload a file with the public key, instead use the key generated in the field **Public key for pasting into OpenSSH authorized_keys file**. The corresponding private key (.ppk) can be used in PuTTY to connect to the development endpoint. To connect to the development endpoint with SSH on Windows, convert the private key from .ppk format to OpenSSH .pem format using the PuTTYgen **Conversion** menu. For more information, see Connecting to Your Linux Instance from Windows Using PuTTY.

6. In **Review**, choose **Finish**. After the development endpoint is created, wait for its provisioning status to move to **READY**.

You are now ready to try out the tutorials in this section:

- Tutorial: Set Up a Local Apache Zeppelin Notebook to Test and Debug ETL Scripts
- Tutorial: Set Up an Apache Zeppelin Notebook on Amazon EC2
- Tutorial: Use a REPL Shell with Your Development Endpoint

Tutorial: Set Up a Local Apache Zeppelin Notebook to Test and Debug ETL Scripts

In this tutorial, you connect an Apache Zeppelin Notebook on your local machine to a development endpoint so that you can interactively run, debug, and test AWS Glue ETL (extract, transform, and load) scripts before deploying them.

The tutorial assumes that you have already taken the steps outlined in Tutorial Prerequisites.

Installing an Apache Zeppelin Notebook

1. Make sure that you have an up-to-date version of Java installed on your local machine (see the Java home page for the latest version).

   If you are running on Microsoft Windows, make sure that the `JAVA_HOME` environment variable points to the right Java directory. It's possible to update Java without updating this variable, and if it points to a folder that no longer exists, Zeppelin fails to start.

2. Download Apache Zeppelin (the version with all interpreters) from the Zeppelin download page onto your local machine.

   On the menu bar of the download page, choose **Quick Start**, and follow the installation instructions. Start Zeppelin in the way that's appropriate for your operating system as documented on the Quick Start page. Leave the terminal window that starts the notebook server open while you are using Zeppelin. When the server has started successfully, you can see a line in the console that ends with "Done, zeppelin server started."

3. Open Zeppelin in your browser by navigating to `http://localhost:8080`.

4. In Zeppelin in the browser, open the drop-down menu at **anonymous** in the upper-right corner of the page, and choose **Interpreter**. On the interpreters page, search for `spark`, and choose **edit** on the right. Make the following changes:

   - Select the **Connect to existing process** check box, and then set **Host** to `localhost` and **Port** to 9007 (or whatever other port you are using for port forwarding).
   - In **Properties**, set **master** to `yarn-client`.
   - If there is a `spark.executor.memory` property, delete it by choosing the **x** in the **action** column.
   - If there is a `spark.driver.memory` property, delete it by choosing the **x** in the **action** column.

   Choose **Save** at the bottom of the page, and then choose **OK** to confirm that you want to update the interpreter and restart it. Use the browser back button to return to the Zeppelin start page.

Initiating SSH Port Forwarding to Connect to Your DevEndpoint

Next, use SSH local port forwarding to forward a local port (here, 9007) to remote destination 169.254.76.1:9007.

Open a terminal window that gives you access to the SSH secure-shell protocol. On Microsoft Windows, you can use the BASH shell provided by Git for Windows, or install Cygwin.

Run the following SSH command, modified as follows:

- Replace `private-key-file-path` with a path to the `.pem` file that contains the private key corresponding to the public key that you used to create your development endpoint.
- If you are forwarding a different port than 9007, replace 9007 with the port number that you are actually using locally (the second 9007 is the remote port).

- Replace `dev-endpoint-public-dns` with the public DNS address of your development endpoint. To find this address, navigate to your development endpoint in the AWS Glue console, choose the name, and copy the **Public address** that's listed in the **Endpoint details** page.

```
1 ssh -i private-key-file-path -NTL 9007:169.254.76.1:9007 glue@dev-endpoint-public-dns
```

You will likely see a warning message like the following:

```
1 The authenticity of host 'ec2-xx-xxx-xxx-xx.us-west-2.compute.amazonaws.com (xx.xxx.xxx.xx)'
2 can't be established.  ECDSA key fingerprint is SHA256:4e97875Brt+1wKzRko+
    JflSnp21X7aTP3BcFnHYLEts.
3 Are you sure you want to continue connecting (yes/no)?
```

Type **yes** and leave the terminal window open while you use your Zeppelin notebook.

Running a Simple Script Fragment in a Notebook Paragraph

In the Zeppelin start page, choose **Create new note**. Name the new note `Legislators`, and confirm `spark` as the interpreter.

Type the following script fragment into your notebook and run it. It uses the person's metadata in the AWS Glue Data Catalog to create a DynamicFrame from your sample data. It then prints out the item count and the schema of this data.

```
1 %pyspark
2 import sys
3 from pyspark.context import SparkContext
4 from awsglue.context import GlueContext
5 from awsglue.transforms import *
6
7 # Create a Glue context
8 glueContext = GlueContext(SparkContext.getOrCreate())
9
10 # Create a DynamicFrame using the 'persons_json' table
11 persons_DyF = glueContext.create_dynamic_frame.from_catalog(database="legislators", table_name="
    persons_json")
12
13 # Print out information about this data
14 print "Count:  ", persons_DyF.count()
15 persons_DyF.printSchema()
```

The output of the script is as follows:

```
1  Count:  1961
2  root
3  |-- family_name: string
4  |-- name: string
5  |-- links: array
6  |    |-- element: struct
7  |    |    |-- note: string
8  |    |    |-- url: string
9  |-- gender: string
10 |-- image: string
11 |-- identifiers: array
12 |    |-- element: struct
13 |    |    |-- scheme: string
```

```
14  |    |    |-- identifier: string
15  |-- other_names: array
16  |    |-- element: struct
17  |    |    |-- note: string
18  |    |    |-- name: string
19  |    |    |-- lang: string
20  |-- sort_name: string
21  |-- images: array
22  |    |-- element: struct
23  |    |    |-- url: string
24  |-- given_name: string
25  |-- birth_date: string
26  |-- id: string
27  |-- contact_details: array
28  |    |-- element: struct
29  |    |    |-- type: string
30  |    |    |-- value: string
31  |-- death_date: string
```

Troubleshooting Your Local Notebook Connection

- If you encounter a *connection refused* error, you might be using a development endpoint that is out of date. Try creating a new development endpoint and reconnecting.

- If your connection times out or stops working for any reason, you may need to take the following steps to restore it:

  1. In Zeppelin, in the drop-down menu in the upper-right corner of the page, choose **Interpretors**. On the interpreters page, search for `spark`. Choose **edit**, and clear the **Connect to existing process** check box. Choose **Save** at the bottom of the page.

  2. Initiate SSH port forwarding as described earlier.

  3. In Zeppelin, re-enable the `spark` interpreter's **Connect to existing process** settings, and then save again.

  Resetting the interpreter like this should restore the connection. Another way to accomplish this is to choose **restart** for the Spark interpreter on the **Interpreters** page. Then wait for up to 30 seconds to ensure that the remote interpreter has restarted.

Tutorial: Set Up an Apache Zeppelin Notebook on Amazon EC2

In this tutorial, you create an Apache Zeppelin Notebook server that is hosted on an Amazon EC2 instance. The notebook connects to one of your development endpoints so that you can interactively run, debug, and test AWS Glue ETL (extract, transform, and load) scripts before deploying them.

The tutorial assumes that you have already taken the steps outlined in Tutorial Prerequisites.

Creating an Apache Zeppelin Notebook Server on an Amazon EC2 Instance

To create a notebook server on Amazon EC2, you must have permission to create resources in AWS CloudFormation, Amazon EC2, and other services. For more information about required user permissions, see Step 3: Attach a Policy to IAM Users That Access AWS Glue.

1. On the AWS Glue console, choose **Dev endpoints** to go to the development endpoints list.

2. Choose an endpoint by selecting the box next to it. Then choose **Actions**, and choose **Create notebook server**.

   To host the notebook server, an Amazon EC2 instance is spun up using an AWS CloudFormation stack on your development endpoint, and a Zeppelin notebook HTTP server is started on port 443.

3. Enter an AWS CloudFormation stack server name such as `demo-cf`, using only alphanumeric characters and hyphens.

4. Choose an IAM role that you have set up with a trust relationship to Amazon EC2, as documented in Step 5: Create an IAM Role for Notebooks.

5. Choose an Amazon EC2 key pair that you have generated on the Amazon EC2 console (https://console. aws.amazon.com/ec2/), or choose **Create EC2 key pair** to generate a new one. Remember where you have downloaded and saved the private key portion of the pair. This key pair is different from the SSH key you used when creating your development endpoint (the keys that Amazon EC2 uses are 2048-bit SSH-2 RSA keys). For more information about Amazon EC2 keys, see Amazon EC2 Key Pairs.

   It is to generally a good practice to ensure that the private-key file is write-protected so that it is not accidentally modified. On macOS and Linux systems, do this by opening a terminal and entering `chmod 400 private-key-file path`. On Windows, open the console and enter `attrib -r private-key -file path`.

6. Choose a user name and password to access your Zeppelin notebook.

7. Choose an Amazon S3 path for your notebook state to be stored in.

8. Choose **Create**.

You can view the status of the AWS CloudFormation stack in the AWS CloudFormation console **Events** tab (https://console.aws.amazon.com/cloudformation). You can view the Amazon EC2 instances created by AWS CloudFormation in the Amazon EC2 console (https://console.aws.amazon.com/ec2/). Search for instances that are tagged with the key name **aws-glue-dev-endpoint** and value of the name of your development endpoint.

After the notebook server is created, its status changes to **CREATE_COMPLETE** in the Amazon EC2 console. Details about your server also appear in the development endpoint details page. When the creation is complete, you can connect to a notebook on the new server.

Note
For any notebook server that you create that is associated with a development endpoint, you manage it. Therefore, if you delete the development endpoint, to delete the notebook server, you must delete the AWS CloudFormation stack on the AWS CloudFormation console.

Connecting to Your Notebook Server on Amazon EC2

1. In the AWS Glue console, choose Dev endpoints to navigate to the development endpoints list. Choose the name of the development endpoint for which you created a notebook server. Choosing the name opens its details page.

2. At the bottom of the **Endpoint details** page, copy the URL labeled **Notebook Server URL**.

3. Open a web browser, and paste in the notebook server URL. This lets you access the server using HTTPS on port 443. Your browser may not recognize the server's certificate, in which case you have to override its protection and proceed anyway.

4. Log in to Zeppelin using the user name and password that you provided when you created the notebook server.

Running a Simple Script Fragment in a Notebook Paragraph

1. Choose **Create new note** and name it **Legislators**. Confirm spark as the **Default Interpreter**.

2. You can verify that your notebook is now set up correctly by typing the statement spark.version and running it. This returns the version of Apache Spark that is running on your notebook server.

3. Type the following script into the next paragraph in your notebook and run it. This script reads metadata from the **persons_json** table that your crawler created, creates a DynamicFrame from the underlying data, and displays the number of records and the schema of the data.

```
1 %pyspark
2 import sys
3 from pyspark.context import SparkContext
4 from awsglue.context import GlueContext
5 from awsglue.transforms import *
6 from awsglue.utils import getResolvedOptions
7
8 # Create a Glue context
9 glueContext = GlueContext(SparkContext.getOrCreate())
10
11 # Create a DynamicFrame using the 'persons_json' table
12 persons_DyF = glueContext.create_dynamic_frame.from_catalog(database="legislators",
       table_name="persons_json")
13
14 # Print out information about this data
15 print "Count:  ", persons_DyF.count()
16 persons_DyF.printSchema()
```

The output of the script should be:

```
1  Count:  1961
2  root
3  |-- family_name: string
4  |-- name: string
5  |-- links: array
6  |    |-- element: struct
7  |    |    |-- note: string
8  |    |    |-- url: string
9  |-- gender: string
10 |-- image: string
11 |-- identifiers: array
```

```
12  |     |-- element: struct
13  |     |     |-- scheme: string
14  |     |     |-- identifier: string
15  |-- other_names: array
16  |     |-- element: struct
17  |     |     |-- note: string
18  |     |     |-- name: string
19  |     |     |-- lang: string
20  |-- sort_name: string
21  |-- images: array
22  |     |-- element: struct
23  |     |     |-- url: string
24  |-- given_name: string
25  |-- birth_date: string
26  |-- id: string
27  |-- contact_details: array
28  |     |-- element: struct
29  |     |     |-- type: string
30  |     |     |-- value: string
31  |-- death_date: string
```

Tutorial: Use a REPL Shell with Your Development Endpoint

In AWS Glue, you can create a development endpoint and then invoke a REPL (Read–Evaluate–Print Loop) shell to run PySpark code incrementally so that you can interactively debug your ETL scripts before deploying them.

The tutorial assumes that you have already taken the steps outlined in Tutorial Prerequisites.

1. In the AWS Glue console, choose **Dev endpoints** to navigate to the development endpoints list. Choose the name of a development endpoint to open its details page.

2. Copy the SSH command labeled **SSH to Python REPL**, and paste it into a text editor. Replace the `<private-key.pem>` text with the path to the private-key `.pem` file that corresponds to the public key that you used to create the development endpoint. Use forward slashes rather than backslashes as delimiters in the path.

3. On your local computer, open a terminal window that can run SSH commands, and paste in the edited SSH command. Run the command. The output will look like this:

```
 1 download: s3://aws-glue-jes-prod-us-east-1-assets/etl/jars/glue-assembly.jar to ../../usr/
     share/aws/glue/etl/jars/glue-assembly.jar
 2 download: s3://aws-glue-jes-prod-us-east-1-assets/etl/python/PyGlue.zip to ../../usr/share/
     aws/glue/etl/python/PyGlue.zip
 3 Python 2.7.12 (default, Sep  1 2016, 22:14:00)
 4 [GCC 4.8.3 20140911 (Red Hat 4.8.3-9)] on linux2
 5 Type "help", "copyright", "credits" or "license" for more information.
 6 Setting default log level to "WARN".
 7 To adjust logging level use sc.setLogLevel(newLevel). For SparkR, use setLogLevel(newLevel)
   .
 8 SLF4J: Class path contains multiple SLF4J bindings.
 9 SLF4J: Found binding in [jar:file:/usr/share/aws/glue/etl/jars/glue-assembly.jar!/org/slf4j
     /impl/StaticLoggerBinder.class]
10 SLF4J: Found binding in [jar:file:/usr/lib/spark/jars/slf4j-log4j12-1.7.16.jar!/org/slf4j/
     impl/StaticLoggerBinder.class]
11 SLF4J: See http://www.slf4j.org/codes.html#multiple_bindings for an explanation.
12 SLF4J: Actual binding is of type [org.slf4j.impl.Log4jLoggerFactory]
13 Welcome to
14       ____              __
15      / __/__  ___ _____/ /__
16     _\ \/ _ \/ _ `/ __/  '_/
17    /__ / .__/\_,_/_/ /_/\_\   version 2.1.0
18       /_/
19
20 Using Python version 2.7.12 (default, Sep  1 2016 22:14:00)
21 SparkSession available as 'spark'.
22 >>>
```

4. Test that the REPL shell is working correctly by typing the statement, `print spark.version`. As long as that displays the Spark version, your REPL is now ready to use.

5. Now you can try executing the following simple script, line by line, in the shell:

```
1 import sys
2 from pyspark.context import SparkContext
3 from awsglue.context import GlueContext
4 from awsglue.transforms import *
5 glueContext = GlueContext(SparkContext.getOrCreate())
```

```
6 persons_DyF = glueContext.create_dynamic_frame.from_catalog(database="legislators",
      table_name="persons_json")
7 print "Count:  ", persons_DyF.count()
8 persons_DyF.printSchema()
```

Tutorial: Set Up PyCharm Professional with a Development Endpoint

This tutorial shows you how to connect the PyCharm Professional Python IDE running on your local machine to a development endpoint so that you can interactively run, debug, and test AWS Glue ETL (extract, transfer, and load) scripts before deploying them.

To connect to a development endpoint interactively, you must have PyCharm Professional installed. You can't do this using the free edition.

The tutorial assumes that you have already taken the steps outlined in Tutorial Prerequisites.

Connecting PyCharm Professional to a Development Endpoint

1. Create a new pure-Python project in PyCharm named `legislators`.

2. Create a file named `get_person_schema.py` in the project with the following content:

```
1  import sys
2  import pydevd
3  from pyspark.context import SparkContext
4  from awsglue.context import GlueContext
5  from awsglue.transforms import *
6
7  def main():
8      # Invoke pydevd
9      pydevd.settrace('169.254.76.0', port=9001, stdoutToServer=True, stderrToServer=True)
10
11     # Create a Glue context
12     glueContext = GlueContext(SparkContext.getOrCreate())
13
14     # Create a DynamicFrame using the 'persons_json' table
15     persons_DyF = glueContext.create_dynamic_frame.from_catalog(database="legislators",
           table_name="persons_json")
16
17     # Print out information about this data
18     print "Count:  ", persons_DyF.count()
19     persons_DyF.printSchema()
20
21 if __name__ == "__main__":
22 main()
```

3. Download the AWS Glue Python library file, `PyGlue.zip`, from `https://s3.amazonaws.com/aws-glue-jes-prod-us-east-1-assets/etl/python/PyGlue.zip` to a convenient location on your local machine.

4. Add `PyGlue.zip` as a content root for your project in PyCharm:

   - In PyCharm, choose **File**, **Settings** to open the **Settings** dialog box. (You can also use the gear-and-wrench icon on the toolbar, or press Ctrl+Alt+S.)
   - Expand the `legislators` project and choose **Project Structure**. Then in the right pane, choose + **Add Content Root**.
   - Navigate to the location where you saved `PyGlue.zip`, select it, then choose **Apply**.

   The **Settings** screen should look something like the following:

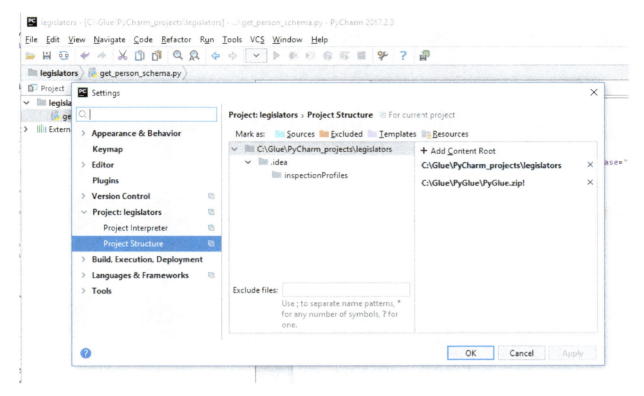

Leave the **Settings** dialog box open after you choose **Apply**.

5. Configure deployment options to upload the local script to your development endpoint using SFTP (this capability is available only in PyCharm Professional):

- In the **Settings** dialog box, expand the **Build, Execution, Deployment** section. Choose the **Deployment** subsection.
- Choose the **+** icon at the top of the middle pane to add a new server. Give it a name and set its **Type** to SFTP.
- Set the **SFTP host** to the **Public address** of your development endpoint, as listed on its details page (choose the name of your development endpoint in the AWS Glue console to display the details page).
- Set the **User name** to glue.
- Set the **Auth type** to **Key pair (OpenSSH or Putty)**. Set the **Private key file** by browsing to the location where your development endpoint's private key file is located. Note that PyCharm only supports DSA, RSA and ECDSA OpenSSH key types. You can use an up-to-date version of ssh-keygen to generate a key-pair type that PyCharm accepts.
- Choose **Test SFTP connection**, and allow the connection to be tested. If the connection succeeds, choose **Apply**.

The **Settings** screen should now look something like the following:

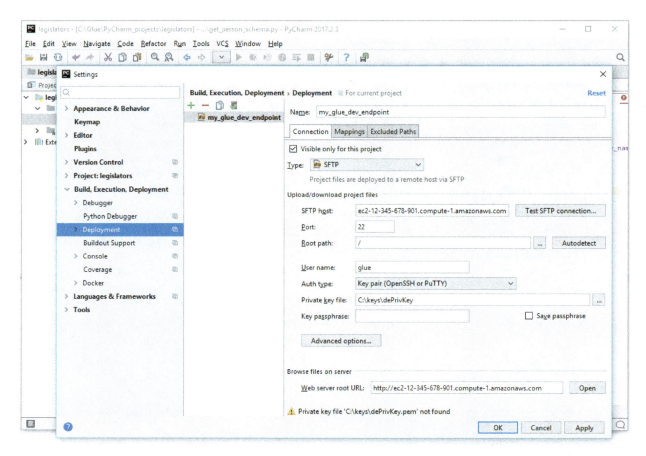

Again, leave the **Settings** dialog box open after you choose **Apply**.

6. Map the local directory to a remote directory for deployment:

- In the right pane of the **Deployment** page, choose the middle tab at the top, labeled **Mappings**.
- In the **Deployment Path** column, enter a path under `/home/glue/scripts/` for deployment of your project path.
- Choose **Apply**.

The **Settings** screen should now look something like the following:

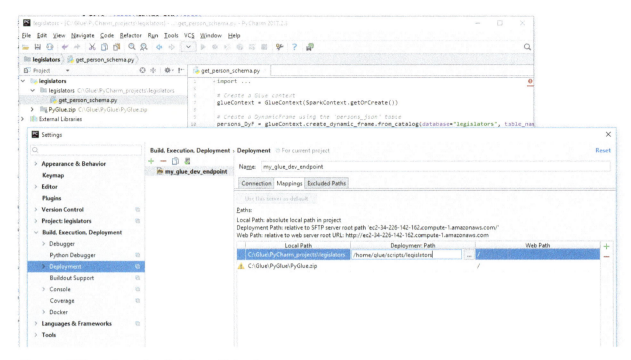

Choose **OK** to close the **Settings**dialog box.

Deploying the Script to Your Development Endpoint

To deploy your script to the development endpoint, choose **Tools**, **Deployment**, and then choose the name under which you set up your development endpoint, as shown in the following image:

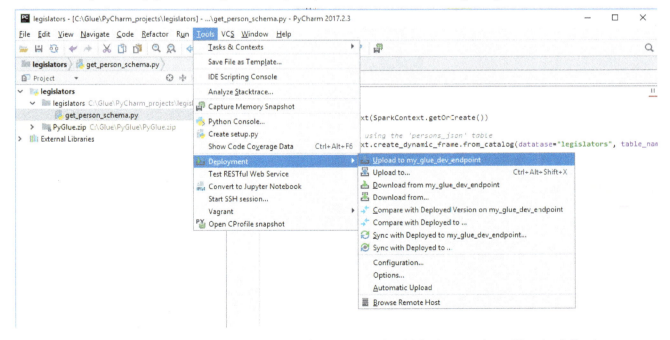

After your script has been deployed, the bottom of the screen should look something like the following:

Starting the Debug Server on `localhost` and a Local Port

To start the debug server, take the following steps:

1. Choose **Run**, **Edit Configuration**.

2. Expand **Defaults** in the left pane, and choose **Python Remote Debug**.

3. Enter a port number, such as 9001, for the **Port**:

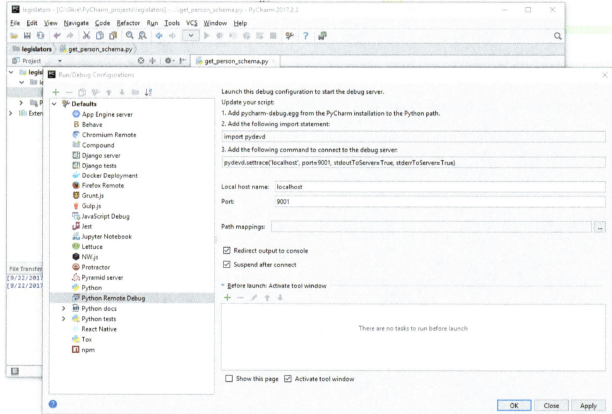

4. Note items 2 and 3 in the instructions in this screen. The script file that you created does import `pydevd`. But in the call to `settrace`, it replaces `localhost` with **169.254.76.0**, which is a special link local IP address that is accessible to your development endpoint.

5. Choose **Apply** to save this default configuration.

6. Choose the **+** icon at the top of the screen to create a new configuration based on the default that you just saved. In the drop-down menu, choose **Python Remote Debug**. Name this configuration **demoDevEndpoint**, and choose **OK**.

7. On the **Run** menu, choose **Debug 'demoDevEndpoint'**. Your screen should now look something like the following:

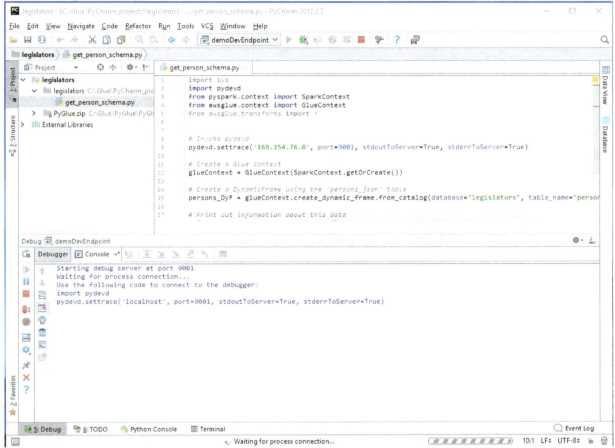

Initiating Port Forwarding

To invoke silent-mode remote port forwarding over SSH, open a terminal window that supports SSH, such as Bash (or on Windows, Git Bash). Type this command with the replacements that follow:

```
1 ssh -i private-key-file-path -nNT -g -R :9001:localhost:9001 glue@ec2-12-345-678-9.compute-1.
     amazonaws.com
```

Replacements

- Replace `private-key-file-path` with the path to the private-key `.pem` file that corresponds to your development endpoint's public key.
- Replace `ec2-12-345-678-9.compute-1.amazonaws.com` with the public address of your development endpoint. You can find the public address in the AWS Glue console by choosing **Dev endpoints**. Then choose the name of the development endpoint to open its **Endpoint details** page.

Running Your Script on the Development Endpoint

To run your script on your development endpoint, open another terminal window that supports SSH, and type this command with the replacements that follow:

```
1 ssh -i private-key-file-path \
```

```
2      glue@ec2-12-345-678-9.compute-1.amazonaws.com \
3      -t gluepython deployed-script-path/script-name
```

Replacements

- Replace `private-key-file-path` with the path to the private-key `.pem` file that corresponds to your development endpoint's public key.
- Replace `ec2-12-345-678-9.compute-1.amazonaws.com` with the public address of your development endpoint. You can find the public address in the AWS Glue console by navigating to **Dev endpoints**. Then choose the name of the development endpoint to open its **Endpoint details** page.
- Replace `deployed-script-path` with the path that you entered in the **Deployment Mappings** tab (for example, `/home/glue/scripts/legislators/`).
- Replace `script-name` with the name of the script that you uploaded (for example, `get_person_schema.py`).

PyCharm now prompts you to provide a local source file equivalent to the one being debugged remotely:

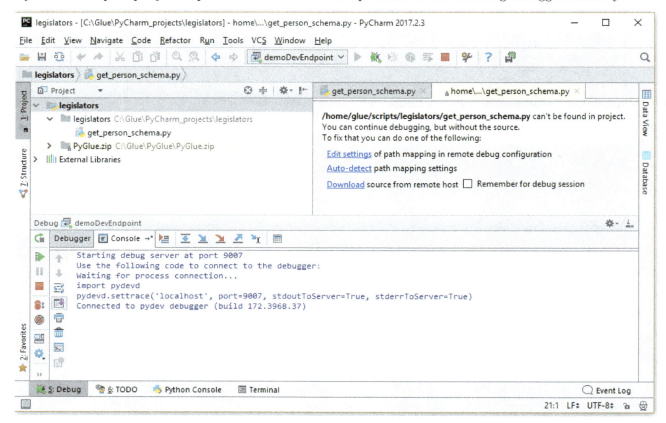

Choose **Autodetect**.

You are now set up to debug your script remotely on your development endpoint.

Working with Development Endpoints on the AWS Glue Console

A development endpoint is an environment that you can use to develop and test your AWS Glue scripts. The **Dev endpoints** tab on the AWS Glue console lists all the development endpoints that you have created. You can add, delete, or rotate the SSH key of a development endpoint. You can also create notebooks that use the development endpoint.

To display details for a development endpoint, choose the endpoint in the list. Endpoint details include the information you defined when you created it using the **Add endpoint** wizard. They also include information that you need to connect to the endpoint and any notebooks that use the endpoint.

Follow the instructions in the tutorial topics to learn the details about how to use your development endpoint with notebooks.

The following are some of the development endpoint properties:

Endpoint name
The unique name that you give the endpoint when you create it.

Provisioning status
Describes whether the endpoint is being created (**PROVISIONING**), ready to be used (**READY**), in the process of terminating (**UNHEALTHY_TERMINATING**), terminated (**UNHEALTHY_TERMINATED**), failed (**FAILED**), or being updated (**UPDATING**).

Failure reason
Reason for the development endpoint failure.

Public address
Address to connect to the development endpoint.

Public key contents
Current public SSH key associated with the development endpoint.

SSH to Python REPL
You can open a terminal window on your computer (laptop) and type this command to interact with the development endpoint in as a Read-Eval-Print Loop (REPL) shell.

SSH to Scala REPL
You can open a terminal window on your computer (laptop) and type this command to interact with the development endpoint in as a Read-Eval-Print Loop (REPL) shell.

SSH tunnel to remote interpreter
You can open a terminal window on your computer (laptop) and type this command to open a tunnel to the development endpoint. Then you can open your local Apache Zeppelin notebook and point to the development endpoint as a remote interpreter. Once the interpreter is set up, all notes within the notebook can use it.

Last modified time
Last time this development endpoint was modified.

Running for
Amount of time the development endpoint has been provisioned and READY.

Adding an Endpoint

To add an endpoint, sign in to the AWS Management Console and open the AWS Glue console at https://console.aws.amazon.com/glue/. Choose the **Dev endpoints** tab, and then choose **Add endpoint**.

Follow the steps in the AWS Glue **Add endpoint** wizard to provide the properties that are required to create an endpoint. When you create your development endpoint, save your SSH private key to access the your development endpoint later. The following are some optional fields you might provide:

Data processing units (DPUs)
You can specify the number of DPUs AWS Glue uses for your development endpoint.

Python library path
Comma-separated Amazon Simple Storage Service (Amazon S3) paths to Python libraries that are required by your script.
Only pure Python libraries can be used. Libraries that rely on C extensions, such as the pandas Python Data Analysis Library, are not yet supported.

Dependent jars path
Comma-separated Amazon S3 paths to JAR files that are required by the script.
Currently, only pure Java or Scala (2.11) libraries can be used.

Creating a Notebook Hosted on Amazon EC2

You can install an Apache Zeppelin Notebook on your local machine and use it to debug and test ETL scripts on a development endpoint. Alternatively, you can host the Zeppelin Notebook on an Amazon EC2 instance.

The AWS Glue **Create notebook server** window requests the properties required to create a notebook server to use an Apache Zeppelin notebook.

Note
For any notebook server that you create that is associated with a development endpoint, you manage it. Therefore, if you delete the development endpoint, to delete the notebook server, you must delete the AWS CloudFormation stack on the AWS CloudFormation console.

You provide the following properties.

CloudFormation stack name
The name of your notebook that is created in the AWS CloudFormation stack on the development endpoint. The name is prefixed with `aws-glue-`. This notebook runs on an Amazon EC2 instance. The Zeppelin HTTP server is started on port 443.

IAM role
A role with a trust relationship to Amazon EC2 that matches the Amazon EC2 instance profile exactly. Create the role in the IAM console, select **Amazon EC2**, and attach a policy for the notebook, such as **AWSGlueServiceNotebookRoleDefault**. For more information, see Step 5: Create an IAM Role for Notebooks.
For more information about instance profiles, see Using Instance Profiles.

EC2 key pair
The Amazon EC2 key that is used to access the notebook. You can create a key pair on the Amazon EC2 console (https://console.aws.amazon.com/ec2/). For more information, see Amazon EC2 Key Pairs.

SSH private key to access development endpoint
The private key used to connect to the development endpoint associated with the notebook server. This private key corresponds to the current SSH public key of the development endpoint.

Notebook username
The user name that you use to access the Zeppelin notebook.

Notebook password
The password that you use to access the Zeppelin notebook. It must not contain characters interpreted by the operating environment, such as, quotes and backticks.

Notebook S3 path
The location where the state of the notebook is stored. The Amazon S3 path to the Zeppelin notebook must follow the format: `s3://bucket-name/username`. Subfolders cannot be included in the path.

Subnet

The available subnets that you can use with your notebook server. An asterisk (*) indicates that the subnet can be accessed from the internet. The subnet must have an internet gateway (igw) in its route table so that it can be reached. For more information, see Setting Up Your Environment for Development Endpoints.

Security groups

The available security groups that you can use with your notebook server. The security group must have inbound rules for HTTPS (port 443) and SSH (port 22). Ensure that the rule's source is either 0.0.0.0/0 or the IP address of the machine connecting to the notebook.

Notebook server tags

The AWS CloudFormation stack is always tagged with a key **aws-glue-dev-endpoint** and the value of the name of the development endpoint. You can add more tags to the AWS CloudFormation stack.

The AWS Glue **Development endpoints** details window displays a section for each notebook created on the development endpoint. The following properties are shown.

EC instance

The name of Amazon EC2 instance that is created to host your notebook. This links to the Amazon EC2 console (https://console.aws.amazon.com/ec2/) where the instance is tagged with the key **aws-glue-dev-endpoint** and value of the name of the development endpoint.

SSH to EC2 server command

Type this command in a terminal window to connect to the Amazon EC2 instance that is running your notebook.

Notebook Server URL

Type this URL in a browser to connect to your notebook on a local port.

CloudFormation stack

The name of the AWS CloudFormation stack used to create the notebook server.

Running and Monitoring AWS Glue

You can automate the running of your ETL (extract, transform, and load) jobs. AWS Glue also provides metrics for crawlers and jobs that you can monitor. After you set up the AWS Glue Data Catalog with the required metadata, AWS Glue provides statistics about the health of your environment. You can automate the invocation of crawlers and jobs with a time-based schedule based on cron. You can also trigger jobs when an event-based trigger fires.

The main objective of AWS Glue is to provide an easier way to extract and transform your data from source to target. To accomplish this objective, an ETL job follows these typical steps (as shown in the diagram that follows):

1. A trigger fires to initiate a job run. This event can be set up on a recurring schedule or to satisfy a dependency.

2. The job extracts data from your source. If required, connection properties are used to access your source.

3. The job transforms your data using a script that you created and the values of any arguments. The script contains the Scala or PySpark Python code that transforms your data.

4. The transformed data is loaded to your data targets. If required, connection properties are used to access the target.

5. Statistics are collected about the job run and are written to your Data Catalog.

The following diagram shows the ETL workflow containing these five steps.

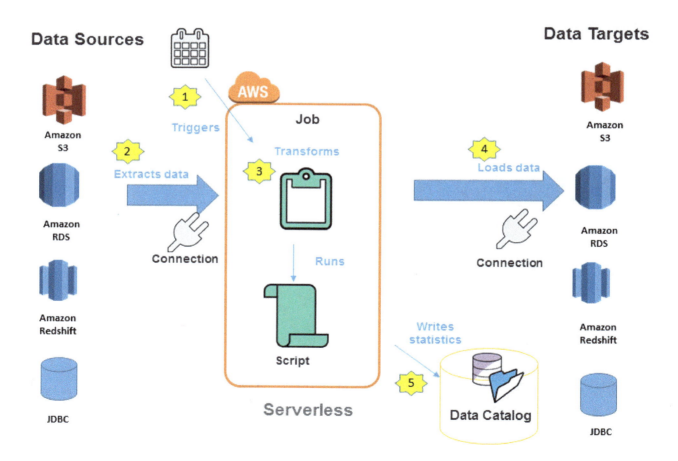

Topics

- Automated Monitoring Tools
- Time-Based Schedules for Jobs and Crawlers
- Job Bookmarks
- Automating AWS Glue with CloudWatch Events
- Logging AWS Glue Operations Using AWS CloudTrail

Automated Monitoring Tools

Monitoring is an important part of maintaining the reliability, availability, and performance of AWS Glue and your other AWS solutions. AWS provides monitoring tools that you can use to watch AWS Glue, report when something is wrong, and take action automatically when appropriate:

You can use the following automated monitoring tools to watch AWS Glue and report when something is wrong:

- **Amazon CloudWatch Events** delivers a near real-time stream of system events that describe changes in AWS resources. CloudWatch Events enables automated event-driven computing. You can write rules that watch for certain events and trigger automated actions in other AWS services when these events occur. For more information, see the Amazon CloudWatch Events User Guide.
- **Amazon CloudWatch Logs** enables you to monitor, store, and access your log files from Amazon EC2 instances, AWS CloudTrail, and other sources. CloudWatch Logs can monitor information in the log files and notify you when certain thresholds are met. You can also archive your log data in highly durable storage. For more information, see the Amazon CloudWatch Logs User Guide.
- **AWS CloudTrail** captures API calls and related events made by or on behalf of your AWS account and delivers the log files to an Amazon S3 bucket that you specify. You can identify which users and accounts call AWS, the source IP address from which the calls are made, and when the calls occur. For more information, see the AWS CloudTrail User Guide.

Time-Based Schedules for Jobs and Crawlers

You can define a time-based schedule for your crawlers and jobs in AWS Glue. The definition of these schedules uses the Unix-like cron syntax. You specify time in Coordinated Universal Time (UTC), and the minimum precision for a schedule is 5 minutes.

Cron Expressions

Cron expressions have six required fields, which are separated by white space.

Syntax

```
1 cron(fields)
```

Fields	Values	Wildcards
Minutes	0–59	, - * /
Hours	0–23	, - * /
Day-of-month	1–31	, - * ? / L W
Month	1–12 or JAN-DEC	, - * /
Day-of-week	1–7 or SUN-SAT	, - * ? / L
Year	1970–2199	, - * /

Wildcards

- The **,** (comma) wildcard includes additional values. In the `Month` field, `JAN,FEB,MAR` would include January, February, and March.
- The **-** (dash) wildcard specifies ranges. In the `Day` field, 1–15 would include days 1 through 15 of the specified month.
- The ***** (asterisk) wildcard includes all values in the field. In the `Hours` field, ***** would include every hour.
- The **/** (forward slash) wildcard specifies increments. In the `Minutes` field, you could enter **1/10** to specify every 10th minute, starting from the first minute of the hour (for example, the 11th, 21st, and 31st minute).
- The **?** (question mark) wildcard specifies one or another. In the `Day-of-month` field you could enter **7**, and if you didn't care what day of the week the seventh was, you could enter **?** in the Day-of-week field.
- The **L** wildcard in the `Day-of-month` or `Day-of-week` fields specifies the last day of the month or week.
- The **W** wildcard in the `Day-of-month` field specifies a weekday. In the `Day-of-month` field, `3W` specifies the day closest to the third weekday of the month.

Limits

- You can't specify the `Day-of-month` and `Day-of-week` fields in the same cron expression. If you specify a value in one of the fields, you must use a **?** (question mark) in the other.
- Cron expressions that lead to rates faster than 5 minutes are not supported. The support for specifying both a day-of-week and a day-of-month value is not yet complete (you must currently use the '?' character in one of these fields).

Examples
When creating a schedule, you can use the following sample cron strings.

Minutes	Hours	Day of month	Month	Day of week	Year	Meaning
0	10	*	*	?	*	Run at 10:00 am (UTC) every day

Minutes	Hours	Day of month	Month	Day of week	Year	Meaning
15	12	*	*	?	*	Run at 12:15 pm (UTC) every day
0	18	?	*	MON-FRI	*	Run at 6:00 pm (UTC) every Monday through Friday
0	8	1	*	?	*	Run at 8:00 am (UTC) every first day of the month
0/15	*	*	*	?	*	Run every 15 minutes
0/10	*	?	*	MON-FRI	*	Run every 10 minutes Monday through Friday
0/5	8–17	?	*	MON-FRI	*	Run every 5 minutes Monday through Friday between 8:00 am and 5:55 pm (UTC)

Job Bookmarks

AWS Glue keeps track of data that has already been processed by a previous run of an extract, transform, and load (ETL) job. This persisted state information is called a *job bookmark*. A job bookmark is composed of the states for various elements of jobs, such as sources, transformations, and targets. For example, your ETL job might read new partitions in an Amazon S3 file. AWS Glue tracks which partitions have successfully been processed by the job to prevent duplicate processing and duplicate data in the job's target data store.

Currently, job bookmarks are implemented for some Amazon Simple Storage Service (Amazon S3) sources and the Relationalize transform. AWS Glue supports job bookmarks for Amazon S3 source formats of JSON, CSV, Avro, and XML. Parquet and ORC are not supported.

In the AWS Glue console, a job bookmark option is passed as a parameter when the job is started.

Job bookmark	Description
Enable	Keep track of previously processed data. When a job runs, process new data since the last checkpoint.
Disable	Always process the entire dataset. You are responsible for managing the output from previous job runs. This is the default.
Pause	Process incremental data since the last run. Don't update the state information so that every subsequent run processes data since the last bookmark. You are responsible for managing the output from previous job runs.

For details about the parameters passed to a job, and specifically for a job bookmark, see Special Parameters Used by AWS Glue.

AWS Glue keeps track of job bookmarks by job name. If you delete a job, the job bookmark remains. To delete a job bookmark, you need to contact AWS Support.

If you intend to reuse a job name, reset the job bookmark. To reset the job bookmark state, use the AWS Glue console, AWS Glue API named ResetJobBookmark Action (Python: reset_job_bookmark), or the AWS CLI. For example, with the CLI you can enter the folllowing command.

```
1    reset-job-bookmark  --job-name my-job-name
```

Many of the AWS Glue PySpark dynamic frame methods include an optional parameter named `transformation_ctx`, which is used to identify state information for a job bookmark. For job bookmarks to work properly, enable the job bookmark parameter and set the `transformation_ctx`. If you do not pass in the `transformation_ctx` parameter, then job bookmarks are not enabled for a dynamic frame or table used in the method. For example, if you have an ETL job that reads and joins two Amazon S3 sources, you might choose to pass the `transformation_ctx` parameter only to those methods that you want to enable bookmarks. If you reset the job bookmark for a job, it resets all transformations associated with the job regardless of the `transformation_ctx` used. For more information about the `DynamicFrameReader` class, see DynamicFrameReader Class. For more information about PySpark extensions, see AWS Glue PySpark Extensions Reference.

Automating AWS Glue with CloudWatch Events

You can use Amazon CloudWatch Events to automate your AWS services and respond automatically to system events such as application availability issues or resource changes. Events from AWS services are delivered to CloudWatch Events in near real time. You can write simple rules to indicate which events are of interest to you, and what automated actions to take when an event matches a rule. The actions that can be automatically triggered include the following:

- Invoking an AWS Lambda function
- Invoking Amazon EC2 Run Command
- Relaying the event to Amazon Kinesis Data Streams
- Activating an AWS Step Functions state machine
- Notifying an Amazon SNS topic or an AWS SMS queue

Some examples of using CloudWatch Events with AWS Glue include the following:

- Activating a Lambda function when an ETL job succeeds
- Notifying an Amazon SNS topic when an ETL job fails

The following CloudWatch Events are generated by AWS Glue.

- Events for `"detail-type"`:`"Glue Job State Change"` are generated for SUCCEEDED, FAILED, and STOPPED.
- Events for `"detail-type"`:`"Glue Job Run Status"` are generated for RUNNING, STARTING, and STOPPING job runs when they exceed the job delay notification threshold.
- Events for `"detail-type"`:`"Glue Crawler State Change"` are generated for Started, Succeeded, and Failed.

For more information, see the Amazon CloudWatch Events User Guide. For events specific to AWS Glue, see AWS Glue Events.

Logging AWS Glue Operations Using AWS CloudTrail

AWS Glue is integrated with AWS CloudTrail, a service that provides a record of actions taken by a user, a role, or an AWS service in AWS Glue. If you create a trail, you can enable continuous delivery of CloudTrail events to an Amazon S3 bucket, Amazon CloudWatch Logs, and Amazon CloudWatch Events. Using the information collected by CloudTrail, you can determine the request that was made to AWS Glue, the IP address from which the request was made, who made the request, when it was made, and additional details.

To learn more about CloudTrail, including how to configure and enable it, see the AWS CloudTrail User Guide.

AWS Glue Information in CloudTrail

Every event or log entry contains information about who generated the request. The identity information helps you determine the following:

- Whether the request was made with root or IAM user credentials.
- Whether the request was made with temporary security credentials for a role or federated user.
- Whether the request was made by another AWS service.

For more information, see the CloudTrail userIdentity Element.

You can also create a trail and store your log files in one of your Amazon S3 buckets for as long as you want. A trail is a configuration that enables delivery of events as log files to an Amazon S3 bucket that you specify. You can then define Amazon S3 lifecycle rules to archive or delete log files automatically. By default, your log files are encrypted with Amazon S3 server-side encryption (SSE).

An event in a CloudTrail log file represents a single request from any source. It includes information about the requested action, the date and time of the action, request parameters, and so on. These events don't necessarily appear in the order the requests were made, or in any particular order at all.

All AWS Glue actions are logged by CloudTrail. For example, calls to `CreateDatabase`, `CreateTable`, and `CreateScript` all generate entries in the CloudTrail log files.

However, CloudTrail doesn't log all information regarding calls. For example, it doesn't log certain sensitive information, such as the `ConnectionProperties` used in connection requests, and it logs a `null` instead of the responses returned by the following APIs:

1 BatchGetPartition	GetCrawlers	GetJobs	GetTable
2 CreateScript	GetCrawlerMetrics	GetJobRun	GetTables
3 GetCatalogImportStatus	GetDatabase	GetJobRuns	GetTableVersions
4 GetClassifier	GetDatabases	GetMapping	GetTrigger
5 GetClassifiers	GetDataflowGraph	GetObjects	GetTriggers
6 GetConnection	GetDevEndpoint	GetPartition	GetUserDefinedFunction
7 GetConnections	GetDevEndpoints	GetPartitions	GetUserDefinedFunctions
8 GetCrawler	GetJob	GetPlan	

To be notified of log file delivery, configure CloudTrail to publish Amazon SNS notifications when new log files are delivered. For more information, see Configuring Amazon SNS Notifications for CloudTrail.

You can also aggregate AWS Glue log files from multiple AWS Regions and multiple AWS accounts into a single Amazon S3 bucket. For more information, see Receiving CloudTrail Log Files from Multiple Regions and Receiving CloudTrail Log Files from Multiple Accounts.

CloudTrail Log File Entries for AWS Glue

The following example shows the kind of CloudTrail log entry that a `DeleteCrawler` call generates:

```json
{
  "eventVersion": "1.05",
  "userIdentity": {
    "type": "IAMUser",
    "principalId": "AKIAIOSFODNN7EXAMPLE",
    "arn": "arn:aws:iam::123456789012:user/johndoe",
    "accountId": "123456789012",
    "accessKeyId": "AKIAIOSFODNN7EXAMPLE",
    "userName": "johndoe"
  },
  "eventTime": "2017-10-11T22:29:49Z",
  "eventSource": "glue.amazonaws.com",
  "eventName": "DeleteCrawler",
  "awsRegion": "us-east-1",
  "sourceIPAddress": "72.21.198.64",
  "userAgent": "aws-cli/1.11.148 Python/3.6.1 Darwin/16.7.0 botocore/1.7.6",
  "requestParameters": {
    "name": "tes-alpha"
  },
  "responseElements": null,
  "requestID": "b16f4050-aed3-11e7-b0b3-75564a46954f",
  "eventID": "e73dd117-cfd1-47d1-9e2f-d1271cad838c",
  "eventType": "AwsApiCall",
  "recipientAccountId": "123456789012"
}
```

This example shows the kind of CloudTrail log entry that a **CreateConnection** call generates:

```json
{
  "eventVersion": "1.05",
  "userIdentity": {
    "type": "IAMUser",
    "principalId": "AKIAIOSFODNN7EXAMPLE",
    "arn": "arn:aws:iam::123456789012:user/johndoe",
    "accountId": "123456789012",
    "accessKeyId": "AKIAIOSFODNN7EXAMPLE",
    "userName": "johndoe"
  },
  "eventTime": "2017-10-13T00:19:19Z",
  "eventSource": "glue.amazonaws.com",
  "eventName": "CreateConnection",
  "awsRegion": "us-east-1",
  "sourceIPAddress": "72.21.198.66",
  "userAgent": "aws-cli/1.11.148 Python/3.6.1 Darwin/16.7.0 botocore/1.7.6",
  "requestParameters": {
    "connectionInput": {
      "name": "test-connection-alpha",
      "connectionType": "JDBC",
      "physicalConnectionRequirements": {
        "subnetId": "subnet-323232",
        "availabilityZone": "us-east-1a",
        "securityGroupIdList": [
          "sg-12121212"
        ]
      }
```

```
28        }
29     },
30     "responseElements": null,
31     "requestID": "27136ebc-afac-11e7-a7d6-ab217e5c3f19",
32     "eventID": "e8b3baeb-c511-4597-880f-c16210c60a4a",
33     "eventType": "AwsApiCall",
34     "recipientAccountId": "123456789012"
35 }
```

AWS Glue Troubleshooting

Topics

- Gathering AWS Glue Troubleshooting Information
- Troubleshooting Connection Issues in AWS Glue
- Troubleshooting Errors in AWS Glue
- AWS Glue Limits

Gathering AWS Glue Troubleshooting Information

If you encounter errors or unexpected behavior in AWS Glue and need to contact AWS Support, you should first gather information about names, IDs, and logs that are associated with the failed action. Having this information available enables AWS Support to help you resolve the problems you're experiencing.

Along with your *account ID*, gather the following information for each of these types of failures:

When a crawler fails, gather the following information:

- Crawler name

  Logs from crawler runs are located in CloudWatch Logs under `/aws-glue/crawlers`.

When a test connection fails, gather the following information:

- Connection name
- Connection ID
- JDBC connection string in the form `jdbc:protocol://host:port/database-name`.

  Logs from test connections are located in CloudWatch Logs under `/aws-glue/testconnection`.

When a job fails, gather the following information:

- Job name
- Job run ID in the form `jr_xxxxx`.

  Logs from job runs are located in CloudWatch Logs under `/aws-glue/jobs`.

Troubleshooting Connection Issues in AWS Glue

When an AWS Glue crawler or a job uses connection properties to access a data store, you might encounter errors when you try to connect. AWS Glue uses private IP addresses in the subnet when it creates elastic network interfaces in your specified virtual private cloud (VPC) and subnet. Security groups specified in the connection are applied on each of the elastic network interfaces. Check to see whether security groups allow outbound access and if they allow connectivity to the database cluster.

In addition, Apache Spark requires bi-directional connectivity among driver and executor nodes. One of the security groups needs to allow ingress rules on all TCP ports. You can prevent it from being open to the world by restricting the source of the security group to itself with a self-referencing security group.

Here are some typical actions you can take to troubleshoot connection problems:

- Check the port address of your connection.
- Check the user name and password string in your connection.
- For a JDBC data store, verify that it allows incoming connections.
- Verify that your data store can be accessed within your VPC.

Troubleshooting Errors in AWS Glue

If you encounter errors in AWS Glue, use the following solutions to help you find the source of the problems and fix them.

Note
The AWS Glue GitHub repository contains additional troubleshooting guidance in AWS Glue Frequently Asked Questions.

Error: Resource Unavailable

If AWS Glue returns a resource unavailable message, you can view error messages or logs to help you learn more about the issue. The following tasks describe general methods for troubleshooting.

- For any connections and development endpoints that you use, check that your cluster has not run out of elastic network interfaces.

Error: Could Not Find S3 Endpoint or NAT Gateway for subnetId in VPC

Check the subnet ID and VPC ID in the message to help you diagnose the issue.

- Check that you have an Amazon S3 VPC endpoint set up, which is required with AWS Glue. In addition, check your NAT gateway if that's part of your configuration. For more information, see Amazon VPC Endpoints for Amazon S3.

Error: Inbound Rule in Security Group Required

At least one security group must open all ingress ports. To limit traffic, the source security group in your inbound rule can be restricted to the same security group.

- For any connections that you use, check your security group for an inbound rule that is self-referencing. For more information, see Setting Up Your Environment to Access Data Stores.
- When you are using a development endpoint, check your security group for an inbound rule that is self-referencing. For more information, see Setting Up Your Environment to Access Data Stores.

Error: Outbound Rule in Security Group Required

At least one security group must open all egress ports. To limit traffic, the source security group in your outbound rule can be restricted to the same security group.

- For any connections that you use, check your security group for an outbound rule that is self-referencing. For more information, see Setting Up Your Environment to Access Data Stores.
- When you are using a development endpoint, check your security group for an outbound rule that is self-referencing. For more information, see Setting Up Your Environment to Access Data Stores.

Error: Custom DNS Resolution Failures

When using a custom DNS for internet name resolution, both forward DNS lookup and reverse DNS lookup must be implemented. Otherwise, you might receive errors similar to: *Reverse dns resolution of ip failure* or *Dns resolution of dns failed*. If AWS Glue returns a message, you can view error messages or logs to help you learn more about the issue. The following tasks describe general methods for troubleshooting.

- A custom DNS configuration without reverse lookup can cause AWS Glue to fail. Check your DNS configuration. If you are using Route 53 or Microsoft Active Directory, make sure that there are forward and reverse lookups. For more information, see Setting Up DNS in Your VPC.

Error: Job run failed because the role passed should be given assume role permissions for the AWS Glue Service

The user who defines a job must have permission for `iam:PassRole` for AWS Glue.

- When a user creates an AWS Glue job, confirm that the user's role contains a policy that contains `iam:PassRole` for AWS Glue. For more information, see Step 3: Attach a Policy to IAM Users That Access AWS Glue.

Error: DescribeVpcEndpoints Action Is Unauthorized. Unable to Validate VPC ID vpc-id

- Check the policy passed to AWS Glue for the `ec2:DescribeVpcEndpoints` permission.

Error: DescribeRouteTables Action Is Unauthorized. Unable to Validate Subnet Id: subnet-id in VPC id: vpc-id

- Check the policy passed to AWS Glue for the `ec2:DescribeRouteTables` permission.

Error: Failed to Call ec2:DescribeSubnets

- Check the policy passed to AWS Glue for the `ec2:DescribeSubnets` permission.

Error: Failed to Call ec2:DescribeSecurityGroups

- Check the policy passed to AWS Glue for the `ec2:DescribeSecurityGroups` permission.

Error: Could Not Find Subnet for AZ

- The Availability Zone might not be available to AWS Glue. Create and use a new subnet in a different Availability Zone from the one specified in the message.

Error: Job Run Exception for Connection List with Multiple Subnet or AZ

When running a job, validation fails with the exception: `CONNECTION_LIST_CONNECTION_WITH_MULTIPLE_SUBNET_ID` and `CONNECTION_LIST_CONNECTION_WITH_MULTIPLE_AZ`.

- If your job has multiple connections, they can't be in different Availability Zones or subnets. Ensure that all connections in a job are in the same Availability Zone, or edit the job to remove connections so that only connections that are in the same Availability Zone are required.

Error: Job Run Exception When Writing to a JDBC Target

When you are running a job that writes to a JDBC target, the job might encounter errors in the following scenarios:

- If your job writes to a Microsoft SQL Server table, and the table has columns defined as type `Boolean`, then the table must be predefined in the SQL Server database. When you define the job on the AWS Glue console using a SQL Server target with the option **Create tables in your data target**, don't map any source columns to a target column with data type `Boolean`. You might encounter an error when the job runs.

  You can avoid the error by doing the following:

  - Choose an existing table with the **Boolean** column.
  - Edit the `ApplyMapping` transform and map the **Boolean** column in the source to a number or string in the target.
  - Edit the `ApplyMapping` transform to remove the **Boolean** column from the source.

- If your job writes to an Oracle table, you might need to adjust the length of names of Oracle objects. In some versions of Oracle, the maximum identifier length is limited to 30 bytes or 128 bytes. This limit affects the table names and column names of Oracle target data stores.

  You can avoid the error by doing the following:

  - Name Oracle target tables within the limit for your version.
  - The default column names are generated from the field names in the data. To handle the case when the column names are longer than the limit, use `ApplyMapping` or `RenameField` transforms to change the name of the column to be within the limit.

Error: Amazon S3 Timeout

If AWS Glue returns a connect timed out error, it might be because it is trying to access an Amazon S3 bucket in another AWS Region.

- An Amazon S3 VPC endpoint can only route traffic to buckets within an AWS Region. If you need to connect to buckets in other Regions, a possible workaround is to use a NAT gateway. For more information, see NAT Gateways.

Error: Amazon S3 Access Denied

If AWS Glue returns an access denied error to an Amazon S3 bucket or object, it might be because the IAM role provided does not have a policy with permission to your data store.

- An ETL job must have access to an Amazon S3 data store used as a source or target. A crawler must have access to an Amazon S3 data store that it crawls. For more information, see Step 2: Create an IAM Role for AWS Glue.

Error: Amazon S3 Access Key ID Does Not Exist

If AWS Glue returns an access key ID does not exist error when running a job, it might be because of one of the following reasons:

- An ETL job uses an IAM role to access data stores, confirm that the IAM role for your job was not deleted before the job started.
- An IAM role contains permissions to access your data stores, confirm that any attached Amazon S3 policy containing `s3:ListBucket` is correct.

Error: Job run fails when accessing Amazon S3 with an `s3a://` URI

If a job run returns an an error like *Failed to parse XML document with handler class *, it might be because of a failure trying to list hundreds of files using the using an `s3a://` URI. Access your data store using an `s3://` URI instead. The following exception trace highlights the errors to look for:

```
1.  com.amazonaws.SdkClientException: Failed to parse XML document with handler class com.
    amazonaws.services.s3.model.transform.XmlResponsesSaxParser$ListBucketHandler
2.  at com.amazonaws.services.s3.model.transform.XmlResponsesSaxParser.parseXmlInputStream(
    XmlResponsesSaxParser.java:161)
3.  at com.amazonaws.services.s3.model.transform.XmlResponsesSaxParser.
    parseListBucketObjectsResponse(XmlResponsesSaxParser.java:317)
4.  at com.amazonaws.services.s3.model.transform.Unmarshallers$ListObjectsUnmarshaller.
    unmarshall(Unmarshallers.java:70)
5.  at com.amazonaws.services.s3.model.transform.Unmarshallers$ListObjectsUnmarshaller.
    unmarshall(Unmarshallers.java:59)
6.  at com.amazonaws.services.s3.internal.S3XmlResponseHandler.handle(S3XmlResponseHandler.java
    :62)
7.  at com.amazonaws.services.s3.internal.S3XmlResponseHandler.handle(S3XmlResponseHandler.java
    :31)
8.  at com.amazonaws.http.response.AwsResponseHandlerAdapter.handle(AwsResponseHandlerAdapter.
    java:70)
9.  at com.amazonaws.http.AmazonHttpClient$RequestExecutor.handleResponse(AmazonHttpClient.java
    :1554)
10. at com.amazonaws.http.AmazonHttpClient$RequestExecutor.executeOneRequest(AmazonHttpClient.
    java:1272)
11. at com.amazonaws.http.AmazonHttpClient$RequestExecutor.executeHelper(AmazonHttpClient.java
    :1056)
12. at com.amazonaws.http.AmazonHttpClient$RequestExecutor.doExecute(AmazonHttpClient.java:743)
13. at com.amazonaws.http.AmazonHttpClient$RequestExecutor.executeWithTimer(AmazonHttpClient.
    java:717)
14. at com.amazonaws.http.AmazonHttpClient$RequestExecutor.execute(AmazonHttpClient.java:699)
15. at com.amazonaws.http.AmazonHttpClient$RequestExecutor.access$500(AmazonHttpClient.java:667)
16. at com.amazonaws.http.AmazonHttpClient$RequestExecutionBuilderImpl.execute(AmazonHttpClient.
    java:649)
17. at com.amazonaws.http.AmazonHttpClient.execute(AmazonHttpClient.java:513)
18. at com.amazonaws.services.s3.AmazonS3Client.invoke(AmazonS3Client.java:4325)
19. at com.amazonaws.services.s3.AmazonS3Client.invoke(AmazonS3Client.java:4272)
20. at com.amazonaws.services.s3.AmazonS3Client.invoke(AmazonS3Client.java:4266)
21. at com.amazonaws.services.s3.AmazonS3Client.listObjects(AmazonS3Client.java:834)
22. at org.apache.hadoop.fs.s3a.S3AFileSystem.getFileStatus(S3AFileSystem.java:971)
23. at org.apache.hadoop.fs.s3a.S3AFileSystem.deleteUnnecessaryFakeDirectories(S3AFileSystem.
    java:1155)
24. at org.apache.hadoop.fs.s3a.S3AFileSystem.finishedWrite(S3AFileSystem.java:1144)
25. at org.apache.hadoop.fs.s3a.S3AOutputStream.close(S3AOutputStream.java:142)
26. at org.apache.hadoop.fs.FSDataOutputStream$PositionCache.close(FSDataOutputStream.java:74)
27. at org.apache.hadoop.fs.FSDataOutputStream.close(FSDataOutputStream.java:108)
28. at org.apache.parquet.hadoop.ParquetFileWriter.end(ParquetFileWriter.java:467)
29. at org.apache.parquet.hadoop.InternalParquetRecordWriter.close(InternalParquetRecordWriter.
    java:117)
30. at org.apache.parquet.hadoop.ParquetRecordWriter.close(ParquetRecordWriter.java:112)
31. at org.apache.spark.sql.execution.datasources.parquet.ParquetOutputWriter.close(
    ParquetOutputWriter.scala:44)
32. at org.apache.spark.sql.execution.datasources.FileFormatWriter$SingleDirectoryWriteTask.
    releaseResources(FileFormatWriter.scala:252)
```

```
33  33. at org.apache.spark.sql.execution.datasources.
        FileFormatWriter$$anonfun$org$apache$spark$sql$execution$datasources$FileFormatWriter$$executeTas
        .apply(FileFormatWriter.scala:191)
34  34. at org.apache.spark.sql.execution.datasources.
        FileFormatWriter$$anonfun$org$apache$spark$sql$execution$datasources$FileFormatWriter$$executeTas
        .apply(FileFormatWriter.scala:188)
35  35. at org.apache.spark.util.Utils$.tryWithSafeFinallyAndFailureCallbacks(Utils.scala:1341)
36  36. at org.apache.spark.sql.execution.datasources.FileFormatWriter$.
        org$apache$spark$sql$execution$datasources$FileFormatWriter$$executeTask(FileFormatWriter.
        scala:193)
37  37. at org.apache.spark.sql.execution.datasources.FileFormatWriter$$anonfun$write$1$$anonfun$3.
        apply(FileFormatWriter.scala:129)
38  38. at org.apache.spark.sql.execution.datasources.FileFormatWriter$$anonfun$write$1$$anonfun$3.
        apply(FileFormatWriter.scala:128)
39  39. at org.apache.spark.scheduler.ResultTask.runTask(ResultTask.scala:87)
40  40. at org.apache.spark.scheduler.Task.run(Task.scala:99)
41  41. at org.apache.spark.executor.Executor$TaskRunner.run(Executor.scala:282)
42  42. at java.util.concurrent.ThreadPoolExecutor.runWorker(ThreadPoolExecutor.java:1149)
43  43. at java.util.concurrent.ThreadPoolExecutor$Worker.run(ThreadPoolExecutor.java:624)
44  44. at java.lang.Thread.run(Thread.java:748)
```

Error: No Private DNS for Network Interface Found

If a job fails or a development endpoint fails to provision, it might be because of a problem in the network setup.

- If you are using the Amazon provided DNS, the value of enableDnsHostnames must be set to true. For more information, see DNS.

Error: Development Endpoint Provisioning Failed

If AWS Glue fails to successfully provision a development endpoint, it might be because of a problem in the network setup.

- When you define a development endpoint, the VPC, subnet, and security groups are validated to confirm that they meet certain requirements.
- If you provided the optional SSH public key, check that it is a valid SSH public key.
- Check in the VPC console that your VPC uses a valid **DHCP option set**. For more information, see DHCP option sets.
- If after a few minutes, the development endpoint **Provisioning status** changes to FAILED and the failure reason is DNS related, for example, Reverse dns resolution of ip 10.5.237.213 failed, check your DNS setup. For more information, see Setting Up DNS in Your VPC.
- If the cluster remains in the PROVISIONING state, contact AWS Support.

Error: Notebook Server CREATE_FAILED

If AWS Glue fails to create the notebook server for a development endpoint, it might be because of one of the following problems:

- AWS Glue passes an IAM role to Amazon EC2 when it is setting up the notebook server. The IAM role must have a trust relationship to Amazon EC2.
- The IAM role must have an instance profile of the same name. When you create the role for Amazon EC2 with the IAM console, the instance profile with the same name is automatically created. Check for an error

in the log regarding an invalid instance profile name `iamInstanceProfile.name`. For more information, see Using Instance Profiles.

- Check that your role has permission to access `aws-glue*` buckets in the policy that you pass to create the notebook server.

Error: Local Notebook Fails to Start

If your local notebook fails to start and reports errors that a directory or folder cannot be found, it might be because of one of the following problems:

- If you are running on Microsoft Windows, make sure that the `JAVA_HOME` environment variable points to the correct Java directory. It's possible to update Java without updating this variable, and if it points to a folder that no longer exists, Zeppelin notebooks fail to start.

Error: Notebook Usage Errors

When using an Apache Zeppelin notebook, you might encounter errors due to your setup or environment.

- You provide an IAM role with an attached policy when you created the notebook server. If the policy does not include all the required permissions, you might get an error such as `assumed-role/name-of-role/i -0bf0fa9d038087062 is not authorized to perform some-action AccessDeniedException`. Check the policy that is passed to your notebook server in the IAM console.
- If the Zeppelin notebook does not render correctly in your web browser, check the Zeppelin requirements for browser support. For example, there might be specific versions and setup required for the Safari browser. You might need to update your browser or use a different browser.

Error: Running Crawler Failed

If AWS Glue fails to successfully run a crawler to catalog your data, it might be because of one of the following reasons. First check if an error is listed in the AWS Glue console crawlers list. Check if there is an exclamation icon next to the crawler name and hover over the icon to see any associated messages.

- Check the logs for the crawler run in CloudWatch Logs under `/aws-glue/crawlers`.

Error: Upgrading Athena Data Catalog

If you encounter errors while upgrading your Athena Data Catalog to the AWS Glue Data Catalog, see the Amazon Athena User Guide topic Upgrading to the AWS Glue Data Catalog Step-by-Step.

AWS Glue Limits

Note
You can contact AWS Support to request a limit increase for the limits listed here.

Resource	Default Limit
Number of databases per account	10,000
Number of tables per database	100,000
Number of partitions per table	1,000,000
Number of table versions per table	100,000
Number of tables per account	1,000,000
Number of partitions per account	10,000,000
Number of table versions per account	1,000,000
Number of connections per account	1,000
Number of crawlers per account	25
Number of jobs per account	25
Number of triggers per account	25
Number of concurrent job runs per account	30
Number of concurrent job runs per job	3
Number of jobs per trigger	10
Number of development endpoints per account	2
Maximum DPUs used by a development endpoint at one time	5
Maximum DPUs used by a role at one time	100

Programming ETL Scripts

AWS Glue makes it easy to write or autogenerate extract, transform, and load (ETL) scripts, as well as test and run them. This section describes the extensions to Apache Spark that AWS Glue has introduced, and provides examples of how to code and run ETL scripts in Python and Scala.

General Information about Programming AWS Glue ETL Scripts

The following sections describe techniques and values that apply generally to AWS Glue ETL programming in any language.

Topics

- Special Parameters Used by AWS Glue
- Connection Types and Options for ETL Output in AWS Glue
- Format Options for ETL Output in AWS Glue
- Managing Partitions for ETL Output in AWS Glue
- Reading Input Files in Larger Groups

Special Parameters Used by AWS Glue

There are a number of argument names that are recognized and used by AWS Glue, that you can use to set up the script environment for your Jobs and JobRuns:

- `--job-language` — The script programming language. This must be either `scala` or `python`. If this parameter is not present, the default is `python`.
- `--class` — The Scala class that serves as the entry point for your Scala script. This only applies if your `--job-language` is set to `scala`.
- `--scriptLocation` — The S3 location where your ETL script is located (in a form like `s3://path/to/my/script.py`). This overrides a script location set in the JobCommand object.
- `--extra-py-files` — S3 path(s) to additional Python modules that AWS Glue will add to the Python path before executing your script. Multiple values must be complete paths separated by a comma (`,`). Note that only pure Python modules will work currently. Extension modules written in C or other languages are not supported.
- `--extra-jars` — S3 path(s) to additional Java .jar file(s) that AWS Glue will add to the Java classpath before executing your script. Multiple values must be complete paths separated by a comma (`,`).
- `--extra-files` — S3 path(s) to additional files such as configuration files that AWS Glue will copy to the working directory of your script before executing it. Multiple values must be complete paths separated by a comma (`,`).
- `--job-bookmark-option` — Controls the behavior of a job bookmark. The following option values can be set:

[See the AWS documentation website for more details]

For example, to enable a job bookmark, pass the argument:

```
1  '--job-bookmark-option': 'job-bookmark-enable'
```

- `--TempDir` — Specifies an S3 path to a bucket that can be used as a temporary directory for the Job.

  For example, to set a temporary directory, pass the argument:

  ```
  1  '--TempDir': 's3-path-to-directory'
  ```

There are also several argument names used by AWS Glue internally that you should never set:

- `--conf` — Internal to AWS Glue. Do not set!
- `--debug` — Internal to AWS Glue. Do not set!
- `--mode` — Internal to AWS Glue. Do not set!
- `--JOB_NAME` — Internal to AWS Glue. Do not set!

Connection Types and Options for ETL Output in AWS Glue

Various AWS Glue PySpark and Scala methods and transforms specify connection parameters using a `connectionType` parameter and a `connectionOptions` parameter.

The `connectionType` parameter can take the following values, and the associated "connectionOptions" parameter values for each type are documented below:

In general, these are for ETL input and do not apply to ETL sinks.

- "connectionType": "s3": Designates a connection to Amazon Simple Storage Service (Amazon S3).
- "connectionType": "parquet": Designates a connection to files stored in Amazon S3 in the Apache Parquet file format.
- "connectionType": "orc": Designates a connection to files stored in Amazon S3 in the Apache Hive Optimized Row Columnar (ORC) file format.
- "connectionType": "mysql": Designates a connection to a MySQL database (see JDBC connectionType values).
- "connectionType": "redshift": Designates a connection to an Amazon Redshift database (see JDBC connectionType values).
- "connectionType": "oracle": Designates a connection to an Oracle database (see JDBC connectionType values).
- "connectionType": "sqlserver": Designates a connection to a Microsoft SQL Server database (see JDBC connectionType values).
- "connectionType": "postgresql": Designates a connection to a PostgreSQL database (see JDBC connectionType values).

"connectionType": "s3"

Designates a connection to Amazon Simple Storage Service (Amazon S3).

Use the following `connectionOptions` with `"connectionType"`: `"s3"`:

- `"paths"`: (Required) A list of the Amazon S3 paths from which to read.
- `"exclusions"`: (Optional) A string containing a JSON list of Unix-style glob patterns to exclude. for example "[\"**.pdf\"]" would exclude all pdf files. More information about the glob syntax supported by AWS Glue can be found at Using Include and Exclude Patterns.
- `"compressionType"`: (Optional) Specifies how the data is compressed. This is generally not necessary if the data has a standard file extension. Possible values are `"gzip"` and `"bzip"`).
- `"groupFiles"`: (Optional) Grouping files is enabled by default when the input contains more than 50,000 files. To disable grouping with fewer than 50,000 files, set this parameter to `"inPartition"`. To disable grouping when there are more than 50,000 files, set this parameter to `"none"`.
- `"groupSize"`: (Optional) The target group size in bytes. The default is computed based on the input data size and the size of your cluster. When there are fewer than 50,000 input files, `"groupFiles"` must be set to `"inPartition"` for this to take effect.
- `"recurse"`: (Optional) If set to true, recursively reads files in all subdirectories under the specified paths.
- `"maxBand"`: (Optional, Advanced) This option controls the duration in seconds after which s3 listing is likely to be consistent. Files with modification timestamps falling within the last `maxBand` seconds are tracked specially when using JobBookmarks to account for S3 eventual consistency. Most users do not need to set this option. The default is 900 seconds.
- `"maxFilesInBand"`: (Optional, Advanced) This option specifies the maximum number of files to save from the last `maxBand` seconds. If this number is exceeded, extra files are skipped and only processed in the next job run. Most users do not need to set this option.

"connectionType": "parquet"

Designates a connection to files stored in Amazon Simple Storage Service (Amazon S3) in the Apache Parquet file format.

Use the following `connectionOptions` with `"connectionType"`: `"parquet"`:

- **paths**: (Required) A list of the Amazon S3 paths from which to read.
- *(Other option name/value pairs)*: Any additional options, including formatting options, are passed directly to the SparkSQL DataSource.

"connectionType": "orc"

Designates a connection to files stored in Amazon S3 in the Apache Hive Optimized Row Columnar (ORC) file format.

Use the following `connectionOptions` with `"connectionType"`: `"orc"`:

- **paths**: (Required) A list of the Amazon S3 paths from which to read.
- *(Other option name/value pairs)*: Any additional options, including formatting options, are passed directly to the SparkSQL DataSource.

JDBC connectionType values

These include the following:

- `"connectionType"`: `"mysql"`: Designates a connection to a MySQL database.
- `"connectionType"`: `"redshift"`: Designates a connection to an Amazon Redshift database.
- `"connectionType"`: `"oracle"`: Designates a connection to an Oracle database.
- `"connectionType"`: `"sqlserver"`: Designates a connection to a Microsoft SQL Server database.
- `"connectionType"`: `"postgresql"`: Designates a connection to a PostgreSQL database.

Use these `connectionOptions` with JDBC connections:

- `"url"`: (Required) The JDBC URL for the database.
- `"dbtable"`: The database table to read from.
- `"tempdir"`: (Required for Amazon Redshift, optional for other JDBC types) The Amazon S3 path where temporary data can be staged when copying out of the database.
- `"user"`: (Required) The username to use when connecting.
- `"password"`: (Required) The password to use when connecting.

All other option name/value pairs that are included in `connectionOptions` for a JDBC connection, including formatting options, are passed directly to the underlying SparkSQL DataSource.

Format Options for ETL Output in AWS Glue

Various AWS Glue PySpark and Scala methods and transforms specify their input and/or output format using a `format` parameter and a `format_options` parameter. These parameters can take the following values:

format="avro"

This value designates the Apache Avro data format.

There are no `format_options` values for `format="avro"`.

format="csv"

This value designates `comma-separated-values` as the data format (for example, see RFC 4180 and RFC 7111).

You can use the following `format_options` values with `format="csv"`:

- `separator`: Specifies the delimiter character. The default is a comma: `','`.
- `escaper`: Specifies a character to use for escaping. The default value is `"none"`.
- `quoteChar`: Specifies the character to use for quoting. The default is a double quote: `'"'`. Set this to `'-1'` to disable quoting entirely.
- `multiline`: A Boolean value that specifies whether a single record can span multiple lines. This can occur when a field contains a quoted new-line character. You must set this option to "true" if any record spans multiple lines. The default value is `"false"`, which allows for more aggressive file-splitting during parsing.
- `withHeader`: A Boolean value that specifies whether to treat the first line as a header. The default value is `"false"`. This option can be used in the `DynamicFrameReader` class.
- `writeHeader`: A Boolean value that specifies whether to write the header to output. The default value is `"true"`. This option can be used in the `DynamicFrameWriter` class.
- `skipFirst`: A Boolean value that specifies whether to skip the first data line. The default value is `"false"`.

format="ion"

This value designates Amazon Ion as the data format. (For more information, see the Amazon Ion Specification.)

Currently, AWS Glue does not support "ion" for output.

There are no `format_options` values for `format="ion"`.

format="grokLog"

This value designates a log data format specified by one or more Logstash grok patterns (for example, see Logstash Reference (6.2): Grok filter plugin).

Currently, AWS Glue does not support "groklog" for output.

You can use the following `format_options` values with `format="grokLog"`:

- `logFormat`: Specifies the grok pattern that matches the log's format.
- `customPatterns`: Specifies additional grok patterns used here.
- `MISSING`: Specifies the signal to use in identifying missing values. The default is `'-'`.
- `LineCount`: Specifies the number of lines in each log record. The default is `'1'`, and currently only single-line records are supported.
- `StrictMode`: A Boolean value that specifies whether strict mode is enabled. In strict mode, the reader doesn't do automatic type conversion or recovery. The default value is `"false"`.

format="json"

This value designates a JSON (JavaScript Object Notation) data format.

You can use the following `format_options` values with `format="json"`:

- `jsonPath`: A JsonPath expression that identifies an object to be written. For example, the following JsonPath expression targets the `id` field of a JSON object:

```
1  format="json", format_options={"jsonPath": "$.id"}
```

- `multiline`: A Boolean value that specifies whether a single record can span multiple lines. This can occur when a field contains a quoted new-line character. You must set this option to "true" if any record spans multiple lines. The default value is `"false"`, which allows for more aggressive file-splitting during parsing.

format="orc"

This value designates Apache ORC as the data format. (For more information, see the LanguageManual ORC.)

There are no `format_options` values for `format="orc"`. However, any options that are accepted by the underlying SparkSQL code can be passed to it by way of the `connection_options` map parameter.

format="parquet"

This value designates Apache Parquet as the data format.

There are no `format_options` values for `format="parquet"`. However, any options that are accepted by the underlying SparkSQL code can be passed to it by way of the `connection_options` map parameter.

format="xml"

This value designates XML as the data format, parsed through a fork of the XML Data Source for Apache Spark parser.

Currently, AWS Glue does not support "xml" for output.

You can use the following `format_options` values with `format="xml"`:

- `rowtag`: Specifies the XML tag in the file to treat as a row. Row tags cannot be self-closing.
- `encoding`: Specifies the character encoding. The default value is `"UTF-8"`.
- `excludeAttribute`: A Boolean value that specifies whether you want to exclude attributes in elements or not. The default value is `"false"`.
- `treatEmptyValuesAsNulls`: A Boolean value that specifies whether to treat white space as a null value. The default value is `"false"`.
- `attributePrefix`: A prefix for attributes to differentiate them from elements. This prefix is used for field names. The default value is `"_"`.
- `valueTag`: The tag used for a value when there are attributes in the element that have no child. The default is `"_VALUE"`.
- `ignoreSurroundingSpaces`: A Boolean value that specifies whether the white space that surrounds values should be ignored. The default value is `"false"`.

Managing Partitions for ETL Output in AWS Glue

Partitioning is an important technique for organizing datasets so they can be queried efficiently. It organizes data in a hierarchical directory structure based on the distinct values of one or more columns.

For example, you might decide to partition your application logs in Amazon Simple Storage Service (Amazon S3) by date, broken down by year, month, and day. Files that correspond to a single day's worth of data are then placed under a prefix such as `s3://my_bucket/logs/year=2018/month=01/day=23/`. Systems like Amazon Athena, Amazon Redshift Spectrum, and now AWS Glue can use these partitions to filter data by partition value without having to read all the underlying data from Amazon S3.

Crawlers not only infer file types and schemas, they also automatically identify the partition structure of your dataset when they populate the AWS Glue Data Catalog. The resulting partition columns are available for querying in AWS Glue ETL jobs or query engines like Amazon Athena.

After you crawl a table, you can view the partitions that the crawler created by navigating to the table in the AWS Glue console and choosing **View Partitions**.

For Apache Hive-style partitioned paths in `key=val` style, crawlers automatically populate the column name in the Data Catalog using default names like `partition_0`, `partition_1`, and so on. To change the default names in the console, navigate to the table, choose **Edit Schema**, and modify the names of the partition columns there.

In your ETL scripts, you can then filter on the partition columns.

Pre-Filtering Using Pushdown Predicates

In many cases, you can use a pushdown predicate to filter on partitions without having to list and read all the files in your dataset. Instead of reading the entire dataset and then filtering in a DynamicFrame, you can apply the filter directly on the partition metadata in the Data Catalog. Then you only list and read what you actually need into a DynamicFrame.

For example, in Python you could write the following:

```
1  glue_context.create_dynamic_frame.from_catalog(
2      database = "my_S3_data_set",
3      table_name = "catalog_data_table",
4      push_down_predicate = my_partition_predicate)
```

This creates a DynamicFrame that loads only the partitions in the Data Catalog that satisfy the predicate expression. Depending on how small a subset of your data you are loading, this can save a great deal of processing time.

The predicate expression can be any Boolean expression supported by Spark SQL. Anything you could put in a `WHERE` clause in a Spark SQL query will work. For more information, see the Apache Spark SQL documentation, and in particular, the Scala SQL functions reference.

In addition to Hive-style partitioning for Amazon S3 paths, Apache Parquet and Apache ORC file formats further partition each file into blocks of data that represent column values. Each block also stores statistics for the records that it contains, such as min/max for column values. AWS Glue supports pushdown predicates for both Hive-style partitions and block partitions in these formats. In this way, you can prune unnecessary Amazon S3 partitions in Parquet and ORC formats, and skip blocks that you determine are unnecessary using column statistics.

Writing Partitions

By default, a DynamicFrame is not partitioned when it is written. All of the output files are written at the top level of the specified output path. Until recently, the only way to write a DynamicFrame into partitions was to convert it to a Spark SQL DataFrame before writing.

However, DynamicFrames now support native partitioning using a sequence of keys, using the **partitionKeys** option when you create a sink. For example, the following Python code writes out a dataset to Amazon S3 in the Parquet format, into directories partitioned by the type field. From there, you can process these partitions using other systems, such as Amazon Athena.

```
1 glue_context.write_dynamic_frame.from_options(
2     frame = projectedEvents,
3     connection_type = "s3",
4     connection_options = {"path": "$outpath", "partitionKeys": ["type"]},
5     format = "parquet")
```

Reading Input Files in Larger Groups

You can set properties of your tables to enable an AWS Glue ETL job to group files when they are read from an Amazon S3 data store. These properties enable each ETL task to read a group of input files into a single in-memory partition, this is especially useful when there is a large number of small files in your Amazon S3 data store. When you set certain properties, you instruct AWS Glue to group files within an Amazon S3 data partition and set the size of the groups to be read. You can also set these options when reading from an Amazon S3 data store with the `create_dynamic_frame_from_options` method.

To enable grouping files for a table, you set key-value pairs in the parameters field of your table structure. Use JSON notation to set a value for the parameter field of your table. For more information about editing the properties of a table, see Viewing and Editing Table Details.

You can use this method to enable grouping for tables in the Data Catalog with Amazon S3 data stores.

groupFiles
Set **groupFiles** to `inPartition` to enable the grouping of files within an Amazon S3 data partition. AWS Glue automatically enables grouping if there are more than 50,000 input files. For example:

```
1    '--groupFiles': 'inPartition'
```

groupSize
Set **groupSize** to the target size of groups in bytes. The **groupSize** property is optional, if not provided, AWS Glue calculates a size to use all the CPU cores in the cluster while still reducing the overall number of ETL tasks and in-memory partitions.
For example, to set the group size to 1 MB:

```
1    '--groupSize': '1024 * 1024'
```

If you are reading from Amazon S3 directly using the `create_dynamic_frame_from_options` method, add these connection options. For example, the following attempts to group files into 1 MB groups:

```
1 df = glueContext.create_dynamic_frame_from_options("s3", {'paths': ["s3://s3path/"], 'groupFiles
    ': 'inPartition', 'groupSize': 1024 * 1024}, format="json")
```

Program AWS Glue ETL Scripts in Python

You can find Python code examples and utilities for AWS Glue in the AWS Glue samples repository on the GitHub website.

Using Python with AWS Glue

AWS Glue supports an extension of the PySpark Python dialect for scripting extract, transform, and load (ETL) jobs. This section describes how to use Python in ETL scripts and with the AWS Glue API.

- Setting Up to Use Python with AWS Glue
- Calling AWS Glue APIs in Python
- Using Python Libraries with AWS Glue
- AWS Glue Python Code Samples

AWS Glue PySpark Extensions

AWS Glue has created the following extensions to the PySpark Python dialect.

- Accessing Parameters Using `getResolvedOptions`
- PySpark Extension Types
- DynamicFrame Class
- DynamicFrameCollection Class
- DynamicFrameWriter Class
- DynamicFrameReader Class
- GlueContext Class

AWS Glue PySpark Transforms

AWS Glue has created the following transform Classes to use in PySpark ETL operations.

- GlueTransform Base Class
- ApplyMapping Class
- DropFields Class
- DropNullFields Class
- ErrorsAsDynamicFrame Class
- Filter Class
- Join Class
- Map Class
- MapToCollection Class
- Relationalize Class
- RenameField Class
- ResolveChoice Class
- SelectFields Class
- SelectFromCollection Class
- Spigot Class
- SplitFields Class
- SplitRows Class
- Unbox Class
- UnnestFrame Class

Setting Up to Use Python with AWS Glue

Use Python 2.7 rather than Python 3 to develop your ETL scripts. The AWS Glue development endpoints that provide interactive testing and development do not work with Python 3 yet.

To set up your system for using Python with AWS Glue

Follow these steps to install Python and to be able to invoke the AWS Glue APIs.

1. If you don't already have Python 2.7 installed, download and install it from the Python.org download page.

2. Install the AWS Command Line Interface (AWS CLI) as documented in the AWS CLI documentation.

   The AWS CLI is not directly necessary for using Python. However, installing and configuring it is a convenient way to set up AWS with your account credentials and verify that they work.

3. Install the AWS SDK for Python (Boto 3), as documented in the Boto3 Quickstart.

   Boto 3 resource APIs are not yet available for AWS Glue. Currently, only the Boto 3 client APIs can be used.

   For more information about Boto 3, see AWS SDK for Python (Boto 3) Getting Started.

You can find Python code examples and utilities for AWS Glue in the AWS Glue samples repository on the GitHub website.

Calling AWS Glue APIs in Python

Note that Boto 3 resource APIs are not yet available for AWS Glue. Currently, only the Boto 3 client APIs can be used.

AWS Glue API Names in Python

AWS Glue API names in Java and other programming languages are generally CamelCased. However, when called from Python, these generic names are changed to lowercase, with the parts of the name separated by underscore characters to make them more "Pythonic". In the AWS Glue API reference documentation, these Pythonic names are listed in parentheses after the generic CamelCased names.

However, although the AWS Glue API names themselves are transformed to lowercase, their parameter names remain capitalized. It is important to remember this, because parameters should be passed by name when calling AWS Glue APIs, as described in the following section.

Passing and Accessing Python Parameters in AWS Glue

In Python calls to AWS Glue APIs, it's best to pass parameters explicitly by name. For example:

```
1  job = glue.create_job(Name='sample', Role='Glue_DefaultRole',
2                        command={'Name': 'glueetl',
3                                 'ScriptLocation': 's3://my_script_bucket/scripts/my_etl_script.py
                                 '})
```

It is helpful to understand that Python creates a dictionary of the name/value tuples that you specify as arguments to an ETL script in a Job Structure or JobRun Structure. Boto 3 then passes them to AWS Glue in JSON format by way of a REST API call. This means that you cannot rely on the order of the arguments when you access them in your script.

For example, suppose that you're starting a JobRun in a Python Lambda handler function, and you want to specify several parameters. Your code might look something like the following:

```
1  from datetime import datetime, timedelta
2
3  client = boto3.client('glue')
4
5  def lambda_handler(event, context):
6    last_hour_date_time = datetime.now() - timedelta(hours = 1)
7    day_partition_value = last_hour_date_time.strftime("%Y-%m-%d")
8    hour_partition_value = last_hour_date_time.strftime("%-H")
9
10   response = client.start_job_run(
11             JobName = 'my_test_Job',
12             Arguments = {
13               '--day_partition_key':   'partition_0',
14               '--hour_partition_key':  'partition_1',
15               '--day_partition_value':  day_partition_value,
16               '--hour_partition_value': hour_partition_value } )
```

To access these parameters reliably in your ETL script, specify them by name using AWS Glue's getResolvedOptions function and then access them from the resulting dictionary:

```
1  import sys
2  from awsglue.utils import getResolvedOptions
```

```
 3
 4 args = getResolvedOptions(sys.argv,
 5                              ['JOB_NAME',
 6                               'day_partition_key',
 7                               'hour_partition_key',
 8                               'day_partition_value',
 9                               'hour_partition_value'])
10 print "The day partition key is: ", args['day_partition_key']
11 print "and the day partition value is: ", args['day_partition_value']
```

Example: Create and Run a Job

The following example shows how call the AWS Glue APIs using Python, to create and run an ETL job.

To create and run a job

1. Create an instance of the AWS Glue client:

```
1 import boto3
2 glue = boto3.client(service_name='glue', region_name='us-east-1',
3               endpoint_url='https://glue.us-east-1.amazonaws.com')
```

2. Create a job. You must use glueetl as the name for the ETL command, as shown in the following code:

```
1 myJob = glue.create_job(Name='sample', Role='Glue_DefaultRole',
2                         Command={'Name': 'glueetl',
3                                  'ScriptLocation': 's3://my_script_bucket/scripts/
                                     my_etl_script.py'})
```

3. Start a new run of the job that you created in the previous step:

```
1 myNewJobRun = glue.start_job_run(JobName=myJob['Name'])
```

4. Get the job status:

```
1 status = glue.get_job_run(JobName=myJob['Name'], RunId=myNewJobRun['JobRunId'])
```

5. Print the current state of the job run:

```
1 print status['myNewJobRun']['JobRunState']
```

Using Python Libraries with AWS Glue

You can use Python extension modules and libraries with your AWS Glue ETL scripts as long as they are written in pure Python. C libraries such as `pandas` are not supported at the present time, nor are extensions written in other languages.

Zipping Libraries for Inclusion

Unless a library is contained in a single `.py` file, it should be packaged in a `.zip` archive. The package directory should be at the root of the archive, and must contain an `__init__.py` file for the package. Python will then be able to import the package in the normal way.

If your library only consists of a single Python module in one `.py` file, you do not need to place it in a `.zip` file.

Loading Python Libraries in a Development Endpoint

If you are using different library sets for different ETL scripts, you can either set up a separate development endpoint for each set, or you can overwrite the library `.zip` file(s) that your development endpoint loads every time you switch scripts.

You can use the console to specify one or more library .zip files for a development endpoint when you create it. After assigning a name and an IAM role, choose **Script Libraries and job parameters (optional)** and enter the full Amazon S3 path to your library `.zip` file in the **Python library path** box. For example:

```
1  s3://bucket/prefix/site-packages.zip
```

If you want, you can specify multiple full paths to files, separating them with commas but no spaces, like this:

```
1  s3://bucket/prefix/lib_A.zip,s3://bucket_B/prefix/lib_X.zip
```

If you update these `.zip` files later, you can use the console to re-import them into your development endpoint. Navigate to the developer endpoint in question, check the box beside it, and choose **Update ETL libraries** from the **Action** menu.

In a similar way, you can specify library files using the AWS Glue APIs. When you create a development endpoint by calling CreateDevEndpoint Action (Python: create_dev_endpoint), you can specify one or more full paths to libraries in the `ExtraPythonLibsS3Path` parameter, in a call that looks this:

```
1  dep = glue.create_dev_endpoint(
2              EndpointName="testDevEndpoint",
3              RoleArn="arn:aws:iam::123456789012",
4              SecurityGroupIds="sg-7f5ad1ff",
5              SubnetId="subnet-c12fdba4",
6              PublicKey="ssh-rsa AAAAB3NzaC1yc2EAAAADAQABAAABAQCtp04H/y...",
7              NumberOfNodes=3,
8              ExtraPythonLibsS3Path="s3://bucket/prefix/lib_A.zip,s3://bucket_B/prefix/lib_X.zip
                  ")
```

When you update a development endpoint, you can also update the libraries it loads using a DevEndpointCustomLibraries object and setting the `UpdateEtlLibraries` parameter to `True` when calling UpdateDevEndpoint (update_dev_endpoint).

If you are using a Zeppelin Notebook with your development endpoint, you will need to call the following PySpark function before importing a package or packages from your `.zip` file:

```
1  sc.addPyFile"(/home/glue/downloads/python/yourZipFileName."zip)
```

Using Python Libraries in a Job or JobRun

When you are creating a new Job on the console, you can specify one or more library .zip files by choosing **Script Libraries and job parameters (optional)** and entering the full Amazon S3 library path(s) in the same way you would when creating a development endpoint:

```
1 s3://bucket/prefix/lib_A.zip,s3://bucket_B/prefix/lib_X.zip
```

If you are calling CreateJob (create_job), you can specify one or more full paths to default libraries using the `--extra-py-files` default parameter, like this:

```
1 job = glue.create_job(Name='sampleJob',
2                        Role='Glue_DefaultRole',
3                        Command={'Name': 'glueetl',
4                                 'ScriptLocation': 's3://my_script_bucket/scripts/my_etl_script.py
                                 '},
5                        DefaultArguments={'--extra-py-files': 's3://bucket/prefix/lib_A.zip,s3://
                                 bucket_B/prefix/lib_X.zip'})
```

Then when you are starting a JobRun, you can override the default library setting with a different one:

```
1 runId = glue.start_job_run(JobName='sampleJob',
2                            Arguments={'--extra-py-files': 's3://bucket/prefix/lib_B.zip'})
```

AWS Glue Python Code Samples

- Code Example: Joining and Relationalizing Data
- Code Example: Data Preparation Using ResolveChoice, Lambda, and ApplyMapping

Code Example: Joining and Relationalizing Data

This example uses a dataset that was downloaded from http://everypolitician.org/ to the `sample-dataset` bucket in Amazon Simple Storage Service (Amazon S3): `s3://awsglue-datasets/examples/us-legislators/all`. The dataset contains data in JSON format about United States legislators and the seats that they have held in the US House of Representatives and Senate, and has been modified slightly for purposes of this tutorial.

You can find the source code for this example in the `join_and_relationalize.py` file in the AWS Glue samples repository on the GitHub website.

Using this data, this tutorial shows you how to do the following:

- Use an AWS Glue crawler to classify objects that are stored in an Amazon S3 bucket and save their schemas into the AWS Glue Data Catalog.
- Examine the table metadata and schemas that result from the crawl.
- Write a Python extract, transfer, and load (ETL) script that uses the metadata in the Data Catalog to do the following:
  - Join the data in the different source files together into a single data table (that is, denormalize the data).
  - Filter the joined table into separate tables by type of legislator.
  - Write out the resulting data to separate Apache Parquet files for later analysis.

The easiest way to debug Python or PySpark scripts is to create a development endpoint and run your code there. We recommend that you start by setting up a development endpoint to work in. For more information, see Working with Development Endpoints on the AWS Glue Console.

Step 1: Crawl the Data in the Amazon S3 Bucket

1. Sign in to the AWS Management Console, and open the AWS Glue console at https://console.aws.amazon.com/glue/.

2. Following the steps in Working with Crawlers on the AWS Glue Console, create a new crawler that can crawl the `s3://awsglue-datasets/examples/us-legislators/all` dataset into a database named `legislators` in the AWS Glue Data Catalog.

3. Run the new crawler, and then check the `legislators` database.

   The crawler creates the following metadata tables:

   - `persons_json`
   - `memberships_json`
   - `organizations_json`
   - `events_json`
   - `areas_json`
   - `countries_r_json`

   This is a semi-normalized collection of tables containing legislators and their histories.

Step 2: Add Boilerplate Script to the Development Endpoint Notebook

Paste the following boilerplate script into the development endpoint notebook to import the AWS Glue libraries that you need, and set up a single `GlueContext`:

```
1  import sys
2  from awsglue.transforms import *
3  from awsglue.utils import getResolvedOptions
4  from pyspark.context import SparkContext
```

```
5 from awsglue.context import GlueContext
6 from awsglue.job import Job
7
8 glueContext = GlueContext(SparkContext.getOrCreate())
```

Step 3: Examine the Schemas in the Data Catalog

Next, you can easily examine the schemas that the crawler recorded in the AWS Glue Data Catalog. For example, to see the schema of the persons_json table, add the following in your notebook:

```
1 persons = glueContext.create_dynamic_frame.from_catalog(
2              database="legislators",
3              table_name="persons_json")
4 print "Count: ", persons.count()
5 persons.printSchema()
```

Here's the output from the print calls:

```
1 Count:  1961
2 root
3 |-- family_name: string
4 |-- name: string
5 |-- links: array
6 |    |-- element: struct
7 |    |    |-- note: string
8 |    |    |-- url: string
9 |-- gender: string
10 |-- image: string
11 |-- identifiers: array
12 |    |-- element: struct
13 |    |    |-- scheme: string
14 |    |    |-- identifier: string
15 |-- other_names: array
16 |    |-- element: struct
17 |    |    |-- note: string
18 |    |    |-- name: string
19 |    |    |-- lang: string
20 |-- sort_name: string
21 |-- images: array
22 |    |-- element: struct
23 |    |    |-- url: string
24 |-- given_name: string
25 |-- birth_date: string
26 |-- id: string
27 |-- contact_details: array
28 |    |-- element: struct
29 |    |    |-- type: string
30 |    |    |-- value: string
31 |-- death_date: string
```

Each person in the table is a member of some US congressional body.

To view the schema of the memberships_json table, type the following:

```
1 memberships = glueContext.create_dynamic_frame.from_catalog(
```

```
2                    database="legislators",
3                    table_name="memberships_json")
4 print "Count: ", memberships.count()
5 memberships.printSchema()
```

The output is as follows:

```
1 Count:  10439
2 root
3 |-- area_id: string
4 |-- on_behalf_of_id: string
5 |-- organization_id: string
6 |-- role: string
7 |-- person_id: string
8 |-- legislative_period_id: string
9 |-- start_date: string
10 |-- end_date: string
```

The organizations are parties and the two chambers of Congress, the Senate and House of Representatives. To view the schema of the organizations_json table, type the following:

```
1 orgs = glueContext.create_dynamic_frame.from_catalog(
2          database="legislators",
3          table_name="organizations_json")
4 print "Count: ", orgs.count()
5 orgs.printSchema()
```

The output is as follows:

```
1 Count:  13
2 root
3 |-- classification: string
4 |-- links: array
5 |    |-- element: struct
6 |    |    |-- note: string
7 |    |    |-- url: string
8 |-- image: string
9 |-- identifiers: array
10 |    |-- element: struct
11 |    |    |-- scheme: string
12 |    |    |-- identifier: string
13 |-- other_names: array
14 |    |-- element: struct
15 |    |    |-- lang: string
16 |    |    |-- note: string
17 |    |    |-- name: string
18 |-- id: string
19 |-- name: string
20 |-- seats: int
21 |-- type: string
```

Step 4: Filter the Data

Next, keep only the fields that you want, and rename id to org_id. The dataset is small enough that you can view the whole thing.

The `toDF()` converts a `DynamicFrame` to an Apache Spark `DataFrame`, so you can apply the transforms that already exist in Apache Spark SQL:

```
1 orgs = orgs.drop_fields(['other_names',
2                          'identifiers']).rename_field(
3                      'id', 'org_id').rename_field(
4                      'name', 'org_name')
5 orgs.toDF().show()
```

The following shows the output:

```
+--------------+--------------------+--------------------+--------------------+-----+----------+----
|classification|              org_id|            org_name|               links|seats|      type
|          |              image|
+--------------+--------------------+--------------------+--------------------+-----+----------+----
|         party|            party/al|                  AL|                null| null|      null
|          |              null|
|         party|       party/democrat|            Democrat|[[website,http://...| null|      null
|       |https://upload.wi...|
|         party|party/democrat-li...|    Democrat-Liberal|[[website,http://...| null|      null
|          |              null|
|   legislature|d56acebe-8fdc-47b...|House of Represen...|                null|  435|lower house
|          |              null|
|         party|    party/independent|         Independent|                null| null|      null
|          |              null|
|         party|party/new_progres...|    New Progressive|[[website,http://...| null|      null
|       |https://upload.wi...|
|         party|party/popular_dem...|     Popular Democrat|[[website,http://...| null|      null
|          |              null|
|         party|     party/republican|          Republican|[[website,http://...| null|      null
|       |https://upload.wi...|
|         party|party/republican-...|Republican-Conser...|[[website,http://...| null|      null
|          |              null|
|         party|       party/democrat|            Democrat|[[website,http://...| null|      null
|       |https://upload.wi...|
|         party|    party/independent|         Independent|                null| null|      null
|          |              null|
|         party|     party/republican|          Republican|[[website,http://...| null|      null
|       |https://upload.wi...|
|   legislature|8fa6c3d2-71dc-478...|              Senate|                null|  100|upper house
|          |              null|
+--------------+--------------------+--------------------+--------------------+-----+----------+----
```

Type the following to view the `organizations` that appear in `memberships`:

```
1 memberships.select_fields(['organization_id']).toDF().distinct().show()
```

The following shows the output:

```
1 +--------------------+
2 |     organization_id|
3 +--------------------+
4 |d56acebe-8fdc-47b...|
5 |8fa6c3d2-71dc-478...|
```

```
6  +--------------------+
```

Step 5: Put It All Together

Now, use AWS Glue to join these relational tables and create one full history table of legislator `memberships` and their corresponding `organizations`.

1. First, join `persons` and `memberships` on `id` and `person_id`.

2. Next, join the result with `orgs` on `org_id` and `organization_id`.

3. Then, drop the redundant fields, `person_id` and `org_id`.

You can do all these operations in one (extended) line of code:

```
1  l_history = Join.apply(orgs,
2                         Join.apply(persons, memberships, 'id', 'person_id'),
3                         'org_id', 'organization_id').drop_fields(['person_id', 'org_id'])
4  print "Count: ", l_history.count()
5  l_history.printSchema()
```

The output is as follows:

```
1  Count:  10439
2  root
3  |-- role: string
4  |-- seats: int
5  |-- org_name: string
6  |-- links: array
7  |    |-- element: struct
8  |    |    |-- note: string
9  |    |    |-- url: string
10 |-- type: string
11 |-- sort_name: string
12 |-- area_id: string
13 |-- images: array
14 |    |-- element: struct
15 |    |    |-- url: string
16 |-- on_behalf_of_id: string
17 |-- other_names: array
18 |    |-- element: struct
19 |    |    |-- note: string
20 |    |    |-- name: string
21 |    |    |-- lang: string
22 |-- contact_details: array
23 |    |-- element: struct
24 |    |    |-- type: string
25 |    |    |-- value: string
26 |-- name: string
27 |-- birth_date: string
28 |-- organization_id: string
29 |-- gender: string
30 |-- classification: string
31 |-- death_date: string
32 |-- legislative_period_id: string
33 |-- identifiers: array
```

```
34 |      |-- element: struct
35 |      |      |-- scheme: string
36 |      |      |-- identifier: string
37 |-- image: string
38 |-- given_name: string
39 |-- family_name: string
40 |-- id: string
41 |-- start_date: string
42 |-- end_date: string
```

You now have the final table that you can use for analysis. You can write it out in a compact, efficient format for analytics—namely Parquet—that you can run SQL over in AWS Glue, Amazon Athena, or Amazon Redshift Spectrum.

The following call writes the table across multiple files to support fast parallel reads when doing analysis later:

```
1 glueContext.write_dynamic_frame.from_options(frame = l_history,
2          connection_type = "s3",
3          connection_options = {"path": "s3://glue-sample-target/output-dir/legislator_history
                  "},
4          format = "parquet")
```

To put all the history data into a single file, you must convert it to a data frame, repartition it, and write it out:

```
1 s_history = l_history.toDF().repartition(1)
2 s_history.write.parquet('s3://glue-sample-target/output-dir/legislator_single')
```

Or, if you want to separate it by the Senate and the House:

```
1 l_history.toDF().write.parquet('s3://glue-sample-target/output-dir/legislator_part',
2                                  partitionBy=['org_name'])
```

Step 6: Write the Data to Relational Databases

AWS Glue makes it easy to write the data to relational databases like Amazon Redshift, even with semi-structured data. It offers a transform `relationalize`, which flattens `DynamicFrames` no matter how complex the objects in the frame might be.

Using the `l_history` DynamicFrame in this example, pass in the name of a root table (`hist_root`) and a temporary working path to `relationalize`. This returns a `DynamicFrameCollection`. You can then list the names of the `DynamicFrames` in that collection:

```
1 dfc = l_history.relationalize("hist_root", "s3://glue-sample-target/temp-dir/")
2 dfc.keys()
```

The following is the output of the `keys` call:

```
1 [u'hist_root', u'hist_root_contact_details', u'hist_root_links',
2  u'hist_root_other_names', u'hist_root_images', u'hist_root_identifiers']
```

`Relationalize` broke the history table out into six new tables: a root table that contains a record for each object in the `DynamicFrame`, and auxiliary tables for the arrays. Array handling in relational databases is often suboptimal, especially as those arrays become large. Separating the arrays into different tables makes the queries go much faster.

Next, look at the separation by examining `contact_details`:

```
1 l_history.select_fields('contact_details').printSchema()
2 dfc.select('hist_root_contact_details').toDF().where("id = 10 or id = 75").orderBy(['id','index
  ']).show()
```

The following is the output of the **show** call:

```
1 root
2 |-- contact_details: array
3 |    |-- element: struct
4 |    |    |-- type: string
5 |    |    |-- value: string
6 +---+-----+----------------------+----------------------+
7 | id|index|contact_details.val.type|contact_details.val.value|
8 +---+-----+----------------------+----------------------+
9 | 10|    0|                   fax|                      |
10 | 10|    1|                      |          202-225-1314|
11 | 10|    2|                 phone|                      |
12 | 10|    3|                      |          202-225-3772|
13 | 10|    4|               twitter|                      |
14 | 10|    5|                      |       MikeRossUpdates|
15 | 75|    0|                   fax|                      |
16 | 75|    1|                      |          202-225-7856|
17 | 75|    2|                 phone|                      |
18 | 75|    3|                      |          202-225-2711|
19 | 75|    4|               twitter|                      |
20 | 75|    5|                      |             SenCapito|
21 +---+-----+----------------------+----------------------+
```

The **contact_details** field was an array of structs in the original **DynamicFrame**. Each element of those arrays is a separate row in the auxiliary table, indexed by **index**. The **id** here is a foreign key into the **hist_root** table with the key **contact_details**:

```
1 dfc.select('hist_root').toDF().where(
2     "contact_details = 10 or contact_details = 75").select(
3         ['id', 'given_name', 'family_name', 'contact_details']).show()
```

The following is the output:

```
1 +--------------------+----------+-----------+---------------+
2 |                  id|given_name|family_name|contact_details|
3 +--------------------+----------+-----------+---------------+
4 |f4fc30ee-7b42-432...|      Mike|       Ross|             10|
5 |e3c60f34-7d1b-4c0...|   Shelley|     Capito|             75|
6 +--------------------+----------+-----------+---------------+
```

Notice in these commands that **toDF()** and then a **where** expression are used to filter for the rows that you want to see.

So, joining the **hist_root** table with the auxiliary tables lets you do the following:

- Load data into databases without array support.
- Query each individual item in an array using SQL.

You already have a connection set up named **redshift3**. For information about how to create your own connection, see Adding a Connection to Your Data Store.

Next, write this collection into Amazon Redshift by cycling through the **DynamicFrames** one at a time:

```
1 for df_name in dfc.keys():
2     m_df = dfc.select(df_name)
3     print "Writing to Redshift table: ", df_name
4     glueContext.write_dynamic_frame.from_jdbc_conf(frame = m_df,
5                                         catalog_connection = "redshift3",
6                                         connection_options = {"dbtable": df_name, "
                                              database": "testdb"},
7                                         redshift_tmp_dir = "s3://glue-sample-target/
                                              temp-dir/")
```

Here's what the tables look like in Amazon Redshift. (You connected to Amazon Redshift through psql.)

```
1 testdb=# \d
2                      List of relations
3  schema |           name            | type  |   owner
4 --------+---------------------------+-------+-----------
5  public | hist_root                 | table | test_user
6  public | hist_root_contact_details | table | test_user
7  public | hist_root_identifiers     | table | test_user
8  public | hist_root_images          | table | test_user
9  public | hist_root_links           | table | test_user
10 public | hist_root_other_names     | table | test_user
11 (6 rows)
12
13 testdb=# \d hist_root_contact_details
14          Table "public.hist_root_contact_details"
15            Column            |           Type            | Modifiers
16 ---------------------------+---------------------------+-----------
17 id                         | bigint                    |
18 index                      | integer                   |
19 contact_details.val.type   | character varying(65535)  |
20 contact_details.val.value  | character varying(65535)  |
21
22 testdb=# \d hist_root
23              Table "public.hist_root"
24         Column         |           Type            | Modifiers
25 ----------------------+---------------------------+-----------
26 role                  | character varying(65535)  |
27 seats                 | integer                   |
28 org_name              | character varying(65535)  |
29 links                 | bigint                    |
30 type                  | character varying(65535)  |
31 sort_name             | character varying(65535)  |
32 area_id               | character varying(65535)  |
33 images                | bigint                    |
34 on_behalf_of_id       | character varying(65535)  |
35 other_names           | bigint                    |
36 birth_date            | character varying(65535)  |
37 name                  | character varying(65535)  |
38 organization_id       | character varying(65535)  |
39 gender                | character varying(65535)  |
40 classification        | character varying(65535)  |
41 legislative_period_id | character varying(65535)  |
42 identifiers           | bigint                    |
43 given_name            | character varying(65535)  |
```

```
44  image                   | character varying(65535) |
45  family_name             | character varying(65535) |
46  id                      | character varying(65535) |
47  death_date              | character varying(65535) |
48  start_date              | character varying(65535) |
49  contact_details         | bigint                   |
50  end_date                | character varying(65535) |
```

Now you can query these tables using SQL in Amazon Redshift:

```
1  testdb=# select * from hist_root_contact_details where id = 10 or id = 75 order by id, index;
```

The following shows the result:

```
1  id | index | contact_details.val.type | contact_details.val.value
2  ---+-------+--------------------------+--------------------------
3  10 |     0 | fax                      | 202-224-6020
4  10 |     1 | phone                    | 202-224-3744
5  10 |     2 | twitter                  | ChuckGrassley
6  75 |     0 | fax                      | 202-224-4680
7  75 |     1 | phone                    | 202-224-4642
8  75 |     2 | twitter                  | SenJackReed
9  (6 rows)
```

Conclusion

Overall, AWS Glue is very flexible. It lets you accomplish, in a few lines of code, what normally would take days to write. You can find the entire source-to-target ETL scripts in the Python file `join_and_relationalize.py` in the AWS Glue samples on GitHub.

Code Example: Data Preparation Using ResolveChoice, Lambda, and ApplyMapping

The dataset that is used in this example consists of Medicare Provider payment data downloaded from two `Data.CMS.gov` sites: Inpatient Prospective Payment System Provider Summary for the Top 100 Diagnosis-Related Groups - FY2011), and Inpatient Charge Data FY 2011. After downloading it, we modified the data to introduce a couple of erroneous records at the end of the file. This modified file is located in a public Amazon S3 bucket at `s3://awsglue-datasets/examples/medicare/Medicare_Hospital_Provider.csv`.

You can find the source code for this example in the `data_cleaning_and_lambda.py` file in the AWS Glue examples GitHub repository.

The easiest way to debug Python or PySpark scripts is to create a development endpoint and run your code there. We recommend that you start by setting up a development endpoint to work in. For more information, see Working with Development Endpoints on the AWS Glue Console.

Step 1: Crawl the Data in the Amazon S3 Bucket

1. Sign in to the AWS Management Console and open the AWS Glue console at https://console.aws.amazon.com/glue/.

2. Following the process described in Working with Crawlers on the AWS Glue Console, create a new crawler that can crawl the `s3://awsglue-datasets/examples/medicare/Medicare_Hospital_Provider.csv` file, and can place the resulting metadata into a database named `payments` in the AWS Glue Data Catalog.

3. Run the new crawler, and then check the `payments` database. You should find that the crawler has created a metadata table named `medicare` in the database after reading the first 2 MB of data in the file.

   The schema of the new `medicare` table is as follows:

```
1  Column  name                              Data type
2  ==================================================
3  drg definition                               string
4  provider id                                  bigint
5  provider name                                string
6  provider street address                      string
7  provider city                                string
8  provider state                               string
9  provider zip code                            bigint
10 hospital referral region description         string
11 total discharges                             bigint
12 average covered charges                      string
13 average total payments                       string
14 average medicare payments                    string
```

Step 2: Add Boilerplate Script to the Development Endpoint Notebook

Paste the following boilerplate script into the development endpoint notebook to import the AWS Glue libraries that you need, and set up a single `GlueContext`:

```
1 import sys
2 from awsglue.transforms import *
3 from awsglue.utils import getResolvedOptions
4 from pyspark.context import SparkContext
```

```
5 from awsglue.context import GlueContext
6 from awsglue.job import Job
7
8 glueContext = GlueContext(SparkContext.getOrCreate())
```

Step 3: Compare Different Schema Parsings

Next, you can see if the schema that was recognized by an Apache Spark `DataFrame` is the same as the one that your AWS Glue crawler recorded. Run this code:

```
1 medicare = spark.read.format(
2     "com.databricks.spark.csv").option(
3     "header", "true").option(
4     "inferSchema", "true").load(
5     's3://awsglue-datasets/examples/medicare/Medicare_Hospital_Provider.csv')
6 medicare.printSchema()
```

Here's the output from the `printSchema` call:

```
1  root
2   |-- DRG Definition: string (nullable = true)
3   |-- Provider Id: string (nullable = true)
4   |-- Provider Name: string (nullable = true)
5   |-- Provider Street Address: string (nullable = true)
6   |-- Provider City: string (nullable = true)
7   |-- Provider State: string (nullable = true)
8   |-- Provider Zip Code: integer (nullable = true)
9   |-- Hospital Referral Region Description: string (nullable = true)
10  |--  Total Discharges : integer (nullable = true)
11  |--  Average Covered Charges : string (nullable = true)
12  |--  Average Total Payments : string (nullable = true)
13  |-- Average Medicare Payments: string (nullable = true)
```

Next, look at the schema that an AWS Glue `DynamicFrame` generates:

```
1 medicare_dynamicframe = glueContext.create_dynamic_frame.from_catalog(
2         database = "payments",
3         table_name = "medicare")
4 medicare_dynamicframe.printSchema()
```

The output from `printSchema` is as follows:

```
1  root
2   |-- drg definition: string
3   |-- provider id: choice
4   |      |-- long
5   |      |-- string
6   |-- provider name: string
7   |-- provider street address: string
8   |-- provider city: string
9   |-- provider state: string
10  |-- provider zip code: long
11  |-- hospital referral region description: string
12  |-- total discharges: long
13  |-- average covered charges: string
```

```
14  |-- average total payments: string
15  |-- average medicare payments: string
```

The `DynamicFrame` generates a schema in which `provider id` could be either a `long` or a `string` type. The `DataFrame` schema lists `Provider Id` as being a `string` type, and the Data Catalog lists `provider id` as being a `bigint` type.

Which one is correct? There are two records at the end of the file (out of 160,000 records) with `string` values in that column. These are the erroneous records that were introduced to illustrate a problem.

To address this kind of problem, the AWS Glue `DynamicFrame` introduces the concept of a *choice* type. In this case, the `DynamicFrame` shows that both `long` and `string` values can appear in that column. The AWS Glue crawler missed the `string` values because it considered only a 2 MB prefix of the data. The Apache Spark `DataFrame` considered the whole dataset, but it was forced to assign the most general type to the column, namely `string`. In fact, Spark often resorts to the most general case when there are complex types or variations with which it is unfamiliar.

To query the `provider id` column, resolve the choice type first. You can use the `resolveChoice` transform method in your `DynamicFrame` to convert those `string` values to `long` values with a `cast:long` option:

```
1  medicare_res = medicare_dynamicframe.resolveChoice(specs = [('provider id','cast:long')])
2  medicare_res.printSchema()
```

The `printSchema` output is now:

```
1   root
2   |-- drg definition: string
3   |-- provider id: long
4   |-- provider name: string
5   |-- provider street address: string
6   |-- provider city: string
7   |-- provider state: string
8   |-- provider zip code: long
9   |-- hospital referral region description: string
10  |-- total discharges: long
11  |-- average covered charges: string
12  |-- average total payments: string
13  |-- average medicare payments: string
```

Where the value was a `string` that could not be cast, AWS Glue inserted a `null`.

Another option is to convert the choice type to a `struct`, which keeps values of both types.

Next, look at the rows that were anomalous:

```
1  medicare_res.toDF().where("'provider id' is NULL").show()
```

You see the following:

```
1  +-------------------+-----------+--------------+---------------------+-------------+------------+-------------
2  |     drg definition|provider id|  provider name|provider street address|provider city|provider
     state|provider zip code|hospital referral region description|total discharges|average
     covered charges|average total payments|average medicare payments|
3  +-------------------+-----------+--------------+---------------------+-------------+------------+-------------
4  |948 - SIGNS & SYM...|       null|           INC|      1050 DIVISION ST|     MAUSTON|
            WI|            53948|                                 WI - Madison|              12|
           $11961.41|                              $4619.00|                             $3775.33|
```

```
5 |948 - SIGNS & SYM...|        null| INC- ST JOSEPH|      5000 W CHAMBERS ST|    MILWAUKEE|
            WI|       53210|                        WI - Milwaukee|              14|
              $10514.28|              $5562.50|              $4522.78|
6 +-------------------+----------+---------------+-----------------------+------------+--------------
```

Now remove the two malformed records, as follows:

```
1 medicare_dataframe = medicare_res.toDF()
2 medicare_dataframe = medicare_dataframe.where("'provider id' is NOT NULL")
```

Step 4: Map the Data and Use Apache Spark Lambda Functions

AWS Glue does not yet directly support Lambda functions, also known as user-defined functions. But you can always convert a `DynamicFrame` to and from an Apache Spark `DataFrame` to take advantage of Spark functionality in addition to the special features of `DynamicFrames`.

Next, turn the payment information into numbers, so analytic engines like Amazon Redshift or Amazon Athena can do their number crunching faster:

```
1 from pyspark.sql.functions import udf
2 from pyspark.sql.types import StringType
3
4 chop_f = udf(lambda x: x[1:], StringType())
5 medicare_dataframe = medicare_dataframe.withColumn(
6         "ACC", chop_f(
7             medicare_dataframe["average covered charges"])).withColumn(
8             "ATP", chop_f(
9                 medicare_dataframe["average total payments"])).withColumn(
10                "AMP", chop_f(
11                    medicare_dataframe["average medicare payments"]))
12 medicare_dataframe.select(['ACC', 'ATP', 'AMP']).show()
```

The output from the `show` call is as follows:

```
1  +--------+-------+-------+
2  |     ACC|    ATP|    AMP|
3  +--------+-------+-------+
4  |32963.07|5777.24|4763.73|
5  |15131.85|5787.57|4976.71|
6  |37560.37|5434.95|4453.79|
7  |13998.28|5417.56|4129.16|
8  |31633.27|5658.33|4851.44|
9  |16920.79|6653.80|5374.14|
10 |11977.13|5834.74|4761.41|
11 |35841.09|8031.12|5858.50|
12 |28523.39|6113.38|5228.40|
13 |75233.38|5541.05|4386.94|
14 |67327.92|5461.57|4493.57|
15 |39607.28|5356.28|4408.20|
16 |22862.23|5374.65|4186.02|
17 |31110.85|5366.23|4376.23|
18 |25411.33|5282.93|4383.73|
19 | 9234.51|5676.55|4509.11|
20 |15895.85|5930.11|3972.85|
```

```
21 |19721.16|6192.54|5179.38|
22 |10710.88|4968.00|3898.88|
23 |51343.75|5996.00|4962.45|
24 +--------+-------+-------+
25 only showing top 20 rows
```

These are all still strings in the data. We can use the powerful `apply_mapping` transform method to drop, rename, cast, and nest the data so that other data programming languages and systems can easily access it:

```
1 medicare_tmp_dyf = DynamicFrame.fromDF(medicare_dataframe, glueContext, "nested")
2 medicare_nest_dyf = medicare_tmp_dyf.apply_mapping([('drg definition', 'string', 'drg', 'string
      '),
3                    ('provider id', 'long', 'provider.id', 'long'),
4                    ('provider name', 'string', 'provider.name', 'string'),
5                    ('provider city', 'string', 'provider.city', 'string'),
6                    ('provider state', 'string', 'provider.state', 'string'),
7                    ('provider zip code', 'long', 'provider.zip', 'long'),
8                    ('hospital referral region description', 'string','rr', 'string'),
9                    ('ACC', 'string', 'charges.covered', 'double'),
10                   ('ATP', 'string', 'charges.total_pay', 'double'),
11                   ('AMP', 'string', 'charges.medicare_pay', 'double')])
12 medicare_nest_dyf.printSchema()
```

The `printSchema` output is as follows:

```
1 root
2 |-- drg: string
3 |-- provider: struct
4 |     |-- id: long
5 |     |-- name: string
6 |     |-- city: string
7 |     |-- state: string
8 |     |-- zip: long
9 |-- rr: string
10 |-- charges: struct
11 |     |-- covered: double
12 |     |-- total_pay: double
13 |     |-- medicare_pay: double
```

Turning the data back into a Spark `DataFrame`, you can show what it looks like now:

```
1 medicare_nest_dyf.toDF().show()
```

The output is as follows:

```
1 +-------------------+-------------------+---------------+-------------------+
2 |                drg|           provider|             rr|            charges|
3 +-------------------+-------------------+---------------+-------------------+
4 |039 - EXTRACRANIA...|[10001,SOUTHEAST ...|     AL - Dothan|[32963.07,5777.24...|
5 |039 - EXTRACRANIA...|[10005,MARSHALL M...|AL - Birmingham|[15131.85,5787.57...|
6 |039 - EXTRACRANIA...|[10006,ELIZA COFF...|AL - Birmingham|[37560.37,5434.95...|
7 |039 - EXTRACRANIA...|[10011,ST VINCENT...|AL - Birmingham|[13998.28,5417.56...|
8 |039 - EXTRACRANIA...|[10016,SHELBY BAP...|AL - Birmingham|[31633.27,5658.33...|
9 |039 - EXTRACRANIA...|[10023,BAPTIST ME...|AL - Montgomery|[16920.79,6653.8,...|
10 |039 - EXTRACRANIA...|[10029,EAST ALABA...|AL - Birmingham|[11977.13,5834.74...|
11 |039 - EXTRACRANIA...|[10033,UNIVERSITY...|AL - Birmingham|[35841.09,8031.12...|
12 |039 - EXTRACRANIA...|[10039,HUNTSVILLE...|AL - Huntsville|[28523.39,6113.38...|
```

```
13  |039 - EXTRACRANIA...|[10040,GADSDEN RE...|AL - Birmingham|[75233.38,5541.05...|
14  |039 - EXTRACRANIA...|[10046,RIVERVIEW ...|AL - Birmingham|[67327.92,5461.57...|
15  |039 - EXTRACRANIA...|[10055,FLOWERS HO...|    AL - Dothan|[39607.28,5356.28...|
16  |039 - EXTRACRANIA...|[10056,ST VINCENT...|AL - Birmingham|[22862.23,5374.65...|
17  |039 - EXTRACRANIA...|[10078,NORTHEAST ...|AL - Birmingham|[31110.85,5366.23...|
18  |039 - EXTRACRANIA...|[10083,SOUTH BALD...|    AL - Mobile|[25411.33,5282.93...|
19  |039 - EXTRACRANIA...|[10085,DECATUR GE...|AL - Huntsville|[9234.51,5676.55,...|
20  |039 - EXTRACRANIA...|[10090,PROVIDENCE...|    AL - Mobile|[15895.85,5930.11...|
21  |039 - EXTRACRANIA...|[10092,D C H REGI...|AL - Tuscaloosa|[19721.16,6192.54...|
22  |039 - EXTRACRANIA...|[10100,THOMAS HOS...|    AL - Mobile|[10710.88,4968.0,...|
23  |039 - EXTRACRANIA...|[10103,BAPTIST ME...|AL - Birmingham|[51343.75,5996.0,...|
24  +-------------------+-------------------+--------------+-------------------+
25  only showing top 20 rows
```

Step 5: Write the Data to Apache Parquet

AWS Glue makes it easy to write the data in a format such as Apache Parquet that relational databases can effectively consume:

```
1  glueContext.write_dynamic_frame.from_options(
2        frame = medicare_nest_dyf,
3        connection_type = "s3",
4        connection_options = {"path": "s3://glue-sample-target/output-dir/medicare_parquet"},
5        format = "parquet")
```

AWS Glue PySpark Extensions Reference

AWS Glue has created the following extensions to the PySpark Python dialect.

- Accessing Parameters Using `getResolvedOptions`
- PySpark Extension Types
- DynamicFrame Class
- DynamicFrameCollection Class
- DynamicFrameWriter Class
- DynamicFrameReader Class
- GlueContext Class

Accessing Parameters Using `getResolvedOptions`

The AWS Glue `getResolvedOptions(args, options)` utility function gives you access to the arguments that are passed to your script when you run a job. To use this function, start by importing it from the AWS Glue `utils` module, along with the `sys` module:

```
1 import sys
2 from awsglue.utils import getResolvedOptions
```

`getResolvedOptions(args, options)`

- `args` – The list of arguments contained in `sys.argv`.
- `options` – A Python array of the argument names that you want to retrieve.

Example Retrieving arguments passed to a JobRun

Suppose that you created a JobRun in a script, perhaps within a Lambda function:

```
1 response = client.start_job_run(
2             JobName = 'my_test_Job',
3             Arguments = {
4               '--day_partition_key':   'partition_0',
5               '--hour_partition_key':  'partition_1',
6               '--day_partition_value':  day_partition_value,
7               '--hour_partition_value': hour_partition_value } )
```

To retrieve the arguments that are passed, you can use the `getResolvedOptions` function as follows:

```
1 import sys
2 from awsglue.utils import getResolvedOptions
3
4 args = getResolvedOptions(sys.argv,
5                           ['JOB_NAME',
6                            'day_partition_key',
7                            'hour_partition_key',
8                            'day_partition_value',
9                            'hour_partition_value'])
10 print "The day-partition key is: ", args['day_partition_key']
11 print "and the day-partition value is: ", args['day_partition_value']
```

PySpark Extension Types

The types that are used by the AWS Glue PySpark extensions.

DataType

The base class for the other AWS Glue types.

`__init__(properties={})`

- `properties` – Properties of the data type (optional).

`typeName(cls)`

Returns the type of the AWS Glue type class (that is, the class name with "Type" removed from the end).

- `cls` – An AWS Glue class instance derived from `DataType`.

`jsonValue( )`

Returns a JSON object that contains the data type and properties of the class:

```
1  {
2    "dataType": typeName,
3    "properties": properties
4  }
```

AtomicType and Simple Derivatives

Inherits from and extends the DataType class, and serves as the base class for all the AWS Glue atomic data types.

`fromJsonValue(cls, json_value)`

Initializes a class instance with values from a JSON object.

- `cls` – An AWS Glue type class instance to initialize.
- `json_value` – The JSON object to load key-value pairs from.

The following types are simple derivatives of the AtomicType class:

- `BinaryType` – Binary data.
- `BooleanType` – Boolean values.
- `ByteType` – A byte value.
- `DateType` – A datetime value.
- `DoubleType` – A floating-point double value.
- `IntegerType` – An integer value.
- `LongType` – A long integer value.
- `NullType` – A null value.
- `ShortType` – A short integer value.
- `StringType` – A text string.
- `TimestampType` – A timestamp value (typically in seconds from 1/1/1970).
- `UnknownType` – A value of unidentified type.

DecimalType(AtomicType)

Inherits from and extends the AtomicType class to represent a decimal number (a number expressed in decimal digits, as opposed to binary base-2 numbers).

`__init__(precision=10, scale=2, properties={})`

- `precision` – The number of digits in the decimal number (optional; the default is 10).
- `scale` – The number of digits to the right of the decimal point (optional; the default is 2).
- `properties` – The properties of the decimal number (optional).

EnumType(AtomicType)

Inherits from and extends the AtomicType class to represent an enumeration of valid options.

`__init__(options)`

- `options` – A list of the options being enumerated.

Collection Types

- ArrayType(DataType)
- ChoiceType(DataType)
- MapType(DataType)
- Field(Object)
- StructType(DataType)
- EntityType(DataType)

ArrayType(DataType)

`__init__(elementType=UnknownType(), properties={})`

- `elementType` – The type of elements in the array (optional; the default is UnknownType).
- `properties` – Properties of the array (optional).

ChoiceType(DataType)

`__init__(choices=[], properties={})`

- `choices` – A list of possible choices (optional).
- `properties` – Properties of these choices (optional).

`add(new_choice)`

Adds a new choice to the list of possible choices.

- `new_choice` – The choice to add to the list of possible choices.

`merge(new_choices)`

Merges a list of new choices with the existing list of choices.

- `new_choices` – A list of new choices to merge with existing choices.

MapType(DataType)

`__init__(valueType=UnknownType, properties={})`

- `valueType` – The type of values in the map (optional; the default is UnknownType).
- `properties` – Properties of the map (optional).

Field(Object)

Creates a field object out of an object that derives from DataType.

`__init__(name, dataType, properties={})`

- `name` – The name to be assigned to the field.
- `dataType` – The object to create a field from.
- `properties` – Properties of the field (optional).

StructType(DataType)

Defines a data structure (`struct`).

`__init__(fields=[], properties={})`

- `fields` – A list of the fields (of type `Field`) to include in the structure (optional).
- `properties` – Properties of the structure (optional).

`add(field)`

- `field` – An object of type `Field` to add to the structure.

`hasField(field)`

Returns `True` if this structure has a field of the same name, or `False` if not.

- `field` – A field name, or an object of type `Field` whose name is used.

`getField(field)`

- `field` – A field name or an object of type `Field` whose name is used. If the structure has a field of the same name, it is returned.

EntityType(DataType)

`__init__(entity, base_type, properties)`

This class is not yet implemented.

Other Types

- DataSource(object)
- DataSink(object)

DataSource(object)

__init__(j_source, sql_ctx, name)

- `j_source` – The data source.
- `sql_ctx` – The SQL context.
- `name` – The data-source name.

setFormat(format, **options)

- `format` – The format to set for the data source.
- `options` – A collection of options to set for the data source.

getFrame()

Returns a `DynamicFrame` for the data source.

DataSink(object)

__init__(j_sink, sql_ctx)

- `j_sink` – The sink to create.
- `sql_ctx` – The SQL context for the data sink.

setFormat(format, **options)

- `format` – The format to set for the data sink.
- `options` – A collection of options to set for the data sink.

setAccumulableSize(size)

- `size` – The accumulable size to set, in bytes.

writeFrame(dynamic_frame, info="")

- `dynamic_frame` – The `DynamicFrame` to write.
- `info` – Information about the `DynamicFrame` (optional).

write(dynamic_frame_or_dfc, info="")

Writes a `DynamicFrame` or a `DynamicFrameCollection`.

- `dynamic_frame_or_dfc` – Either a `DynamicFrame` object or a `DynamicFrameCollection` object to be written.
- `info` – Information about the `DynamicFrame` or `DynamicFrames` to be written (optional).

DynamicFrame Class

One of the major abstractions in Apache Spark is the SparkSQL `DataFrame`, which is similar to the `DataFrame` construct found in R and Pandas. A `DataFrame` is similar to a table and supports functional-style (map/reduce/-filter/etc.) operations and SQL operations (select, project, aggregate).

`DataFrames` are powerful and widely used, but they have limitations with respect to extract, transform, and load (ETL) operations. Most significantly, they require a schema to be specified before any data is loaded. SparkSQL addresses this by making two passes over the data—the first to infer the schema, and the second to load the data. However, this inference is limited and doesn't address the realities of messy data. For example, the same field might be of a different type in different records. Apache Spark often gives up and reports the type as `string` using the original field text. This might not be correct, and you might want finer control over how schema discrepancies are resolved. And for large datasets, an additional pass over the source data might be prohibitively expensive.

To address these limitations, AWS Glue introduces the `DynamicFrame`. A `DynamicFrame` is similar to a `DataFrame`, except that each record is self-describing, so no schema is required initially. Instead, AWS Glue computes a schema on-the-fly when required, and explicitly encodes schema inconsistencies using a choice (or union) type. You can resolve these inconsistencies to make your datasets compatible with data stores that require a fixed schema.

Similarly, a `DynamicRecord` represents a logical record within a `DynamicFrame`. It is like a row in a Spark `DataFrame`, except that it is self-describing and can be used for data that does not conform to a fixed schema.

You can convert `DynamicFrames` to and from `DataFrames` once you resolve any schema inconsistencies.

— Construction —

- __init__
- fromDF
- toDF

__init__

`__init__(jdf, glue_ctx, name)`

- `jdf` – A reference to the data frame in the Java Virtual Machine (JVM).
- `glue_ctx` – A GlueContext Class object.
- `name` – An optional name string, empty by default.

fromDF

`fromDF(dataframe, glue_ctx, name)`

Converts a `DataFrame` to a `DynamicFrame` by converting `DataFrame` fields to `DynamicRecord` fields. Returns the new DynamicFrame.

A `DynamicRecord` represents a logical record in a `DynamicFrame`. It is similar to a row in a Spark `DataFrame`, except that it is self-describing and can be used for data that does not conform to a fixed schema.

- `dataframe` – The Apache Spark SQL `DataFrame` to convert (required).
- `glue_ctx` – The GlueContext Class object that specifies the context for this transform (required).
- `name` – The name of the resulting `DynamicFrame` (required).

toDF

toDF(options)

Converts a `DynamicFrame` to an Apache Spark `DataFrame` by converting `DynamicRecords` into `DataFrame` fields. Returns the new `DataFrame`.

A `DynamicRecord` represents a logical record in a `DynamicFrame`. It is similar to a row in a Spark `DataFrame`, except that it is self-describing and can be used for data that does not conform to a fixed schema.

- options – A list of options. Specify the target type if you choose the `Project` and `Cast` action type. Examples include the following:

```
1 >>>toDF([ResolveOption("a.b.c", "KeepAsStruct")])
2 >>>toDF([ResolveOption("a.b.c", "Project", DoubleType())])
```

— Information —

- count
- schema
- printSchema
- show

count

`count( )` – Returns the number of rows in the underlying `DataFrame`.

schema

`schema( )` – Returns the schema of this `DynamicFrame`, or if that is not available, the schema of the underlying `DataFrame`.

printSchema

`printSchema( )` – Prints the schema of the underlying `DataFrame`.

show

`show(num_rows)` – Prints a specified number of rows from the underlying `DataFrame`.

— Transforms —

- apply_mapping
- drop_fields
- filter
- join
- map
- relationalize
- rename_field
- resolveChoice
- select_fields

- spigot
- split_fields
- split_rows
- unbox
- unnest
- write

apply_mapping

`apply_mapping(mappings, transformation_ctx="", info="", stageThreshold=0, totalThreshold=0)`

Applies a declarative mapping to this `DynamicFrame` and returns a new `DynamicFrame` with those mappings applied.

- `mappings` – A list of mapping tuples, each consisting of: (source column, source type, target column, target type). Required.
- `transformation_ctx` – A unique string that is used to identify state information (optional).
- `info` – A string to be associated with error reporting for this transformation (optional).
- `stageThreshold` – The number of errors encountered during this transformation at which the process should error out (optional: zero by default, indicating that the process should not error out).
- `totalThreshold` – The number of errors encountered up to and including this transformation at which the process should error out (optional: zero by default, indicating that the process should not error out).

drop_fields

`drop_fields(paths, transformation_ctx="", info="", stageThreshold=0, totalThreshold=0)`

Calls the FlatMap Class transform to remove fields from a `DynamicFrame`. Returns a new `DynamicFrame` with the specified fields dropped.

- `paths` – A list of strings, each containing the full path to a field node you want to drop.
- `transformation_ctx` – A unique string that is used to identify state information (optional).
- `info` – A string to be associated with error reporting for this transformation (optional).
- `stageThreshold` – The number of errors encountered during this transformation at which the process should error out (optional: zero by default, indicating that the process should not error out).
- `totalThreshold` – The number of errors encountered up to and including this transformation at which the process should error out (optional: zero by default, indicating that the process should not error out).

filter

`filter(f, transformation_ctx="", info="", stageThreshold=0, totalThreshold=0)`

Returns a new `DynamicFrame` built by selecting all `DynamicRecords` within the input `DynamicFrame` that satisfy the specified predicate function `f`.

- `f` – The predicate function to apply to the `DynamicFrame`. The function must take a `DynamicRecord` as an argument and return True if the `DynamicRecord` meets the filter requirements, or False if not (required).

  A `DynamicRecord` represents a logical record in a `DynamicFrame`. It is similar to a row in a Spark `DataFrame`, except that it is self-describing and can be used for data that does not conform to a fixed schema.

- `transformation_ctx` – A unique string that is used to identify state information (optional).

- `info` – A string to be associated with error reporting for this transformation (optional).

- `stageThreshold` – The number of errors encountered during this transformation at which the process should error out (optional: zero by default, indicating that the process should not error out).

- **totalThreshold** – The number of errors encountered up to and including this transformation at which the process should error out (optional: zero by default, indicating that the process should not error out).

For an example of how to use the `filter` transform, see Filter Class.

join

```
join(paths1, paths2, frame2, transformation_ctx="", info="", stageThreshold=0,
totalThreshold=0)
```

Performs an equality join with another `DynamicFrame` and returns the resulting `DynamicFrame`.

- **paths1** – A list of the keys in this frame to join.
- **paths2** – A list of the keys in the other frame to join.
- **frame2** – The other `DynamicFrame` to join.
- **transformation_ctx** – A unique string that is used to identify state information (optional).
- **info** – A string to be associated with error reporting for this transformation (optional).
- **stageThreshold** – The number of errors encountered during this transformation at which the process should error out (optional: zero by default, indicating that the process should not error out).
- **totalThreshold** – The number of errors encountered up to and including this transformation at which the process should error out (optional: zero by default, indicating that the process should not error out).

map

```
map(f, transformation_ctx="", info="", stageThreshold=0, totalThreshold=0)
```

Returns a new `DynamicFrame` that results from applying the specified mapping function to all records in the original `DynamicFrame`.

- **f** – The mapping function to apply to all records in the `DynamicFrame`. The function must take a `DynamicRecord` as an argument and return a new `DynamicRecord` (required).

  A `DynamicRecord` represents a logical record in a `DynamicFrame`. It is similar to a row in an Apache Spark `DataFrame`, except that it is self-describing and can be used for data that does not conform to a fixed schema.

- **transformation_ctx** – A unique string that is used to identify state information (optional).

- **info** – A string associated with errors in the transformation (optional).

- **stageThreshold** – The maximum number of errors that can occur in the transformation before it errors out (optional; the default is zero).

- **totalThreshold** – The maximum number of errors that can occur overall before processing errors out (optional; the default is zero).

For an example of how to use the `map` transform, see Map Class.

relationalize

```
relationalize(root_table_name, staging_path, options, transformation_ctx="", info="",
stageThreshold=0, totalThreshold=0)
```

Relationalizes a `DynamicFrame` by producing a list of frames that are generated by unnesting nested columns and pivoting array columns. The pivoted array column can be joined to the root table using the joinkey generated during the unnest phase.

- **root_table_name** – The name for the root table.

- `staging_path` – The path at which to store partitions of pivoted tables in CSV format (optional). Pivoted tables are read back from this path.
- `options` – A dictionary of optional parameters.
- `transformation_ctx` – A unique string that is used to identify state information (optional).
- `info` – A string to be associated with error reporting for this transformation (optional).
- `stageThreshold` – The number of errors encountered during this transformation at which the process should error out (optional: zero by default, indicating that the process should not error out).
- `totalThreshold` – The number of errors encountered up to and including this transformation at which the process should error out (optional: zero by default, indicating that the process should not error out).

rename_field

```
rename_field(oldName, newName, transformation_ctx="", info="", stageThreshold=0,
totalThreshold=0)
```

Renames a field in this `DynamicFrame` and returns a new `DynamicFrame` with the field renamed.

- `oldName` – The full path to the node you want to rename.

  If the old name has dots in it, RenameField will not work unless you place back-ticks around it ("`"). For example, to replace `this.old.name` with 'thisNewName', you would call rename_field as follows:

```
1 newDyF = oldDyF.rename_field("`this.old.name`", "thisNewName")
```

- `newName` – The new name, as a full path.
- `transformation_ctx` – A unique string that is used to identify state information (optional).
- `info` – A string to be associated with error reporting for this transformation (optional).
- `stageThreshold` – The number of errors encountered during this transformation at which the process should error out (optional: zero by default, indicating that the process should not error out).
- `totalThreshold` – The number of errors encountered up to and including this transformation at which the process should error out (optional: zero by default, indicating that the process should not error out).

resolveChoice

```
resolveChoice(specs = None, option="", transformation_ctx="", info="", stageThreshold=0,
totalThreshold=0)
```

Resolves a choice type within this `DynamicFrame` and returns the new `DynamicFrame`.

- `specs` – A list of specific ambiguities to resolve, each in the form of a tuple: (`path`, `action`). The `path` value identifies a specific ambiguous element, and the `action` value identifies the corresponding resolution. Only one of the `specs` and `option` parameters can be used. If the `spec` parameter is not `None`, then the `option` parameter must be an empty string. Conversely if the `option` is not an empty string, then the `spec` parameter must be `None`. If neither parameter is provided, AWS Glue tries to parse the schema and use it to resolve ambiguities.

  The `action` portion of a `specs` tuple can specify one of four resolution strategies:
  - `cast`: Allows you to specify a type to cast to (for example, `cast:int`).
  - `make_cols`: Resolves a potential ambiguity by flattening the data. For example, if `columnA` could be an `int` or a `string`, the resolution would be to produce two columns named `columnA_int` and `columnA_string` in the resulting `DynamicFrame`.
  - `make_struct`: Resolves a potential ambiguity by using a struct to represent the data. For example, if data in a column could be an `int` or a `string`, using the `make_struct` action produces a column of structures in the resulting `DynamicFrame` that each contains both an `int` and a `string`.

- **project:** Resolves a potential ambiguity by projecting all the data to one of the possible data types. For example, if data in a column could be an `int` or a `string`, using a `project:string` action produces a column in the resulting `DynamicFrame` where all the `int` values have been converted to strings.

If the `path` identifies an array, place empty square brackets after the name of the array to avoid ambiguity. For example, suppose you are working with data structured as follows:

```
1  "myList": [
2    { "price": 100.00 },
3    { "price": "$100.00" }
4  ]
```

You can select the numeric rather than the string version of the price by setting the `path` to `"myList[].price"`, and the `action` to `"cast:double"`.

- **option** – The default resolution action if the `specs` parameter is `None`. If the `specs` parameter is not `None`, then this must not be set to anything but an empty string.

- **transformation_ctx** – A unique string that is used to identify state information (optional).

- **info** – A string to be associated with error reporting for this transformation (optional).

- **stageThreshold** – The number of errors encountered during this transformation at which the process should error out (optional: zero by default, indicating that the process should not error out).

- **totalThreshold** – The number of errors encountered up to and including this transformation at which the process should error out (optional: zero by default, indicating that the process should not error out).

Example

```
1  df1 = df.resolveChoice(option = "make_cols")
2  df2 = df.resolveChoice(specs = [("a.b", "make_struct"), ("c.d", "cast:double")])
```

select_fields

```
select_fields(paths, transformation_ctx="", info="", stageThreshold=0, totalThreshold=0)
```

Returns a new `DynamicFrame` containing the selected fields.

- **paths** – A list of strings, each of which is a full path to a node that you want to select.
- **transformation_ctx** – A unique string that is used to identify state information (optional).
- **info** – A string to be associated with error reporting for this transformation (optional).
- **stageThreshold** – The number of errors encountered during this transformation at which the process should error out (optional: zero by default, indicating that the process should not error out).
- **totalThreshold** – The number of errors encountered up to and including this transformation at which the process should error out (optional: zero by default, indicating that the process should not error out).

spigot

```
spigot(path, options={})
```

Writes sample records to a specified destination during a transformation, and returns the input `DynamicFrame` with an additional write step.

- **path** – The path to the destination to which to write (required).
- **options** – Key-value pairs specifying options (optional). The `"topk"` option specifies that the first k records should be written. The `"prob"` option specifies the probability of picking any given record, to be used in selecting records to write.

- `transformation_ctx` – A unique string that is used to identify state information (optional).

split_fields

`split_fields(paths, name1, name2, transformation_ctx="", info='", stageThreshold=0, totalThreshold=0)`

Returns a new `DynamicFrameCollection` that contains two `DynamicFrames`: the first containing all the nodes that have been split off, and the second containing the nodes that remain.

- `paths` – A list of strings, each of which is a full path to a node that you want to split into a new `DynamicFrame`.
- `name1` – A name string for the `DynamicFrame` that is split off.
- `name2` – A name string for the `DynamicFrame` that remains after the specified nodes have been split off.
- `transformation_ctx` – A unique string that is used to identify state information (optional).
- `info` – A string to be associated with error reporting for this transformation (optional).
- `stageThreshold` – The number of errors encountered during this transformation at which the process should error out (optional: zero by default, indicating that the process should not error out).
- `totalThreshold` – The number of errors encountered up to and including this transformation at which the process should error out (optional: zero by default, indicating that the process should not error out).

split_rows

Splits one or more rows in a `DynamicFrame` off into a new `DynamicFrame`.

`split_rows(comparison_dict, name1, name2, transformation_ctx="", info="", stageThreshold=0, totalThreshold=0)`

Returns a new `DynamicFrameCollection` containing two `DynamicFrames`: the first containing all the rows that have been split off and the second containing the rows that remain.

- `comparison_dict` – A dictionary in which the key is a path to a column and the value is another dictionary for mapping comparators to values to which the column value are compared. For example, `{"age": {">": 10, "<": 20}}` splits off all rows whose value in the age column is greater than 10 and less than 20.
- `name1` – A name string for the `DynamicFrame` that is split off.
- `name2` – A name string for the `DynamicFrame` that remains after the specified nodes have been split off.
- `transformation_ctx` – A unique string that is used to identify state information (optional).
- `info` – A string to be associated with error reporting for this transformation (optional).
- `stageThreshold` – The number of errors encountered during this transformation at which the process should error out (optional: zero by default, indicating that the process should not error out).
- `totalThreshold` – The number of errors encountered up to and including this transformation at which the process should error out (optional: zero by default, indicating that the process should not error out).

unbox

`unbox(path, format, transformation_ctx="", info="", stageThreshold=0, totalThreshold=0, ** options)`

Unboxes a string field in a `DynamicFrame` and returns a new `DynamicFrame` containing the unboxed `DynamicRecords`.

A `DynamicRecord` represents a logical record in a `DynamicFrame`. It is similar to a row in an Apache Spark `DataFrame`, except that it is self-describing and can be used for data that does not conform to a fixed schema.

- `path` – A full path to the string node you want to unbox.

- **format** – A format specification (optional). This is used for an Amazon Simple Storage Service (Amazon S3) or tape connection that supports multiple formats. See Format Options for ETL Output in AWS Glue for the formats that are supported.
- **transformation_ctx** – A unique string that is used to identify state information (optional).
- **info** – A string to be associated with error reporting for this transformation (optional).
- **stageThreshold** – The number of errors encountered during this transformation at which the process should error out (optional: zero by default, indicating that the process should not error out).
- **totalThreshold** – The number of errors encountered up to and including this transformation at which the process should error out (optional: zero by default, indicating that the process should not error out).
- **options** – One or more of the following:
  - **separator** – A string containing the separator character.
  - **escaper** – A string containing the escape character.
  - **skipFirst** – A Boolean value indicating whether to skip the first instance.
  - **withSchema** – A string containing the schema; must be called using `StructType.json( )`.
  - **withHeader** – A Boolean value indicating whether a header is included.

For example: `unbox("a.b.c", "csv", separator="|")`

unnest

Unnests nested objects in a `DynamicFrame`, making them top-level objects, and returns a new unnested `DynamicFrame`.

`unnest(transformation_ctx="", info="", stageThreshold=0, totalThreshold=0)`

Unnests nested objects in a `DynamicFrame`, making them top-level objects, and returns a new unnested `DynamicFrame`.

- **transformation_ctx** – A unique string that is used to identify state information (optional).
- **info** – A string to be associated with error reporting for this transformation (optional).
- **stageThreshold** – The number of errors encountered during this transformation at which the process should error out (optional: zero by default, indicating that the process should not error out).
- **totalThreshold** – The number of errors encountered up to and including this transformation at which the process should error out (optional: zero by default, indicating that the process should not error out).

For example: `unnest( )`

write

`write(connection_type, connection_options, format, format_options, accumulator_size)`

Gets a DataSink(object) of the specified connection type from the GlueContext Class of this `DynamicFrame`, and uses it to format and write the contents of this `DynamicFrame`. Returns the new `DynamicFrame` formatted and written as specified.

- **connection_type** – The connection type to use. Valid values include s3, `mysql`, `postgresql`, `redshift`, `sqlserver`, and `oracle`.

- **connection_options** – The connection option to use (optional). For a `connection_type` of s3, an Amazon S3 path is defined.

```
1 connection_options = {"path": "s3://aws-glue-target/temp"}
```

For JDBC connections, several properties must be defined. Note that the database name must be part of the URL. It can optionally be included in the connection options.

```
1 connection_options = {"url": "jdbc-url/database", "user": "username", "password": "password
     ","dbtable": "table-name", "redshiftTmpDir": "s3-tempdir-path"}
```

- `format` – A format specification (optional). This is used for an Amazon Simple Storage Service (Amazon S3) or tape connection that supports multiple formats. See Format Options for ETL Output in AWS Glue for the formats that are supported.

- `format_options` – Format options for the specified format. See Format Options for ETL Output in AWS Glue for the formats that are supported.

- `accumulator_size` – The accumulable size to use (optional).

— Errors —

- assertErrorThreshold
- errorsAsDynamicFrame
- errorsCount
- stageErrorsCount

assertErrorThreshold

`assertErrorThreshold( )` – An assert for errors in the transformations that created this `DynamicFrame`. Returns an `Exception` from the underlying `DataFrame`.

errorsAsDynamicFrame

`errorsAsDynamicFrame( )` – Returns a `DynamicFrame` that has error records nested inside.

errorsCount

`errorsCount( )` – Returns the total number of errors in a `DynamicFrame`.

stageErrorsCount

`stageErrorsCount` – Returns the number of errors that occurred in the process of generating this `DynamicFrame`.

DynamicFrameCollection Class

A `DynamicFrameCollection` is a dictionary of DynamicFrame Class objects, in which the keys are the names of the `DynamicFrames` and the values are the `DynamicFrame` objects.

___init___

`__init__(dynamic_frames, glue_ctx)`

- `dynamic_frames` – A dictionary of DynamicFrame Class objects.
- `glue_ctx` – A GlueContext Class object.

keys

`keys( )` – Returns a list of the keys in this collection, which generally consists of the names of the corresponding `DynamicFrame` values.

values

`values(key)` – Returns a list of the `DynamicFrame` values in this collection.

select

`select(key)`

Returns the `DynamicFrame` that corresponds to the specfied key (which is generally the name of the `DynamicFrame`).

- `key` – A key in the `DynamicFrameCollection`, which usually represents the name of a `DynamicFrame`.

map

`map(callable, transformation_ctx="")`

Uses a passed-in function to create and return a new `DynamicFrameCollection` based on the `DynamicFrames` in this collection.

- `callable` – A function that takes a `DynamicFrame` and the specified transformation context as parameters and returns a `DynamicFrame`.
- `transformation_ctx` – A transformation context to be used by the callable (optional).

flatmap

`flatmap(f, transformation_ctx="")`

Uses a passed-in function to create and return a new `DynamicFrameCollection` based on the `DynamicFrames` in this collection.

- `f` – A function that takes a `DynamicFrame` as a parameter and returns a `DynamicFrame` or `DynamicFrameCollection`.
- `transformation_ctx` – A transformation context to be used by the function (optional).

DynamicFrameWriter Class

Methods

- __init__
- from_options
- from_catalog
- from_jdbc_conf

__init__

`__init__(glue_context)`

- `glue_context` – The GlueContext Class to use.

from_options

`from_options(frame, connection_type, connection_options={}, format=None, format_options={}, transformation_ctx="")`

Writes a `DynamicFrame` using the specified connection and format.

- `frame` – The `DynamicFrame` to write.

- `connection_type` – The connection type. Valid values include `s3`, `mysql`, `postgresql`, `redshift`, `sqlserver`, and `oracle`.

- `connection_options` – Connection options, such as path and database table (optional). For a `connection_type` of `s3`, an Amazon S3 path is defined.

```
1 connection_options = {"path": "s3://aws-glue-target/temp"}
```

For JDBC connections, several properties must be defined. Note that the database name must be part of the URL. It can optionally be included in the connection options.

```
1 connection_options = {"url": "jdbc-url/database", "user": "username", "password": "password
   ","dbtable": "table-name", "redshiftTmpDir": "s3-tempdir-path"}
```

- `format` – A format specification (optional). This is used for an Amazon Simple Storage Service (Amazon S3) or tape connection that supports multiple formats. See Format Options for ETL Output in AWS Glue for the formats that are supported.

- `format_options` – Format options for the specified format. See Format Options for ETL Output in AWS Glue for the formats that are supported.

- `transformation_ctx` – A transformation context to use (optional).

from_catalog

`from_catalog(frame, name_space, table_name, redshift_tmp_dir="", transformation_ctx="")`

Writes a `DynamicFrame` using the specified catalog database and table name.

- `frame` – The `DynamicFrame` to write.
- `name_space` – The database to use.
- `table_name` – The `table_name` to use.
- `redshift_tmp_dir` – An Amazon Redshift temporary directory to use (optional).

- `transformation_ctx` – A transformation context to use (optional).

from__jdbc__conf

```
from_jdbc_conf(frame, catalog_connection, connection_options={}, redshift_tmp_dir = "",
transformation_ctx="")
```

Writes a `DynamicFrame` using the specified JDBC connection information.

- `frame` – The `DynamicFrame` to write.
- `catalog_connection` – A catalog connection to use.
- `connection_options` – Connection options, such as path and database table (optional).
- `redshift_tmp_dir` – An Amazon Redshift temporary directory to use (optional).
- `transformation_ctx` – A transformation context to use (optional).

DynamicFrameReader Class

— Methods —

- ___init___
- from_rdd
- from_options
- from_catalog

___init___

`__init__(glue_context)`

- `glue_context` – The GlueContext Class to use.

from_rdd

`from_rdd(data, name, schema=None, sampleRatio=None)`

Reads a `DynamicFrame` from a Resilient Distributed Dataset (RDD).

- `data` – The dataset to read from.
- `name` – The name to read from.
- `schema` – The schema to read (optional).
- `sampleRatio` – The sample ratio (optional).

from_options

`from_options(connection_type, connection_options={}, format=None, format_options={}, transformation_ctx="")`

Reads a `DynamicFrame` using the specified connection and format.

- `connection_type` – The connection type. Valid values include `s3`, `mysql`, `postgresql`, `redshift`, `sqlserver`, and `oracle`.

- `connection_options` – Connection options, such as path and database table (optional). For a `connection_type` of s3, Amazon S3 paths are defined in an array.

  1 `connection_options = {"paths": [ "s3://mybucket/object_a", "s3://mybucket/object_b"]}`

  For JDBC connections, several properties must be defined. Note that the database name must be part of the URL. It can optionally be included in the connection options.

  1 `connection_options = {"url": "jdbc-url/database", "user": "username", "password": "password","dbtable": "table-name", "redshiftTmpDir": "s3-tempdir-path"}`

- `format` – A format specification (optional). This is used for an Amazon Simple Storage Service (Amazon S3) or tape connection that supports multiple formats. See Format Options for ETL Output in AWS Glue for the formats that are supported.

- `format_options` – Format options for the specified format. See Format Options for ETL Output in AWS Glue for the formats that are supported.

- `transformation_ctx` – The transformation context to use (optional).

from_catalog

```
from_catalog(name_space, table_name, redshift_tmp_dir = "", transformation_ctx="")
```

Reads a `DynamicFrame` using the specified catalog namespace and table name.

- `name_space` – The database to read from.
- `table_name` – The name of the table to read from.
- `redshift_tmp_dir` – An Amazon Redshift temporary directory to use (optional).
- `transformation_ctx` – The transformation context to use (optional).

GlueContext Class

Wraps the Apache SparkSQL SQLContext object, and thereby provides mechanisms for interacting with the Apache Spark platform.

Creating

- ___init___
- getSource
- create_dynamic_frame_from_rdd
- create_dynamic_frame_from_catalog
- create_dynamic_frame_from_options

___init___

`__init__(sparkContext)`

- sparkContext – The Apache Spark context to use.

getSource

`getSource(connection_type, transformation_ctx = "", **options)`

Creates a `DataSource` object that can be used to read `DynamicFrames` from external sources.

- connection_type – The connection type to use, such as Amazon S3, Amazon Redshift, and JDBC. Valid values include s3, mysql, postgresql, redshift, sqlserver, and oracle.
- transformation_ctx – The transformation context to use (optional).
- options – A collection of optional name-value pairs.

The following is an example of using `getSource`:

```
1 >>> data_source = context.getSource("file", paths=["/in/path"])
2 >>> data_source.setFormat("json")
3 >>> myFrame = data_source.getFrame()
```

create_dynamic_frame_from_rdd

`create_dynamic_frame_from_rdd(data, name, schema=None, sample_ratio=None, transformation_ctx ="")`

Returns a `DynamicFrame` that is created from an Apache Spark Resilient Distributed Dataset (RDD).

- data – The data source to use.
- name – The name of the data to use.
- schema – The schema to use (optional).
- sample_ratio – The sample ratio to use (optional).
- transformation_ctx – The transformation context to use (optional).

create_dynamic_frame_from_catalog

```
create_dynamic_frame_from_catalog(database, table_name, redshift_tmp_dir, transformation_ctx
  = "")
```

Returns a `DynamicFrame` that is created using a catalog database and table name.

- `Database` – The database to read from.
- `table_name` – The name of the table to read from.
- `redshift_tmp_dir` – An Amazon Redshift temporary directory to use (optional).
- `transformation_ctx` – The transformation context to use (optional).

create_dynamic_frame_from_options

```
create_dynamic_frame_from_options(connection_type, connection_options={}, format=None,
format_options={}, transformation_ctx = "")
```

Returns a `DynamicFrame` created with the specified connection and format.

- `connection_type` – The connection type, such as Amazon S3, Amazon Redshift, and JDBC. Valid values include `s3`, `mysql`, `postgresql`, `redshift`, `sqlserver`, and `oracle`.

- `connection_options` – Connection options, such as path and database table (optional). For a `connection_type` of s3, an Amazon S3 path is defined.

```
1 connection_options = {"paths": ["s3://aws-glue-target/temp"]}
```

For JDBC connections, several properties must be defined. Note that the database name must be part of the URL. It can optionally be included in the connection options.

```
1 connection_options = {"url": "jdbc-url/database", "user": "username", "password": "password
    ","dbtable": "table-name", "redshiftTmpDir": "s3-tempdir-path"}
```

- `format` – A format specification (optional). This is used for an Amazon Simple Storage Service (Amazon S3) or tape connection that supports multiple formats. See Format Options for ETL Output in AWS Glue for the formats that are supported.

- `format_options` – Format options for the specified format. See Format Options for ETL Output in AWS Glue for the formats that are supported.

- `transformation_ctx` – The transformation context to use (optional).

Writing

- getSink
- write_dynamic_frame_from_options
- write_from_options
- write_dynamic_frame_from_catalog
- write_dynamic_frame_from_jdbc_conf
- write_from_jdbc_conf

getSink

```
getSink(connection_type, format = None, transformation_ctx = "", **options)
```

Gets a `DataSink` object that can be used to write `DynamicFrames` to external sources. Check the SparkSQL `format` first to be sure to get the expected sink.

- connection_type – The connection type to use, such as Amazon S3, Amazon Redshift, and JDBC. Valid values include s3, mysql, postgresql, redshift, sqlserver, and oracle.
- format – The SparkSQL format to use (optional).
- transformation_ctx – The transformation context to use (optional).
- options – A collection of option name-value pairs.

For example:

```
1 >>> data_sink = context.getSink("s3")
2 >>> data_sink.setFormat("json"),
3 >>> data_sink.writeFrame(myFrame)
```

write_dynamic_frame_from_options

```
write_dynamic_frame_from_options(frame, connection_type, connection_options={}, format=None,
 format_options={}, transformation_ctx = "")
```

Writes and returns a DynamicFrame using the specified connection and format.

- frame – The DynamicFrame to write.

- connection_type – The connection type, such as Amazon S3, Amazon Redshift, and JDBC. Valid values include s3, mysql, postgresql, redshift, sqlserver, and oracle.

- connection_options – Connection options, such as path and database table (optional). For a connection_type of s3, an Amazon S3 path is defined.

```
1 connection_options = {"path": "s3://aws-glue-target/temp"}
```

  For JDBC connections, several properties must be defined. Note that the database name must be part of the URL. It can optionally be included in the connection options.

```
1 connection_options = {"url": "jdbc-url/database", "user": "username", "password": "password
    ","dbtable": "table-name", "redshiftTmpDir": "s3-tempdir-path"}
```

- format – A format specification (optional). This is used for an Amazon Simple Storage Service (Amazon S3) or tape connection that supports multiple formats. See Format Options for ETL Output in AWS Glue for the formats that are supported.

- format_options – Format options for the specified format. See Format Options for ETL Output in AWS Glue for the formats that are supported.

- transformation_ctx – A transformation context to use (optional).

write_from_options

```
write_from_options(frame_or_dfc, connection_type, connection_options={}, format={},
format_options={}, transformation_ctx = "")
```

Writes and returns a DynamicFrame or DynamicFrameCollection that is created with the specified connection and format information.

- frame_or_dfc – The DynamicFrame or DynamicFrameCollection to write.

- connection_type – The connection type, such as Amazon S3, Amazon Redshift, and JDBC. Valid values include s3, mysql, postgresql, redshift, sqlserver, and oracle.

- connection_options – Connection options, such as path and database table (optional). For a connection_type of s3, an Amazon S3 path is defined.

```
1 connection_options = {"path": "s3://aws-glue-target/temp"}
```

For JDBC connections, several properties must be defined. Note that the database name must be part of the URL. It can optionally be included in the connection options.

```
1 connection_options = {"url": "jdbc-url/database", "user": "username", "password": "password
    ","dbtable": "table-name", "redshiftTmpDir": "s3-tempdir-path"}
```

- `format` – A format specification (optional). This is used for an Amazon Simple Storage Service (Amazon S3) or tape connection that supports multiple formats. See Format Options for ETL Output in AWS Glue for the formats that are supported.

- `format_options` – Format options for the specified format. See Format Options for ETL Output in AWS Glue for the formats that are supported.

- `transformation_ctx` – A transformation context to use (optional).

write_dynamic_frame_from_catalog

```
write_dynamic_frame_from_catalog(frame, database, table_name, redshift_tmp_dir,
transformation_ctx = "")
```

Writes and returns a `DynamicFrame` using a catalog database and a table name.

- `frame` – The `DynamicFrame` to write.
- `Database` – The database to read from.
- `table_name` – The name of the table to read from.
- `redshift_tmp_dir` – An Amazon Redshift temporary directory to use (optional).
- `transformation_ctx` – The transformation context to use (optional).

write_dynamic_frame_from_jdbc_conf

```
write_dynamic_frame_from_jdbc_conf(frame, catalog_connection, connection_options={},
redshift_tmp_dir = "", transformation_ctx = "")
```

Writes and returns a `DynamicFrame` using the specified JDBC connection information.

- `frame` – The `DynamicFrame` to write.
- `catalog_connection` – A catalog connection to use.
- `connection_options` – Connection options, such as path and database table (optional).
- `redshift_tmp_dir` – An Amazon Redshift temporary directory to use (optional).
- `transformation_ctx` – A transformation context to use (optional).

write_from_jdbc_conf

```
write_from_jdbc_conf(frame_or_dfc, catalog_connection, connection_options={},
redshift_tmp_dir = "", transformation_ctx = "")
```

Writes and returns a `DynamicFrame` or `DynamicFrameCollection` using the specified JDBC connection information.

- `frame_or_dfc` – The `DynamicFrame` or `DynamicFrameCollection` to write.
- `catalog_connection` – A catalog connection to use.
- `connection_options` – Connection options, such as path and database table (optional).
- `redshift_tmp_dir` – An Amazon Redshift temporary directory to use (optional).
- `transformation_ctx` – A transformation context to use (optional).

AWS Glue PySpark Transforms Reference

AWS Glue has created the following transform Classes to use in PySpark ETL operations.

- GlueTransform Base Class
- ApplyMapping Class
- DropFields Class
- DropNullFields Class
- ErrorsAsDynamicFrame Class
- Filter Class
- Join Class
- Map Class
- MapToCollection Class
- Relationalize Class
- RenameField Class
- ResolveChoice Class
- SelectFields Class
- SelectFromCollection Class
- Spigot Class
- SplitFields Class
- SplitRows Class
- Unbox Class
- UnnestFrame Class

GlueTransform Base Class

The base class that all the `awsglue.transforms` classes inherit from.

The classes all define a `__call__` method. They either override the `GlueTransform` class methods listed in the following sections, or they are called using the class name by default.

Methods

- apply(cls, *args, **kwargs)
- name(cls)
- describeArgs(cls)
- describeReturn(cls)
- describeTransform(cls)
- describeErrors(cls)
- describe(cls)

apply(cls, *args, **kwargs)

Applies the transform by calling the transform class, and returns the result.

- `cls` – The `self` class object.

name(cls)

Returns the name of the derived transform class.

- `cls` – The `self` class object.

describeArgs(cls)

- `cls` – The `self` class object.

Returns a list of dictionaries, each corresponding to a named argument, in the following format:

```
[
  {
    "name": "(name of argument)",
    "type": "(type of argument)",
    "description": "(description of argument)",
    "optional": "(Boolean, True if the argument is optional)",
    "defaultValue": "(Default value string, or None)(String; the default value, or None)"
  },
  ...
]
```

Raises a `NotImplementedError` exception when called in a derived transform where it is not implemented.

describeReturn(cls)

- `cls` – The `self` class object.

Returns a dictionary with information about the return type, in the following format:

```
1 {
2   "type": "(return type)",
3   "description": "(description of output)"
4 }
```

Raises a `NotImplementedError` exception when called in a derived transform where it is not implemented.

describeTransform(cls)

Returns a string describing the transform.

- `cls` – The `self` class object.

Raises a `NotImplementedError` exception when called in a derived transform where it is not implemented.

describeErrors(cls)

- `cls` – The `self` class object.

Returns a list of dictionaries, each describing a possible exception thrown by this transform, in the following format:

```
1 [
2   {
3     "type": "(type of error)",
4     "description": "(description of error)"
5   },
6 ...
7 ]
```

describe(cls)

- `cls` – The `self` class object.

Returns an object with the following format:

```
1 {
2   "transform" : {
3     "name" : cls.name( ),
4     "args" : cls.describeArgs( ),
5     "returns" : cls.describeReturn( ),
6     "raises" : cls.describeErrors( ),
7     "location" : "internal"
8   }
9 }
```

ApplyMapping Class

Applies a mapping in a `DynamicFrame`.

Methods

- ___call___
- apply
- name
- describeArgs
- describeReturn
- describeTransform
- describeErrors
- describe

___call___(frame, mappings, transformation_ctx = "", info = "", stageThreshold = 0, totalThreshold = 0)

Applies a declarative mapping to a specified `DynamicFrame`.

- `frame` – The `DynamicFrame` in which to apply the mapping (required).
- `mappings` – A list of mapping tuples, each consisting of: (source column, source type, target column, target type). Required.
- `transformation_ctx` – A unique string that is used to identify state information (optional).
- `info` – A string associated with errors in the transformation (optional).
- `stageThreshold` – The maximum number of errors that can occur in the transformation before it errors out (optional; the default is zero).
- `totalThreshold` – The maximum number of errors that can occur overall before processing errors out (optional; the default is zero).

Returns a new `DynamicFrame` in which the mapping has been applied.

apply(cls, *args, **kwargs)

Inherited from `GlueTransform` apply.

name(cls)

Inherited from `GlueTransform` name.

describeArgs(cls)

Inherited from `GlueTransform` describeArgs.

describeReturn(cls)

Inherited from `GlueTransform` describeReturn.

describeTransform(cls)

Inherited from `GlueTransform` describeTransform.

describeErrors(cls)

Inherited from `GlueTransform` describeErrors.

describe(cls)

Inherited from `GlueTransform` describe.

DropFields Class

Drops fields within a `DynamicFrame`.

Methods

- ___call___
- apply
- name
- describeArgs
- describeReturn
- describeTransform
- describeErrors
- describe

___call___(frame, paths, transformation_ctx = "", info = "", stageThreshold = 0, totalThreshold = 0)

Drops nodes within a `DynamicFrame`.

- `frame` – The `DynamicFrame` in which to drop the nodes (required).
- `paths` – A list of full paths to the nodes to drop (required).
- `transformation_ctx` – A unique string that is used to identify state information (optional).
- `info` – A string associated with errors in the transformation (optional).
- `stageThreshold` – The maximum number of errors that can occur in the transformation before it errors out (optional; the default is zero).
- `totalThreshold` – The maximum number of errors that can occur overall before processing errors out (optional; the default is zero).

Returns a new `DynamicFrame` without the specified fields.

apply(cls, *args, **kwargs)

Inherited from `GlueTransform` apply.

name(cls)

Inherited from `GlueTransform` name.

describeArgs(cls)

Inherited from `GlueTransform` describeArgs.

describeReturn(cls)

Inherited from `GlueTransform` describeReturn.

describeTransform(cls)

Inherited from `GlueTransform` describeTransform.

describeErrors(cls)

Inherited from `GlueTransform` describeErrors.

describe(cls)

Inherited from `GlueTransform` describe.

DropNullFields Class

Drops all null fields in a `DynamicFrame` whose type is `NullType`. These are fields with missing or null values in every record in the `DynamicFrame` data set.

Methods

- ___call___
- apply
- name
- describeArgs
- describeReturn
- describeTransform
- describeErrors
- describe

___call___(frame, transformation_ctx = "", info = "", stageThreshold = 0, totalThreshold = 0)

Drops all null fields in a `DynamicFrame` whose type is `NullType`. These are fields with missing or null values in every record in the `DynamicFrame` data set.

- `frame` – The `DynamicFrame` in which to drop null fields (required).
- `transformation_ctx` – A unique string that is used to identify state information (optional).
- `info` – A string associated with errors in the transformation (optional).
- `stageThreshold` – The maximum number of errors that can occur in the transformation before it errors out (optional; the default is zero).
- `totalThreshold` – The maximum number of errors that can occur overall before processing errors out (optional; the default is zero).

Returns a new `DynamicFrame` with no null fields.

apply(cls, *args, **kwargs)

- `cls` – cls

name(cls)

- `cls` – cls

describeArgs(cls)

- `cls` – cls

describeReturn(cls)

- `cls` – cls

describeTransform(cls)

- cls – cls

describeErrors(cls)

- cls – cls

describe(cls)

- cls – cls

ErrorsAsDynamicFrame Class

Returns a `DynamicFrame` that contains nested error records leading up to the creation of the source `DynamicFrame`.

Methods

- __call__
- apply
- name
- describeArgs
- describeReturn
- describeTransform
- describeErrors
- describe

__call__(frame)

Returns a `DynamicFrame` that contains nested error records relating to the source `DynamicFrame`.

- `frame` – The source `DynamicFrame` (required).

apply(cls, *args, **kwargs)

- `cls` – cls

name(cls)

- `cls` – cls

describeArgs(cls)

- `cls` – cls

describeReturn(cls)

- `cls` – cls

describeTransform(cls)

- `cls` – cls

describeErrors(cls)

- `cls` – cls

describe(cls)

- cls – cls

Filter Class

Builds a new `DynamicFrame` by selecting records from the input `DynamicFrame` that satisfy a specified predicate function.

Methods

- ___call___
- apply
- name
- describeArgs
- describeReturn
- describeTransform
- describeErrors
- describe
- Example Code

___call___(frame, f, transformation_ctx="", info="", stageThreshold=0, totalThreshold=0))

Returns a new `DynamicFrame` built by selecting records from the input `DynamicFrame` that satisfy a specified predicate function.

- `frame` – The source `DynamicFrame` to apply the specified filter function to (required).

- `f` – The predicate function to apply to each `DynamicRecord` in the `DynamicFrame`. The function must take a `DynamicRecord` as its argument and return True if the `DynamicRecord` meets the filter requirements, or False if it does not (required).

  A `DynamicRecord` represents a logical record in a `DynamicFrame`. It is similar to a row in a Spark `DataFrame`, except that it is self-describing and can be used for data that does not conform to a fixed schema.

- `transformation_ctx` – A unique string that is used to identify state information (optional).

- `info` – A string associated with errors in the transformation (optional).

- `stageThreshold` – The maximum number of errors that can occur in the transformation before it errors out (optional; the default is zero).

- `totalThreshold` – The maximum number of errors that can occur overall before processing errors out (optional; the default is zero).

apply(cls, *args, **kwargs)

Inherited from `GlueTransform` apply.

name(cls)

Inherited from `GlueTransform` name.

describeArgs(cls)

Inherited from `GlueTransform` describeArgs.

describeReturn(cls)

Inherited from `GlueTransform` describeReturn.

describeTransform(cls)

Inherited from `GlueTransform` describeTransform.

describeErrors(cls)

Inherited from `GlueTransform` describeErrors.

describe(cls)

Inherited from `GlueTransform` describe.

AWS Glue Python Example

This example filters sample data using the `Filter` transform and a simple Lambda function. The dataset used here consists of Medicare Provider payment data downloaded from two `Data.CMS.gov` sites: Inpatient Prospective Payment System Provider Summary for the Top 100 Diagnosis-Related Groups - FY2011), and Inpatient Charge Data FY 2011.

After downloading the sample data, we modified it to introduce a couple of erroneous records at the end of the file. This modified file is located in a public Amazon S3 bucket at `s3://awsglue-datasets/examples/medicare/Medicare_Hospital_Provider.csv`. For another example that uses this dataset, see Code Example: Data Preparation Using ResolveChoice, Lambda, and ApplyMapping.

Begin by creating a `DynamicFrame` for the data:

```
1 %pyspark
2 from awsglue.context import GlueContext
3 from awsglue.transforms import *
4 from pyspark.context import SparkContext
5
6 glueContext = GlueContext(SparkContext.getOrCreate())
7
8 dyF = glueContext.create_dynamic_frame.from_options(
9         's3',
10        {'paths': ['s3://awsglue-datasets/examples/medicare/Medicare_Hospital_Provider.csv']},
11        'csv',
12        {'withHeader': True})
13
14 print "Full record count:  ", dyF.count()
15 dyF.printSchema()
```

The output should be as follows:

```
1 Full record count:   163065L
2 root
3 |-- DRG Definition: string
4 |-- Provider Id: string
5 |-- Provider Name: string
```

```
 6 |-- Provider Street Address: string
 7 |-- Provider City: string
 8 |-- Provider State: string
 9 |-- Provider Zip Code: string
10 |-- Hospital Referral Region Description: string
11 |-- Total Discharges: string
12 |-- Average Covered Charges: string
13 |-- Average Total Payments: string
14 |-- Average Medicare Payments: string
```

Next, use the `Filter` transform to condense the dataset, retaining only those entries that are from Sacramento, California, or from Montgomery, Alabama. The filter transform works with any filter function that takes a `DynamicRecord` as input and returns True if the `DynamicRecord` meets the filter requirements, or False if not.

Note

You can use Python's dot notation to access many fields in a `DynamicRecord`. For example, you can access the `column_A` field in `dynamic_record_X` as: `dynamic_record_X.column_A`.

However, this technique doesn't work with field names that contain anything besides alphanumeric characters and underscores. For fields that contain other characters, such as spaces or periods, you must fall back to Python's dictionary notation. For example, to access a field named `col-B`, use: `dynamic_record_X["col-B"]`.

You can use a simple Lambda function with the `Filter` transform to remove all `DynamicRecords` that don't originate in Sacramento or Montgomery. To confirm that this worked, print out the number of records that remain:

```
1 sac_or_mon_dyF = Filter.apply(frame = dyF,
2                               f = lambda x: x["Provider State"] in ["CA", "AL"] and x["Provider
                                  City"] in ["SACRAMENTO", "MONTGOMERY"])
3 print "Filtered record count: ", sac_or_mon_dyF.count()
```

The output that you get looks like the following:

```
Filtered record count:  564L
```

FlatMap Class

Applies a transform to each `DynamicFrame` in a collection and flattens the results.

Methods

- ___call___
- apply
- name
- describeArgs
- describeReturn
- describeTransform
- describeErrors
- describe

___call___(dfc, BaseTransform, frame_name, transformation_ctx = "", **base_kwargs)

Applies a transform to each `DynamicFrame` in a collection and flattens the results.

- `dfc` – The `DynamicFrameCollection` over which to flatmap (required).
- `BaseTransform` – A transform derived from `GlueTransform` to apply to each member of the collection (required).
- `frame_name` – The argument name to pass the elements of the collection to (required).
- `transformation_ctx` – A unique string that is used to identify state information (optional).
- `base_kwargs` – Arguments to pass to the base transform (required).

Returns a new `DynamicFrameCollection` created by applying the transform to each `DynamicFrame` in the source `DynamicFrameCollection`.

apply(cls, *args, **kwargs)

Inherited from `GlueTransform` apply.

name(cls)

Inherited from `GlueTransform` name.

describeArgs(cls)

Inherited from `GlueTransform` describeArgs.

describeReturn(cls)

Inherited from `GlueTransform` describeReturn.

describeTransform(cls)

Inherited from `GlueTransform` describeTransform.

describeErrors(cls)

Inherited from `GlueTransform` describeErrors.

describe(cls)

Inherited from `GlueTransform` describe.

Join Class

Performs an equality join on two `DynamicFrames`.

Methods

- `__call__`
- apply
- name
- describeArgs
- describeReturn
- describeTransform
- describeErrors
- describe

`__call__`(frame1, frame2, keys1, keys2, transformation_ctx = "")

Performs an equality join on two `DynamicFrames`.

- `frame1` – The first `DynamicFrame` to join (required).
- `frame2` – The second `DynamicFrame` to join (required).
- `keys1` – The keys to join on for the first frame (required).
- `keys2` – The keys to join on for the second frame (required).
- `transformation_ctx` – A unique string that is used to identify state information (optional).

Returns a new `DynamicFrame` obtained by joining the two `DynamicFrames`.

apply(cls, *args, **kwargs)

Inherited from `GlueTransform` apply

name(cls)

Inherited from `GlueTransform` name

describeArgs(cls)

Inherited from `GlueTransform` describeArgs

describeReturn(cls)

Inherited from `GlueTransform` describeReturn

describeTransform(cls)

Inherited from `GlueTransform` describeTransform

describeErrors(cls)

Inherited from `GlueTransform` describeErrors

describe(cls)

Inherited from `GlueTransform` describe

Map Class

Builds a new `DynamicFrame` by applying a function to all records in the input `DynamicFrame`.

Methods

- ___call___
- apply
- name
- describeArgs
- describeReturn
- describeTransform
- describeErrors
- describe
- Example Code

___call___(frame, f, transformation_ctx="", info="", stageThreshold=0, totalThreshold=0)

Returns a new `DynamicFrame` that results from applying the specified function to all `DynamicRecords` in the original `DynamicFrame`.

- `frame` – The original `DynamicFrame` to which to apply the mapping function (required).

- `f` – The function to apply to all `DynamicRecords` in the `DynamicFrame`. The function must take a `DynamicRecord` as an argument and return a new `DynamicRecord` produced by the mapping (required).

  A `DynamicRecord` represents a logical record in a `DynamicFrame`. It is similar to a row in an Apache Spark `DataFrame`, except that it is self-describing and can be used for data that does not conform to a fixed schema.

- `transformation_ctx` – A unique string that is used to identify state information (optional).

- `info` – A string associated with errors in the transformation (optional).

- `stageThreshold` – The maximum number of errors that can occur in the transformation before it errors out (optional; the default is zero).

- `totalThreshold` – The maximum number of errors that can occur overall before processing errors out (optional; the default is zero).

Returns a new `DynamicFrame` that results from applying the specified function to all `DynamicRecords` in the original `DynamicFrame`.

apply(cls, *args, **kwargs)

Inherited from `GlueTransform` apply.

name(cls)

Inherited from `GlueTransform` name.

describeArgs(cls)

Inherited from `GlueTransform` describeArgs.

describeReturn(cls)

Inherited from `GlueTransform` describeReturn.

describeTransform(cls)

Inherited from `GlueTransform` describeTransform.

describeErrors(cls)

Inherited from `GlueTransform` describeErrors.

describe(cls)

Inherited from `GlueTransform` describe.

AWS Glue Python Example

This example uses the `Map` transform to merge several fields into one `struct` type. The dataset that is used here consists of Medicare Provider payment data downloaded from two `Data.CMS.gov` sites: Inpatient Prospective Payment System Provider Summary for the Top 100 Diagnosis-Related Groups - FY2011), and Inpatient Charge Data FY 2011.

After downloading the sample data, we modified it to introduce a couple of erroneous records at the end of the file. This modified file is located in a public Amazon S3 bucket at `s3://awsglue-datasets/examples/medicare/Medicare_Hospital_Provider.csv`. For another example that uses this dataset, see Code Example: Data Preparation Using ResolveChoice, Lambda, and ApplyMapping.

Begin by creating a `DynamicFrame` for the data:

```
1  from awsglue.context import GlueContext
2  from awsglue.transforms import *
3  from pyspark.context import SparkContext
4
5  glueContext = GlueContext(SparkContext.getOrCreate())
6
7  dyF = glueContext.create_dynamic_frame.from_options(
8        's3',
9        {'paths': ['s3://awsglue-datasets/examples/medicare/Medicare_Hospital_Provider.csv']},
10       'csv',
11       {'withHeader': True})
12
13 print "Full record count:  ", dyF.count()
14 dyF.printSchema()
```

The output of this code should be as follows:

```
1 Full record count:  163065L
2 root
3 |-- DRG Definition: string
4 |-- Provider Id: string
5 |-- Provider Name: string
6 |-- Provider Street Address: string
7 |-- Provider City: string
8 |-- Provider State: string
9 |-- Provider Zip Code: string
10 |-- Hospital Referral Region Description: string
11 |-- Total Discharges: string
12 |-- Average Covered Charges: string
13 |-- Average Total Payments: string
14 |-- Average Medicare Payments: string
```

Next, create a mapping function to merge provider-address fields in a `DynamicRecord` into a `struct`, and then delete the individual address fields:

```
1 def MergeAddress(rec):
2    rec["Address"] = {}
3    rec["Address"]["Street"] = rec["Provider Street Address"]
4    rec["Address"]["City"] = rec["Provider City"]
5    rec["Address"]["State"] = rec["Provider State"]
6    rec["Address"]["Zip.Code"] = rec["Provider Zip Code"]
7    rec["Address"]["Array"] = [rec["Provider Street Address"], rec["Provider City"], rec["Provider
          State"], rec["Provider Zip Code"]]
8    del rec["Provider Street Address"]
9    del rec["Provider City"]
10   del rec["Provider State"]
11   del rec["Provider Zip Code"]
12   return rec
```

In this mapping function, the line `rec["Address"] = {}` creates a dictionary in the input `DynamicRecord` that contains the new structure.

Note
Python `map` fields are *not* supported here. For example, you can't have a line like the following:
`rec["Addresses"] = [] # ILLEGAL!`

The lines that are like `rec["Address"]["Street"] = rec["Provider Street Address"]` add fields to the new structure using Python dictionary syntax.

After the address lines are added to the new structure, the lines that are like `del rec["Provider Street Address"]` remove the individual fields from the `DynamicRecord`.

Now you can use the `Map` transform to apply your mapping function to all `DynamicRecords` in the `DynamicFrame`.

```
1 mapped_dyF = Map.apply(frame = dyF, f = MergeAddress)
2 mapped_dyF.printSchema()
```

The output is as follows:

```
1 root
2 |-- Average Total Payments: string
3 |-- Average Covered Charges: string
4 |-- DRG Definition: string
5 |-- Average Medicare Payments: string
6 |-- Hospital Referral Region Description: string
```

```
 7 |-- Address: struct
 8 |  |-- Zip.Code: string
 9 |  |-- City: string
10 |  |-- Array: array
11 |  |  |-- element: string
12 |  |-- State: string
13 |  |-- Street: string
14 |-- Provider Id: string
15 |-- Total Discharges: string
16 |-- Provider Name: string
```

MapToCollection Class

Applies a transform to each `DynamicFrame` in the specified `DynamicFrameCollection`.

Methods

- __call__
- apply
- name
- describeArgs
- describeReturn
- describeTransform
- describeErrors
- describe

__call__(dfc, BaseTransform, frame_name, transformation_ctx = "", **base_kwargs)

Applies a transform function to each `DynamicFrame` in the specified `DynamicFrameCollection`.

- `dfc` – The `DynamicFrameCollection` over which to apply the transform function (required).
- `callable` – A callable transform function to apply to each member of the collection (required).
- `transformation_ctx` – A unique string that is used to identify state information (optional).

Returns a new `DynamicFrameCollection` created by applying the transform to each `DynamicFrame` in the source `DynamicFrameCollection`.

apply(cls, *args, **kwargs)

Inherited from `GlueTransform` apply

name(cls)

Inherited from `GlueTransform` name.

describeArgs(cls)

Inherited from `GlueTransform` describeArgs.

describeReturn(cls)

Inherited from `GlueTransform` describeReturn.

describeTransform(cls)

Inherited from `GlueTransform` describeTransform.

describeErrors(cls)

Inherited from `GlueTransform` describeErrors.

describe(cls)

Inherited from `GlueTransform` describe.

Relationalize Class

Flattens nested schema in a `DynamicFrame` and pivots out array columns from the flattened frame.

Methods

- ___call___
- apply
- name
- describeArgs
- describeReturn
- describeTransform
- describeErrors
- describe

___call___(frame, staging_path=None, name='roottable', options=None, transformation_ctx = "", info = "", stageThreshold = 0, totalThreshold = 0)

Relationalizes a `DynamicFrame` and produces a list of frames that are generated by unnesting nested columns and pivoting array columns. The pivoted array column can be joined to the root table using the joinkey generated in the unnest phase.

- `frame` – The `DynamicFrame` to relationalize (required).
- `staging_path` – The path at which to store partitions of pivoted tables in CSV format (optional). Pivoted tables are read back from this path.
- `name` – The name of the root table (optional).
- `options` – A dictionary of optional parameters.
- `transformation_ctx` – A unique string that is used to identify state information (optional).
- `info` – A string associated with errors in the transformation (optional).
- `stageThreshold` – The maximum number of errors that can occur in the transformation before it errors out (optional; the default is zero).
- `totalThreshold` – The maximum number of errors that can occur overall before processing errors out (optional; the default is zero).

Return a `DynamicFrameCollection` containing the `DynamicFrames` produced by from the relationalize operation.

apply(cls, *args, **kwargs)

Inherited from `GlueTransform` apply.

name(cls)

Inherited from `GlueTransform` name.

describeArgs(cls)

Inherited from `GlueTransform` describeArgs.

describeReturn(cls)

Inherited from `GlueTransform` describeReturn.

describeTransform(cls)

Inherited from `GlueTransform` describeTransform.

describeErrors(cls)

Inherited from `GlueTransform` describeErrors.

describe(cls)

Inherited from `GlueTransform` describe.

RenameField Class

Renames a node within a `DynamicFrame`.

Methods

- ___call___
- apply
- name
- describeArgs
- describeReturn
- describeTransform
- describeErrors
- describe

___call___(frame, old_name, new_name, transformation_ctx = "", info = "", stageThreshold = 0, totalThreshold = 0)

Renames a node within a `DynamicFrame`.

- `frame` – The `DynamicFrame` in which to rename a node (required).

- `old_name` – Full path to the node to rename (required).

  If the old name has dots in it, RenameField will not work unless you place back-ticks around it ("`"). For example, to replace `this.old.name` with 'thisNewName', you would call RenameField as follows:

  ```
  1 newDyF = RenameField(oldDyF, "`this.old.name`", "thisNewName")
  ```

- `new_name` – New name, including full path (required).

- `transformation_ctx` – A unique string that is used to identify state information (optional).

- `info` – A string associated with errors in the transformation (optional).

- `stageThreshold` – The maximum number of errors that can occur in the transformation before it errors out (optional; the default is zero).

- `totalThreshold` – The maximum number of errors that can occur overall before processing errors out (optional; the default is zero).

Returns a `DynamicFrame` with the specified field renamed.

apply(cls, *args, **kwargs)

Inherited from `GlueTransform` apply.

name(cls)

Inherited from `GlueTransform` name.

describeArgs(cls)

Inherited from `GlueTransform` describeArgs.

describeReturn(cls)

Inherited from `GlueTransform` describeReturn.

describeTransform(cls)

Inherited from `GlueTransform` describeTransform.

describeErrors(cls)

Inherited from `GlueTransform` describeErrors.

describe(cls)

Inherited from `GlueTransform` describe.

ResolveChoice Class

Resolves a choice type within a `DynamicFrame`.

Methods

- ___call___
- apply
- name
- describeArgs
- describeReturn
- describeTransform
- describeErrors
- describe

___call___(frame, specs = None, choice = "", transformation_ctx = "", info = "", stageThreshold = 0, totalThreshold = 0)

Provides information for resolving ambiguous types within a `DynamicFrame`. Returns the resulting `DynamicFrame`.

- `frame` – The `DynamicFrame` in which to resolve the choice type (required).

- `specs` – A list of specific ambiguities to resolve, each in the form of a tuple:`(path, action)`. The `path` value identifies a specific ambiguous element, and the `action` value identifies the corresponding resolution. Only one of the `spec` and `choice` parameters can be used. If the `spec` parameter is not `None`, then the `choice` parameter must be an empty string. Conversely if the `choice` is not an empty string, then the `spec` parameter must be `None`. If neither parameter is provided, AWS Glue tries to parse the schema and use it to resolve ambiguities.

  The `action` portion of a `specs` tuple can specify one of four resolution strategies:

  - `cast`: Allows you to specify a type to cast to (for example, `cast:int`).
  - `make_cols`: Resolves a potential ambiguity by flattening the data. For example, if `columnA` could be an `int` or a `string`, the resolution is to produce two columns named `columnA_int` and `columnA_string` in the resulting `DynamicFrame`.
  - `make_struct`: Resolves a potential ambiguity by using a struct to represent the data. For example, if data in a column could be an `int` or a `string`, using the `make_struct` action produces a column of structures in the resulting `DynamicFrame` with each containing both an `int` and a `string`.
  - `project`: Resolves a potential ambiguity by projecting all the data to one of the possible data types. For example, if data in a column could be an `int` or a `string`, using a `project:string` action produces a column in the resulting `DynamicFrame` where all the `int` values are converted to strings.

  If the `path` identifies an array, place empty square brackets after the name of the array to avoid ambiguity. For example, suppose you are working with data structured as follows:

```
1 "myList": [
2   { "price": 100.00 },
3   { "price": "$100.00" }
4 ]
```

  You can select the numeric rather than the string version of the price by setting the `path` to `"myList[]. price"`, and the `action` to `"cast:double"`.

- `choice` – The default resolution action if the `specs` parameter is `None`. If the `specs` parameter is not `None`, then this must not be set to anything but an empty string.

- `transformation_ctx` – A unique string that is used to identify state information (optional).

- `info` – A string associated with errors in the transformation (optional).

- `stageThreshold` – The maximum number of errors that can occur in the transformation before it errors out (optional; the default is zero).

- `totalThreshold` – The maximum number of errors that can occur overall before processing errors out (optional; the default is zero).

Returns a `DynamicFrame` with the resolved choice.

Example

```
1 df1 = ResolveChoice.apply(df, choice = "make_cols")
2 df2 = ResolveChoice.apply(df, specs = [("a.b", "make_struct"), ("c.d", "cast:double")])
```

apply(cls, *args, **kwargs)

Inherited from `GlueTransform` apply.

name(cls)

Inherited from `GlueTransform` name.

describeArgs(cls)

Inherited from `GlueTransform` describeArgs.

describeReturn(cls)

Inherited from `GlueTransform` describeReturn.

describeTransform(cls)

Inherited from `GlueTransform` describeTransform.

describeErrors(cls)

Inherited from `GlueTransform` describeErrors.

describe(cls)

Inherited from `GlueTransform` describe.

SelectFields Class

Gets fields in a `DynamicFrame`.

Methods

- ___call___
- apply
- name
- describeArgs
- describeReturn
- describeTransform
- describeErrors
- describe

___call___(frame, paths, transformation_ctx = "", info = "", stageThreshold = 0, totalThreshold = 0)

Gets fields (nodes) in a `DynamicFrame`.

- `frame` – The `DynamicFrame` in which to select fields (required).
- `paths` – A list of full paths to the fields to select (required).
- `transformation_ctx` – A unique string that is used to identify state information (optional).
- `info` – A string associated with errors in the transformation (optional).
- `stageThreshold` – The maximum number of errors that can occur in the transformation before it errors out (optional; the default is zero).
- `totalThreshold` – The maximum number of errors that can occur overall before processing errors out (optional; the default is zero).

Returns a new `DynamicFrame` containing only the specified fields.

apply(cls, *args, **kwargs)

Inherited from `GlueTransform` apply.

name(cls)

Inherited from `GlueTransform` name.

describeArgs(cls)

Inherited from `GlueTransform` describeArgs.

describeReturn(cls)

Inherited from `GlueTransform` describeReturn.

describeTransform(cls)

Inherited from `GlueTransform` describeTransform.

describeErrors(cls)

Inherited from `GlueTransform` describeErrors.

describe(cls)

Inherited from `GlueTransform` describe.

SelectFromCollection Class

Selects one `DynamicFrame` in a `DynamicFrameCollection`.

Methods

- ___call___
- apply
- name
- describeArgs
- describeReturn
- describeTransform
- describeErrors
- describe

___call___(dfc, key, transformation_ctx = "")

Gets one `DynamicFrame` from a `DynamicFrameCollection`.

- `dfc` – The key of the `DynamicFrame` to select (required).
- `transformation_ctx` – A unique string that is used to identify state information (optional).

Returns the specified `DynamicFrame`.

apply(cls, *args, **kwargs)

Inherited from `GlueTransform` apply.

name(cls)

Inherited from `GlueTransform` name.

describeArgs(cls)

Inherited from `GlueTransform` describeArgs.

describeReturn(cls)

Inherited from `GlueTransform` describeReturn.

describeTransform(cls)

Inherited from `GlueTransform` describeTransform.

describeErrors(cls)

Inherited from `GlueTransform` describeErrors.

describe(cls)

Inherited from `GlueTransform` describe.

Spigot Class

Writes sample records to a specified destination during a transformation.

Methods

- __call__
- apply
- name
- describeArgs
- describeReturn
- describeTransform
- describeErrors
- describe

__call__(frame, path, options, transformation_ctx = "")

Writes sample records to a specified destination during a transformation.

- `frame` – The `DynamicFrame` to spigot (required).
- `path` – The path to the destination to write to (required).
- `options` – JSON key-value pairs specifying options (optional). The `"topk"` option specifies that the first k records should be written. The `"prob"` option specifies the probability of picking any given record, to be used in selecting records to write.
- `transformation_ctx` – A unique string that is used to identify state information (optional).

Returns the input `DynamicFrame` with an additional write step.

apply(cls, *args, **kwargs)

Inherited from `GlueTransform` apply

name(cls)

Inherited from `GlueTransform` name

describeArgs(cls)

Inherited from `GlueTransform` describeArgs

describeReturn(cls)

Inherited from `GlueTransform` describeReturn

describeTransform(cls)

Inherited from `GlueTransform` describeTransform

describeErrors(cls)

Inherited from `GlueTransform` describeErrors

describe(cls)

Inherited from `GlueTransform` describe

SplitFields Class

Splits a `DynamicFrame` into two new ones, by specified fields.

Methods

- ___call___
- apply
- name
- describeArgs
- describeReturn
- describeTransform
- describeErrors
- describe

___call___(frame, paths, name1 = None, name2 = None, transformation_ctx = "", info = "", stageThreshold = 0, totalThreshold = 0)

Splits one or more fields in a `DynamicFrame` off into a new `DynamicFrame` and creates another new `DynamicFrame` containing the fields that remain.

- `frame` – The source `DynamicFrame` to split into two new ones (required).
- `paths` – A list of full paths to the fields to be split (required).
- `name1` – The name to assign to the `DynamicFrame` that will contain the fields to be split off (optional). If no name is supplied, the name of the source frame is used with "1" appended.
- `name2` – The name to assign to the `DynamicFrame` that will contain the fields that remain after the specified fields are split off (optional). If no name is provided, the name of the source frame is used with "2" appended.
- `transformation_ctx` – A unique string that is used to identify state information (optional).
- `info` – A string associated with errors in the transformation (optional).
- `stageThreshold` – The maximum number of errors that can occur in the transformation before it errors out (optional; the default is zero).
- `totalThreshold` – The maximum number of errors that can occur overall before processing errors out (optional; the default is zero).

Returns a `DynamicFrameCollection` containing two `DynamicFrames`: one contains only the specified fields to split off, and the other contains the remaining fields.

apply(cls, *args, **kwargs)

Inherited from `GlueTransform` apply.

name(cls)

Inherited from `GlueTransform` name.

describeArgs(cls)

Inherited from `GlueTransform` describeArgs.

describeReturn(cls)

Inherited from `GlueTransform` describeReturn.

describeTransform(cls)

Inherited from `GlueTransform` describeTransform.

describeErrors(cls)

Inherited from `GlueTransform` describeErrors.

describe(cls)

Inherited from `GlueTransform` describe.

SplitRows Class

Splits a `DynamicFrame` in two by specified rows.

Methods

- ___call___
- apply
- name
- describeArgs
- describeReturn
- describeTransform
- describeErrors
- describe

___call___(frame, comparison_dict, name1="frame1", name2="frame2", transformation_ctx = "", info = None, stageThreshold = 0, totalThreshold = 0)

Splits one or more rows in a `DynamicFrame` off into a new `DynamicFrame`.

- `frame` – The source `DynamicFrame` to split into two new ones (required).
- `comparison_dict` – A dictionary where the key is the full path to a column, and the value is another dictionary mapping comparators to the value to which the column values are compared. For example, `{"age": {">": 10, "<": 20}}` splits rows where the value of "age" is between 10 and 20, exclusive, from rows where "age" is outside that range (required).
- `name1` – The name to assign to the `DynamicFrame` that will contain the rows to be split off (optional).
- `name2` – The name to assign to the `DynamicFrame` that will contain the rows that remain after the specified rows are split off (optional).
- `transformation_ctx` – A unique string that is used to identify state information (optional).
- `info` – A string associated with errors in the transformation (optional).
- `stageThreshold` – The maximum number of errors that can occur in the transformation before it errors out (optional; the default is zero).
- `totalThreshold` – The maximum number of errors that can occur overall before processing errors out (optional; the default is zero).

Returns a `DynamicFrameCollection` that contains two `DynamicFrames`: one contains only the specified rows to be split, and the other contains all remaining rows.

apply(cls, *args, **kwargs)

Inherited from `GlueTransform` apply.

name(cls)

Inherited from `GlueTransform` name.

describeArgs(cls)

Inherited from `GlueTransform` describeArgs.

describeReturn(cls)

Inherited from `GlueTransform` describeReturn.

describeTransform(cls)

Inherited from `GlueTransform` describeTransform.

describeErrors(cls)

Inherited from `GlueTransform` describeErrors.

describe(cls)

Inherited from `GlueTransform` describe.

Unbox Class

Unboxes a string field in a `DynamicFrame`.

Methods

- ___call___
- apply
- name
- describeArgs
- describeReturn
- describeTransform
- describeErrors
- describe

___call___(frame, path, format, transformation_ctx = "", info="", stageThreshold=0, totalThreshold=0, **options)

Unboxes a string field in a `DynamicFrame`.

- `frame` – The `DynamicFrame` in which to unbox a field. (required).
- `path` – The full path to the `StringNode` to unbox (required).
- `format` – A format specification (optional). This is used for an Amazon Simple Storage Service (Amazon S3) or tape connection that supports multiple formats. See Format Options for ETL Output in AWS Glue for the formats that are supported.
- `transformation_ctx` – A unique string that is used to identify state information (optional).
- `info` – A string associated with errors in the transformation (optional).
- `stageThreshold` – The maximum number of errors that can occur in the transformation before it errors out (optional; the default is zero).
- `totalThreshold` – The maximum number of errors that can occur overall before processing errors out (optional; the default is zero).
- `separator` – A separator token (optional).
- `escaper` – An escape token (optional).
- `skipFirst` – `True` if the first line of data should be skipped, or `False` if it should not be skipped (optional).
- withSchema" – A string containing schema for the data to be unboxed (optional). This should always be created using `StructType.json`.
- `withHeader` – `True` if the data being unpacked includes a header, or `False` if not (optional).

Returns a new `DynamicFrame` with unboxed `DynamicRecords`.

apply(cls, *args, **kwargs)

Inherited from `GlueTransform` apply.

name(cls)

Inherited from `GlueTransform` name.

describeArgs(cls)

Inherited from `GlueTransform` describeArgs.

describeReturn(cls)

Inherited from `GlueTransform` describeReturn.

describeTransform(cls)

Inherited from `GlueTransform` describeTransform.

describeErrors(cls)

Inherited from `GlueTransform` describeErrors.

describe(cls)

Inherited from `GlueTransform` describe.

UnnestFrame Class

Unnests a `DynamicFrame`, flattens nested objects to top-level elements, and generates joinkeys for array objects.

Methods

- ___call___
- apply
- name
- describeArgs
- describeReturn
- describeTransform
- describeErrors
- describe

___call___(frame, transformation_ctx = "", info="", stageThreshold=0, totalThreshold=0)

Unnests a `DynamicFrame`. Flattens nested objects to top-level elements, and generates joinkeys for array objects.

- `frame` – The DynamicFrame to unnest (required).
- `transformation_ctx` – A unique string that is used to identify state information (optional).
- `info` – A string associated with errors in the transformation (optional).
- `stageThreshold` – The maximum number of errors that can occur in the transformation before it errors out (optional; the default is zero).
- `totalThreshold` – The maximum number of errors that can occur overall before processing errors out (optional; the default is zero).

Returns the unnested `DynamicFrame`.

apply(cls, *args, **kwargs)

Inherited from `GlueTransform` apply.

name(cls)

Inherited from `GlueTransform` name.

describeArgs(cls)

Inherited from `GlueTransform` describeArgs.

describeReturn(cls)

Inherited from `GlueTransform` describeReturn.

describeTransform(cls)

Inherited from `GlueTransform` describeTransform.

describeErrors(cls)

Inherited from `GlueTransform` describeErrors.

describe(cls)

Inherited from `GlueTransform` describe.

Programming AWS Glue ETL Scripts in Scala

You can find Scala code examples and utilities for AWS Glue in the AWS Glue samples repository on the GitHub website.

AWS Glue supports an extension of the PySpark Scala dialect for scripting extract, transform, and load (ETL) jobs. The following sections describe how to use the AWS Glue Scala library and the AWS Glue API in ETL scripts, and provide reference documentation for the library.

Contents

- Using Scala
  - Testing on a DevEndpoint Notebook
  - Testing on a DevEndpoint REPL
- Scala API List
  - com.amazonaws.services.glue
  - com.amazonaws.services.glue.types
  - com.amazonaws.services.glue.util
  - ChoiceOption
    - ChoiceOption Trait
    - ChoiceOption Object
      - apply
    - ChoiceOptionWithResolver
    - MatchCatalogSchemaChoiceOption
  - DataSink
    - writeDynamicFrame
    - pyWriteDynamicFrame
    - supportsFormat
    - setFormat
    - withFormat
    - setAccumulableSize
    - getOutputErrorRecordsAccumulable
    - errorsAsDynamicFrame
    - DataSink Object
      - recordMetrics
  - DataSource trait
  - DynamicFrame
    - DynamicFrame Class
      - errorsCount
      - applyMapping
      - assertErrorThreshold
      - count
      - dropField
      - dropFields
      - dropNulls
      - errorsAsDynamicFrame
      - filter
      - getName
      - getNumPartitions
      - getSchemaIfComputed
      - isSchemaComputed
      - javaToPython
      - join
      - map
      - printSchema

- recomputeSchema
- relationalize
- renameField
- repartition
- resolveChoice
- schema
- selectField
- selectFields
- show
- spigot
- splitFields
- def splitRows
- stageErrorsCount
- toDF
- unbox
- unnest
- withFrameSchema
- def withName
- withTransformationContext
  - DynamicFrame Object
    - def apply
    - def emptyDynamicFrame
    - def fromPythonRDD
    - def ignoreErrors
    - def inlineErrors
    - def newFrameWithErrors
- DynamicRecord
  - addField
  - dropField
  - setError
  - isError
  - getError
  - clearError
  - write
  - readFields
  - clone
  - schema
  - getRoot
  - toJson
  - getFieldNode
  - getField
  - hashCode
  - equals
  - DynamicRecord object
    - apply
  - RecordTraverser trait
- GlueContext
  - getCatalogSink
  - getCatalogSource
  - getJDBCSink
  - getSink
  - getSinkWithFormat
  - getSource
  - getSourceWithFormat

- getSparkSession
- this
- this
- this
- MappingSpec
  - MappingSpec Case Class
  - MappingSpec Object
  - orderingByTarget
  - apply
  - apply
  - apply
- ResolveSpec
  - ResolveSpec Object
    - def
    - def
  - ResolveSpec Case Class
    - def Methods
- ArrayNode
  - ArrayNode Case Class
    - def Methods
- BinaryNode
  - BinaryNode Case Class
    - val Fields
    - def Methods
- BooleanNode
  - BooleanNode Case Class
    - val Fields
    - def Methods
- ByteNode
  - ByteNode Case Class
    - val Fields
    - def Methods
- DateNode
  - DateNode Case Class
    - val Fields
    - def Methods
- DecimalNode
  - DecimalNode Case Class
    - val Fields
    - def Methods
- DoubleNode
  - DoubleNode Case Class
    - val Fields
    - def Methods
- DynamicNode
  - DynamicNode Class
    - def Methods
  - DynamicNode Object
    - def Methods
- FloatNode
  - FloatNode Case Class
    - val Fields
    - def Methods
- IntegerNode

- IntegerNode Case Class
  - val Fields
  - def Methods
- LongNode
  - LongNode Case Class
    - val Fields
    - def Methods
- MapLikeNode
  - MapLikeNode Class
    - def Methods
- MapNode
  - MapNode Case Class
    - def Methods
- NullNode
  - NullNode Class
  - NullNode Case Object
- ObjectNode
  - ObjectNode Object
    - def Methods
  - ObjectNode Case Class
    - def Methods
- ScalarNode
  - ScalarNode Class
    - def Methods
  - ScalarNode Object
    - def Methods
- ShortNode
  - ShortNode Case Class
    - val Fields
    - def Methods
- StringNode
  - StringNode Case Class
    - val Fields
    - def Methods
- TimestampNode
  - TimestampNode Case Class
    - val Fields
    - def Methods
- GlueArgParser
  - GlueArgParser Object
    - def Methods
- Job
  - Job Object
    - def Methods

Using Scala to Program AWS Glue ETL Scripts

You can automatically generate a Scala extract, transform, and load (ETL) program using the AWS Glue console, and modify it as needed before assigning it to a job. Or, you can write your own program from scratch. For more information, see Adding Jobs in AWS Glue. AWS Glue then compiles your Scala program on the server before running the associated job.

To ensure that your program compiles without errors and runs as expected, it's important that you load it on a development endpoint in a REPL (Read-Eval-Print Loop) or an Apache Zeppelin Notebook and test it there before running it in a job. Because the compile process occurs on the server, you will not have good visibility into any problems that happen there.

Testing a Scala ETL Program in a Zeppelin Notebook on a Development Endpoint

To test a Scala program on an AWS Glue development endpoint, set up the development endpoint as described in Using Development Endpoints.

Next, connect it to an Apache Zeppelin Notebook that is either running locally on your machine or remotely on an Amazon EC2 notebook server. To install a local version of a Zeppelin Notebook, follow the instructions in Tutorial: Local Zeppelin Notebook.

The only difference between running Scala code and running PySpark code on your Notebook is that you should start each paragraph on the Notebook with the the following:

```
1 %spark
```

This prevents the Notebook server from defaulting to the PySpark flavor of the Spark interpreter.

Testing a Scala ETL Program in a Scala REPL

You can test a Scala program on a development endpoint using the AWS Glue Scala REPL. Follow the instructions in Tutorial: Use a REPL Shell, except at the end of the SSH-to-REPL command, replace -t gluepyspark with -t glue-spark-shell. This invokes the AWS Glue Scala REPL.

To close the REPL when you are finished, type sys.exit.

APIs in the AWS Glue Scala Library

AWS Glue supports an extension of the PySpark Scala dialect for scripting extract, transform, and load (ETL) jobs. The following sections describe the APIs in the AWS Glue Scala library.

com.amazonaws.services.glue

The **com.amazonaws.services.glue** package in the AWS Glue Scala library contains the following APIs:

- ChoiceOption
- DataSink
- DataSource trait
- DynamicFrame
- DynamicRecord
- GlueContext
- MappingSpec
- ResolveSpec

com.amazonaws.services.glue.types

The **com.amazonaws.services.glue.types** package in the AWS Glue Scala library contains the following APIs:

- ArrayNode
- BinaryNode
- BooleanNode
- ByteNode
- DateNode
- DecimalNode
- DoubleNode
- DynamicNode
- FloatNode
- IntegerNode
- LongNode
- MapLikeNode
- MapNode
- NullNode
- ObjectNode
- ScalarNode
- ShortNode
- StringNode
- TimestampNode

com.amazonaws.services.glue.util

The **com.amazonaws.services.glue.util** package in the AWS Glue Scala library contains the following APIs:

- GlueArgParser
- Job

MappingSpec

Package: com.amazonaws.services.glue

MappingSpec Case Class

```
1 case class MappingSpec( sourcePath: SchemaPath,
2                         sourceType: DataType,
3                         targetPath: SchemaPath,
4                         targetType: DataTyp
5                         ) extends Product4[String, String, String, String] {
6   override def _1: String = sourcePath.toString
7   override def _2: String = ExtendedTypeName.fromDataType(sourceType)
8   override def _3: String = targetPath.toString
9   override def _4: String = ExtendedTypeName.fromDataType(targetType)
10 }
```

- sourcePath — The SchemaPath of the source field.
- sourceType — The DataType of the source field.
- targetPath — The SchemaPath of the target field.
- targetType — The DataType of the target field.

A MappingSpec specifies a mapping from a source path and a source data type to a target path and a target data type. The value at the source path in the source frame appears in the target frame at the target path. The source data type is cast to the target data type.

It extends from Product4 so that you can handle any Product4 in your applyMapping interface.

MappingSpec Object

```
1 object MappingSpec
```

The MappingSpec object has the following members:

val orderingByTarget

```
1 val orderingByTarget: Ordering[MappingSpec]
```

def apply

```
1 def apply( sourcePath : String,
2            sourceType : DataType,
3            targetPath : String,
4            targetType : DataType
5          ) : MappingSpec
```

Creates a MappingSpec.

- sourcePath — A string representation of the source path.
- sourceType — The source DataType.
- targetPath — A string representation of the target path.
- targetType — The target DataType.

Returns a MappingSpec.

def apply

```
1 def apply( sourcePath : String,
2            sourceTypeString : String,
3            targetPath : String,
4            targetTypeString : String
5          ) : MappingSpec
```

Creates a `MappingSpec`.

- `sourcePath` — A string representation of the source path.
- `sourceType` — A string representation of the source data type.
- `targetPath` — A string representation of the target path.
- `targetType` — A string representation of the target data type.

Returns a `MappingSpec`.

def apply

```
1 def apply( product : Product4[String, String, String, String] ) : MappingSpec
```

Creates a `MappingSpec`.

- `product` — The `Product4` of the source path, source data type, target path, and target data type.

Returns a `MappingSpec`.

AWS Glue Scala ChoiceOption APIs

Topics

- ChoiceOption Trait
- ChoiceOption Object
- case class ChoiceOptionWithResolver
- case class MatchCatalogSchemaChoiceOption

Package: com.amazonaws.services.glue

ChoiceOption Trait

```
1 trait ChoiceOption extends Serializable
```

ChoiceOption Object

ChoiceOption

```
1 object ChoiceOption
```

A general strategy to resolve choice applicable to all `ChoiceType` nodes in a `DynamicFrame`.

- `val CAST`
- `val MAKE_COLS`
- `val MAKE_STRUCT`
- `val MATCH_CATALOG`
- `val PROJECT`

def apply

```
1 def apply(choice: String): ChoiceOption
```

case class ChoiceOptionWithResolver

```
1 case class ChoiceOptionWithResolver(name: String, choiceResolver: ChoiceResolver) extends
    ChoiceOption {}
```

case class MatchCatalogSchemaChoiceOption

```
1 case class MatchCatalogSchemaChoiceOption() extends ChoiceOption {}
```

Abstract DataSink Class

Topics

- def writeDynamicFrame
- def pyWriteDynamicFrame
- def supportsFormat
- def setFormat
- def withFormat
- def setAccumulableSize
- def getOutputErrorRecordsAccumulable

- def errorsAsDynamicFrame
- DataSink Object

Package: com.amazonaws.services.glue

```
1 abstract class DataSink
```

The writer analog to a `DataSource`. `DataSink` encapsulates a destination and a format that a `DynamicFrame` can be written to.

def writeDynamicFrame

```
1 def writeDynamicFrame( frame : DynamicFrame,
2                        callSite : CallSite = CallSite("Not provided", "")
3                      ) : DynamicFrame
```

def pyWriteDynamicFrame

```
1 def pyWriteDynamicFrame( frame : DynamicFrame,
2                          site : String = "Not provided",
3                          info : String = "" )
```

def supportsFormat

```
1 def supportsFormat( format : String ) : Boolean
```

def setFormat

```
1 def setFormat( format : String,
2               options : JsonOptions
3             ) : Unit
```

def withFormat

```
1 def withFormat( format : String,
2               options : JsonOptions = JsonOptions.empty
3             ) : DataSink
```

def setAccumulableSize

```
1 def setAccumulableSize( size : Int ) : Unit
```

def getOutputErrorRecordsAccumulable

```
1 def getOutputErrorRecordsAccumulable : Accumulable[List[OutputError], OutputError]
```

def errorsAsDynamicFrame

```
1 def errorsAsDynamicFrame : DynamicFrame
```

DataSink Object

```
1 object DataSink
```

def recordMetrics

```
1 def recordMetrics( frame : DynamicFrame,
2                    ctxt : String
3                   ) : DynamicFrame
```

AWS Glue Scala DataSource Trait

Package: com.amazonaws.services.glue

A high-level interface for producing a DynamicFrame.

```
1 trait DataSource {
2
3   def getDynamicFrame : DynamicFrame
4
5   def getDynamicFrame( minPartitions : Int,
6                        targetPartitions : Int
7                       ) : DynamicFrame
8
9   def glueContext : GlueContext
10
11  def setFormat( format : String,
12                 options : String
13               ) : Unit
14
15  def setFormat( format : String,
16                 options : JsonOptions
17               ) : Unit
18
19  def supportsFormat( format : String ) : Boolean
20
21  def withFormat( format : String,
22                  options : JsonOptions = JsonOptions.empty
23                ) : DataSource
24 }
```

AWS Glue Scala DynamicFrame APIs

Package: com.amazonaws.services.glue

Contents

- AWS Glue Scala DynamicFrame Class
    - val errorsCount
    - def applyMapping
    - def assertErrorThreshold
    - def count
    - def dropField
    - def dropFields
    - def dropNulls
    - def errorsAsDynamicFrame
    - def filter
    - def getName
    - def getNumPartitions
    - def getSchemaIfComputed
    - def isSchemaComputed
    - def javaToPython
    - def join
    - def map
    - def printSchema
    - def recomputeSchema
    - def relationalize
    - def renameField
    - def repartition
    - def resolveChoice
    - def schema
    - def selectField
    - def selectFields
    - def show
    - def spigot
    - def splitFields
    - def splitRows
    - def stageErrorsCount
    - def toDF
    - def unbox
    - def unnest
    - def withFrameSchema
    - def withName
    - def withTransformationContext
- The DynamicFrame Object
    - def apply
    - def emptyDynamicFrame
    - def fromPythonRDD
    - def ignoreErrors
    - def inlineErrors
    - def newFrameWithErrors

AWS Glue Scala DynamicFrame Class

Package: com.amazonaws.services.glue

```
1  class DynamicFrame extends Serializable with Logging  (
2          val glueContext : GlueContext,
3          _records : RDD[DynamicRecord],
4          val name : String = s"",
5          val transformationContext : String = DynamicFrame.UNDEFINED,
6          callSite : CallSite = CallSite("Not provided", ""),
7          stageThreshold : Long = 0,
8          totalThreshold : Long = 0,
9          prevErrors : => Long = 0,
10         errorExpr : => Unit = {} )
```

A `DynamicFrame` is a distributed collection of self-describing DynamicRecord objects.

DynamicFrames are designed to provide a flexible data model for ETL (extract, transform, and load) operations. They don't require a schema to create, and you can use them to read and transform data that contains messy or inconsistent values and types. A schema can be computed on demand for those operations that need one.

DynamicFrames provide a range of transformations for data cleaning and ETL. They also support conversion to and from SparkSQL DataFrames to integrate with existing code and the many analytics operations that DataFrames provide.

The following parameters are shared across many of the AWS Glue transformations that construct DynamicFrames:

- `transformationContext` — The identifier for this `DynamicFrame`. The `transformationContext` is used as a key for job bookmark state that is persisted across runs.
- `callSite` — Provides context information for error reporting. These values are automatically set when calling from Python.
- `stageThreshold` — The maximum number of error records that are allowed from the computation of this `DynamicFrame` before throwing an exception, excluding records that are present in the previous `DynamicFrame`.
- `totalThreshold` — The maximum number of total error records before an exception is thrown, including those from previous frames.

val errorsCount

```
1  val errorsCount
```

The number of error records in this `DynamicFrame`. This includes errors from previous operations.

def applyMapping

```
1  def applyMapping( mappings : Seq[Product4[String, String, String, String]],
2          caseSensitive : Boolean = true,
3          transformationContext : String = "",
4          callSite : CallSite = CallSite("Not provided", ""),
5          stageThreshold : Long = 0,
6          totalThreshold : Long = 0
7      ) : DynamicFrame
```

- `mappings` — A sequence of mappings to construct a new `DynamicFrame`.
- `caseSensitive` — Whether to treat source columns as case sensitive. Setting this to false might help when integrating with case-insensitive stores like the AWS Glue Data Catalog.

Selects, projects, and casts columns based on a sequence of mappings.

Each mapping is made up of a source column and type and a target column and type. Mappings can be specified as either a four-tuple (`source_path`, `source_type`,`target_path`, `target_type`) or a MappingSpec object containing the same information.

In addition to using mappings for simple projections and casting, you can use them to nest or unnest fields by separating components of the path with '.' (period).

For example, suppose that you have a `DynamicFrame` with the following schema:

```
{{{
  root
  |-- name: string
  |-- age: int
  |-- address: struct
  |      |-- state: string
  |      |-- zip: int
}}}
```

You can make the following call to unnest the `state` and `zip` fields:

```
{{{
  df.applyMapping(
    Seq(("name", "string", "name", "string"),
        ("age", "int", "age", "int"),
        ("address.state", "string", "state", "string"),
        ("address.zip", "int", "zip", "int")))
}}}
```

The resulting schema is as follows:

```
{{{
  root
   |-- name: string
   |-- age: int
   |-- state: string
   |-- zip: int
}}}
```

You can also use `applyMapping` to re-nest columns. For example, the following inverts the previous transformation and creates a struct named `address` in the target:

```
{{{
  df.applyMapping(
    Seq(("name", "string", "name", "string"),
        ("age", "int", "age", "int"),
        ("state", "string", "address.state", "string"),
        ("zip", "int", "address.zip", "int")))
}}}
```

Field names that contain '.' (period) characters can be quoted by using backticks (' ').

Note
Currently, you can't use the `applyMapping` method to map columns that are nested under arrays.

def assertErrorThreshold

```
1 def assertErrorThreshold : Unit
```

An action that forces computation and verifies that the number of error records falls below `stageThreshold` and `totalThreshold`. Throws an exception if either condition fails.

def count

```
1 lazy
2 def count
```

Returns the number of elements in this `DynamicFrame`.

def dropField

```
1 def dropField( path : String,
2                transformationContext : String = "",
3                callSite : CallSite = CallSite("Not provided", ""),
4                stageThreshold : Long = 0,
5                totalThreshold : Long = 0
6              ) : DynamicFrame
```

Returns a new `DynamicFrame` with the specified column removed.

def dropFields

```
1 def dropFields( fieldNames : Seq[String],    // The column names to drop.
2                transformationContext : String = "",
3                callSite : CallSite = CallSite("Not provided", ""),
4                stageThreshold : Long = 0,
5                totalThreshold : Long = 0
6              ) : DynamicFrame
```

Returns a new `DynamicFrame` with the specified columns removed.

You can use this method to delete nested columns, including those inside of arrays, but not to drop specific array elements.

def dropNulls

```
1 def dropNulls( transformationContext : String = "",
2                callSite : CallSite = CallSite("Not provided", ""),
3                stageThreshold : Long = 0,
4                totalThreshold : Long = 0 )
```

Returns a new `DynamicFrame` with all null columns removed.

Note
This only removes columns of type `NullType`. Individual null values in other columns are not removed or modified.

def errorsAsDynamicFrame

```
1 def errorsAsDynamicFrame
```

Returns a new `DynamicFrame` containing the error records from this `DynamicFrame`.

def filter

```
1 def filter( f : DynamicRecord => Boolean,
2            errorMsg : String = "",
3            transformationContext : String = "",
4            callSite : CallSite = CallSite("Not provided"),
5            stageThreshold : Long = 0,
6            totalThreshold : Long = 0
7          ) : DynamicFrame
```

Constructs a new DynamicFrame containing only those records for which the function 'f' returns true. The filter function 'f' should not mutate the input record.

def getName

```
1 def getName : String
```

Returns the name of this DynamicFrame.

def getNumPartitions

```
1 def getNumPartitions
```

Returns the number of partitions in this DynamicFrame.

def getSchemaIfComputed

```
1 def getSchemaIfComputed : Option[Schema]
```

Returns the schema if it has already been computed. Does not scan the data if the schema has not already been computed.

def isSchemaComputed

```
1 def isSchemaComputed : Boolean
```

Returns true if the schema has been computed for this DynamicFrame, or false if not. If this method returns false, then calling the schema method requires another pass over the records in this DynamicFrame.

def javaToPython

```
1 def javaToPython : JavaRDD[Array[Byte]]
```

def join

```
1 def join( keys1 : Seq[String],
2          keys2 : Seq[String],
3          frame2 : DynamicFrame,
4          transformationContext : String = "",
5          callSite : CallSite = CallSite("Not provided", ""),
6          stageThreshold : Long = 0,
7          totalThreshold : Long = 0
8        ) : DynamicFrame
```

- keys1 — The columns in this DynamicFrame to use for the join.
- keys2 — The columns in frame2 to use for the join. Must be the same length as keys1.
- frame2 — The DynamicFrame to join against.

Returns the result of performing an equijoin with frame2 using the specified keys.

def map

```
1 def map( f : DynamicRecord => DynamicRecord,
2          errorMsg : String = "",
3          transformationContext : String = "",
4          callSite : CallSite = CallSite("Not provided", ""),
5          stageThreshold : Long = 0,
6          totalThreshold : Long = 0
7        ) : DynamicFrame
```

Returns a new `DynamicFrame` constructed by applying the specified function 'f' to each record in this `DynamicFrame`.

This method copies each record before applying the specified function, so it is safe to mutate the records. If the mapping function throws an exception on a given record, that record is marked as an error, and the stack trace is saved as a column in the error record.

def printSchema

```
1 def printSchema : Unit
```

Prints the schema of this `DynamicFrame` to `stdout` in a human-readable format.

def recomputeSchema

```
1 def recomputeSchema : Schema
```

Forces a schema recomputation. This requires a scan over the data, but it may "tighten" the schema if there are some fields in the current schema that are not present in the data.

Returns the recomputed schema.

def relationalize

```
1 def relationalize( rootTableName : String,
2                    stagingPath : String,
3                    options : JsonOptions = JsonOptions.empty,
4                    transformationContext : String = "",
5                    callSite : CallSite = CallSite("Not provided"),
6                    stageThreshold : Long = 0,
7                    totalThreshold : Long = 0
8                  ) : Seq[DynamicFrame]
```

- `rootTableName` — The name to use for the base `DynamicFrame` in the output. `DynamicFrames` that are created by pivoting arrays start with this as a prefix.
- `stagingPath` — The Amazon Simple Storage Service (Amazon S3) path for writing intermediate data.
- `options` — Relationalize options and configuration. Currently unused.

Flattens all nested structures and pivots arrays into separate tables.

You can use this operation to prepare deeply nested data for ingestion into a relational database. Nested structs are flattened in the same manner as the unnest transform. Additionally, arrays are pivoted into separate tables with each array element becoming a row. For example, suppose that you have a `DynamicFrame` with the following data:

```
1 {"name": "Nancy", "age": 47, "friends": ["Fred", "Lakshmi"]}
2 {"name": "Stephanie", "age": 28, "friends": ["Yao", "Phil", "Alvin"]}
3 {"name": "Nathan", "age": 54, "friends": ["Nicolai", "Karen"]}
```

Execute the following code:

```
df.relationalize("people", "s3:/my_bucket/my_path", JsonOptions.empty)
```

This produces two tables. The first table is named "people" and contains the following:

```
{"name": "Nancy", "age": 47, "friends": 1}
{"name": "Stephanie", "age": 28, "friends": 2}
{"name": "Nathan", "age": 54, "friends": 3)
```

Here, the friends array has been replaced with an auto-generated join key. A separate table named `people.friends` is created with the following content:

```
{"id": 1, "index": 0, "val": "Fred"}
{"id": 1, "index": 1, "val": "Lakshmi"}
{"id": 2, "index": 0, "val": "Yao"}
{"id": 2, "index": 1, "val": "Phil"}
{"id": 2, "index": 2, "val": "Alvin"}
{"id": 3, "index": 0, "val": "Nicolai"}
{"id": 3, "index": 1, "val": "Karen"}
```

In this table, 'id' is a join key that identifies which record the array element came from, 'index' refers to the position in the original array, and 'val' is the actual array entry.

The `relationalize` method returns the sequence of `DynamicFrame`s created by applying this process recursively to all arrays.

Note
The AWS Glue library automatically generates join keys for new tables. To ensure that join keys are unique across job runs, you must enable job bookmarks.

def renameField

```
def renameField( oldName : String,
                 newName : String,
                 transformationContext : String = "",
                 callSite : CallSite = CallSite("Not provided", ""),
                 stageThreshold : Long = 0,
                 totalThreshold : Long = 0
               ) : DynamicFrame
```

- `oldName` — The original name of the column.
- `newName` — The new name of the column.

Returns a new `DynamicFrame` with the specified field renamed.

You can use this method to rename nested fields. For example, the following code would rename `state` to `state_code` inside the address struct:

```
df.renameField("address.state", "address.state_code")
```

def repartition

```
1 def repartition( numPartitions : Int,
2                  transformationContext : String = "",
3                  callSite : CallSite = CallSite("Not provided", "'"),
4                  stageThreshold : Long = 0,
5                  totalThreshold : Long = 0
6               ) : DynamicFrame
```

Returns a new `DynamicFrame` with `numPartitions` partitions.

def resolveChoice

```
1 def resolveChoice( specs : Seq[Product2[String, String]] = Seq.empty[ResolveSpec],
2                    choiceOption : Option[ChoiceOption] = None,
3                    database : Option[String] = None,
4                    tableName : Option[String] = None,
5                    transformationContext : String = "",
6                    callSite : CallSite = CallSite("Not provided", ""),
7                    stageThreshold : Long = 0,
8                    totalThreshold : Long = 0
9                 ) : DynamicFrame
```

- `choiceOption` — An action to apply to all `ChoiceType` columns not listed in the specs sequence.
- `database` — The Data Catalog database to use with the `match_catalog` action.
- `tableName` — The Data Catalog table to use with the `match_catalog` action.

Returns a new `DynamicFrame` by replacing one or more `ChoiceTypes` with a more specific type.

There are two ways to use `resolveChoice`. The first is to specify a sequence of specific columns and how to resolve them. These are specified as tuples made up of (column, action) pairs.

The following are the possible actions:

- `cast:type` — Attempts to cast all values to the specified type.
- `make_cols` — Converts each distinct type to a column with the name `columnName_type`.
- `make_struct` — Converts a column to a struct with keys for each distinct type.
- `project:type` — Retains only values of the specified type.

The other mode for `resolveChoice` is to specify a single resolution for all `ChoiceTypes`. You can use this in cases where the complete list of `ChoiceTypes` is unknown before execution. In addition to the actions listed preceding, this mode also supports the following action:

- `match_catalog` — Attempts to cast each `ChoiceType` to the corresponding type in the specified catalog table.

Examples:

Resolve the `user.id` column by casting to an int, and make the `address` field retain only structs:

```
1 {{{
2   df.resolveChoice(specs = Seq(("user.id", "cast:int"), ("address", "project:struct")))
3 }}}
```

Resolve all `ChoiceTypes` by converting each choice to a separate column:

```
1 {{{
2   df.resolveChoice(choiceOption = Some(ChoiceOption("make_cols")))
3 }}}
```

Resolve all `ChoiceTypes` by casting to the types in the specified catalog table:

```
{{{
  df.resolveChoice(choiceOption = Some(ChoiceOption("match_catalog")),
                   database = Some("my_database"),
                   tableName = Some("my_table"))
}}}
```

def schema

```
def schema : Schema
```

Returns the schema of this `DynamicFrame`.

The returned schema is guaranteed to contain every field that is present in a record in this `DynamicFrame`. But in a small number of cases, it might also contain additional fields. You can use the unnest method to "tighten" the schema based on the records in this `DynamicFrame`.

def selectField

```
def selectField( fieldName : String,
                 transformationContext : String = "",
                 callSite : CallSite = CallSite("Not provided", ""),
                 stageThreshold : Long = 0,
                 totalThreshold : Long = 0
               ) : DynamicFrame
```

Returns a single field as a `DynamicFrame`.

def selectFields

```
def selectFields( paths : Seq[String],
                  transformationContext : String = "",
                  callSite : CallSite = CallSite("Not provided", ""),
                  stageThreshold : Long = 0,
                  totalThreshold : Long = 0
                ) : DynamicFrame
```

- paths — The sequence of column names to select.

Returns a new `DynamicFrame` containing the specified columns.

Note
You can only use the `selectFields` method to select top-level columns. You can use the applyMapping method to select nested columns.

def show

```
def show( numRows : Int = 20 ) : Unit
```

- numRows — The number of rows to print.

Prints rows from this `DynamicFrame` in JSON format.

def spigot

```
1 def spigot( path : String,
2             options : JsonOptions = new JsonOptions("{}"),
3             transformationContext : String = "",
4             callSite : CallSite = CallSite("Not provided"),
5             stageThreshold : Long = 0,
6             totalThreshold : Long = 0
7           ) : DynamicFrame
```

Passthrough transformation that returns the same records but writes out a subset of records as a side effect.

- path — The path in Amazon S3 to write output to, in the form s3://bucket//path.
- options — An optional JsonOptions map describing the sampling behavior.

Returns a DynamicFrame that contains the same records as this one.

By default, writes 100 arbitrary records to the location specified by path. You can customize this behavior by using the options map. Valid keys include the following:

- topk — Specifies the total number of records written out. The default is 100.
- prob — Specifies the probability that an individual record is included. Default is 1.

For example, the following call would sample the dataset by selecting each record with a 20 percent probability and stopping after 200 records have been written:

```
1 {{{
2   df.spigot("s3://my_bucket/my_path", JsonOptions(Map("topk" -&gt; 200, "prob" -&gt; 0.2)))
3 }}}
```

def splitFields

```
1 def splitFields( paths : Seq[String],
2                  transformationContext : String = "",
3                  callSite : CallSite = CallSite("Not provided", ""),
4                  stageThreshold : Long = 0,
5                  totalThreshold : Long = 0
6                ) : Seq[DynamicFrame]
```

- paths — The paths to include in the first DynamicFrame.

Returns a sequence of two DynamicFrames. The first DynamicFrame contains the specified paths, and the second contains all other columns.

def splitRows

```
1 def splitRows( paths : Seq[String],
2               values : Seq[Any],
3               operators : Seq[String],
4               transformationContext : String,
5               callSite : CallSite,
6               stageThreshold : Long,
7               totalThreshold : Long
8             ) : Seq[DynamicFrame]
```

Splits rows based on predicates that compare columns to constants.

- `paths` — The columns to use for comparison.
- `values` — The constant values to use for comparison.
- `operators` — The operators to use for comparison.

Returns a sequence of two `DynamicFrame`s. The first contains rows for which the predicate is true and the second contains those for which it is false.

Predicates are specified using three sequences: 'paths' contains the (possibly nested) column names, 'values' contains the constant values to compare to, and 'operators' contains the operators to use for comparison. All three sequences must be the same length: The nth operator is used to compare the nth column with the nth value.

Each operator must be one of "!=", "=", "<=", "<", ">=", or ">".

As an example, the following call would split a `DynamicFrame` so that the first output frame would contain records of people over 65 from the United States, and the second would contain all other records:

```
{{{
  df.splitRows(Seq("age", "address.country"), Seq(65, "USA"), Seq("&gt;=", "="))
}}}
```

def stageErrorsCount

```
def stageErrorsCount
```

Returns the number of error records created while computing this `DynamicFrame`. This excludes errors from previous operations that were passed into this `DynamicFrame` as input.

def toDF

```
def toDF( specs : Seq[ResolveSpec] = Seq.empty[ResolveSpec] ) : DataFrame
```

Converts this `DynamicFrame` to an Apache Spark SQL `DataFrame` with the same schema and records.

Note
Because `DataFrame`s don't support `ChoiceType`s, this method automatically converts `ChoiceType` columns into `StructType`s. For more information and options for resolving choice, see resolveChoice.

def unbox

```
def unbox( path : String,
           format : String,
           optionString : String = "{}",
           transformationContext : String = "",
           callSite : CallSite = CallSite("Not provided"),
           stageThreshold : Long = 0,
           totalThreshold : Long = 0
         ) : DynamicFrame
```

- `path` — The column to parse. Must be a string or binary.
- `format` — The format to use for parsing.
- `optionString` — Options to pass to the format, such as the CSV separator.

Parses an embedded string or binary column according to the specified format. Parsed columns are nested under a struct with the original column name.

For example, suppose that you have a CSV file with an embedded JSON column:

```
1 name, age, address
2 Sally, 36, {"state": "NE", "city": "Omaha"}
3 ...
```

After an initial parse, you would get a **DynamicFrame** with the following schema:

```
1 {{{
2   root
3   |-- name: string
4   |-- age: int
5   |-- address: string
6 }}}
```

You can call **unbox** on the address column to parse the specific components:

```
1 {{{
2   df.unbox("address", "json")
3 }}}
```

This gives us a **DynamicFrame** with the following schema:

```
1 {{{
2   root
3   |-- name: string
4   |-- age: int
5   |-- address: struct
6   |      |-- state: string
7   |      |-- city: string
8 }}}
```

def unnest

```
1 def unnest( transformationContext : String = "",
2             callSite : CallSite = CallSite("Not Provided"),
3             stageThreshold : Long = 0,
4             totalThreshold : Long = 0
5           ) : DynamicFrame
```

Returns a new **DynamicFrame** with all nested structures flattened. Names are constructed using the '.' (period) character.

For example, suppose that you have a **DynamicFrame** with the following schema:

```
1 {{{
2   root
3   |-- name: string
4   |-- age: int
5   |-- address: struct
6   |      |-- state: string
7   |      |-- city: string
8 }}}
```

The following call unnests the address struct:

```
1 {{{
2   df.unnest()
3 }}}
```

The resulting schema is as follows:

```
1 {{{
2   root
3   |-- name: string
4   |-- age: int
5   |-- address.state: string
6   |-- address.city: string
7 }}}
```

This method also unnests nested structs inside of arrays. But for historical reasons, the names of such fields are prepended with the name of the enclosing array and ".val".

def withFrameSchema

```
1 def withFrameSchema( getSchema : () => Schema ) : DynamicFrame
```

- getSchema — A function that returns the schema to use. Specified as a zero-parameter function to defer potentially expensive computation.

Sets the schema of this DynamicFrame to the specified value. This is primarily used internally to avoid costly schema recomputation. The passed-in schema must contain all columns present in the data.

def withName

```
1 def withName( name : String ) : DynamicFrame
```

- name — The new name to use.

Returns a copy of this DynamicFrame with a new name.

def withTransformationContext

```
1 def withTransformationContext( ctx : String ) : DynamicFrame
```

Returns a copy of this DynamicFrame with the specified transformation context.

The DynamicFrame Object

Package: com.amazonaws.services.glue

```
1 object DynamicFrame
```

def apply

```
1 def apply( df : DataFrame,
2           glueContext : GlueContext
3         ) : DynamicFrame
```

def emptyDynamicFrame

```
1 def emptyDynamicFrame( glueContext : GlueContext ) : DynamicFrame
```

def fromPythonRDD

```
1 def fromPythonRDD( rdd : JavaRDD[Array[Byte]],
2                    glueContext : GlueContext
3               ) : DynamicFrame
```

def ignoreErrors

```
1 def ignoreErrors( fn : DynamicRecord => DynamicRecord ) : DynamicRecord
```

def inlineErrors

```
1 def inlineErrors( msg : String,
2                   callSite : CallSite
3               ) : (DynamicRecord => DynamicRecord)
```

def newFrameWithErrors

```
1 def newFrameWithErrors( prevFrame : DynamicFrame,
2                         rdd : RDD[DynamicRecord],
3                         name : String = "",
4                         transformationContext : String = "",
5                         callSite : CallSite,
6                         stageThreshold : Long,
7                         totalThreshold : Long
8                     ) : DynamicFrame
```

AWS Glue Scala DynamicRecord Class

Topics

- def addField
- def dropField
- def setError
- def isError
- def getError
- def clearError
- def write
- def readFields
- def clone
- def schema
- def getRoot
- def toJson
- def getFieldNode
- def getField
- def hashCode
- def equals
- DynamicRecord Object
- RecordTraverser Trait

Package: com.amazonaws.services.glue

```
1 class DynamicRecord extends Serializable with Writable with Cloneable
```

305

A `DynamicRecord` is a self-describing data structure that represents a row of data in the dataset that is being processed. It is self-describing in the sense that you can get the schema of the row that is represented by the `DynamicRecord` by inspecting the record itself. A `DynamicRecord` is similar to a `Row` in Apache Spark.

def addField

```
1 def addField( path : String,
2              dynamicNode : DynamicNode
3            ) : Unit
```

Adds a DynamicNode to the specified path.

- `path` — The path for the field to be added.
- `dynamicNode` — The DynamicNode to be added at the specified path.

def dropField

```
1  def dropField(path: String, underRename: Boolean = false): Option[DynamicNode]
```

Drops a DynamicNode from the specified path and returns the dropped node if there is not an array in the specified path.

- `path` — The path to the field to drop.
- `underRename` — True if `dropField` is called as part of a rename transform, or false otherwise (false by default).

Returns a `scala.Option` Option (DynamicNode).

def setError

```
1 def setError( error : Error )
```

Sets this record as an error record, as specified by the `error` parameter.

Returns a `DynamicRecord`.

def isError

```
1 def isError
```

Checks whether this record is an error record.

def getError

```
1 def getError
```

Gets the `Error` if the record is an error record. Returns `scala.Some` Some (Error) if this record is an error record, or otherwise `scala.None` .

def clearError

```
1 def clearError
```

Set the `Error` to `scala.None.None` .

def write

```
1 override def write( out : DataOutput ) : Unit
```

def readFields

```
1 override def readFields( in : DataInput ) : Unit
```

def clone

```
1 override def clone : DynamicRecord
```

Clones this record to a new `DynamicRecord` and returns it.

def schema

```
1 def schema
```

Gets the `Schema` by inspecting the record.

def getRoot

```
1 def getRoot : ObjectNode
```

Gets the root `ObjectNode` for the record.

def toJson

```
1 def toJson : String
```

Gets the JSON string for the record.

def getFieldNode

```
1 def getFieldNode( path : String ) : Option[DynamicNode]
```

Gets the field's value at the specified `path` as an option of `DynamicNode`.

Returns `scala.Some` Some (DynamicNode) if the field exists, or otherwise `scala.None.None` .

def getField

```
1 def getField( path : String ) : Option[Any]
```

Gets the field's value at the specified `path` as an option of `DynamicNode`.

Returns `scala.Some` Some (value).

def hashCode

```
1 override def hashCode : Int
```

def equals

```
1 override def equals( other : Any )
```

DynamicRecord Object

```
1 object DynamicRecord
```

def apply

```
1 def apply( row : Row,
2            schema : SparkStructType )
```

Apply method to convert an Apache Spark SQL Row to a DynamicRecord.

- row — A Spark SQL Row.
- schema — The Schema of that row.

Returns a DynamicRecord.

RecordTraverser Trait

```
1  trait RecordTraverser {
2    def nullValue(): Unit
3    def byteValue(value: Byte): Unit
4    def binaryValue(value: Array[Byte]): Unit
5    def booleanValue(value: Boolean): Unit
6    def shortValue(value: Short) : Unit
7    def intValue(value: Int) : Unit
8    def longValue(value: Long) : Unit
9    def floatValue(value: Float): Unit
10   def doubleValue(value: Double): Unit
11   def decimalValue(value: BigDecimal): Unit
12   def stringValue(value: String): Unit
13   def dateValue(value: Date): Unit
14   def timestampValue(value: Timestamp): Unit
15   def objectStart(length: Int): Unit
16   def objectKey(key: String): Unit
17   def objectEnd(): Unit
18   def mapStart(length: Int): Unit
19   def mapKey(key: String): Unit
20   def mapEnd(): Unit
21   def arrayStart(length: Int): Unit
22   def arrayEnd(): Unit
23 }
```

AWS Glue Scala GlueContext APIs

Package: com.amazonaws.services.glue

```
1 class GlueContext extends SQLContext(sc) (
2         @transient val sc : SparkContext,
3         val defaultSourcePartitioner : PartitioningStrategy )
```

GlueContext is the entry point for reading and writing a DynamicFrame from and to Amazon Simple Storage Service (Amazon S3), the AWS Glue Data Catalog, JDBC, and so on. This class provides utility functions to create DataSource trait and DataSink objects that can in turn be used to read and write DynamicFrames.

308

You can also use `GlueContext` to set a target number of partitions (default 20) in the `DynamicFrame` if the number of partitions created from the source is less than a minimum threshold for partitions (default 10).

def getCatalogSink

```
1 def getCatalogSink( database : String,
2                     tableName : String,
3                     redshiftTmpDir : String = "",
4                     transformationContext : String = ""
5                   ) : DataSink
```

Creates a DataSink that writes to a location specified in a table that is defined in the Data Catalog.

- `database` — The database name in the Data Catalog.
- `tableName` — The table name in the Data Catalog.
- `redshiftTmpDir` — The temporary staging directory to be used with certain data sinks. Set to empty by default.
- `transformationContext` — The transformation context that is associated with the sink to be used by job bookmarks. Set to empty by default.

Returns the `DataSink`.

def getCatalogSource

```
1 def getCatalogSource( database : String,
2                       tableName : String,
3                       redshiftTmpDir : String = "",
4                       transformationContext : String = ""
5                     ) : DataSource
```

Creates a DataSource trait that reads data from a table definition in the Data Catalog.

- `database` — The database name in the Data Catalog.
- `tableName` — The table name in the Data Catalog.
- `redshiftTmpDir` — The temporary staging directory to be used with certain data sinks. Set to empty by default.
- `transformationContext` — The transformation context that is associated with the sink to be used by job bookmarks. Set to empty by default.

Returns the `DataSource`.

def getJDBCSink

```
1 def getJDBCSink( catalogConnection : String,
2                  options : JsonOptions,
3                  redshiftTmpDir : String = "",
4                  transformationContext : String = ""
5                ) : DataSink
```

Creates a DataSink that writes to a JDBC database that is specified in a `Connection` object in the Data Catalog. The `Connection` object has information to connect to a JDBC sink, including the URL, user name, password, VPC, subnet, and security groups.

- `catalogConnection` — The name of the connection in the Data Catalog that contains the JDBC URL to write to.

- options — A string of JSON name-value pairs that provide additional information that is required to write to a JDBC data store. This includes:
    - *dbtable* (required) — The name of the JDBC table.
    - *database* (required) — The name of the JDBC database.
    - Any additional options passed directly to the SparkSQL JDBC writer.
- redshiftTmpDir — A temporary staging directory to be used with certain data sinks. Set to empty by default.
- transformationContext — The transformation context that is associated with the sink to be used by job bookmarks. Set to empty by default.

Example code:

```
1 getJDBCSink(catalogConnection = "my-connection-name", options = JsonOptions("""{"dbtable": "my-jdbc-table", "database": "my-jdbc-db"}"""), redshiftTmpDir = "", transformationContext = "datasink4")
```

Returns the DataSink.

def getSink

```
1 def getSink( connectionType : String,
2              options : JsonOptions,
3              transformationContext : String = ""
4            ) : DataSink
```

Creates a DataSink that writes data to a destination like Amazon Simple Storage Service (Amazon S3), JDBC, or the AWS Glue Data Catalog.

- connectionType — The type of the connection.
- options — A string of JSON name-value pairs that provide additional information to establish the connection with the data sink.
- transformationContext — The transformation context that is associated with the sink to be used by job bookmarks. Set to empty by default.

Returns the DataSink.

def getSinkWithFormat

```
1 def getSinkWithFormat( connectionType : String,
2                        options : JsonOptions,
3                        transformationContext : String = "",
4                        format : String = null,
5                        formatOptions : JsonOptions = JsonOptions.empty
6                      ) : DataSink
```

Creates a DataSink that writes data to a destination like Amazon S3, JDBC, or the Data Catalog, and also sets the format for the data to be written out to the destination.

- connectionType — The type of the connection. Refer to DataSink for a list of supported connection types.
- options — A string of JSON name-value pairs that provide additional information to establish a connection with the data sink.
- transformationContext — The transformation context that is associated with the sink to be used by job bookmarks. Set to empty by default.
- format — The format of the data to be written out to the destination.

310

- `formatOptions` — A string of JSON name-value pairs that provide additional options for formatting data at the destination. See Format Options.

Returns the `DataSink`.

def getSource

```
1 def getSource( connectionType : String,
2                connectionOptions : JsonOptions,
3                transformationContext : String = ""
4              ) : DataSource
```

Creates a DataSource trait that reads data from a source like Amazon S3, JDBC, or the AWS Glue Data Catalog.

- `connectionType` — The type of the data source. Can be one of "s3", "mysql", "redshift", "oracle", "sqlserver", "postgresql", "parquet", or "orc".
- `connectionOptions` — A string of JSON name-value pairs that provide additional information for establishing a connection with the data source.
  - `connectionOptions` when the `connectionType` is "s3":
    - *paths* (required) — List of Amazon S3 paths to read.
    - *compressionType* (optional) — Compression type of the data. This is generally not required if the data has a standard file extension. Possible values are "gzip" and "bzip".
    - *exclusions* (optional) — A string containing a JSON list of glob patterns to exclude. For example "[\"**.pdf\"]" excludes all PDF files.
    - *maxBand* (optional) — This advanced option controls the duration in seconds after which AWS Glue expects an Amazon S3 listing to be consistent. Files with modification timestamps falling within the last maxBand seconds are tracked when using job bookmarks to account for Amazon S3 eventual consistency. It is rare to set this option. The default is 900 seconds.
    - *maxFilesInBand* (optional) — This advanced option specifies the maximum number of files to save from the last maxBand seconds. If this number is exceeded, extra files are skipped and processed only in the next job run.
    - *groupFiles* (optional) — Grouping files is enabled by default when the input contains more than 50,000 files. To disable grouping with fewer than 50,000 files, set this parameter to "inPartition". To disable grouping when there are more than 50,000 files, set this parameter to "none".
    - *groupSize* (optional) — The target group size in bytes. The default is computed based on the input data size and the size of your cluster. When there are fewer than 50,000 input files, groupFiles must be set to "inPartition" for this option to take effect.
    - *recurse* (optional) — If set to true, recursively read files in any subdirectory of the specified paths.
  - `connectionOptions` when the `connectionType` is "parquet" or "orc":
    - *paths* (required) — List of Amazon S3 paths to read.
    - Any additional options are passed directly to the SparkSQL DataSource.
  - `connectionOptions` when the `connectionType` is "redshift":
    - *url* (required) — The JDBC URL for an Amazon Redshift database.
    - *dbtable* (required) — The Amazon Redshift table to read.
    - *tempdir* (required) — The Amazon S3 path where temporary data can be staged when copying out of Amazon Redshift.
    - *user* (required) — The username to use when connecting to the Amazon Redshift cluster.
    - *password* (required) — The password to use when connecting to the Amazon Redshift cluster.
- `transformationContext` — The transformation context that is associated with the sink to be used by job bookmarks. Set to empty by default.

Returns the `DataSource`.

def getSourceWithFormat

```
1 def getSourceWithFormat( connectionType : String,
2                          options : JsonOptions,
3                          transformationContext : String = "",
4                          format : String = null,
5                          formatOptions : JsonOptions = JsonOptions.empty
6                        ) : DataSource
```

Creates a DataSource trait that reads data from a source like Amazon S3, JDBC, or the AWS Glue Data Catalog, and also sets the format of data stored in the source.

- connectionType — The type of the data source. Can be one of "s3", "mysql", "redshift", "oracle", "sqlserver", "postgresql", "parquet", or "orc".
- options — A string of JSON name-value pairs that provide additional information for establishing a connection with the data source.
- transformationContext — The transformation context that is associated with the sink to be used by job bookmarks. Set to empty by default.
- format — The format of the data that is stored at the source. When the connectionType is "s3", you can also specify format. Can be one of "avro", "csv", "grokLog", "ion", "json", "xml", "parquet", or "orc".
- formatOptions — A string of JSON name-value pairs that provide additional options for parsing data at the source. See Format Options.

Returns the DataSource.

def getSparkSession

```
1 def getSparkSession : SparkSession
```

Gets the SparkSession object associated with this GlueContext. Use this SparkSession object to register tables and UDFs for use with DataFrame created from DynamicFrames.

Returns the SparkSession.

def this

```
1 def this( sc : SparkContext,
2           minPartitions : Int,
3           targetPartitions : Int )
```

Creates a GlueContext object using the specified SparkContext, minimum partitions, and target partitions.

- sc — The SparkContext.
- minPartitions — The minimum number of partitions.
- targetPartitions — The target number of partitions.

Returns the GlueContext.

def this

```
1 def this( sc : SparkContext )
```

Creates a GlueContext object with the provided SparkContext. Sets the minimum partitions to 10 and target partitions to 20.

- sc — The SparkContext.

Returns the GlueContext.

def this

```
1 def this( sparkContext : JavaSparkContext )
```

Creates a `GlueContext` object with the provided `JavaSparkContext`. Sets the minimum partitions to 10 and target partitions to 20.

- sparkContext — The `JavaSparkContext`.

Returns the `GlueContext`.

AWS Glue Scala ResolveSpec APIs

Topics

- ResolveSpec Object
- ResolveSpec Case Class

Package: com.amazonaws.services.glue

ResolveSpec Object

ResolveSpec

```
1 object ResolveSpec
```

def

```
1 def apply( path : String,
2           action : String
3         ) : ResolveSpec
```

Creates a `ResolveSpec`.

- `path` — A string representation of the choice field that needs to be resolved.
- `action` — A resolution action. The action can be one of the following: `Project`, `KeepAsStruct`, or `Cast`.

Returns the `ResolveSpec`.

def

```
1 def apply( product : Product2[String, String] ) : ResolveSpec
```

Creates a `ResolveSpec`.

- `product` — `Product2` of: source path, resolution action.

Returns the `ResolveSpec`.

ResolveSpec Case Class

```
1 case class ResolveSpec extends Product2[String, String]  (
2           path : SchemaPath,
3           action : String )
```

Creates a `ResolveSpec`.

- `path` — The `SchemaPath` of the choice field that needs to be resolved.
- `action` — A resolution action. The action can be one of the following: `Project`, `KeepAsStruct`, or `Cast`.

```
1 def _1 : String
```

```
1 def _2 : String
```

AWS Glue Scala ArrayNode APIs

Package: com.amazonaws.services.glue.types

ArrayNode Case Class

ArrayNode

```
1 case class ArrayNode extends DynamicNode (
2            value : ArrayBuffer[DynamicNode] )
```

ArrayNode def Methods

```
1 def add( node : DynamicNode )
```

```
1 def clone
```

```
1 def equals( other : Any )
```

```
1 def get( index : Int ) : Option[DynamicNode]
```

```
1 def getValue
```

```
1 def hashCode : Int
```

```
1 def isEmpty : Boolean
```

```
1 def nodeType
```

```
1 def remove( index : Int )
```

```
1 def this
```

```
1 def toIterator : Iterator[DynamicNode]
```

```
1 def toJson : String
```

```
1 def update( index : Int,
2            node : DynamicNode )
```

AWS Glue Scala BinaryNode APIs

Package: com.amazonaws.services.glue.types

BinaryNode Case Class

BinaryNode

```
1 case class BinaryNode extends ScalarNode(value, TypeCode.BINARY)  (
2          value : Array[Byte] )
```

BinaryNode val Fields

- ordering

BinaryNode def Methods

```
1 def clone
```

```
1 def equals( other : Any )
```

```
1 def hashCode : Int
```

AWS Glue Scala BooleanNode APIs

Package: com.amazonaws.services.glue.types

BooleanNode Case Class

BooleanNode

```
1 case class BooleanNode extends ScalarNode(value, TypeCode.BOOLEAN)  (
2          value : Boolean )
```

BooleanNode val Fields

- ordering

BooleanNode def Methods

```
1 def equals( other : Any )
```

AWS Glue Scala ByteNode APIs

Package: com.amazonaws.services.glue.types

ByteNode Case Class

ByteNode

```
1 case class ByteNode extends ScalarNode(value, TypeCode.BYTE)  (
2          value : Byte )
```

ByteNode val Fields

- ordering

ByteNode def Methods

```
1 def equals( other : Any )
```

AWS Glue Scala DateNode APIs

Package: com.amazonaws.services.glue.types

DateNode Case Class

DateNode

```
1 case class DateNode extends ScalarNode(value, TypeCode.DATE) (
2          value : Date )
```

DateNode val Fields

- ordering

DateNode def Methods

```
1 def equals( other : Any )
```

```
1 def this( value : Int )
```

AWS Glue Scala DecimalNode APIs

Package: com.amazonaws.services.glue.types

DecimalNode Case Class

DecimalNode

```
1 case class DecimalNode extends ScalarNode(value, TypeCode.DECIMAL) (
2          value : BigDecimal )
```

DecimalNode val Fields

- ordering

DecimalNode def Methods

```
1 def equals( other : Any )
```

```
1 def this( value : Decimal )
```

AWS Glue Scala DoubleNode APIs

Package: com.amazonaws.services.glue.types

DoubleNode Case Class

DoubleNode

```
1 case class DoubleNode extends ScalarNode(value, TypeCode.DOUBLE)  (
2          value : Double )
```

DoubleNode val Fields

* ordering

DoubleNode def Methods

```
1 def equals( other : Any )
```

AWS Glue Scala DynamicNode APIs

Topics
* DynamicNode Class
* DynamicNode Object

Package: com.amazonaws.services.glue.types

DynamicNode Class

DynamicNode

```
1 class DynamicNode extends Serializable with Cloneable
```

DynamicNode def Methods

```
1 def getValue : Any
```

Get plain value and bind to the current record:

```
1 def nodeType : TypeCode
```

```
1 def toJson : String
```

Method for debug:

```
1  def toRow( schema : Schema,
2             options : Map[String, ResolveOption]
3         ) : Row
```

```
1  def typeName : String
```

DynamicNode Object

DynamicNode

```
1  object DynamicNode
```

DynamicNode def Methods

```
1  def quote( field : String,
2             useQuotes : Boolean
3         ) : String
```

```
1  def quote( node : DynamicNode,
2             useQuotes : Boolean
3         ) : String
```

AWS Glue Scala FloatNode APIs

Package: com.amazonaws.services.glue.types

FloatNode Case Class

FloatNode

```
1  case class FloatNode extends ScalarNode(value, TypeCode.FLOAT)  (
2             value : Float )
```

FloatNode val Fields

- ordering

FloatNode def Methods

```
1  def equals( other : Any )
```

AWS Glue Scala IntegerNode APIs

Package: com.amazonaws.services.glue.types

IntegerNode Case Class

IntegerNode

```
1  case class IntegerNode extends ScalarNode(value, TypeCode.INT)  (
2             value : Int )
```

IntegerNode val Fields

- ordering

IntegerNode def Methods

```
1 def equals( other : Any )
```

AWS Glue Scala LongNode APIs

Package: com.amazonaws.services.glue.types

LongNode Case Class

LongNode

```
1 case class LongNode extends ScalarNode(value, TypeCode.LONG)  (
2         value : Long )
```

LongNode val Fields

- ordering

LongNode def Methods

```
1 def equals( other : Any )
```

AWS Glue Scala MapLikeNode APIs

Package: com.amazonaws.services.glue.types

MapLikeNode Class

MapLikeNode

```
1 class MapLikeNode extends DynamicNode  (
2         value : mutable.Map[String, DynamicNode] )
```

MapLikeNode def Methods

```
1 def clear : Unit
```

```
1 def get( name : String ) : Option[DynamicNode]
```

```
1 def getValue
```

```
1 def has( name : String ) : Boolean
```

```
1 def isEmpty : Boolean
```

```
1 def put( name : String,
2         node : DynamicNode
3       ) : Option[DynamicNode]
```

```
1 def remove( name : String ) : Option[DynamicNode]
```

```
1 def toIterator : Iterator[(String, DynamicNode)]
```

```
1 def toJson : String
```

```
1 def toJson( useQuotes : Boolean ) : String
```

Example: Given this JSON:

```
1 {"foo": "bar"}
```

If useQuotes == true, toJson yields {"foo": "bar"}. If useQuotes == false, toJson yields {foo: bar}
@return.

AWS Glue Scala MapNode APIs

Package: com.amazonaws.services.glue.types

MapNode Case Class

MapNode

```
1 case class MapNode extends MapLikeNode(value)  (
2           value : mutable.Map[String, DynamicNode] )
```

MapNode def Methods

```
1 def clone
```

```
1 def equals( other : Any )
```

```
1 def hashCode : Int
```

```
1 def nodeType
```

```
1 def this
```

AWS Glue Scala NullNode APIs

Topics

- NullNode Class
- NullNode Case Object

Package: com.amazonaws.services.glue.types

NullNode Class

NullNode

```
1 class NullNode
```

NullNode Case Object

NullNode

```
1 case object NullNode extends NullNode
```

AWS Glue Scala ObjectNode APIs

Topics

- ObjectNode Object
- ObjectNode Case Class

Package: com.amazonaws.services.glue.types

ObjectNode Object

ObjectNode

```
1 object ObjectNode
```

ObjectNode def Methods

```
1 def apply( frameKeys : Set[String],
2            v1 : mutable.Map[String, DynamicNode],
3            v2 : mutable.Map[String, DynamicNode],
4            resolveWith : String
5        ) : ObjectNode
```

ObjectNode Case Class

ObjectNode

```
1 case class ObjectNode extends MapLikeNode(value)  (
2            val value : mutable.Map[String, DynamicNode] )
```

ObjectNode def Methods

```
1 def clone
```

```
1 def equals( other : Any )
```

```
1 def hashCode : Int
```

```
1 def nodeType
```

```
1 def this
```

AWS Glue Scala ScalarNode APIs

Topics

- ScalarNode Class
- ScalarNode Object

Package: com.amazonaws.services.glue.types

ScalarNode Class

ScalarNode

```
1 class ScalarNode extends DynamicNode  (
2          value : Any,
3          scalarType : TypeCode )
```

ScalarNode def Methods

```
1 def compare( other : Any,
2           operator : String
3           ) : Boolean
```

```
1 def getValue
```

```
1 def hashCode : Int
```

```
1 def nodeType
```

```
1 def toJson
```

ScalarNode Object

ScalarNode

```
1 object ScalarNode
```

ScalarNode def Methods

```
1 def apply( v : Any ) : DynamicNode
```

```
1 def compare( tv : Ordered[T],
2           other : T,
3           operator : String
4           ) : Boolean
```

```
1 def compareAny( v : Any,
2              y : Any,
3              o : String )
```

```
1 def withEscapedSpecialCharacters( jsonToEscape : String ) : String
```

AWS Glue Scala ShortNode APIs

Package: com.amazonaws.services.glue.types

ShortNode Case Class

ShortNode

```
1 case class ShortNode extends ScalarNode(value, TypeCode.SHORT)  (
2          value : Short )
```

ShortNode val Fields

- ordering

ShortNode def Methods

```
1 def equals( other : Any )
```

AWS Glue Scala StringNode APIs

Package: com.amazonaws.services.glue.types

StringNode Case Class

StringNode

```
1 case class StringNode extends ScalarNode(value, TypeCode.STRING)  (
2          value : String )
```

StringNode val Fields

- ordering

StringNode def Methods

```
1 def equals( other : Any )
```

```
1 def this( value : UTF8String )
```

AWS Glue Scala TimestampNode APIs

Package: com.amazonaws.services.glue.types

TimestampNode Case Class

TimestampNode

```
1 case class TimestampNode extends ScalarNode(value, TypeCode.TIMESTAMP)  (
2          value : Timestamp )
```

TimestampNode val Fields

- ordering

TimestampNode def Methods

```
1 def equals( other : Any )
```

```
1 def this( value : Long )
```

AWS Glue Scala GlueArgParser APIs

Package: com.amazonaws.services.glue.util

GlueArgParser Object

GlueArgParser

```
1 object GlueArgParser
```

This is strictly consistent with the Python version of utils.getResolvedOptions in the AWSGlueDataplanePython package.

GlueArgParser def Methods

```
1 def getResolvedOptions( args : Array[String],
2                         options : Array[String]
3                       ) : Map[String, String]
```

```
1 def initParser( userOptionsSet : mutable.Set[String] ) : ArgumentParser
```

AWS Glue Scala Job APIs

Package: com.amazonaws.services.glue.util

Job Object

Job

```
1 object Job
```

Job def Methods

```
1 def commit
```

```
1 def init( jobName : String,
2           glueContext : GlueContext,
3           args : java.util.Map[String, String] = Map[String, String]().asJava
4         ) : this.type
```

```
1 def init( jobName : String,
2           glueContext : GlueContext,
3           endpoint : String,
4           args : java.util.Map[String, String]
5         ) : this.type
```

```
1 def isInitialized
```

```
1 def reset
```

```
1 def runId
```

AWS Glue API

Contents

- Catalog API
  - Database API
    - Data Types
    - Database Structure
    - DatabaseInput Structure
    - Operations
    - CreateDatabase Action (Python: create_database)
    - UpdateDatabase Action (Python: update_database)
    - DeleteDatabase Action (Python: delete_database)
    - GetDatabase Action (Python: get_database)
    - GetDatabases Action (Python: get_databases)
  - Table API
    - Data Types
    - Table Structure
    - TableInput Structure
    - Column Structure
    - StorageDescriptor Structure
    - SerDeInfo Structure
    - Order Structure
    - SkewedInfo Structure
    - TableVersion Structure
    - TableError Structure
    - TableVersionError Structure
    - Operations
    - CreateTable Action (Python: create_table)
    - UpdateTable Action (Python: update_table)
    - DeleteTable Action (Python: delete_table)
    - BatchDeleteTable Action (Python: batch_delete_table)
    - GetTable Action (Python: get_table)
    - GetTables Action (Python: get_tables)
    - GetTableVersion Action (Python: get_table_version)
    - GetTableVersions Action (Python: get_table_versions)
    - DeleteTableVersion Action (Python: delete_table_version)
    - BatchDeleteTableVersion Action (Python: batch_delete_table_version)
  - Partition API
    - Data Types
    - Partition Structure
    - PartitionInput Structure
    - PartitionSpecWithSharedStorageDescriptor Structure
    - PartitionListComposingSpec Structure
    - PartitionSpecProxy Structure
    - PartitionValueList Structure
    - Segment Structure
    - PartitionError Structure

- Operations
- CreatePartition Action (Python: create_partition)
- BatchCreatePartition Action (Python: batch_create_partition)
- UpdatePartition Action (Python: update_partition)
- DeletePartition Action (Python: delete_partition)
- BatchDeletePartition Action (Python: batch_delete_partition)
- GetPartition Action (Python: get_partition)
- GetPartitions Action (Python: get_partitions)
- BatchGetPartition Action (Python: batch_get_partition)
- Connection API
  - Data Types
  - Connection Structure
  - ConnectionInput Structure
  - PhysicalConnectionRequirements Structure
  - GetConnectionsFilter Structure
  - Operations
  - CreateConnection Action (Python: create_connection)
  - DeleteConnection Action (Python: delete_connection)
  - GetConnection Action (Python: get_connection)
  - GetConnections Action (Python: get_connections)
  - UpdateConnection Action (Python: update_connection)
  - BatchDeleteConnection Action (Python: batch_delete_connection)
- User-Defined Function API
  - Data Types
  - UserDefinedFunction Structure
  - UserDefinedFunctionInput Structure
  - Operations
  - CreateUserDefinedFunction Action (Python: create_user_defined_function)
  - UpdateUserDefinedFunction Action (Python: update_user_defined_function)
  - DeleteUserDefinedFunction Action (Python: delete_user_defined_function)
  - GetUserDefinedFunction Action (Python: get_user_defined_function)
  - GetUserDefinedFunctions Action (Python: get_user_defined_functions)
- Importing an Athena Catalog to AWS Glue
  - Data Types
  - CatalogImportStatus Structure
  - Operations
  - ImportCatalogToGlue Action (Python: import_catalog_to_glue)
  - GetCatalogImportStatus Action (Python: get_catalog_import_status)
- Crawlers and Classifiers API
  - Classifier API
    - Data Types
    - Classifier Structure
    - GrokClassifier Structure
    - XMLClassifier Structure
    - JsonClassifier Structure
    - CreateGrokClassifierRequest Structure
    - UpdateGrokClassifierRequest Structure
    - CreateXMLClassifierRequest Structure
    - UpdateXMLClassifierRequest Structure
    - CreateJsonClassifierRequest Structure
    - UpdateJsonClassifierRequest Structure
    - Operations
    - CreateClassifier Action (Python: create_classifier)
    - DeleteClassifier Action (Python: delete_classifier)

- GetClassifier Action (Python: get_classifier)
- GetClassifiers Action (Python: get_classifiers)
- UpdateClassifier Action (Python: update_classifier)
  - Crawler API
    - Data Types
    - Crawler Structure
    - Schedule Structure
    - CrawlerTargets Structure
    - S3Target Structure
    - JdbcTarget Structure
    - CrawlerMetrics Structure
    - SchemaChangePolicy Structure
    - LastCrawlInfo Structure
    - Operations
    - CreateCrawler Action (Python: create_crawler)
    - DeleteCrawler Action (Python: delete_crawler)
    - GetCrawler Action (Python: get_crawler)
    - GetCrawlers Action (Python: get_crawlers)
    - GetCrawlerMetrics Action (Python: get_crawler_metrics)
    - UpdateCrawler Action (Python: update_crawler)
    - StartCrawler Action (Python: start_crawler)
    - StopCrawler Action (Python: stop_crawler)
  - Crawler Scheduler API
    - Data Types
    - Schedule Structure
    - Operations
    - UpdateCrawlerSchedule Action (Python: update_crawler_schedule)
    - StartCrawlerSchedule Action (Python: start_crawler_schedule)
    - StopCrawlerSchedule Action (Python: stop_crawler_schedule)
- AWS Glue API for Autogenerating ETL Scripts
  - Data Types
  - CodeGenNode Structure
  - CodeGenNodeArg Structure
  - CodeGenEdge Structure
  - Location Structure
  - CatalogEntry Structure
  - MappingEntry Structure
  - Operations
  - CreateScript Action (Python: create_script)
  - GetDataflowGraph Action (Python: get_dataflow_graph)
  - GetMapping Action (Python: get_mapping)
  - GetPlan Action (Python: get_plan)
- Jobs API
  - Jobs
    - Data Types
    - Job Structure
    - ExecutionProperty Structure
    - NotificationProperty Structure
    - JobCommand Structure
    - ConnectionsList Structure
    - JobUpdate Structure
    - Operations
    - CreateJob Action (Python: create_job)
    - UpdateJob Action (Python: update_job)

- GetJob Action (Python: get_job)
- GetJobs Action (Python: get_jobs)
- DeleteJob Action (Python: delete_job)
- Job Runs
  - Data Types
  - JobRun Structure
  - Predecessor Structure
  - JobBookmarkEntry Structure
  - BatchStopJobRunSuccessfulSubmission Structure
  - BatchStopJobRunError Structure
  - Operations
  - StartJobRun Action (Python: start_job_run)
  - BatchStopJobRun Action (Python: batch_stop_job_run)
  - GetJobRun Action (Python: get_job_run)
  - GetJobRuns Action (Python: get_job_runs)
  - ResetJobBookmark Action (Python: reset_job_bookmark)
- Triggers
  - Data Types
  - Trigger Structure
  - TriggerUpdate Structure
  - Predicate Structure
  - Condition Structure
  - Action Structure
  - Operations
  - CreateTrigger Action (Python: create_trigger)
  - StartTrigger Action (Python: start_trigger)
  - GetTrigger Action (Python: get_trigger)
  - GetTriggers Action (Python: get_triggers)
  - UpdateTrigger Action (Python: update_trigger)
  - StopTrigger Action (Python: stop_trigger)
  - DeleteTrigger Action (Python: delete_trigger)
- AWS Glue Development Endpoints API
  - Data Types
  - DevEndpoint Structure
  - DevEndpointCustomLibraries Structure
  - Operations
  - CreateDevEndpoint Action (Python: create_dev_endpoint)
  - UpdateDevEndpoint Action (Python: update_dev_endpoint)
  - DeleteDevEndpoint Action (Python: delete_dev_endpoint)
  - GetDevEndpoint Action (Python: get_dev_endpoint)
  - GetDevEndpoints Action (Python: get_dev_endpoints)
- Common Data Types
  - Tag Structure
  - DecimalNumber Structure
  - ErrorDetail Structure
  - PropertyPredicate Structure
  - ResourceUri Structure
  - String Patterns
- Exceptions
  - AccessDeniedException Structure
  - AlreadyExistsException Structure
  - ConcurrentModificationException Structure
  - ConcurrentRunsExceededException Structure
  - CrawlerNotRunningException Structure

- CrawlerRunningException Structure
- CrawlerStoppingException Structure
- EntityNotFoundException Structure
- IdempotentParameterMismatchException Structure
- InternalServiceException Structure
- InvalidExecutionEngineException Structure
- InvalidInputException Structure
- InvalidTaskStatusTransitionException Structure
- JobDefinitionErrorException Structure
- JobRunInTerminalStateException Structure
- JobRunInvalidStateTransitionException Structure
- JobRunNotInTerminalStateException Structure
- LateRunnerException Structure
- NoScheduleException Structure
- OperationTimeoutException Structure
- ResourceNumberLimitExceededException Structure
- SchedulerNotRunningException Structure
- SchedulerRunningException Structure
- SchedulerTransitioningException Structure
- UnrecognizedRunnerException Structure
- ValidationException Structure
- VersionMismatchException Structure

Catalog API

Topics

- Database API
- Table API
- Partition API
- Connection API
- User-Defined Function API
- Importing an Athena Catalog to AWS Glue

Database API

Data Types

- Database Structure
- DatabaseInput Structure

Database Structure

The `Database` object represents a logical grouping of tables that may reside in a Hive metastore or an RDBMS.

Fields

- `Name` – UTF-8 string, not less than 1 or more than 255 bytes long, matching the Single-line string pattern. Required.

  Name of the database. For Hive compatibility, this is folded to lowercase when it is stored.

- `Description` – Description string, not more than 2048 bytes long, matching the URI address multi-line string pattern.

  Description of the database.

- `LocationUri` – Uniform resource identifier (uri), not less than 1 or more than 1024 bytes long, matching the URI address multi-line string pattern.

  The location of the database (for example, an HDFS path).

- `Parameters` – A map array of key-value pairs

  Each key is a Key string, not less than 1 or more than 255 bytes long, matching the Single-line string pattern.

  Each value is a UTF-8 string, not more than 512000 bytes long.

  These key-value pairs define parameters and properties of the database.

- `CreateTime` – Timestamp.

  The time at which the metadata database was created in the catalog.

DatabaseInput Structure

The structure used to create or update a database.

Fields

- `Name` – UTF-8 string, not less than 1 or more than 255 bytes long, matching the Single-line string pattern. Required.

  Name of the database. For Hive compatibility, this is folded to lowercase when it is stored.

- `Description` – Description string, not more than 2048 bytes long, matching the URI address multi-line string pattern.

  Description of the database

- `LocationUri` – Uniform resource identifier (uri), not less than 1 or more than 1024 bytes long, matching the URI address multi-line string pattern.

  The location of the database (for example, an HDFS path).

- `Parameters` – A map array of key-value pairs

  Each key is a Key string, not less than 1 or more than 255 bytes long, matching the Single-line string pattern.

  Each value is a UTF-8 string, not more than 512000 bytes long.

  Thes key-value pairs define parameters and properties of the database.

Operations

- CreateDatabase Action (Python: create_database)
- UpdateDatabase Action (Python: update_database)
- DeleteDatabase Action (Python: delete_database)
- GetDatabase Action (Python: get_database)
- GetDatabases Action (Python: get_databases)

CreateDatabase Action (Python: create_database)

Creates a new database in a Data Catalog.

Request

- `CatalogId` – Catalog id string, not less than 1 or more than 255 bytes long, matching the Single-line string pattern.

  The ID of the Data Catalog in which to create the database. If none is supplied, the AWS account ID is used by default.

- `DatabaseInput` – A DatabaseInput object. Required.

  A `DatabaseInput` object defining the metadata database to create in the catalog.

Response

- *No Response parameters.*

Errors

- `InvalidInputException`
- `AlreadyExistsException`
- `ResourceNumberLimitExceededException`
- `InternalServiceException`
- `OperationTimeoutException`
- `GlueEncryptionException`

UpdateDatabase Action (Python: update_database)

Updates an existing database definition in a Data Catalog.

Request

- `CatalogId` – Catalog id string, not less than 1 or more than 255 bytes long, matching the Single-line string pattern.

  The ID of the Data Catalog in which the metadata database resides. If none is supplied, the AWS account ID is used by default.

- `Name` – UTF-8 string, not less than 1 or more than 255 bytes long, matching the Single-line string pattern. Required.

  The name of the database to update in the catalog. For Hive compatibility, this is folded to lowercase.

- `DatabaseInput` – A DatabaseInput object. Required.

  A `DatabaseInput` object specifying the new definition of the metadata database in the catalog.

Response

- *No Response parameters.*

Errors

- `EntityNotFoundException`
- `InvalidInputException`
- `InternalServiceException`
- `OperationTimeoutException`
- `GlueEncryptionException`

DeleteDatabase Action (Python: delete_database)

Removes a specified Database from a Data Catalog.

Note
After completing this operation, you will no longer have access to the tables (and all table versions and partitions that might belong to the tables) and the user-defined functions in the deleted database. AWS Glue deletes these "orphaned" resources asynchronously in a timely manner, at the discretion of the service.
To ensure immediate deletion of all related resources, before calling `DeleteDatabase`, use `DeleteTableVersion` or `BatchDeleteTableVersion`, `DeletePartition` or `BatchDeletePartition`, `DeleteUserDefinedFunction`, and `DeleteTable` or `BatchDeleteTable`, to delete any resources that belong to the database.

Request

- `CatalogId` – Catalog id string, not less than 1 or more than 255 bytes long, matching the Single-line string pattern.

  The ID of the Data Catalog in which the database resides. If none is supplied, the AWS account ID is used by default.

- `Name` – UTF-8 string, not less than 1 or more than 255 bytes long, matching the Single-line string pattern. Required.

  The name of the Database to delete. For Hive compatibility, this must be all lowercase.

Response

- *No Response parameters.*

Errors

- `EntityNotFoundException`
- `InvalidInputException`
- `InternalServiceException`
- `OperationTimeoutException`

GetDatabase Action (Python: get_database)

Retrieves the definition of a specified database.

Request

- `CatalogId` – Catalog id string, not less than 1 or more than 255 bytes long, matching the Single-line string pattern.

  The ID of the Data Catalog in which the database resides. If none is supplied, the AWS account ID is used by default.

- `Name` – UTF-8 string, not less than 1 or more than 255 bytes long, matching the Single-line string pattern. Required.

  The name of the database to retrieve. For Hive compatibility, this should be all lowercase.

Response

- `Database` – A Database object.

  The definition of the specified database in the catalog.

Errors

- `InvalidInputException`
- `EntityNotFoundException`
- `InternalServiceException`
- `OperationTimeoutException`
- `GlueEncryptionException`

GetDatabases Action (Python: get_databases)

Retrieves all Databases defined in a given Data Catalog.

Request

- `CatalogId` – Catalog id string, not less than 1 or more than 255 bytes long, matching the Single-line string pattern.

  The ID of the Data Catalog from which to retrieve `Databases`. If none is supplied, the AWS account ID is used by default.

- `NextToken` – UTF-8 string.

  A continuation token, if this is a continuation call.

- `MaxResults` – Number (integer), not less than 1 or more than 1000.

  The maximum number of databases to return in one response.

Response

- `DatabaseList` – An array of Databases. Required.

  A list of `Database` objects from the specified catalog.

- `NextToken` – UTF-8 string.

  A continuation token for paginating the returned list of tokens, returned if the current segment of the list is not the last.

Errors

- `InvalidInputException`
- `InternalServiceException`
- `OperationTimeoutException`
- `GlueEncryptionException`

Table API

Data Types

- Table Structure
- TableInput Structure
- Column Structure
- StorageDescriptor Structure
- SerDeInfo Structure
- Order Structure
- SkewedInfo Structure
- TableVersion Structure
- TableError Structure
- TableVersionError Structure

Table Structure

Represents a collection of related data organized in columns and rows.

Fields

- `Name` – UTF-8 string, not less than 1 or more than 255 bytes long, matching the Single-line string pattern. Required.

  Name of the table. For Hive compatibility, this must be entirely lowercase.

- `DatabaseName` – UTF-8 string, not less than 1 or more than 255 bytes long, matching the Single-line string pattern.

  Name of the metadata database where the table metadata resides. For Hive compatibility, this must be all lowercase.

- `Description` – Description string, not more than 2048 bytes long, matching the URI address multi-line string pattern.

  Description of the table.

- `Owner` – UTF-8 string, not less than 1 or more than 255 bytes long, matching the Single-line string pattern.

  Owner of the table.

- `CreateTime` – Timestamp.

  Time when the table definition was created in the Data Catalog.

- `UpdateTime` – Timestamp.

  Last time the table was updated.

- `LastAccessTime` – Timestamp.

  Last time the table was accessed. This is usually taken from HDFS, and may not be reliable.

- `LastAnalyzedTime` – Timestamp.

  Last time column statistics were computed for this table.

- `Retention` – Number (integer), at least 0.

  Retention time for this table.

- `StorageDescriptor` – A StorageDescriptor object.

  A storage descriptor containing information about the physical storage of this table.

- `PartitionKeys` – An array of Columns.

  A list of columns by which the table is partitioned. Only primitive types are supported as partition keys.

- `ViewOriginalText` – UTF-8 string, not more than 409600 bytes long.

  If the table is a view, the original text of the view; otherwise `null`.

- `ViewExpandedText` – UTF-8 string, not more than 409600 bytes long.

  If the table is a view, the expanded text of the view; otherwise `null`.

- `TableType` – UTF-8 string, not more than 255 bytes long.

  The type of this table (`EXTERNAL_TABLE`, `VIRTUAL_VIEW`, etc.).

- `Parameters` – A map array of key-value pairs

  Each key is a Key string, not less than 1 or more than 255 bytes long, matching the Single-line string pattern.

  Each value is a UTF-8 string, not more than 512000 bytes long.

  These key-value pairs define properties associated with the table.

- `CreatedBy` – UTF-8 string, not less than 1 or more than 255 bytes long, matching the Single-line string pattern.

  Person or entity who created the table.

TableInput Structure

Structure used to create or update the table.

Fields

- `Name` – UTF-8 string, not less than 1 or more than 255 bytes long, matching the Single-line string pattern. Required.

  Name of the table. For Hive compatibility, this is folded to lowercase when it is stored.

- `Description` – Description string, not more than 2048 bytes long, matching the URI address multi-line string pattern.

  Description of the table.

- `Owner` – UTF-8 string, not less than 1 or more than 255 bytes long, matching the Single-line string pattern.

  Owner of the table.

- `LastAccessTime` – Timestamp.

  Last time the table was accessed.

- `LastAnalyzedTime` – Timestamp.

  Last time column statistics were computed for this table.

- `Retention` – Number (integer), at least 0.

  Retention time for this table.

- `StorageDescriptor` – A StorageDescriptor object.

  A storage descriptor containing information about the physical storage of this table.

338

- **PartitionKeys** – An array of Columns.

  A list of columns by which the table is partitioned. Only primitive types are supported as partition keys.

- **ViewOriginalText** – UTF-8 string, not more than 409600 bytes long.

  If the table is a view, the original text of the view; otherwise **null**.

- **ViewExpandedText** – UTF-8 string, not more than 409600 bytes long.

  If the table is a view, the expanded text of the view; otherwise **null**.

- **TableType** – UTF-8 string, not more than 255 bytes long.

  The type of this table (**EXTERNAL_TABLE**, **VIRTUAL_VIEW**, etc.).

- **Parameters** – A map array of key-value pairs

  Each key is a Key string, not less than 1 or more than 255 bytes long, matching the Single-line string pattern.

  Each value is a UTF-8 string, not more than 512000 bytes long.

  These key-value pairs define properties associated with the table.

Column Structure

A column in a **Table**.

Fields

- **Name** – UTF-8 string, not less than 1 or more than 1024 bytes long, matching the Single-line string pattern. Required.

  The name of the **Column**.

- **Type** – UTF-8 string, not more than 131072 bytes long, matching the Single-line string pattern.

  The datatype of data in the **Column**.

- **Comment** – Comment string, not more than 255 bytes long, matching the Single-line string pattern.

  Free-form text comment.

StorageDescriptor Structure

Describes the physical storage of table data.

Fields

- **Columns** – An array of Columns.

  A list of the **Columns** in the table.

- **Location** – Location string, not more than 2056 bytes long, matching the URI address multi-line string pattern.

  The physical location of the table. By default this takes the form of the warehouse location, followed by the database location in the warehouse, followed by the table name.

- **InputFormat** – Format string, not more than 128 bytes long, matching the Single-line string pattern.

  The input format: **SequenceFileInputFormat** (binary), or **TextInputFormat**, or a custom format.

- `OutputFormat` – Format string, not more than 128 bytes long, matching the Single-line string pattern.

  The output format: `SequenceFileOutputFormat` (binary), or `IgnoreKeyTextOutputFormat`, or a custom format.

- `Compressed` – Boolean.

  True if the data in the table is compressed, or False if not.

- `NumberOfBuckets` – Number (integer).

  Must be specified if the table contains any dimension columns.

- `SerdeInfo` – A SerDeInfo object.

  Serialization/deserialization (SerDe) information.

- `BucketColumns` – An array of UTF-8 strings.

  A list of reducer grouping columns, clustering columns, and bucketing columns in the table.

- `SortColumns` – An array of Orders.

  A list specifying the sort order of each bucket in the table.

- `Parameters` – A map array of key-value pairs

  Each key is a Key string, not less than 1 or more than 255 bytes long, matching the Single-line string pattern.

  Each value is a UTF-8 string, not more than 512000 bytes long.

  User-supplied properties in key-value form.

- `SkewedInfo` – A SkewedInfo object.

  Information about values that appear very frequently in a column (skewed values).

- `StoredAsSubDirectories` – Boolean.

  True if the table data is stored in subdirectories, or False if not.

SerDeInfo Structure

Information about a serialization/deserialization program (SerDe) which serves as an extractor and loader.

Fields

- `Name` – UTF-8 string, not less than 1 or more than 255 bytes long, matching the Single-line string pattern.

  Name of the SerDe.

- `SerializationLibrary` – UTF-8 string, not less than 1 or more than 255 bytes long, matching the Single-line string pattern.

  Usually the class that implements the SerDe. An example is: `org.apache.hadoop.hive.serde2.columnar`
  `.ColumnarSerDe`.

- `Parameters` – A map array of key-value pairs

  Each key is a Key string, not less than 1 or more than 255 bytes long, matching the Single-line string pattern.

  Each value is a UTF-8 string, not more than 512000 bytes long.

  These key-value pairs define initialization parameters for the SerDe.

Order Structure

Specifies the sort order of a sorted column.

Fields

- `Column` – UTF-8 string, not less than 1 or more than 255 bytes long, matching the Single-line string pattern. Required.

  The name of the column.

- `SortOrder` – Number (integer), not less than 0 or more than 1. Required.

  Indicates that the column is sorted in ascending order (`== 1`), or in descending order (`==0`).

SkewedInfo Structure

Specifies skewed values in a table. Skewed are ones that occur with very high frequency.

Fields

- `SkewedColumnNames` – An array of UTF-8 strings.

  A list of names of columns that contain skewed values.

- `SkewedColumnValues` – An array of UTF-8 strings.

  A list of values that appear so frequently as to be considered skewed.

- `SkewedColumnValueLocationMaps` – A map array of key-value pairs

  Each key is a UTF-8 string.

  Each value is a UTF-8 string.

  A mapping of skewed values to the columns that contain them.

TableVersion Structure

Specifies a version of a table.

Fields

- `Table` – A Table object.

  The table in question

- `VersionId` – UTF-8 string, not less than 1 or more than 255 bytes long, matching the Single-line string pattern.

  The ID value that identifies this table version.

TableError Structure

An error record for table operations.

Fields

- `TableName` – UTF-8 string, not less than 1 or more than 255 bytes long, matching the Single-line string pattern.

  Name of the table. For Hive compatibility, this must be entirely lowercase.

341

- **ErrorDetail** – An ErrorDetail object.

  Detail about the error.

TableVersionError Structure

An error record for table-version operations.

Fields

- **TableName** – UTF-8 string, not less than 1 or more than 255 bytes long, matching the Single-line string pattern.

  The name of the table in question.

- **VersionId** – UTF-8 string, not less than 1 or more than 255 bytes long, matching the Single-line string pattern.

  The ID value of the version in question.

- **ErrorDetail** – An ErrorDetail object.

  Detail about the error.

Operations

- CreateTable Action (Python: create_table)
- UpdateTable Action (Python: update_table)
- DeleteTable Action (Python: delete_table)
- BatchDeleteTable Action (Python: batch_delete_table)
- GetTable Action (Python: get_table)
- GetTables Action (Python: get_tables)
- GetTableVersion Action (Python: get_table_version)
- GetTableVersions Action (Python: get_table_versions)
- DeleteTableVersion Action (Python: delete_table_version)
- BatchDeleteTableVersion Action (Python: batch_delete_table_version)

CreateTable Action (Python: create_table)

Creates a new table definition in the Data Catalog.

Request

- **CatalogId** – Catalog id string, not less than 1 or more than 255 bytes long, matching the Single-line string pattern.

  The ID of the Data Catalog in which to create the **Table**. If none is supplied, the AWS account ID is used by default.

- **DatabaseName** – UTF-8 string, not less than 1 or more than 255 bytes long, matching the Single-line string pattern. Required.

  The catalog database in which to create the new table. For Hive compatibility, this name is entirely lowercase.

- **TableInput** – A TableInput object. Required.

  The **TableInput** object that defines the metadata table to create in the catalog.

Response

- *No Response parameters.*

Errors

- `AlreadyExistsException`
- `InvalidInputException`
- `EntityNotFoundException`
- `ResourceNumberLimitExceededException`
- `InternalServiceException`
- `OperationTimeoutException`
- `GlueEncryptionException`

UpdateTable Action (Python: update_table)

Updates a metadata table in the Data Catalog.

Request

- `CatalogId` – Catalog id string, not less than 1 or more than 255 bytes long, matching the Single-line string pattern.

  The ID of the Data Catalog where the table resides. If none is supplied, the AWS account ID is used by default.

- `DatabaseName` – UTF-8 string, not less than 1 or more than 255 bytes long, matching the Single-line string pattern. Required.

  The name of the catalog database in which the table resides. For Hive compatibility. this name is entirely lowercase.

- `TableInput` – A TableInput object. Required.

  An updated `TableInput` object to define the metadata table in the catalog.

- `SkipArchive` – Boolean.

  By default, `UpdateTable` always creates an archived version of the table before updating it. If `skipArchive` is set to true, however, `UpdateTable` does not create the archived version.

Response

- *No Response parameters.*

Errors

- `EntityNotFoundException`
- `InvalidInputException`
- `InternalServiceException`
- `OperationTimeoutException`
- `ConcurrentModificationException`
- `ResourceNumberLimitExceededException`
- `GlueEncryptionException`

DeleteTable Action (Python: delete_table)

Removes a table definition from the Data Catalog.

Note
After completing this operation, you will no longer have access to the table versions and partitions that belong to the deleted table. AWS Glue deletes these "orphaned" resources asynchronously in a timely manner, at the discretion of the service.

343

To ensure immediate deletion of all related resources, before calling `DeleteTable`, use `DeleteTableVersion` or `BatchDeleteTableVersion`, and `DeletePartition` or `BatchDeletePartition`, to delete any resources that belong to the table.

Request

- `CatalogId` – Catalog id string, not less than 1 or more than 255 bytes long, matching the Single-line string pattern.

  The ID of the Data Catalog where the table resides. If none is supplied, the AWS account ID is used by default.

- `DatabaseName` – UTF-8 string, not less than 1 or more than 255 bytes long, matching the Single-line string pattern. Required.

  The name of the catalog database in which the table resides. For Hive compatibility, this name is entirely lowercase.

- `Name` – UTF-8 string, not less than 1 or more than 255 bytes long, matching the Single-line string pattern. Required.

  The name of the table to be deleted. For Hive compatibility, this name is entirely lowercase.

Response

- *No Response parameters.*

Errors

- `EntityNotFoundException`
- `InvalidInputException`
- `InternalServiceException`
- `OperationTimeoutException`

BatchDeleteTable Action (Python: batch_delete_table)

Deletes multiple tables at once.

Note

After completing this operation, you will no longer have access to the table versions and partitions that belong to the deleted table. AWS Glue deletes these "orphaned" resources asynchronously in a timely manner, at the discretion of the service.

To ensure immediate deletion of all related resources, before calling `BatchDeleteTable`, use `DeleteTableVersion` or `BatchDeleteTableVersion`, and `DeletePartition` or `BatchDeletePartition`, to delete any resources that belong to the table.

Request

- `CatalogId` – Catalog id string, not less than 1 or more than 255 bytes long, matching the Single-line string pattern.

  The ID of the Data Catalog where the table resides. If none is supplied, the AWS account ID is used by default.

- `DatabaseName` – UTF-8 string, not less than 1 or more than 255 bytes long, matching the Single-line string pattern. Required.

  The name of the catalog database where the tables to delete reside. For Hive compatibility, this name is entirely lowercase.

- `TablesToDelete` – An array of UTF-8 strings, not more than 100 items in the array. Required.

  A list of the table to delete.

Response

- Errors – An array of TableErrors.

  A list of errors encountered in attempting to delete the specified tables.

Errors

- InvalidInputException
- EntityNotFoundException
- InternalServiceException
- OperationTimeoutException

GetTable Action (Python: get_table)

Retrieves the Table definition in a Data Catalog for a specified table.

Request

- CatalogId – Catalog id string, not less than 1 or more than 255 bytes long, matching the Single-line string pattern.

  The ID of the Data Catalog where the table resides. If none is supplied, the AWS account ID is used by default.

- DatabaseName – UTF-8 string, not less than 1 or more than 255 bytes long, matching the Single-line string pattern. Required.

  The name of the database in the catalog in which the table resides. For Hive compatibility, this name is entirely lowercase.

- Name – UTF-8 string, not less than 1 or more than 255 bytes long, matching the Single-line string pattern. Required.

  The name of the table for which to retrieve the definition. For Hive compatibility, this name is entirely lowercase.

Response

- Table – A Table object.

  The Table object that defines the specified table.

Errors

- EntityNotFoundException
- InvalidInputException
- InternalServiceException
- OperationTimeoutException
- GlueEncryptionException

GetTables Action (Python: get_tables)

Retrieves the definitions of some or all of the tables in a given Database.

Request

- CatalogId – Catalog id string, not less than 1 or more than 255 bytes long, matching the Single-line string pattern.

  The ID of the Data Catalog where the tables reside. If none is supplied, the AWS account ID is used by default.

- **DatabaseName** – UTF-8 string, not less than 1 or more than 255 bytes long, matching the Single-line string pattern. Required.

  The database in the catalog whose tables to list. For Hive compatibility, this name is entirely lowercase.

- **Expression** – UTF-8 string, not more than 2048 bytes long, matching the Single-line string pattern.

  A regular expression pattern. If present, only those tables whose names match the pattern are returned.

- **NextToken** – UTF-8 string.

  A continuation token, included if this is a continuation call.

- **MaxResults** – Number (integer), not less than 1 or more than 1000.

  The maximum number of tables to return in a single response.

Response

- **TableList** – An array of Tables.

  A list of the requested **Table** objects.

- **NextToken** – UTF-8 string.

  A continuation token, present if the current list segment is not the last.

Errors

- EntityNotFoundException
- InvalidInputException
- OperationTimeoutException
- InternalServiceException
- GlueEncryptionException

GetTableVersion Action (Python: get_table_version)

Retrieves a specified version of a table.

Request

- **CatalogId** – Catalog id string, not less than 1 or more than 255 bytes long, matching the Single-line string pattern.

  The ID of the Data Catalog where the tables reside. If none is supplied, the AWS account ID is used by default.

- **DatabaseName** – UTF-8 string, not less than 1 or more than 255 bytes long, matching the Single-line string pattern. Required.

  The database in the catalog in which the table resides. For Hive compatibility, this name is entirely lowercase.

- **TableName** – UTF-8 string, not less than 1 or more than 255 bytes long, matching the Single-line string pattern. Required.

  The name of the table. For Hive compatibility, this name is entirely lowercase.

- **VersionId** – UTF-8 string, not less than 1 or more than 255 bytes long, matching the Single-line string pattern.

  The ID value of the table version to be retrieved.

Response

- `TableVersion` – A TableVersion object.

  The requested table version.

Errors

- `EntityNotFoundException`
- `InvalidInputException`
- `InternalServiceException`
- `OperationTimeoutException`
- `GlueEncryptionException`

GetTableVersions Action (Python: get_table_versions)

Retrieves a list of strings that identify available versions of a specified table.

Request

- `CatalogId` – Catalog id string, not less than 1 or more than 255 bytes long, matching the Single-line string pattern.

  The ID of the Data Catalog where the tables reside. If none is supplied, the AWS account ID is used by default.

- `DatabaseName` – UTF-8 string, not less than 1 or more than 255 bytes long, matching the Single-line string pattern. Required.

  The database in the catalog in which the table resides. For Hive compatibility, this name is entirely lowercase.

- `TableName` – UTF-8 string, not less than 1 or more than 255 bytes long, matching the Single-line string pattern. Required.

  The name of the table. For Hive compatibility, this name is entirely lowercase.

- `NextToken` – UTF-8 string.

  A continuation token, if this is not the first call.

- `MaxResults` – Number (integer), not less than 1 or more than 1000.

  The maximum number of table versions to return in one response.

Response

- `TableVersions` – An array of TableVersions.

  A list of strings identifying available versions of the specified table.

- `NextToken` – UTF-8 string.

  A continuation token, if the list of available versions does not include the last one.

Errors

- `EntityNotFoundException`
- `InvalidInputException`
- `InternalServiceException`
- `OperationTimeoutException`
- `GlueEncryptionException`

DeleteTableVersion Action (Python: delete_table_version)

Deletes a specified version of a table.

Request

- `CatalogId` – Catalog id string, not less than 1 or more than 255 bytes long, matching the Single-line string pattern.

  The ID of the Data Catalog where the tables reside. If none is supplied, the AWS account ID is used by default.

- `DatabaseName` – UTF-8 string, not less than 1 or more than 255 bytes long, matching the Single-line string pattern. Required.

  The database in the catalog in which the table resides. For Hive compatibility, this name is entirely lowercase.

- `TableName` – UTF-8 string, not less than 1 or more than 255 bytes long, matching the Single-line string pattern. Required.

  The name of the table. For Hive compatibility, this name is entirely lowercase.

- `VersionId` – UTF-8 string, not less than 1 or more than 255 bytes long, matching the Single-line string pattern. Required.

  The ID of the table version to be deleted.

Response

- *No Response parameters.*

Errors

- `EntityNotFoundException`
- `InvalidInputException`
- `InternalServiceException`
- `OperationTimeoutException`

BatchDeleteTableVersion Action (Python: batch_delete_table_version)

Deletes a specified batch of versions of a table.

Request

- `CatalogId` – Catalog id string, not less than 1 or more than 255 bytes long, matching the Single-line string pattern.

  The ID of the Data Catalog where the tables reside. If none is supplied, the AWS account ID is used by default.

- `DatabaseName` – UTF-8 string, not less than 1 or more than 255 bytes long, matching the Single-line string pattern. Required.

  The database in the catalog in which the table resides. For Hive compatibility, this name is entirely lowercase.

- `TableName` – UTF-8 string, not less than 1 or more than 255 bytes long, matching the Single-line string pattern. Required.

  The name of the table. For Hive compatibility, this name is entirely lowercase.

- `VersionIds` – An array of UTF-8 strings, not more than 100 items in the array. Required.

  A list of the IDs of versions to be deleted.

348

Response

- Errors – An array of TableVersionErrors.

  A list of errors encountered while trying to delete the specified table versions.

Errors

- EntityNotFoundException
- InvalidInputException
- InternalServiceException
- OperationTimeoutException

Partition API

Data Types

- Partition Structure
- PartitionInput Structure
- PartitionSpecWithSharedStorageDescriptor Structure
- PartitionListComposingSpec Structure
- PartitionSpecProxy Structure
- PartitionValueList Structure
- Segment Structure
- PartitionError Structure

Partition Structure

Represents a slice of table data.

Fields

- `Values` – An array of UTF-8 strings, at least 1 item in the array.

  The values of the partition.

- `DatabaseName` – UTF-8 string, not less than 1 or more than 255 bytes long, matching the Single-line string pattern.

  The name of the catalog database where the table in question is located.

- `TableName` – UTF-8 string, not less than 1 or more than 255 bytes long, matching the Single-line string pattern.

  The name of the table in question.

- `CreationTime` – Timestamp.

  The time at which the partition was created.

- `LastAccessTime` – Timestamp.

  The last time at which the partition was accessed.

- `StorageDescriptor` – A StorageDescriptor object.

  Provides information about the physical location where the partition is stored.

- `Parameters` – A map array of key-value pairs

  Each key is a Key string, not less than 1 or more than 255 bytes long, matching the Single-line string pattern.

  Each value is a UTF-8 string, not more than 512000 bytes long.

  These key-value pairs define partition parameters.

- `LastAnalyzedTime` – Timestamp.

  The last time at which column statistics were computed for this partition.

PartitionInput Structure

The structure used to create and update a partion.

Fields

- `Values` – An array of UTF-8 strings, at least 1 item in the array.

  The values of the partition.

- `LastAccessTime` – Timestamp.

  The last time at which the partition was accessed.

- `StorageDescriptor` – A StorageDescriptor object.

  Provides information about the physical location where the partition is stored.

- `Parameters` – A map array of key-value pairs

  Each key is a Key string, not less than 1 or more than 255 bytes long, matching the Single-line string pattern.

  Each value is a UTF-8 string, not more than 512000 bytes long.

  These key-value pairs define partition parameters.

- `LastAnalyzedTime` – Timestamp.

  The last time at which column statistics were computed for this partition.

PartitionSpecWithSharedStorageDescriptor Structure

A partition specification for partitions that share a physical location.

Fields

- `StorageDescriptor` – A StorageDescriptor object.

  The shared physical storage information.

- `Partitions` – An array of Partitions.

  A list of the partitions that share this physical location.

PartitionListComposingSpec Structure

Lists related partitions.

Fields

- `Partitions` – An array of Partitions.

  A list of the partitions in the composing specification.

PartitionSpecProxy Structure

Provides a root path to specified partitions.

Fields

- `DatabaseName` – UTF-8 string, not less than 1 or more than 255 bytes long, matching the Single-line string pattern.

  The catalog database in which the partions reside.

- `TableName` – UTF-8 string, not less than 1 or more than 255 bytes long, matching the Single-line string pattern.

  The name of the table containing the partitions.

- `RootPath` – UTF-8 string, not less than 1 or more than 255 bytes long, matching the Single-line string pattern.

  The root path of the proxy for addressing the partitions.

- `PartitionSpecWithSharedSD` – A PartitionSpecWithSharedStorageDescriptor object.

  A specification of partitions that share the same physical storage location.

- `PartitionListComposingSpec` – A PartitionListComposingSpec object.

  Specifies a list of partitions.

PartitionValueList Structure

Contains a list of values defining partitions.

Fields

- `Values` – An array of UTF-8 strings, at least 1 item in the array. Required.

  The list of values.

Segment Structure

Defines a non-overlapping region of a table's partitions, allowing multiple requests to be executed in parallel.

Fields

- `SegmentNumber` – Number (integer), at least 0. Required.

  The zero-based index number of the this segment. For example, if the total number of segments is 4, SegmentNumber values will range from zero through three.

- `TotalSegments` – Number (integer), not less than 1 or more than 10. Required.

  The total numer of segments.

PartitionError Structure

Contains information about a partition error.

Fields

- `PartitionValues` – An array of UTF-8 strings, at least 1 item in the array.

  The values that define the partition.

- `ErrorDetail` – An ErrorDetail object.

  Details about the partition error.

Operations

- CreatePartition Action (Python: create_partition)
- BatchCreatePartition Action (Python: batch_create_partition)
- UpdatePartition Action (Python: update_partition)
- DeletePartition Action (Python: delete_partition)
- BatchDeletePartition Action (Python: batch_delete_partition)
- GetPartition Action (Python: get_partition)
- GetPartitions Action (Python: get_partitions)
- BatchGetPartition Action (Python: batch_get_partition)

CreatePartition Action (Python: create_partition)

Creates a new partition.

Request

- `CatalogId` – Catalog id string, not less than 1 or more than 255 bytes long, matching the Single-line string pattern.

  The ID of the catalog in which the partion is to be created. Currently this should be the AWS account ID.

- `DatabaseName` – UTF-8 string, not less than 1 or more than 255 bytes long, matching the Single-line string pattern. Required.

  The name of the metadata database in which the partition is to be created.

- `TableName` – UTF-8 string, not less than 1 or more than 255 bytes long, matching the Single-line string pattern. Required.

  The name of the metadata table in which the partition is to be created.

- `PartitionInput` – A PartitionInput object. Required.

  A `PartitionInput` structure defining the partition to be created.

Response

- *No Response parameters.*

Errors

- `InvalidInputException`
- `AlreadyExistsException`
- `ResourceNumberLimitExceededException`
- `InternalServiceException`
- `EntityNotFoundException`
- `OperationTimeoutException`
- `GlueEncryptionException`

BatchCreatePartition Action (Python: batch_create_partition)

Creates one or more partitions in a batch operation.

Request

- `CatalogId` – Catalog id string, not less than 1 or more than 255 bytes long, matching the Single-line string pattern.

  The ID of the catalog in which the partion is to be created. Currently, this should be the AWS account ID.

- **DatabaseName** – UTF-8 string, not less than 1 or more than 255 bytes long, matching the Single-line string pattern. Required.

  The name of the metadata database in which the partition is to be created.

- **TableName** – UTF-8 string, not less than 1 or more than 255 bytes long, matching the Single-line string pattern. Required.

  The name of the metadata table in which the partition is to be created.

- **PartitionInputList** – An array of PartitionInputs, not more than 100 items in the array. Required.

  A list of **PartitionInput** structures that define the partitions to be created.

Response

- **Errors** – An array of PartitionErrors.

  Errors encountered when trying to create the requested partitions.

Errors

- InvalidInputException
- AlreadyExistsException
- ResourceNumberLimitExceededException
- InternalServiceException
- EntityNotFoundException
- OperationTimeoutException
- GlueEncryptionException

UpdatePartition Action (Python: update_partition)

Updates a partition.

Request

- **CatalogId** – Catalog id string, not less than 1 or more than 255 bytes long, matching the Single-line string pattern.

  The ID of the Data Catalog where the partition to be updated resides. If none is supplied, the AWS account ID is used by default.

- **DatabaseName** – UTF-8 string, not less than 1 or more than 255 bytes long, matching the Single-line string pattern. Required.

  The name of the catalog database in which the table in question resides.

- **TableName** – UTF-8 string, not less than 1 or more than 255 bytes long, matching the Single-line string pattern. Required.

  The name of the table where the partition to be updated is located.

- **PartitionValueList** – An array of UTF-8 strings, not more than 100 items in the array. Required.

  A list of the values defining the partition.

- **PartitionInput** – A PartitionInput object. Required.

  The new partition object to which to update the partition.

Response

- *No Response parameters.*

Errors

- EntityNotFoundException
- InvalidInputException
- InternalServiceException
- OperationTimeoutException
- GlueEncryptionException

DeletePartition Action (Python: delete_partition)

Deletes a specified partition.

Request

- `CatalogId` – Catalog id string, not less than 1 or more than 255 bytes long, matching the Single-line string pattern.

  The ID of the Data Catalog where the partition to be deleted resides. If none is supplied, the AWS account ID is used by default.

- `DatabaseName` – UTF-8 string, not less than 1 or more than 255 bytes long, matching the Single-line string pattern. Required.

  The name of the catalog database in which the table in question resides.

- `TableName` – UTF-8 string, not less than 1 or more than 255 bytes long, matching the Single-line string pattern. Required.

  The name of the table where the partition to be deleted is located.

- `PartitionValues` – An array of UTF-8 strings, at least 1 item in the array. Required.

  The values that define the partition.

Response

- *No Response parameters.*

Errors

- EntityNotFoundException
- InvalidInputException
- InternalServiceException
- OperationTimeoutException

BatchDeletePartition Action (Python: batch_delete_partition)

Deletes one or more partitions in a batch operation.

Request

- `CatalogId` – Catalog id string, not less than 1 or more than 255 bytes long, matching the Single-line string pattern.

  The ID of the Data Catalog where the partition to be deleted resides. If none is supplied, the AWS account ID is used by default.

- `DatabaseName` – UTF-8 string, not less than 1 or more than 255 bytes long, matching the Single-line string pattern. Required.

  The name of the catalog database in which the table in question resides.

- `TableName` – UTF-8 string, not less than 1 or more than 255 bytes long, matching the Single-line string pattern. Required.

  The name of the table where the partitions to be deleted is located.

- `PartitionsToDelete` – An array of PartitionValueLists, not more than 25 items in the array. Required.

  A list of `PartitionInput` structures that define the partitions to be deleted.

Response

- `Errors` – An array of PartitionErrors.

  Errors encountered when trying to delete the requested partitions.

Errors

- `InvalidInputException`
- `EntityNotFoundException`
- `InternalServiceException`
- `OperationTimeoutException`

GetPartition Action (Python: get_partition)

Retrieves information about a specified partition.

Request

- `CatalogId` – Catalog id string, not less than 1 or more than 255 bytes long, matching the Single-line string pattern.

  The ID of the Data Catalog where the partition in question resides. If none is supplied, the AWS account ID is used by default.

- `DatabaseName` – UTF-8 string, not less than 1 or more than 255 bytes long, matching the Single-line string pattern. Required.

  The name of the catalog database where the partition resides.

- `TableName` – UTF-8 string, not less than 1 or more than 255 bytes long, matching the Single-line string pattern. Required.

  The name of the partition's table.

- `PartitionValues` – An array of UTF-8 strings, at least 1 item in the array. Required.

  The values that define the partition.

Response

- `Partition` – A Partition object.

  The requested information, in the form of a `Partition` object.

Errors

- `EntityNotFoundException`
- `InvalidInputException`
- `InternalServiceException`
- `OperationTimeoutException`
- `GlueEncryptionException`

GetPartitions Action (Python: get_partitions)

Retrieves information about the partitions in a table.

Request

- `CatalogId` – Catalog id string, not less than 1 or more than 255 bytes long, matching the Single-line string pattern.

  The ID of the Data Catalog where the partitions in question reside. If none is supplied, the AWS account ID is used by default.

- `DatabaseName` – UTF-8 string, not less than 1 or more than 255 bytes long, matching the Single-line string pattern. Required.

  The name of the catalog database where the partitions reside.

- `TableName` – UTF-8 string, not less than 1 or more than 255 bytes long, matching the Single-line string pattern. Required.

  The name of the partitions' table.

- `Expression` – Predicate string, not more than 2048 bytes long, matching the URI address multi-line string pattern.

  An expression filtering the partitions to be returned.

- `NextToken` – UTF-8 string.

  A continuation token, if this is not the first call to retrieve these partitions.

- `Segment` – A Segment object.

  The segment of the table's partitions to scan in this request.

- `MaxResults` – Number (integer), not less than 1 or more than 1000.

  The maximum number of partitions to return in a single response.

Response

- `Partitions` – An array of Partitions.

  A list of requested partitions.

- `NextToken` – UTF-8 string.

  A continuation token, if the returned list of partitions does not does not include the last one.

Errors

- `EntityNotFoundException`
- `InvalidInputException`
- `OperationTimeoutException`
- `InternalServiceException`
- `GlueEncryptionException`

BatchGetPartition Action (Python: batch_get_partition)

Retrieves partitions in a batch request.

Request

- `CatalogId` – Catalog id string, not less than 1 or more than 255 bytes long, matching the Single-line string pattern.

  The ID of the Data Catalog where the partitions in question reside. If none is supplied, the AWS account ID is used by default.

- `DatabaseName` – UTF-8 string, not less than 1 or more than 255 bytes long, matching the Single-line string pattern. Required.

  The name of the catalog database where the partitions reside.

- `TableName` – UTF-8 string, not less than 1 or more than 255 bytes long, matching the Single-line string pattern. Required.

  The name of the partitions' table.

- `PartitionsToGet` – An array of PartitionValueLists, not more than 1000 items in the array. Required.

  A list of partition values identifying the partitions to retrieve.

Response

- `Partitions` – An array of Partitions.

  A list of the requested partitions.

- `UnprocessedKeys` – An array of PartitionValueLists, not more than 1000 items in the array.

  A list of the partition values in the request for which partions were not returned.

Errors

- `InvalidInputException`
- `EntityNotFoundException`
- `OperationTimeoutException`
- `InternalServiceException`
- `GlueEncryptionException`

Connection API

Data Types

- Connection Structure
- ConnectionInput Structure
- PhysicalConnectionRequirements Structure
- GetConnectionsFilter Structure

Connection Structure

Defines a connection to a data source.

Fields

- `Name` – UTF-8 string, not less than 1 or more than 255 bytes long, matching the Single-line string pattern.

  The name of the connection definition.

- `Description` – Description string, not more than 2048 bytes long, matching the URI address multi-line string pattern.

  Description of the connection.

- `ConnectionType` – UTF-8 string (valid values: `JDBC` | `SFTP`).

  The type of the connection. Currently, only JDBC is supported; SFTP is not supported.

- `MatchCriteria` – An array of UTF-8 strings, not more than 10 items in the array.

  A list of criteria that can be used in selecting this connection.

- `ConnectionProperties` – A map array of key-value pairs, not more than 100 pairs

  Each key is a UTF-8 string (valid values: `HOST` | `PORT` | `USERNAME="USER_NAME"` | `PASSWORD` | `ENCRYPTED_PASSWORD` | `JDBC_DRIVER_JAR_URI` | `JDBC_DRIVER_CLASS_NAME` | `JDBC_ENGINE` | `JDBC_ENGINE_VERSION` | `CONFIG_FILES` | `INSTANCE_ID` | `JDBC_CONNECTION_URL` | `JDBC_ENFORCE_SSL`).

  Each value is a Value string.

  These key-value pairs define parameters for the connection:

  - `HOST` - The host URI.
  - `PORT` - The port number.
  - `USER_NAME` - The user name for the connection.
  - `PASSWORD` - A password, if one is used.
  - `ENCRYPTED_PASSWORD` - An encrypted password.
  - `JDBC_DRIVER_JAR_URI` - The URI of the a jar file that contains the JDBC driver to use.
  - `JDBC_DRIVER_CLASS_NAME` - The class name of the JDBC driver to use.
  - `JDBC_ENGINE` - The name of the JDBC engine to use.
  - `JDBC_ENGINE_VERSION` - The version of the JDBC engine to use.
  - `CONFIG_FILES` - The URI of configuration files for the connection.
  - `INSTANCE_ID` - The instance ID to use.
  - `JDBC_CONNECTION_URL` - The URL for the JDBC connection.
  - `JDBC_ENFORCE_SSL` - If present, specifies that SSL must be used for the JDBC connection.

- `PhysicalConnectionRequirements` – A PhysicalConnectionRequirements object.

  A map of physical connection requirements, such as VPC and SecurityGroup, needed for making this connection successfully.

- `CreationTime` – Timestamp.

  The time this connection definition was created.

- `LastUpdatedTime` – Timestamp.

  The last time this connection definition was updated.

- `LastUpdatedBy` – UTF-8 string, not less than 1 or more than 255 bytes long, matching the Single-line string pattern.

  The user, group or role that last updated this connection definition.

ConnectionInput Structure

A structure used to specify a connection to create or update.

Fields

- `Name` – UTF-8 string, not less than 1 or more than 255 bytes long, matching the Single-line string pattern. Required.

  The name of the connection.

- `Description` – Description string, not more than 2048 bytes long, matching the URI address multi-line string pattern.

  Description of the connection.

- `ConnectionType` – UTF-8 string (valid values: `JDBC` | `SFTP`). Required.

  The type of the connection. Currently, only JDBC is supported; SFTP is not supported.

- `MatchCriteria` – An array of UTF-8 strings, not more than 10 items in the array.

  A list of criteria that can be used in selecting this connection.

- `ConnectionProperties` – A map array of key-value pairs, not more than 100 pairs

  Each key is a UTF-8 string (valid values: `HOST` | `PORT` | `USERNAME="USER_NAME"` | `PASSWORD` | `ENCRYPTED_PASSWORD` | `JDBC_DRIVER_JAR_URI` | `JDBC_DRIVER_CLASS_NAME` | `JDBC_ENGINE` | `JDBC_ENGINE_VERSION` | `CONFIG_FILES` | `INSTANCE_ID` | `JDBC_CONNECTION_URL` | `JDBC_ENFORCE_SSL`).

  Each value is a Value string. Required.

  These key-value pairs define parameters for the connection.

- `PhysicalConnectionRequirements` – A PhysicalConnectionRequirements object.

  A map of physical connection requirements, such as VPC and SecurityGroup, needed for making this connection successfully.

PhysicalConnectionRequirements Structure

Specifies the physical requirements for a connection.

Fields

- `SubnetId` – UTF-8 string, not less than 1 or more than 255 bytes long, matching the Single-line string pattern.

  The subnet ID used by the connection.

- `SecurityGroupIdList` – An array of UTF-8 strings, not more than 50 items in the array.

  The security group ID list used by the connection.

- `AvailabilityZone` – UTF-8 string, not less than 1 or more than 255 bytes long, matching the Single-line string pattern.

  The connection's availability zone. This field is redundant, since the specified subnet implies the availability zone to be used. The field must be populated now, but will be deprecated in the future.

GetConnectionsFilter Structure

Filters the connection definitions returned by the `GetConnections` API.

Fields

- `MatchCriteria` – An array of UTF-8 strings, not more than 10 items in the array.

  A criteria string that must match the criteria recorded in the connection definition for that connection definition to be returned.

- `ConnectionType` – UTF-8 string (valid values: `JDBC` | `SFTP`).

  The type of connections to return. Currently, only JDBC is supported; SFTP is not supported.

Operations

- CreateConnection Action (Python: create_connection)
- DeleteConnection Action (Python: delete_connection)
- GetConnection Action (Python: get_connection)
- GetConnections Action (Python: get_connections)
- UpdateConnection Action (Python: update_connection)
- BatchDeleteConnection Action (Python: batch_delete_connection)

CreateConnection Action (Python: create_connection)

Creates a connection definition in the Data Catalog.

Request

- `CatalogId` – Catalog id string, not less than 1 or more than 255 bytes long, matching the Single-line string pattern.

  The ID of the Data Catalog in which to create the connection. If none is supplied, the AWS account ID is used by default.

- `ConnectionInput` – A ConnectionInput object. Required.

  A `ConnectionInput` object defining the connection to create.

Response

- *No Response parameters.*

Errors

- `AlreadyExistsException`
- `InvalidInputException`
- `OperationTimeoutException`
- `ResourceNumberLimitExceededException`

- `GlueEncryptionException`

DeleteConnection Action (Python: delete_connection)

Deletes a connection from the Data Catalog.

Request

- `CatalogId` – Catalog id string, not less than 1 or more than 255 bytes long, matching the Single-line string pattern.

  The ID of the Data Catalog in which the connection resides. If none is supplied, the AWS account ID is used by default.

- `ConnectionName` – UTF-8 string, not less than 1 or more than 255 bytes long, matching the Single-line string pattern. Required.

  The name of the connection to delete.

Response

- *No Response parameters.*

Errors

- `EntityNotFoundException`
- `OperationTimeoutException`
- `InvalidInputException`

GetConnection Action (Python: get_connection)

Retrieves a connection definition from the Data Catalog.

Request

- `CatalogId` – Catalog id string, not less than 1 or more than 255 bytes long, matching the Single-line string pattern.

  The ID of the Data Catalog in which the connection resides. If none is supplied, the AWS account ID is used by default.

- `Name` – UTF-8 string, not less than 1 or more than 255 bytes long, matching the Single-line string pattern. Required.

  The name of the connection definition to retrieve.

Response

- `Connection` – A Connection object.

  The requested connection definition.

Errors

- `EntityNotFoundException`
- `OperationTimeoutException`
- `InvalidInputException`
- `GlueEncryptionException`

GetConnections Action (Python: get_connections)

Retrieves a list of connection definitions from the Data Catalog.

Request

- `CatalogId` – Catalog id string, not less than 1 or more than 255 bytes long, matching the Single-line string pattern.

  The ID of the Data Catalog in which the connections reside. If none is supplied, the AWS account ID is used by default.

- `Filter` – A GetConnectionsFilter object.

  A filter that controls which connections will be returned.

- `NextToken` – UTF-8 string.

  A continuation token, if this is a continuation call.

- `MaxResults` – Number (integer), not less than 1 or more than 1000.

  The maximum number of connections to return in one response.

Response

- `ConnectionList` – An array of Connections.

  A list of requested connection definitions.

- `NextToken` – UTF-8 string.

  A continuation token, if the list of connections returned does not include the last of the filtered connections.

Errors

- `EntityNotFoundException`
- `OperationTimeoutException`
- `InvalidInputException`
- `GlueEncryptionException`

UpdateConnection Action (Python: update_connection)

Updates a connection definition in the Data Catalog.

Request

- `CatalogId` – Catalog id string, not less than 1 or more than 255 bytes long, matching the Single-line string pattern.

  The ID of the Data Catalog in which the connection resides. If none is supplied, the AWS account ID is used by default.

- `Name` – UTF-8 string, not less than 1 or more than 255 bytes long, matching the Single-line string pattern. Required.

  The name of the connection definition to update.

- `ConnectionInput` – A ConnectionInput object. Required.

  A `ConnectionInput` object that redefines the connection in question.

Response

- *No Response parameters.*

Errors

- `InvalidInputException`
- `EntityNotFoundException`
- `OperationTimeoutException`
- `InvalidInputException`
- `GlueEncryptionException`

BatchDeleteConnection Action (Python: batch_delete_connection)

Deletes a list of connection definitions from the Data Catalog.

Request

- `CatalogId` – Catalog id string, not less than 1 or more than 255 bytes long, matching the Single-line string pattern.

  The ID of the Data Catalog in which the connections reside. If none is supplied, the AWS account ID is used by default.

- `ConnectionNameList` – An array of UTF-8 strings, not more than 25 items in the array. Required.

  A list of names of the connections to delete.

Response

- `Succeeded` – An array of UTF-8 strings.

  A list of names of the connection definitions that were successfully deleted.

- `Errors` – A map array of key-value pairs

  Each key is a UTF-8 string, not less than 1 or more than 255 bytes long, matching the Single-line string pattern.

  Each value is a An ErrorDetail object.

  A map of the names of connections that were not successfully deleted to error details.

Errors

- `InternalServiceException`
- `OperationTimeoutException`
- `InvalidInputException`

User-Defined Function API

Data Types

- UserDefinedFunction Structure
- UserDefinedFunctionInput Structure

UserDefinedFunction Structure

Represents the equivalent of a Hive user-defined function (UDF) definition.

Fields

- `FunctionName` – UTF-8 string, not less than 1 or more than 255 bytes long, matching the Single-line string pattern.

  The name of the function.

- `ClassName` – UTF-8 string, not less than 1 or more than 255 bytes long, matching the Single-line string pattern.

  The Java class that contains the function code.

- `OwnerName` – UTF-8 string, not less than 1 or more than 255 bytes long, matching the Single-line string pattern.

  The owner of the function.

- `OwnerType` – UTF-8 string (valid values: `USER` | `ROLE` | `GROUP`).

  The owner type.

- `CreateTime` – Timestamp.

  The time at which the function was created.

- `ResourceUris` – An array of ResourceUris, not more than 1000 items in the array.

  The resource URIs for the function.

UserDefinedFunctionInput Structure

A structure used to create or updata a user-defined function.

Fields

- `FunctionName` – UTF-8 string, not less than 1 or more than 255 bytes long, matching the Single-line string pattern.

  The name of the function.

- `ClassName` – UTF-8 string, not less than 1 or more than 255 bytes long, matching the Single-line string pattern.

  The Java class that contains the function code.

- `OwnerName` – UTF-8 string, not less than 1 or more than 255 bytes long, matching the Single-line string pattern.

  The owner of the function.

- OwnerType – UTF-8 string (valid values: USER | ROLE | GROUP).

  The owner type.

- ResourceUris – An array of ResourceUris, not more than 1000 items in the array.

  The resource URIs for the function.

Operations

- CreateUserDefinedFunction Action (Python: create_user_defined_function)
- UpdateUserDefinedFunction Action (Python: update_user_defined_function)
- DeleteUserDefinedFunction Action (Python: delete_user_defined_function)
- GetUserDefinedFunction Action (Python: get_user_defined_function)
- GetUserDefinedFunctions Action (Python: get_user_defined_functions)

CreateUserDefinedFunction Action (Python: create_user_defined_function)

Creates a new function definition in the Data Catalog.

Request

- CatalogId – Catalog id string, not less than 1 or more than 255 bytes long, matching the Single-line string pattern.

  The ID of the Data Catalog in which to create the function. If none is supplied, the AWS account ID is used by default.

- DatabaseName – UTF-8 string, not less than 1 or more than 255 bytes long, matching the Single-line string pattern. Required.

  The name of the catalog database in which to create the function.

- FunctionInput – An UserDefinedFunctionInput object. Required.

  A FunctionInput object that defines the function to create in the Data Catalog.

Response

- *No Response parameters.*

Errors

- AlreadyExistsException
- InvalidInputException
- InternalServiceException
- EntityNotFoundException
- OperationTimeoutException
- ResourceNumberLimitExceededException
- GlueEncryptionException

UpdateUserDefinedFunction Action (Python: update_user_defined_function)

Updates an existing function definition in the Data Catalog.

Request

- `CatalogId` – Catalog id string, not less than 1 or more than 255 bytes long, matching the Single-line string pattern.

  The ID of the Data Catalog where the function to be updated is located. If none is supplied, the AWS account ID is used by default.

- `DatabaseName` – UTF-8 string, not less than 1 or more than 255 bytes long, matching the Single-line string pattern. Required.

  The name of the catalog database where the function to be updated is located.

- `FunctionName` – UTF-8 string, not less than 1 or more than 255 bytes long, matching the Single-line string pattern. Required.

  The name of the function.

- `FunctionInput` – An UserDefinedFunctionInput object. Required.

  A `FunctionInput` object that re-defines the function in the Data Catalog.

Response

- *No Response parameters.*

Errors

- `EntityNotFoundException`
- `InvalidInputException`
- `InternalServiceException`
- `OperationTimeoutException`
- `GlueEncryptionException`

DeleteUserDefinedFunction Action (Python: delete_user_defined_function)

Deletes an existing function definition from the Data Catalog.

Request

- `CatalogId` – Catalog id string, not less than 1 or more than 255 bytes long, matching the Single-line string pattern.

  The ID of the Data Catalog where the function to be deleted is located. If none is supplied, the AWS account ID is used by default.

- `DatabaseName` – UTF-8 string, not less than 1 or more than 255 bytes long, matching the Single-line string pattern. Required.

  The name of the catalog database where the function is located.

- `FunctionName` – UTF-8 string, not less than 1 or more than 255 bytes long, matching the Single-line string pattern. Required.

  The name of the function definition to be deleted.

Response

- *No Response parameters.*

Errors

- `EntityNotFoundException`
- `InvalidInputException`
- `InternalServiceException`
- `OperationTimeoutException`

GetUserDefinedFunction Action (Python: get_user_defined_function)

Retrieves a specified function definition from the Data Catalog.

Request

- `CatalogId` – Catalog id string, not less than 1 or more than 255 bytes long, matching the Single-line string pattern.

  The ID of the Data Catalog where the function to be retrieved is located. If none is supplied, the AWS account ID is used by default.

- `DatabaseName` – UTF-8 string, not less than 1 or more than 255 bytes long, matching the Single-line string pattern. Required.

  The name of the catalog database where the function is located.

- `FunctionName` – UTF-8 string, not less than 1 or more than 255 bytes long, matching the Single-line string pattern. Required.

  The name of the function.

Response

- `UserDefinedFunction` – An UserDefinedFunction object.

  The requested function definition.

Errors

- `EntityNotFoundException`
- `InvalidInputException`
- `InternalServiceException`
- `OperationTimeoutException`
- `GlueEncryptionException`

GetUserDefinedFunctions Action (Python: get_user_defined_functions)

Retrieves a multiple function definitions from the Data Catalog.

Request

- `CatalogId` – Catalog id string, not less than 1 or more than 255 bytes long, matching the Single-line string pattern.

  The ID of the Data Catalog where the functions to be retrieved are located. If none is supplied, the AWS account ID is used by default.

- `DatabaseName` – UTF-8 string, not less than 1 or more than 255 bytes long, matching the Single-line string pattern. Required.

  The name of the catalog database where the functions are located.

- `Pattern` – UTF-8 string, not less than 1 or more than 255 bytes long, matching the Single-line string pattern. Required.

  An optional function-name pattern string that filters the function definitions returned.

- `NextToken` – UTF-8 string.

  A continuation token, if this is a continuation call.

- `MaxResults` – Number (integer), not less than 1 or more than 1000.

  The maximum number of functions to return in one response.

Response

- `UserDefinedFunctions` – An array of UserDefinedFunctions.

  A list of requested function definitions.

- `NextToken` – UTF-8 string.

  A continuation token, if the list of functions returned does not include the last requested function.

Errors

- `EntityNotFoundException`
- `InvalidInputException`
- `OperationTimeoutException`
- `InternalServiceException`
- `GlueEncryptionException`

Importing an Athena Catalog to AWS Glue

Data Types

- CatalogImportStatus Structure

CatalogImportStatus Structure

A structure containing migration status information.

Fields

- `ImportCompleted` – Boolean.

  True if the migration has completed, or False otherwise.

- `ImportTime` – Timestamp.

  The time that the migration was started.

- `ImportedBy` – UTF-8 string, not less than 1 or more than 255 bytes long, matching the Single-line string pattern.

  The name of the person who initiated the migration.

Operations

- ImportCatalogToGlue Action (Python: import_catalog_to_glue)
- GetCatalogImportStatus Action (Python: get_catalog_import_status)

ImportCatalogToGlue Action (Python: import_catalog_to_glue)

Imports an existing Athena Data Catalog to AWS Glue

Request

- `CatalogId` – Catalog id string, not less than 1 or more than 255 bytes long, matching the Single-line string pattern.

  The ID of the catalog to import. Currently, this should be the AWS account ID.

Response

- *No Response parameters.*

Errors

- `InternalServiceException`
- `OperationTimeoutException`

GetCatalogImportStatus Action (Python: get_catalog_import_status)

Retrieves the status of a migration operation.

Request

- `CatalogId` – Catalog id string, not less than 1 or more than 255 bytes long, matching the Single-line string pattern.

  The ID of the catalog to migrate. Currently, this should be the AWS account ID.

Response

- `ImportStatus` – A CatalogImportStatus object.

  The status of the specified catalog migration.

Errors

- `InternalServiceException`
- `OperationTimeoutException`

Crawlers and Classifiers API

Topics

- Classifier API
- Crawler API
- Crawler Scheduler API

Classifier API

Data Types

- Classifier Structure
- GrokClassifier Structure
- XMLClassifier Structure
- JsonClassifier Structure
- CreateGrokClassifierRequest Structure
- UpdateGrokClassifierRequest Structure
- CreateXMLClassifierRequest Structure
- UpdateXMLClassifierRequest Structure
- CreateJsonClassifierRequest Structure
- UpdateJsonClassifierRequest Structure

Classifier Structure

Classifiers are triggered during a crawl task. A classifier checks whether a given file is in a format it can handle, and if it is, the classifier creates a schema in the form of a `StructType` object that matches that data format.

You can use the standard classifiers that AWS Glue supplies, or you can write your own classifiers to best categorize your data sources and specify the appropriate schemas to use for them. A classifier can be a `grok` classifier, an `XML` classifier, or a `JSON` classifier, as specified in one of the fields in the `Classifier` object.

Fields

- `GrokClassifier` – A GrokClassifier object.

  A `GrokClassifier` object.

- `XMLClassifier` – A XMLClassifier object.

  An `XMLClassifier` object.

- `JsonClassifier` – A JsonClassifier object.

  A `JsonClassifier` object.

GrokClassifier Structure

A classifier that uses `grok` patterns.

Fields

- `Name` – UTF-8 string, not less than 1 or more than 255 bytes long, matching the Single-line string pattern. Required.

  The name of the classifier.

- `Classification` – UTF-8 string. Required.

  An identifier of the data format that the classifier matches, such as Twitter, JSON, Omniture logs, and so on.

- `CreationTime` – Timestamp.

  The time this classifier was registered.

- `LastUpdated` – Timestamp.

  The time this classifier was last updated.

- `Version` – Number (long).

  The version of this classifier.

- `GrokPattern` – UTF-8 string, not less than 1 or more than 2048 bytes long, matching the A Logstash Grok string pattern. Required.

  The grok pattern applied to a data store by this classifier. For more information, see built-in patterns in Writing Custom Classifers.

- `CustomPatterns` – UTF-8 string, not more than 16000 bytes long, matching the URI address multi-line string pattern.

  Optional custom grok patterns defined by this classifier. For more information, see custom patterns in Writing Custom Classifers.

XMLClassifier Structure

A classifier for `XML` content.

Fields

- `Name` – UTF-8 string, not less than 1 or more than 255 bytes long, matching the Single-line string pattern. Required.

  The name of the classifier.

- `Classification` – UTF-8 string. Required.

  An identifier of the data format that the classifier matches.

- `CreationTime` – Timestamp.

  The time this classifier was registered.

- `LastUpdated` – Timestamp.

  The time this classifier was last updated.

- `Version` – Number (long).

  The version of this classifier.

- `RowTag` – UTF-8 string.

  The XML tag designating the element that contains each record in an XML document being parsed. Note that this cannot identify a self-closing element (closed by `/>`). An empty row element that contains only attributes can be parsed as long as it ends with a closing tag (for example, `<row item_a="A" item_b="B"></row>` is okay, but `<row item_a="A" item_b="B" />` is not).

JsonClassifier Structure

A classifier for `JSON` content.

Fields

- `Name` – UTF-8 string, not less than 1 or more than 255 bytes long, matching the Single-line string pattern. Required.

  The name of the classifier.

- `CreationTime` – Timestamp.

  The time this classifier was registered.

- `LastUpdated` – Timestamp.

  The time this classifier was last updated.

- `Version` – Number (long).

  The version of this classifier.

- `JsonPath` – UTF-8 string. Required.

  A `JsonPath` string defining the JSON data for the classifier to classify. AWS Glue supports a subset of JsonPath, as described in Writing JsonPath Custom Classifiers.

CreateGrokClassifierRequest Structure

Specifies a `grok` classifier for `CreateClassifier` to create.

Fields

- `Classification` – UTF-8 string. Required.

  An identifier of the data format that the classifier matches, such as Twitter, JSON, Omniture logs, Amazon CloudWatch Logs, and so on.

- `Name` – UTF-8 string, not less than 1 or more than 255 bytes long, matching the Single-line string pattern. Required.

  The name of the new classifier.

- `GrokPattern` – UTF-8 string, not less than 1 or more than 2048 bytes long, matching the A Logstash Grok string pattern. Required.

  The grok pattern used by this classifier.

- `CustomPatterns` – UTF-8 string, not more than 16000 bytes long, matching the URI address multi-line string pattern.

  Optional custom grok patterns used by this classifier.

UpdateGrokClassifierRequest Structure

Specifies a grok classifier to update when passed to `UpdateClassifier`.

Fields

- `Name` – UTF-8 string, not less than 1 or more than 255 bytes long, matching the Single-line string pattern. Required.

  The name of the `GrokClassifier`.

- `Classification` – UTF-8 string.

  An identifier of the data format that the classifier matches, such as Twitter, JSON, Omniture logs, Amazon CloudWatch Logs, and so on.

- `GrokPattern` – UTF-8 string, not less than 1 or more than 2048 bytes long, matching the A Logstash Grok string pattern.

  The grok pattern used by this classifier.

- `CustomPatterns` – UTF-8 string, not more than 16000 bytes long, matching the URI address multi-line string pattern.

  Optional custom grok patterns used by this classifier.

CreateXMLClassifierRequest Structure

Specifies an XML classifier for `CreateClassifier` to create.

Fields

- `Classification` – UTF-8 string. Required.

  An identifier of the data format that the classifier matches.

- `Name` – UTF-8 string, not less than 1 or more than 255 bytes long, matching the Single-line string pattern. Required.

  The name of the classifier.

- `RowTag` – UTF-8 string.

  The XML tag designating the element that contains each record in an XML document being parsed. Note that this cannot identify a self-closing element (closed by `/>`). An empty row element that contains only attributes can be parsed as long as it ends with a closing tag (for example, `<row item_a="A" item_b="B "></row>` is okay, but `<row item_a="A" item_b="B" />` is not).

UpdateXMLClassifierRequest Structure

Specifies an XML classifier to be updated.

Fields

- `Name` – UTF-8 string, not less than 1 or more than 255 bytes long, matching the Single-line string pattern. Required.

  The name of the classifier.

- `Classification` – UTF-8 string.

  An identifier of the data format that the classifier matches.

- `RowTag` – UTF-8 string.

  The XML tag designating the element that contains each record in an XML document being parsed. Note that this cannot identify a self-closing element (closed by `/>`). An empty row element that contains only attributes can be parsed as long as it ends with a closing tag (for example, `<row item_a="A" item_b="B "></row>` is okay, but `<row item_a="A" item_b="B" />` is not).

CreateJsonClassifierRequest Structure

Specifies a JSON classifier for `CreateClassifier` to create.

Fields

- `Name` – UTF-8 string, not less than 1 or more than 255 bytes long, matching the Single-line string pattern. Required.

  The name of the classifier.

- JsonPath – UTF-8 string. Required.

  A `JsonPath` string defining the JSON data for the classifier to classify. AWS Glue supports a subset of JsonPath, as described in Writing JsonPath Custom Classifiers.

UpdateJsonClassifierRequest Structure

Specifies a JSON classifier to be updated.

Fields

- `Name` – UTF-8 string, not less than 1 or more than 255 bytes long, matching the Single-line string pattern. Required.

  The name of the classifier.

- `JsonPath` – UTF-8 string.

  A `JsonPath` string defining the JSON data for the classifier to classify. AWS Glue supports a subset of JsonPath, as described in Writing JsonPath Custom Classifiers.

Operations

- CreateClassifier Action (Python: create_classifier)
- DeleteClassifier Action (Python: delete_classifier)
- GetClassifier Action (Python: get_classifier)
- GetClassifiers Action (Python: get_classifiers)
- UpdateClassifier Action (Python: update_classifier)

CreateClassifier Action (Python: create_classifier)

Creates a classifier in the user's account. This may be a `GrokClassifier`, an `XMLClassifier`, or abbrev `JsonClassifier`, depending on which field of the request is present.

Request

- `GrokClassifier` – A CreateGrokClassifierRequest object.

  A `GrokClassifier` object specifying the classifier to create.

- `XMLClassifier` – A CreateXMLClassifierRequest object.

  An `XMLClassifier` object specifying the classifier to create.

- `JsonClassifier` – A CreateJsonClassifierRequest object.

  A `JsonClassifier` object specifying the classifier to create.

Response

- *No Response parameters.*

Errors

- `AlreadyExistsException`
- `InvalidInputException`
- `OperationTimeoutException`

DeleteClassifier Action (Python: delete_classifier)

Removes a classifier from the Data Catalog.

Request

- `Name` – UTF-8 string, not less than 1 or more than 255 bytes long, matching the Single-line string pattern. Required.

  Name of the classifier to remove.

Response

- *No Response parameters.*

Errors

- `EntityNotFoundException`
- `OperationTimeoutException`

GetClassifier Action (Python: get_classifier)

Retrieve a classifier by name.

Request

- `Name` – UTF-8 string, not less than 1 or more than 255 bytes long, matching the Single-line string pattern. Required.

  Name of the classifier to retrieve.

Response

- `Classifier` – A Classifier object.

  The requested classifier.

Errors

- `EntityNotFoundException`
- `OperationTimeoutException`

GetClassifiers Action (Python: get_classifiers)

Lists all classifier objects in the Data Catalog.

Request

- `MaxResults` – Number (integer), not less than 1 or more than 1000.

  Size of the list to return (optional).

- `NextToken` – UTF-8 string.

  An optional continuation token.

Response

- `Classifiers` – An array of Classifiers.

  The requested list of classifier objects.

- `NextToken` – UTF-8 string.

  A continuation token.

Errors

- OperationTimeoutException

UpdateClassifier Action (Python: update_classifier)

Modifies an existing classifier (a GrokClassifier, XMLClassifier, or JsonClassifier, depending on which field is present).

Request

- GrokClassifier – An UpdateGrokClassifierRequest object.

  A GrokClassifier object with updated fields.

- XMLClassifier – An UpdateXMLClassifierRequest object.

  An XMLClassifier object with updated fields.

- JsonClassifier – An UpdateJsonClassifierRequest object.

  A JsonClassifier object with updated fields.

Response

- *No Response parameters.*

Errors

- InvalidInputException
- VersionMismatchException
- EntityNotFoundException
- OperationTimeoutException

Crawler API

Data Types

- Crawler Structure
- Schedule Structure
- CrawlerTargets Structure
- S3Target Structure
- JdbcTarget Structure
- CrawlerMetrics Structure
- SchemaChangePolicy Structure
- LastCrawlInfo Structure

Crawler Structure

Specifies a crawler program that examines a data source and uses classifiers to try to determine its schema. If successful, the crawler records metadata concerning the data source in the AWS Glue Data Catalog.

Fields

- `Name` – UTF-8 string, not less than 1 or more than 255 bytes long, matching the Single-line string pattern.

  The crawler name.

- `Role` – UTF-8 string.

  The IAM role (or ARN of an IAM role) used to access customer resources, such as data in Amazon S3.

- `Targets` – A CrawlerTargets object.

  A collection of targets to crawl.

- `DatabaseName` – UTF-8 string.

  The database where metadata is written by this crawler.

- `Description` – Description string, not more than 2048 bytes long, matching the URI address multi-line string pattern.

  A description of the crawler.

- `Classifiers` – An array of UTF-8 strings.

  A list of custom classifiers associated with the crawler.

- `SchemaChangePolicy` – A SchemaChangePolicy object.

  Sets the behavior when the crawler finds a changed or deleted object.

- `State` – UTF-8 string (valid values: `READY` | `RUNNING` | `STOPPING`).

  Indicates whether the crawler is running, or whether a run is pending.

- `TablePrefix` – UTF-8 string, not more than 128 bytes long.

  The prefix added to the names of tables that are created.

- `Schedule` – A Schedule object.

  For scheduled crawlers, the schedule when the crawler runs.

- `CrawlElapsedTime` – Number (long).

  If the crawler is running, contains the total time elapsed since the last crawl began.

380

- `CreationTime` – Timestamp.

  The time when the crawler was created.

- `LastUpdated` – Timestamp.

  The time the crawler was last updated.

- `LastCrawl` – A LastCrawlInfo object.

  The status of the last crawl, and potentially error information if an error occurred.

- `Version` – Number (long).

  The version of the crawler.

- `Configuration` – UTF-8 string.

  Crawler configuration information. This versioned JSON string allows users to specify aspects of a crawler's behavior. For more information, see Configuring a Crawler.

Schedule Structure

A scheduling object using a `cron` statement to schedule an event.

Fields

- `ScheduleExpression` – UTF-8 string.

  A `cron` expression used to specify the schedule (see Time-Based Schedules for Jobs and Crawlers. For example, to run something every day at 12:15 UTC, you would specify: `cron(15 12 * * ? *)`.

- `State` – UTF-8 string (valid values: `SCHEDULED` | `NOT_SCHEDULED` | `TRANSITIONING`).

  The state of the schedule.

CrawlerTargets Structure

Specifies data stores to crawl.

Fields

- `S3Targets` – An array of S3Targets.

  Specifies Amazon S3 targets.

- `JdbcTargets` – An array of JdbcTargets.

  Specifies JDBC targets.

S3Target Structure

Specifies a data store in Amazon S3.

Fields

- `Path` – UTF-8 string.

  The path to the Amazon S3 target.

- `Exclusions` – An array of UTF-8 strings.

  A list of glob patterns used to exclude from the crawl. For more information, see Catalog Tables with a Crawler.

JdbcTarget Structure

Specifies a JDBC data store to crawl.

Fields

- `ConnectionName` – UTF-8 string.

  The name of the connection to use to connect to the JDBC target.

- `Path` – UTF-8 string.

  The path of the JDBC target.

- `Exclusions` – An array of UTF-8 strings.

  A list of glob patterns used to exclude from the crawl. For more information, see Catalog Tables with a Crawler.

CrawlerMetrics Structure

Metrics for a specified crawler.

Fields

- `CrawlerName` – UTF-8 string, not less than 1 or more than 255 bytes long, matching the Single-line string pattern.

  The name of the crawler.

- `TimeLeftSeconds` – Number (double), at least 0.0.

  The estimated time left to complete a running crawl.

- `StillEstimating` – Boolean.

  True if the crawler is still estimating how long it will take to complete this run.

- `LastRuntimeSeconds` – Number (double), at least 0.0.

  The duration of the crawler's most recent run, in seconds.

- `MedianRuntimeSeconds` – Number (double), at least 0.0.

  The median duration of this crawler's runs, in seconds.

- `TablesCreated` – Number (integer), at least 0.

  The number of tables created by this crawler.

- `TablesUpdated` – Number (integer), at least 0.

  The number of tables updated by this crawler.

- `TablesDeleted` – Number (integer), at least 0.

  The number of tables deleted by this crawler.

SchemaChangePolicy Structure

Crawler policy for update and deletion behavior.

Fields

- `UpdateBehavior` – UTF-8 string (valid values: `LOG` | `UPDATE_IN_DATABASE`).

  The update behavior when the crawler finds a changed schema.

- `DeleteBehavior` – UTF-8 string (valid values: `LOG` | `DELETE_FROM_DATABASE` | `DEPRECATE_IN_DATABASE`).

  The deletion behavior when the crawler finds a deleted object.

LastCrawlInfo Structure

Status and error information about the most recent crawl.

Fields

- `Status` – UTF-8 string (valid values: `SUCCEEDED` | `CANCELLED` | `FAILED`).

  Status of the last crawl.

- `ErrorMessage` – Description string, not more than 2048 bytes long, matching the URI address multi-line string pattern.

  If an error occurred, the error information about the last crawl.

- `LogGroup` – UTF-8 string, not less than 1 or more than 512 bytes long, matching the Log group string pattern.

  The log group for the last crawl.

- `LogStream` – UTF-8 string, not less than 1 or more than 512 bytes long, matching the Log-stream string pattern.

  The log stream for the last crawl.

- `MessagePrefix` – UTF-8 string, not less than 1 or more than 255 bytes long, matching the Single-line string pattern.

  The prefix for a message about this crawl.

- `StartTime` – Timestamp.

  The time at which the crawl started.

Operations

- CreateCrawler Action (Python: create_crawler)
- DeleteCrawler Action (Python: delete_crawler)
- GetCrawler Action (Python: get_crawler)
- GetCrawlers Action (Python: get_crawlers)
- GetCrawlerMetrics Action (Python: get_crawler_metrics)
- UpdateCrawler Action (Python: update_crawler)
- StartCrawler Action (Python: start_crawler)
- StopCrawler Action (Python: stop_crawler)

CreateCrawler Action (Python: create_crawler)

Creates a new crawler with specified targets, role, configuration, and optional schedule. At least one crawl target must be specified, in either the *s3Targets* or the *jdbcTargets* field.

Request

- **Name** – UTF-8 string, not less than 1 or more than 255 bytes long, matching the Single-line string pattern. Required.

  Name of the new crawler.

- **Role** – UTF-8 string. Required.

  The IAM role (or ARN of an IAM role) used by the new crawler to access customer resources.

- **DatabaseName** – UTF-8 string. Required.

  The AWS Glue database where results are written, such as: `arn:aws:daylight:us-east-1::database/sometable/*`.

- **Description** – Description string, not more than 2048 bytes long, matching the URI address multi-line string pattern.

  A description of the new crawler.

- **Targets** – A CrawlerTargets object. Required.

  A list of collection of targets to crawl.

- **Schedule** – UTF-8 string.

  A `cron` expression used to specify the schedule (see Time-Based Schedules for Jobs and Crawlers. For example, to run something every day at 12:15 UTC, you would specify: `cron(15 12 * * ? *)`.

- **Classifiers** – An array of UTF-8 strings.

  A list of custom classifiers that the user has registered. By default, all built-in classifiers are included in a crawl, but these custom classifiers always override the default classifiers for a given classification.

- **TablePrefix** – UTF-8 string, not more than 128 bytes long.

  The table prefix used for catalog tables that are created.

- **SchemaChangePolicy** – A SchemaChangePolicy object.

  Policy for the crawler's update and deletion behavior.

- **Configuration** – UTF-8 string.

  Crawler configuration information. This versioned JSON string allows users to specify aspects of a crawler's behavior. For more information, see Configuring a Crawler.

Response

- *No Response parameters.*

Errors

- InvalidInputException
- AlreadyExistsException
- OperationTimeoutException
- ResourceNumberLimitExceededException

DeleteCrawler Action (Python: delete_crawler)

Removes a specified crawler from the Data Catalog, unless the crawler state is RUNNING.

Request

- **Name** – UTF-8 string, not less than 1 or more than 255 bytes long, matching the Single-line string pattern. Required.

  Name of the crawler to remove.

384

Response

- *No Response parameters.*

Errors

- `EntityNotFoundException`
- `CrawlerRunningException`
- `SchedulerTransitioningException`
- `OperationTimeoutException`

GetCrawler Action (Python: get_crawler)

Retrieves metadata for a specified crawler.

Request

- `Name` – UTF-8 string, not less than 1 or more than 255 bytes long, matching the Single-line string pattern. Required.

  Name of the crawler to retrieve metadata for.

Response

- `Crawler` – A Crawler object.

  The metadata for the specified crawler.

Errors

- `EntityNotFoundException`
- `OperationTimeoutException`

GetCrawlers Action (Python: get_crawlers)

Retrieves metadata for all crawlers defined in the customer account.

Request

- `MaxResults` – Number (integer), not less than 1 or more than 1000.

  The number of crawlers to return on each call.

- `NextToken` – UTF-8 string.

  A continuation token, if this is a continuation request.

Response

- `Crawlers` – An array of Crawlers.

  A list of crawler metadata.

- `NextToken` – UTF-8 string.

  A continuation token, if the returned list has not reached the end of those defined in this customer account.

Errors

- `OperationTimeoutException`

GetCrawlerMetrics Action (Python: get_crawler_metrics)

Retrieves metrics about specified crawlers.

Request

- `CrawlerNameList` – An array of UTF-8 strings, not more than 100 items in the array.

  A list of the names of crawlers about which to retrieve metrics.

- `MaxResults` – Number (integer), not less than 1 or more than 1000.

  The maximum size of a list to return.

- `NextToken` – UTF-8 string.

  A continuation token, if this is a continuation call.

Response

- `CrawlerMetricsList` – An array of CrawlerMetricss.

  A list of metrics for the specified crawler.

- `NextToken` – UTF-8 string.

  A continuation token, if the returned list does not contain the last metric available.

Errors

- `OperationTimeoutException`

UpdateCrawler Action (Python: update_crawler)

Updates a crawler. If a crawler is running, you must stop it using `StopCrawler` before updating it.

Request

- `Name` – UTF-8 string, not less than 1 or more than 255 bytes long, matching the Single-line string pattern. Required.

  Name of the new crawler.

- `Role` – UTF-8 string.

  The IAM role (or ARN of an IAM role) used by the new crawler to access customer resources.

- `DatabaseName` – UTF-8 string.

  The AWS Glue database where results are stored, such as: `arn:aws:daylight:us-east-1::database/sometable/*`.

- `Description` – UTF-8 string, not more than 2048 bytes long, matching the URI address multi-line string pattern.

  A description of the new crawler.

- `Targets` – A CrawlerTargets object.

  A list of targets to crawl.

- `Schedule` – UTF-8 string.

  A `cron` expression used to specify the schedule (see Time-Based Schedules for Jobs and Crawlers. For example, to run something every day at 12:15 UTC, you would specify: `cron(15 12 * * ? *)`.

- **Classifiers** – An array of UTF-8 strings.

  A list of custom classifiers that the user has registered. By default, all built-in classifiers are included in a crawl, but these custom classifiers always override the default classifiers for a given classification.

- **TablePrefix** – UTF-8 string, not more than 128 bytes long.

  The table prefix used for catalog tables that are created.

- **SchemaChangePolicy** – A SchemaChangePolicy object.

  Policy for the crawler's update and deletion behavior.

- **Configuration** – UTF-8 string.

  Crawler configuration information. This versioned JSON string allows users to specify aspects of a crawler's behavior. For more information, see Configuring a Crawler.

Response

- *No Response parameters.*

Errors

- InvalidInputException
- VersionMismatchException
- EntityNotFoundException
- CrawlerRunningException
- OperationTimeoutException

StartCrawler Action (Python: start_crawler)

Starts a crawl using the specified crawler, regardless of what is scheduled. If the crawler is already running, returns a CrawlerRunningException.

Request

- **Name** – UTF-8 string, not less than 1 or more than 255 bytes long, matching the Single-line string pattern. Required.

  Name of the crawler to start.

Response

- *No Response parameters.*

Errors

- EntityNotFoundException
- CrawlerRunningException
- OperationTimeoutException

StopCrawler Action (Python: stop_crawler)

If the specified crawler is running, stops the crawl.

Request

- **Name** – UTF-8 string, not less than 1 or more than 255 bytes long, matching the Single-line string pattern. Required.

  Name of the crawler to stop.

Response

- *No Response parameters.*

Errors

- EntityNotFoundException
- CrawlerNotRunningException
- CrawlerStoppingException
- OperationTimeoutException

Crawler Scheduler API

Data Types

- Schedule Structure

Schedule Structure

A scheduling object using a `cron` statement to schedule an event.

Fields

- `ScheduleExpression` – UTF-8 string.

  A `cron` expression used to specify the schedule (see Time-Based Schedules for Jobs and Crawlers. For example, to run something every day at 12:15 UTC, you would specify: `cron(15 12 * * ? *)`.

- `State` – UTF-8 string (valid values: `SCHEDULED` | `NOT_SCHEDULED` | `TRANSITIONING`).

  The state of the schedule.

Operations

- UpdateCrawlerSchedule Action (Python: update_crawler_schedule)
- StartCrawlerSchedule Action (Python: start_crawler_schedule)
- StopCrawlerSchedule Action (Python: stop_crawler_schedule)

UpdateCrawlerSchedule Action (Python: update_crawler_schedule)

Updates the schedule of a crawler using a `cron` expression.

Request

- `CrawlerName` – UTF-8 string, not less than 1 or more than 255 bytes long, matching the Single-line string pattern. Required.

  Name of the crawler whose schedule to update.

- `Schedule` – UTF-8 string.

  The updated `cron` expression used to specify the schedule (see Time-Based Schedules for Jobs and Crawlers. For example, to run something every day at 12:15 UTC, you would specify: `cron(15 12 * * ? *)`.

Response

- *No Response parameters.*

Errors

- EntityNotFoundException
- InvalidInputException
- VersionMismatchException
- SchedulerTransitioningException
- OperationTimeoutException

StartCrawlerSchedule Action (Python: start_crawler_schedule)

Changes the schedule state of the specified crawler to SCHEDULED, unless the crawler is already running or the schedule state is already SCHEDULED.

Request

- CrawlerName – UTF-8 string, not less than 1 or more than 255 bytes long, matching the Single-line string pattern. Required.

  Name of the crawler to schedule.

Response

- *No Response parameters.*

Errors

- EntityNotFoundException
- SchedulerRunningException
- SchedulerTransitioningException
- NoScheduleException
- OperationTimeoutException

StopCrawlerSchedule Action (Python: stop_crawler_schedule)

Sets the schedule state of the specified crawler to NOT_SCHEDULED, but does not stop the crawler if it is already running.

Request

- CrawlerName – UTF-8 string, not less than 1 or more than 255 bytes long, matching the Single-line string pattern. Required.

  Name of the crawler whose schedule state to set.

Response

- *No Response parameters.*

Errors

- EntityNotFoundException
- SchedulerNotRunningException
- SchedulerTransitioningException
- OperationTimeoutException

AWS Glue API for Autogenerating ETL Scripts

Data Types

- CodeGenNode Structure
- CodeGenNodeArg Structure
- CodeGenEdge Structure
- Location Structure
- CatalogEntry Structure
- MappingEntry Structure

CodeGenNode Structure

Represents a node in a directed acyclic graph (DAG)

Fields

- `Id` – UTF-8 string, not less than 1 or more than 255 bytes long, matching the Identifier string pattern. Required.

  A node identifier that is unique within the node's graph.

- `NodeType` – UTF-8 string. Required.

  The type of node this is.

- `Args` – An array of CodeGenNodeArgs, not more than 50 items in the array. Required.

  Properties of the node, in the form of name-value pairs.

- `LineNumber` – Number (integer).

  The line number of the node.

CodeGenNodeArg Structure

An argument or property of a node.

Fields

- `Name` – UTF-8 string. Required.

  The name of the argument or property.

- `Value` – UTF-8 string. Required.

  The value of the argument or property.

- `Param` – Boolean.

  True if the value is used as a parameter.

CodeGenEdge Structure

Represents a directional edge in a directed acyclic graph (DAG).

Fields

- `Source` – UTF-8 string, not less than 1 or more than 255 bytes long, matching the Identifier string pattern. Required.

  The ID of the node at which the edge starts.

- `Target` – UTF-8 string, not less than 1 or more than 255 bytes long, matching the Identifier string pattern. Required.

  The ID of the node at which the edge ends.

- `TargetParameter` – UTF-8 string.

  The target of the edge.

Location Structure

The location of resources.

Fields

- `Jdbc` – An array of CodeGenNodeArgs, not more than 50 items in the array.

  A JDBC location.

- `S3` – An array of CodeGenNodeArgs, not more than 50 items in the array.

  An Amazon S3 location.

CatalogEntry Structure

Specifies a table definition in the Data Catalog.

Fields

- `DatabaseName` – UTF-8 string, not less than 1 or more than 255 bytes long, matching the Single-line string pattern. Required.

  The database in which the table metadata resides.

- `TableName` – UTF-8 string, not less than 1 or more than 255 bytes long, matching the Single-line string pattern. Required.

  The name of the table in question.

MappingEntry Structure

Defines a mapping.

Fields

- `SourceTable` – UTF-8 string.

  The name of the source table.

- `SourcePath` – UTF-8 string.

  The source path.

- `SourceType` – UTF-8 string.

  The source type.

- `TargetTable` – UTF-8 string.

  The target table.

- `TargetPath` – UTF-8 string.

  The target path.

- `TargetType` – UTF-8 string.

  The target type.

Operations

- CreateScript Action (Python: create_script)
- GetDataflowGraph Action (Python: get_dataflow_graph)
- GetMapping Action (Python: get_mapping)
- GetPlan Action (Python: get_plan)

CreateScript Action (Python: create_script)

Transforms a directed acyclic graph (DAG) into code.

Request

- `DagNodes` – An array of CodeGenNodes.

  A list of the nodes in the DAG.

- `DagEdges` – An array of CodeGenEdges.

  A list of the edges in the DAG.

- `Language` – UTF-8 string (valid values: `PYTHON` | `SCALA`).

  The programming language of the resulting code from the DAG.

Response

- `PythonScript` – UTF-8 string.

  The Python script generated from the DAG.

- `ScalaCode` – UTF-8 string.

  The Scala code generated from the DAG.

Errors

- `InvalidInputException`
- `InternalServiceException`
- `OperationTimeoutException`

GetDataflowGraph Action (Python: get_dataflow_graph)

Transforms a Python script into a directed acyclic graph (DAG).

Request

- `PythonScript` – UTF-8 string.

  The Python script to transform.

393

Response

- **DagNodes** – An array of CodeGenNodes.

  A list of the nodes in the resulting DAG.

- **DagEdges** – An array of CodeGenEdges.

  A list of the edges in the resulting DAG.

Errors

- `InvalidInputException`
- `InternalServiceException`
- `OperationTimeoutException`

GetMapping Action (Python: get_mapping)

Creates mappings.

Request

- **Source** – A CatalogEntry object. Required.

  Specifies the source table.

- **Sinks** – An array of CatalogEntrys.

  A list of target tables.

- **Location** – A Location object.

  Parameters for the mapping.

Response

- **Mapping** – An array of MappingEntrys. Required.

  A list of mappings to the specified targets.

Errors

- `InvalidInputException`
- `InternalServiceException`
- `OperationTimeoutException`
- `EntityNotFoundException`

GetPlan Action (Python: get_plan)

Gets code to perform a specified mapping.

Request

- **Mapping** – An array of MappingEntrys. Required.

  The list of mappings from a source table to target tables.

- **Source** – A CatalogEntry object. Required.

  The source table.

- **Sinks** – An array of CatalogEntrys.

  The target tables.

- **Location** – A Location object.

  Parameters for the mapping.

- **Language** – UTF-8 string (valid values: PYTHON | SCALA).

  The programming language of the code to perform the mapping.

Response

- **PythonScript** – UTF-8 string.

  A Python script to perform the mapping.

- **ScalaCode** – UTF-8 string.

  Scala code to perform the mapping.

Errors

- InvalidInputException
- InternalServiceException
- OperationTimeoutException
- EntityNotFoundException

Jobs API

Topics

- Jobs
- Job Runs
- Triggers

Jobs

Data Types

- Job Structure
- ExecutionProperty Structure
- NotificationProperty Structure
- JobCommand Structure
- ConnectionsList Structure
- JobUpdate Structure

Job Structure

Specifies a job definition.

Fields

- `Name` – UTF-8 string, not less than 1 or more than 255 bytes long, matching the Single-line string pattern.

  The name you assign to this job definition.

- `Description` – Description string, not more than 2048 bytes long, matching the URI address multi-line string pattern.

  Description of the job being defined.

- `LogUri` – UTF-8 string.

  This field is reserved for future use.

- `Role` – UTF-8 string.

  The name or ARN of the IAM role associated with this job.

- `CreatedOn` – Timestamp.

  The time and date that this job definition was created.

- `LastModifiedOn` – Timestamp.

  The last point in time when this job definition was modified.

- `ExecutionProperty` – An ExecutionProperty object.

  An ExecutionProperty specifying the maximum number of concurrent runs allowed for this job.

- `Command` – A JobCommand object.

  The JobCommand that executes this job.

- `DefaultArguments` – A map array of key-value pairs

  Each key is a UTF-8 string.

  Each value is a UTF-8 string.

  The default arguments for this job, specified as name-value pairs.

  You can specify arguments here that your own job-execution script consumes, as well as arguments that AWS Glue itself consumes.

  For information about how to specify and consume your own Job arguments, see the Calling AWS Glue APIs in Python topic in the developer guide.

397

For information about the key-value pairs that AWS Glue consumes to set up your job, see the Special Parameters Used by AWS Glue topic in the developer guide.

- `Connections` – A ConnectionsList object.

  The connections used for this job.

- `MaxRetries` – Number (integer).

  The maximum number of times to retry this job after a JobRun fails.

- `AllocatedCapacity` – Number (integer).

  The number of AWS Glue data processing units (DPUs) allocated to runs of this job. From 2 to 100 DPUs can be allocated; the default is 10. A DPU is a relative measure of processing power that consists of 4 vCPUs of compute capacity and 16 GB of memory. For more information, see the AWS Glue pricing page.

- `Timeout` – Number (integer), at least 1.

  The Job timeout in minutes. This is the maximum time that a job run can consume resources before it is terminated and enters `TIMEOUT` status. The default is 2,880 minutes (48 hours).

- `NotificationProperty` – A NotificationProperty object.

  Specifies configuration properties of a job notification.

ExecutionProperty Structure

An execution property of a job.

Fields

- `MaxConcurrentRuns` – Number (integer).

  The maximum number of concurrent runs allowed for the job. The default is 1. An error is returned when this threshold is reached. The maximum value you can specify is controlled by a service limit.

NotificationProperty Structure

Specifies configuration properties of a notification.

Fields

- `NotifyDelayAfter` – Number (integer), at least 1.

  After a job run starts, the number of minutes to wait before sending a job run delay notification.

JobCommand Structure

Specifies code executed when a job is run.

Fields

- `Name` – UTF-8 string.

  The name of the job command: this must be **glueetl**.

- `ScriptLocation` – UTF-8 string.

  Specifies the S3 path to a script that executes a job (required).

ConnectionsList Structure

Specifies the connections used by a job.

Fields

- `Connections` – An array of UTF-8 strings.

  A list of connections used by the job.

JobUpdate Structure

Specifies information used to update an existing job definition. Note that the previous job definition will be completely overwritten by this information.

Fields

- `Description` – Description string, not more than 2048 bytes long, matching the URI address multi-line string pattern.

  Description of the job being defined.

- `LogUri` – UTF-8 string.

  This field is reserved for future use.

- `Role` – UTF-8 string.

  The name or ARN of the IAM role associated with this job (required).

- `ExecutionProperty` – An ExecutionProperty object.

  An ExecutionProperty specifying the maximum number of concurrent runs allowed for this job.

- `Command` – A JobCommand object.

  The JobCommand that executes this job (required).

- `DefaultArguments` – A map array of key-value pairs

  Each key is a UTF-8 string.

  Each value is a UTF-8 string.

  The default arguments for this job.

  You can specify arguments here that your own job-execution script consumes, as well as arguments that AWS Glue itself consumes.

  For information about how to specify and consume your own Job arguments, see the Calling AWS Glue APIs in Python topic in the developer guide.

  For information about the key-value pairs that AWS Glue consumes to set up your job, see the Special Parameters Used by AWS Glue topic in the developer guide.

- `Connections` – A ConnectionsList object.

  The connections used for this job.

- `MaxRetries` – Number (integer).

  The maximum number of times to retry this job if it fails.

- `AllocatedCapacity` – Number (integer).

  The number of AWS Glue data processing units (DPUs) to allocate to this Job. From 2 to 100 DPUs can be allocated; the default is 10. A DPU is a relative measure of processing power that consists of 4 vCPUs of compute capacity and 16 GB of memory. For more information, see the AWS Glue pricing page.

- `Timeout` – Number (integer), at least 1.

  The Job timeout in minutes. This is the maximum time that a job run can consume resources before it is terminated and enters `TIMEOUT` status. The default is 2,880 minutes (48 hours).

- `NotificationProperty` – A NotificationProperty object.

  Specifies configuration properties of a job notification.

Operations

- CreateJob Action (Python: create_job)
- UpdateJob Action (Python: update_job)
- GetJob Action (Python: get_job)
- GetJobs Action (Python: get_jobs)
- DeleteJob Action (Python: delete_job)

CreateJob Action (Python: create_job)

Creates a new job definition.

Request

- `Name` – UTF-8 string, not less than 1 or more than 255 bytes long, matching the Single-line string pattern. Required.

  The name you assign to this job definition. It must be unique in your account.

- `Description` – Description string, not more than 2048 bytes long, matching the URI address multi-line string pattern.

  Description of the job being defined.

- `LogUri` – UTF-8 string.

  This field is reserved for future use.

- `Role` – UTF-8 string. Required.

  The name or ARN of the IAM role associated with this job.

- `ExecutionProperty` – An ExecutionProperty object.

  An ExecutionProperty specifying the maximum number of concurrent runs allowed for this job.

- `Command` – A JobCommand object. Required.

  The JobCommand that executes this job.

- `DefaultArguments` – A map array of key-value pairs

  Each key is a UTF-8 string.

  Each value is a UTF-8 string.

  The default arguments for this job.

You can specify arguments here that your own job-execution script consumes, as well as arguments that AWS Glue itself consumes.

For information about how to specify and consume your own Job arguments, see the Calling AWS Glue APIs in Python topic in the developer guide.

For information about the key-value pairs that AWS Glue consumes to set up your job, see the Special Parameters Used by AWS Glue topic in the developer guide.

- `Connections` – A ConnectionsList object.

  The connections used for this job.

- `MaxRetries` – Number (integer).

  The maximum number of times to retry this job if it fails.

- `AllocatedCapacity` – Number (integer).

  The number of AWS Glue data processing units (DPUs) to allocate to this Job. From 2 to 100 DPUs can be allocated; the default is 10. A DPU is a relative measure of processing power that consists of 4 vCPUs of compute capacity and 16 GB of memory. For more information, see the AWS Glue pricing page.

- `Timeout` – Number (integer), at least 1.

  The Job timeout in minutes. This is the maximum time that a job run can consume resources before it is terminated and enters `TIMEOUT` status. The default is 2,880 minutes (48 hours).

- `NotificationProperty` – A NotificationProperty object.

  Specifies configuration properties of a job notification.

Response

- `Name` – UTF-8 string, not less than 1 or more than 255 bytes long, matching the Single-line string pattern.

  The unique name that was provided for this job definition.

Errors

- `InvalidInputException`
- `IdempotentParameterMismatchException`
- `AlreadyExistsException`
- `InternalServiceException`
- `OperationTimeoutException`
- `ResourceNumberLimitExceededException`
- `ConcurrentModificationException`

UpdateJob Action (Python: update_job)

Updates an existing job definition.

Request

- `JobName` – UTF-8 string, not less than 1 or more than 255 bytes long, matching the Single-line string pattern. Required.

  Name of the job definition to update.

- `JobUpdate` – A JobUpdate object. Required.

  Specifies the values with which to update the job definition.

Response

- `JobName` – UTF-8 string, not less than 1 or more than 255 bytes long, matching the Single-line string pattern.

  Returns the name of the updated job definition.

Errors

- `InvalidInputException`
- `EntityNotFoundException`
- `InternalServiceException`
- `OperationTimeoutException`
- `ConcurrentModificationException`

GetJob Action (Python: get_job)

Retrieves an existing job definition.

Request

- `JobName` – UTF-8 string, not less than 1 or more than 255 bytes long, matching the Single-line string pattern. Required.

  The name of the job definition to retrieve.

Response

- `Job` – A Job object.

  The requested job definition.

Errors

- `InvalidInputException`
- `EntityNotFoundException`
- `InternalServiceException`
- `OperationTimeoutException`

GetJobs Action (Python: get_jobs)

Retrieves all current job definitions.

Request

- `NextToken` – UTF-8 string.

  A continuation token, if this is a continuation call.

- `MaxResults` – Number (integer), not less than 1 or more than 1000.

  The maximum size of the response.

Response

- `Jobs` – An array of Jobs.

  A list of job definitions.

- `NextToken` – UTF-8 string.

  A continuation token, if not all job definitions have yet been returned.

Errors

- `InvalidInputException`

- `EntityNotFoundException`
- `InternalServiceException`
- `OperationTimeoutException`

DeleteJob Action (Python: delete_job)

Deletes a specified job definition. If the job definition is not found, no exception is thrown.

Request

- `JobName` – UTF-8 string, not less than 1 or more than 255 bytes long, matching the Single-line string pattern. Required.

  The name of the job definition to delete.

Response

- `JobName` – UTF-8 string, not less than 1 or more than 255 bytes long, matching the Single-line string pattern.

  The name of the job definition that was deleted.

Errors

- `InvalidInputException`
- `InternalServiceException`
- `OperationTimeoutException`

Job Runs

Data Types

- JobRun Structure
- Predecessor Structure
- JobBookmarkEntry Structure
- BatchStopJobRunSuccessfulSubmission Structure
- BatchStopJobRunError Structure

JobRun Structure

Contains information about a job run.

Fields

- `Id` – UTF-8 string, not less than 1 or more than 255 bytes long, matching the Single-line string pattern.

  The ID of this job run.

- `Attempt` – Number (integer).

  The number of the attempt to run this job.

- `PreviousRunId` – UTF-8 string, not less than 1 or more than 255 bytes long, matching the Single-line string pattern.

  The ID of the previous run of this job. For example, the JobRunId specified in the StartJobRun action.

- `TriggerName` – UTF-8 string, not less than 1 or more than 255 bytes long, matching the Single-line string pattern.

  The name of the trigger that started this job run.

- `JobName` – UTF-8 string, not less than 1 or more than 255 bytes long, matching the Single-line string pattern.

  The name of the job definition being used in this run.

- `StartedOn` – Timestamp.

  The date and time at which this job run was started.

- `LastModifiedOn` – Timestamp.

  The last time this job run was modified.

- `CompletedOn` – Timestamp.

  The date and time this job run completed.

- `JobRunState` – UTF-8 string (valid values: `STARTING` | `RUNNING` | `STOPPING` | `STOPPED` | `SUCCEEDED` | `FAILED` | `TIMEOUT`).

  The current state of the job run.

- `Arguments` – A map array of key-value pairs

  Each key is a UTF-8 string.

  Each value is a UTF-8 string.

  The job arguments associated with this run. These override equivalent default arguments set for the job.

404

You can specify arguments here that your own job-execution script consumes, as well as arguments that AWS Glue itself consumes.

For information about how to specify and consume your own job arguments, see the Calling AWS Glue APIs in Python topic in the developer guide.

For information about the key-value pairs that AWS Glue consumes to set up your job, see the Special Parameters Used by AWS Glue topic in the developer guide.

- `ErrorMessage` – UTF-8 string.

  An error message associated with this job run.

- `PredecessorRuns` – An array of Predecessors.

  A list of predecessors to this job run.

- `AllocatedCapacity` – Number (integer).

  The number of AWS Glue data processing units (DPUs) allocated to this JobRun. From 2 to 100 DPUs can be allocated; the default is 10. A DPU is a relative measure of processing power that consists of 4 vCPUs of compute capacity and 16 GB of memory. For more information, see the AWS Glue pricing page.

- `ExecutionTime` – Number (integer).

  The amount of time (in seconds) that the job run consumed resources.

- `Timeout` – Number (integer), at least 1.

  The JobRun timeout in minutes. This is the maximum time that a job run can consume resources before it is terminated and enters `TIMEOUT` status. The default is 2,880 minutes (48 hours). This overrides the timeout value set in the parent job.

- `NotificationProperty` – A NotificationProperty object.

  Specifies configuration properties of a job run notification.

Predecessor Structure

A job run that was used in the predicate of a conditional trigger that triggered this job run.

Fields

- `JobName` – UTF-8 string, not less than 1 or more than 255 bytes long, matching the Single-line string pattern.

  The name of the job definition used by the predecessor job run.

- `RunId` – UTF-8 string, not less than 1 or more than 255 bytes long, matching the Single-line string pattern.

  The job-run ID of the predecessor job run.

JobBookmarkEntry Structure

Defines a point which a job can resume processing.

Fields

- `JobName` – UTF-8 string.

  Name of the job in question.

- `Version` – Number (integer).

  Version of the job.

- `Run` – Number (integer).

  The run ID number.

- `Attempt` – Number (integer).

  The attempt ID number.

- `JobBookmark` – UTF-8 string.

  The bookmark itself.

BatchStopJobRunSuccessfulSubmission Structure

Records a successful request to stop a specified JobRun.

Fields

- `JobName` – UTF-8 string, not less than 1 or more than 255 bytes long, matching the Single-line string pattern.

  The name of the job definition used in the job run that was stopped.

- `JobRunId` – UTF-8 string, not less than 1 or more than 255 bytes long, matching the Single-line string pattern.

  The JobRunId of the job run that was stopped.

BatchStopJobRunError Structure

Records an error that occurred when attempting to stop a specified job run.

Fields

- `JobName` – UTF-8 string, not less than 1 or more than 255 bytes long, matching the Single-line string pattern.

  The name of the job definition used in the job run in question.

- `JobRunId` – UTF-8 string, not less than 1 or more than 255 bytes long, matching the Single-line string pattern.

  The JobRunId of the job run in question.

- `ErrorDetail` – An ErrorDetail object.

  Specifies details about the error that was encountered.

Operations

- StartJobRun Action (Python: start_job_run)
- BatchStopJobRun Action (Python: batch_stop_job_run)
- GetJobRun Action (Python: get_job_run)
- GetJobRuns Action (Python: get_job_runs)
- ResetJobBookmark Action (Python: reset_job_bookmark)

StartJobRun Action (Python: start_job_run)

Starts a job run using a job definition.

Request

- `JobName` – UTF-8 string, not less than 1 or more than 255 bytes long, matching the Single-line string pattern. Required.

  The name of the job definition to use.

- `JobRunId` – UTF-8 string, not less than 1 or more than 255 bytes long, matching the Single-line string pattern.

  The ID of a previous JobRun to retry.

- `Arguments` – A map array of key-value pairs

  Each key is a UTF-8 string.

  Each value is a UTF-8 string.

  The job arguments specifically for this run. They override the equivalent default arguments set for in the job definition itself.

  You can specify arguments here that your own job-execution script consumes, as well as arguments that AWS Glue itself consumes.

  For information about how to specify and consume your own Job arguments, see the Calling AWS Glue APIs in Python topic in the developer guide.

  For information about the key-value pairs that AWS Glue consumes to set up your job, see the Special Parameters Used by AWS Glue topic in the developer guide.

- `AllocatedCapacity` – Number (integer).

  The number of AWS Glue data processing units (DPUs) to allocate to this JobRun. From 2 to 100 DPUs can be allocated; the default is 10. A DPU is a relative measure of processing power that consists of 4 vCPUs of compute capacity and 16 GB of memory. For more information, see the AWS Glue pricing page.

- `Timeout` – Number (integer), at least 1.

  The JobRun timeout in minutes. This is the maximum time that a job run can consume resources before it is terminated and enters `TIMEOUT` status. The default is 2,880 minutes (48 hours). This overrides the timeout value set in the parent job.

- `NotificationProperty` – A NotificationProperty object.

  Specifies configuration properties of a job run notification.

Response

- `JobRunId` – UTF-8 string, not less than 1 or more than 255 bytes long, matching the Single-line string pattern.

  The ID assigned to this job run.

Errors

- `InvalidInputException`
- `EntityNotFoundException`
- `InternalServiceException`
- `OperationTimeoutException`
- `ResourceNumberLimitExceededException`
- `ConcurrentRunsExceededException`

BatchStopJobRun Action (Python: batch_stop_job_run)

Stops one or more job runs for a specified job definition.

Request

- `JobName` – UTF-8 string, not less than 1 or more than 255 bytes long, matching the Single-line string pattern. Required.

  The name of the job definition for which to stop job runs.

- `JobRunIds` – An array of UTF-8 strings, not less than 1 or more than 25 items in the array. Required.

  A list of the JobRunIds that should be stopped for that job definition.

Response

- `SuccessfulSubmissions` – An array of BatchStopJobRunSuccessfulSubmissions.

  A list of the JobRuns that were successfully submitted for stopping.

- `Errors` – An array of BatchStopJobRunErrors.

  A list of the errors that were encountered in tryng to stop JobRuns, including the JobRunId for which each error was encountered and details about the error.

Errors

- `InvalidInputException`
- `InternalServiceException`
- `OperationTimeoutException`

GetJobRun Action (Python: get_job_run)

Retrieves the metadata for a given job run.

Request

- `JobName` – UTF-8 string, not less than 1 or more than 255 bytes long, matching the Single-line string pattern. Required.

  Name of the job definition being run.

- `RunId` – UTF-8 string, not less than 1 or more than 255 bytes long, matching the Single-line string pattern. Required.

  The ID of the job run.

- `PredecessorsIncluded` – Boolean.

  True if a list of predecessor runs should be returned.

Response

- `JobRun` – A JobRun object.

  The requested job-run metadata.

Errors

- `InvalidInputException`
- `EntityNotFoundException`
- `InternalServiceException`
- `OperationTimeoutException`

GetJobRuns Action (Python: get_job_runs)

Retrieves metadata for all runs of a given job definition.

Request

- `JobName` – UTF-8 string, not less than 1 or more than 255 bytes long, matching the Single-line string pattern. Required.

  The name of the job definition for which to retrieve all job runs.

- `NextToken` – UTF-8 string.

  A continuation token, if this is a continuation call.

- `MaxResults` – Number (integer), not less than 1 or more than 1000.

  The maximum size of the response.

Response

- `JobRuns` – An array of JobRuns.

  A list of job-run metatdata objects.

- `NextToken` – UTF-8 string.

  A continuation token, if not all reequested job runs have been returned.

Errors

- `InvalidInputException`
- `EntityNotFoundException`
- `InternalServiceException`
- `OperationTimeoutException`

ResetJobBookmark Action (Python: reset_job_bookmark)

Resets a bookmark entry.

Request

- `JobName` – UTF-8 string. Required.

  The name of the job in question.

Response

- `JobBookmarkEntry` – A JobBookmarkEntry object.

  The reset bookmark entry.

Errors

- `EntityNotFoundException`
- `InvalidInputException`
- `InternalServiceException`
- `OperationTimeoutException`

Triggers

Data Types

- Trigger Structure
- TriggerUpdate Structure
- Predicate Structure
- Condition Structure
- Action Structure

Trigger Structure

Information about a specific trigger.

Fields

- `Name` – UTF-8 string, not less than 1 or more than 255 bytes long, matching the Single-line string pattern.

  Name of the trigger.

- `Id` – UTF-8 string, not less than 1 or more than 255 bytes long, matching the Single-line string pattern.

  Reserved for future use.

- `Type` – UTF-8 string (valid values: `SCHEDULED` | `CONDITIONAL` | `ON_DEMAND`).

  The type of trigger that this is.

- `State` – UTF-8 string (valid values: `CREATING` | `CREATED` | `ACTIVATING` | `ACTIVATED` | `DEACTIVATING` | `DEACTIVATED` | `DELETING` | `UPDATING`).

  The current state of the trigger.

- `Description` – Description string, not more than 2048 bytes long, matching the URI address multi-line string pattern.

  A description of this trigger.

- `Schedule` – UTF-8 string.

  A `cron` expression used to specify the schedule (see Time-Based Schedules for Jobs and Crawlers. For example, to run something every day at 12:15 UTC, you would specify: `cron(15 12 * * ? *)`.

- `Actions` – An array of Actions.

  The actions initiated by this trigger.

- `Predicate` – A Predicate object.

  The predicate of this trigger, which defines when it will fire.

TriggerUpdate Structure

A structure used to provide information used to update a trigger. This object will update the the previous trigger definition by overwriting it completely.

Fields

- `Name` – UTF-8 string, not less than 1 or more than 255 bytes long, matching the Single-line string pattern.

  Reserved for future use.

- **Description** – Description string, not more than 2048 bytes long, matching the URI address multi-line string pattern.

  A description of this trigger.

- **Schedule** – UTF-8 string.

  A `cron` expression used to specify the schedule (see Time-Based Schedules for Jobs and Crawlers. For example, to run something every day at 12:15 UTC, you would specify: `cron(15 12 * * ? *)`.

- **Actions** – An array of Actions.

  The actions initiated by this trigger.

- **Predicate** – A Predicate object.

  The predicate of this trigger, which defines when it will fire.

Predicate Structure

Defines the predicate of the trigger, which determines when it fires.

Fields

- **Logical** – UTF-8 string (valid values: `AND | ANY`).

  Optional field if only one condition is listed. If multiple conditions are listed, then this field is required.

- **Conditions** – An array of Conditions.

  A list of the conditions that determine when the trigger will fire.

Condition Structure

Defines a condition under which a trigger fires.

Fields

- **LogicalOperator** – UTF-8 string (valid values: `EQUALS`).

  A logical operator.

- **JobName** – UTF-8 string, not less than 1 or more than 255 bytes long, matching the Single-line string pattern.

  The name of the Job to whose JobRuns this condition applies and on which this trigger waits.

- **State** – UTF-8 string (valid values: `STARTING | RUNNING | STOPPING | STOPPED | SUCCEEDED | FAILED | TIMEOUT`).

  The condition state. Currently, the values supported are SUCCEEDED, STOPPED, TIMEOUT and FAILED.

Action Structure

Defines an action to be initiated by a trigger.

Fields

- **JobName** – UTF-8 string, not less than 1 or more than 255 bytes long, matching the Single-line string pattern.

  The name of a job to be executed.

- **Arguments** – A map array of key-value pairs

  Each key is a UTF-8 string.

  Each value is a UTF-8 string.

  Arguments to be passed to the job.

  You can specify arguments here that your own job-execution script consumes, as well as arguments that AWS Glue itself consumes.

  For information about how to specify and consume your own Job arguments, see the Calling AWS Glue APIs in Python topic in the developer guide.

  For information about the key-value pairs that AWS Glue consumes to set up your job, see the Special Parameters Used by AWS Glue topic in the developer guide.

- **Timeout** – Number (integer), at least 1.

  The JobRun timeout in minutes. This is the maximum time that a job run can consume resources before it is terminated and enters `TIMEOUT` status. The default is 2,880 minutes (48 hours). This overrides the timeout value set in the parent job.

- **NotificationProperty** – A NotificationProperty object.

  Specifies configuration properties of a job run notification.

Operations

- CreateTrigger Action (Python: create_trigger)
- StartTrigger Action (Python: start_trigger)
- GetTrigger Action (Python: get_trigger)
- GetTriggers Action (Python: get_triggers)
- UpdateTrigger Action (Python: update_trigger)
- StopTrigger Action (Python: stop_trigger)
- DeleteTrigger Action (Python: delete_trigger)

CreateTrigger Action (Python: create_trigger)

Creates a new trigger.

Request

- **Name** – UTF-8 string, not less than 1 or more than 255 bytes long, matching the Single-line string pattern. Required.

  The name of the trigger.

- **Type** – UTF-8 string (valid values: `SCHEDULED` | `CONDITIONAL` | `ON_DEMAND`). Required.

  The type of the new trigger.

- **Schedule** – UTF-8 string.

  A `cron` expression used to specify the schedule (see Time-Based Schedules for Jobs and Crawlers. For example, to run something every day at 12:15 UTC, you would specify: `cron(15 12 * * ? *)`.

  This field is required when the trigger type is SCHEDULED.

- **Predicate** – A Predicate object.

  A predicate to specify when the new trigger should fire.

This field is required when the trigger type is CONDITIONAL.

- `Actions` – An array of Actions. Required.

  The actions initiated by this trigger when it fires.

- `Description` – Description string, not more than 2048 bytes long, matching the URI address multi-line string pattern.

  A description of the new trigger.

- `StartOnCreation` – Boolean.

  Set to true to start SCHEDULED and CONDITIONAL triggers when created. True not supported for ON_DEMAND triggers.

Response

- `Name` – UTF-8 string, not less than 1 or more than 255 bytes long, matching the Single-line string pattern.

  The name of the trigger.

Errors

- `AlreadyExistsException`
- `InvalidInputException`
- `IdempotentParameterMismatchException`
- `InternalServiceException`
- `OperationTimeoutException`
- `ResourceNumberLimitExceededException`
- `ConcurrentModificationException`

StartTrigger Action (Python: start_trigger)

Starts an existing trigger. See Triggering Jobs for information about how different types of trigger are started.

Request

- `Name` – UTF-8 string, not less than 1 or more than 255 bytes long, matching the Single-line string pattern. Required.

  The name of the trigger to start.

Response

- `Name` – UTF-8 string, not less than 1 or more than 255 bytes long, matching the Single-line string pattern.

  The name of the trigger that was started.

Errors

- `InvalidInputException`
- `InternalServiceException`
- `EntityNotFoundException`
- `OperationTimeoutException`
- `ResourceNumberLimitExceededException`
- `ConcurrentRunsExceededException`

GetTrigger Action (Python: get_trigger)

Retrieves the definition of a trigger.

Request

413

- `Name` – UTF-8 string, not less than 1 or more than 255 bytes long, matching the Single-line string pattern. Required.

  The name of the trigger to retrieve.

Response

- `Trigger` – A Trigger object.

  The requested trigger definition.

Errors

- `EntityNotFoundException`
- `InvalidInputException`
- `InternalServiceException`
- `OperationTimeoutException`

GetTriggers Action (Python: get_triggers)

Gets all the triggers associated with a job.

Request

- `NextToken` – UTF-8 string.

  A continuation token, if this is a continuation call.

- `DependentJobName` – UTF-8 string, not less than 1 or more than 255 bytes long, matching the Single-line string pattern.

  The name of the job for which to retrieve triggers. The trigger that can start this job will be returned, and if there is no such trigger, all triggers will be returned.

- `MaxResults` – Number (integer), not less than 1 or more than 1000.

  The maximum size of the response.

Response

- `Triggers` – An array of Triggers.

  A list of triggers for the specified job.

- `NextToken` – UTF-8 string.

  A continuation token, if not all the requested triggers have yet been returned.

Errors

- `EntityNotFoundException`
- `InvalidInputException`
- `InternalServiceException`
- `OperationTimeoutException`

UpdateTrigger Action (Python: update_trigger)

Updates a trigger definition.

Request

- `Name` – UTF-8 string, not less than 1 or more than 255 bytes long, matching the Single-line string pattern. Required.

  The name of the trigger to update.

- `TriggerUpdate` – A TriggerUpdate object. Required.

  The new values with which to update the trigger.

Response

- `Trigger` – A Trigger object.

  The resulting trigger definition.

Errors

- `InvalidInputException`
- `InternalServiceException`
- `EntityNotFoundException`
- `OperationTimeoutException`
- `ConcurrentModificationException`

StopTrigger Action (Python: stop_trigger)

Stops a specified trigger.

Request

- `Name` – UTF-8 string, not less than 1 or more than 255 bytes long, matching the Single-line string pattern. Required.

  The name of the trigger to stop.

Response

- `Name` – UTF-8 string, not less than 1 or more than 255 bytes long, matching the Single-line string pattern.

  The name of the trigger that was stopped.

Errors

- `InvalidInputException`
- `InternalServiceException`
- `EntityNotFoundException`
- `OperationTimeoutException`
- `ConcurrentModificationException`

DeleteTrigger Action (Python: delete_trigger)

Deletes a specified trigger. If the trigger is not found, no exception is thrown.

Request

- `Name` – UTF-8 string, not less than 1 or more than 255 bytes long, matching the Single-line string pattern. Required.

  The name of the trigger to delete.

Response

- `Name` – UTF-8 string, not less than 1 or more than 255 bytes long, matching the Single-line string pattern.

  The name of the trigger that was deleted.

Errors

- InvalidInputException
- InternalServiceException
- OperationTimeoutException
- ConcurrentModificationException

AWS Glue Development Endpoints API

Data Types

- DevEndpoint Structure
- DevEndpointCustomLibraries Structure

DevEndpoint Structure

A development endpoint where a developer can remotely debug ETL scripts.

Fields

- `EndpointName` – UTF-8 string.

  The name of the DevEndpoint.

- `RoleArn` – UTF-8 string, matching the AWS IAM ARN string pattern.

  The AWS ARN of the IAM role used in this DevEndpoint.

- `SecurityGroupIds` – An array of UTF-8 strings.

  A list of security group identifiers used in this DevEndpoint.

- `SubnetId` – UTF-8 string.

  The subnet ID for this DevEndpoint.

- `YarnEndpointAddress` – UTF-8 string.

  The YARN endpoint address used by this DevEndpoint.

- `PrivateAddress` – UTF-8 string.

  A private DNS to access the DevEndpoint within a VPC, if the DevEndpoint is created within one.

- `ZeppelinRemoteSparkInterpreterPort` – Number (integer).

  The Apache Zeppelin port for the remote Apache Spark interpreter.

- `PublicAddress` – UTF-8 string.

  The public VPC address used by this DevEndpoint.

- `Status` – UTF-8 string.

  The current status of this DevEndpoint.

- `NumberOfNodes` – Number (integer).

  The number of AWS Glue Data Processing Units (DPUs) allocated to this DevEndpoint.

- `AvailabilityZone` – UTF-8 string.

  The AWS availability zone where this DevEndpoint is located.

- `VpcId` – UTF-8 string.

  The ID of the virtual private cloud (VPC) used by this DevEndpoint.

- `ExtraPythonLibsS3Path` – UTF-8 string.

  Path(s) to one or more Python libraries in an S3 bucket that should be loaded in your DevEndpoint. Multiple values must be complete paths separated by a comma.

Please note that only pure Python libraries can currently be used on a DevEndpoint. Libraries that rely on C extensions, such as the pandas Python data analysis library, are not yet supported.

- ExtraJarsS3Path – UTF-8 string.

  Path to one or more Java Jars in an S3 bucket that should be loaded in your DevEndpoint.

  Please note that only pure Java/Scala libraries can currently be used on a DevEndpoint.

- FailureReason – UTF-8 string.

  The reason for a current failure in this DevEndpoint.

- LastUpdateStatus – UTF-8 string.

  The status of the last update.

- CreatedTimestamp – Timestamp.

  The point in time at which this DevEndpoint was created.

- LastModifiedTimestamp – Timestamp.

  The point in time at which this DevEndpoint was last modified.

- PublicKey – UTF-8 string.

  The public key to be used by this DevEndpoint for authentication.

DevEndpointCustomLibraries Structure

Custom libraries to be loaded into a DevEndpoint.

Fields

- ExtraPythonLibsS3Path – UTF-8 string.

  Path(s) to one or more Python libraries in an S3 bucket that should be loaded in your DevEndpoint. Multiple values must be complete paths separated by a comma.

  Please note that only pure Python libraries can currently be used on a DevEndpoint. Libraries that rely on C extensions, such as the pandas Python data analysis library, are not yet supported.

- ExtraJarsS3Path – UTF-8 string.

  Path to one or more Java Jars in an S3 bucket that should be loaded in your DevEndpoint.

  Please note that only pure Java/Scala libraries can currently be used on a DevEndpoint.

Operations

- CreateDevEndpoint Action (Python: create_dev_endpoint)
- UpdateDevEndpoint Action (Python: update_dev_endpoint)
- DeleteDevEndpoint Action (Python: delete_dev_endpoint)
- GetDevEndpoint Action (Python: get_dev_endpoint)
- GetDevEndpoints Action (Python: get_dev_endpoints)

CreateDevEndpoint Action (Python: create_dev_endpoint)

Creates a new DevEndpoint.

Request

- `EndpointName` – UTF-8 string. Required.

  The name to be assigned to the new DevEndpoint.

- `RoleArn` – UTF-8 string, matching the AWS IAM ARN string pattern. Required.

  The IAM role for the DevEndpoint.

- `SecurityGroupIds` – An array of UTF-8 strings.

  Security group IDs for the security groups to be used by the new DevEndpoint.

- `SubnetId` – UTF-8 string.

  The subnet ID for the new DevEndpoint to use.

- `PublicKey` – UTF-8 string.

  The public key to use for authentication.

- `NumberOfNodes` – Number (integer).

  The number of AWS Glue Data Processing Units (DPUs) to allocate to this DevEndpoint.

- `ExtraPythonLibsS3Path` – UTF-8 string.

  Path(s) to one or more Python libraries in an S3 bucket that should be loaded in your DevEndpoint. Multiple values must be complete paths separated by a comma.

  Please note that only pure Python libraries can currently be used on a DevEndpoint. Libraries that rely on C extensions, such as the pandas Python data analysis library, are not yet supported.

- `ExtraJarsS3Path` – UTF-8 string.

  Path to one or more Java Jars in an S3 bucket that should be loaded in your DevEndpoint.

Response

- `EndpointName` – UTF-8 string.

  The name assigned to the new DevEndpoint.

- `Status` – UTF-8 string.

  The current status of the new DevEndpoint.

- `SecurityGroupIds` – An array of UTF-8 strings.

  The security groups assigned to the new DevEndpoint.

- `SubnetId` – UTF-8 string.

  The subnet ID assigned to the new DevEndpoint.

- `RoleArn` – UTF-8 string, matching the AWS IAM ARN string pattern.

  The AWS ARN of the role assigned to the new DevEndpoint.

- `YarnEndpointAddress` – UTF-8 string.

  The address of the YARN endpoint used by this DevEndpoint.

- `ZeppelinRemoteSparkInterpreterPort` – Number (integer).

  The Apache Zeppelin port for the remote Apache Spark interpreter.

- `NumberOfNodes` – Number (integer).

  The number of AWS Glue Data Processing Units (DPUs) allocated to this DevEndpoint.

- AvailabilityZone – UTF-8 string.

  The AWS availability zone where this DevEndpoint is located.

- VpcId – UTF-8 string.

  The ID of the VPC used by this DevEndpoint.

- ExtraPythonLibsS3Path – UTF-8 string.

  Path(s) to one or more Python libraries in an S3 bucket that will be loaded in your DevEndpoint.

- ExtraJarsS3Path – UTF-8 string.

  Path to one or more Java Jars in an S3 bucket that will be loaded in your DevEndpoint.

- FailureReason – UTF-8 string.

  The reason for a current failure in this DevEndpoint.

- CreatedTimestamp – Timestamp.

  The point in time at which this DevEndpoint was created.

Errors

- AccessDeniedException
- AlreadyExistsException
- IdempotentParameterMismatchException
- InternalServiceException
- OperationTimeoutException
- InvalidInputException
- ValidationException
- ResourceNumberLimitExceededException

UpdateDevEndpoint Action (Python: update_dev_endpoint)

Updates a specified DevEndpoint.

Request

- EndpointName – UTF-8 string. Required.

  The name of the DevEndpoint to be updated.

- PublicKey – UTF-8 string.

  The public key for the DevEndpoint to use.

- CustomLibraries – A DevEndpointCustomLibraries object.

  Custom Python or Java libraries to be loaded in the DevEndpoint.

- UpdateEtlLibraries – Boolean.

  True if the list of custom libraries to be loaded in the development endpoint needs to be updated, or False otherwise.

Response

- *No Response parameters.*

Errors

- EntityNotFoundException
- InternalServiceException
- OperationTimeoutException

- InvalidInputException
- ValidationException

DeleteDevEndpoint Action (Python: delete_dev_endpoint)

Deletes a specified DevEndpoint.

Request

- EndpointName – UTF-8 string. Required.

  The name of the DevEndpoint.

Response

- *No Response parameters.*

Errors

- EntityNotFoundException
- InternalServiceException
- OperationTimeoutException
- InvalidInputException

GetDevEndpoint Action (Python: get_dev_endpoint)

Retrieves information about a specified DevEndpoint.

Request

- EndpointName – UTF-8 string. Required.

  Name of the DevEndpoint for which to retrieve information.

Response

- DevEndpoint – A DevEndpoint object.

  A DevEndpoint definition.

Errors

- EntityNotFoundException
- InternalServiceException
- OperationTimeoutException
- InvalidInputException

GetDevEndpoints Action (Python: get_dev_endpoints)

Retrieves all the DevEndpoints in this AWS account.

Request

- MaxResults – Number (integer), not less than 1 or more than 1000.

  The maximum size of information to return.

- NextToken – UTF-8 string.

  A continuation token, if this is a continuation call.

Response

- `DevEndpoints` – An array of DevEndpoints.

  A list of DevEndpoint definitions.

- `NextToken` – UTF-8 string.

  A continuation token, if not all DevEndpoint definitions have yet been returned.

Errors

- `EntityNotFoundException`
- `InternalServiceException`
- `OperationTimeoutException`
- `InvalidInputException`

Common Data Types

Tag Structure

An AWS Tag.

Fields

- `key` – UTF-8 string, not less than 1 or more than 128 bytes long.

  The tag key.

- `value` – UTF-8 string, not more than 256 bytes long.

  The tag value.

DecimalNumber Structure

Contains a numeric value in decimal format.

Fields

- `UnscaledValue` – Blob.

  The unscaled numeric value.

- `Scale` – Number (integer).

  The scale that determines where the decimal point falls in the unscaled value.

ErrorDetail Structure

Contains details about an error.

Fields

- `ErrorCode` – UTF-8 string, not less than 1 or more than 255 bytes lcng, matching the Single-line string pattern.

  The code associated with this error.

- `ErrorMessage` – Description string, not more than 2048 bytes long, matching the URI address multi-line string pattern.

  A message describing the error.

PropertyPredicate Structure

Defines a property predicate.

Fields

- `Key` – Value string.

  The key of the property.

- `Value` – Value string.

  The value of the property.

- Comparator – UTF-8 string (valid values: `EQUALS` | `GREATER_THAN` | `LESS_THAN` | `GREATER_THAN_EQUALS` | `LESS_THAN_EQUALS`).

  The comparator used to compare this property to others.

ResourceUri Structure

URIs for function resources.

Fields

- ResourceType – UTF-8 string (valid values: `JAR` | `FILE` | `ARCHIVE`).

  The type of the resource.

- Uri – Uniform resource identifier (uri), not less than 1 or more than 1024 bytes long, matching the URI address multi-line string pattern.

  The URI for accessing the resource.

String Patterns

The API uses the following regular expressions to define what is valid content for various string parameters and members:

- Single-line string pattern – `"[\u0020-\uD7FF\uE000-\uFFFD\uD800\uDC00-\uDBFF\uDFFF\t]*"`
- URI address multi-line string pattern – `"[\u0020-\uD7FF\uE000-\uFFFD\uD800\uDC00-\uDBFF\uDFFF\r\n\t]*"`
- A Logstash Grok string pattern – `"[\u0020-\uD7FF\uE000-\uFFFD\uD800\uDC00-\uDBFF\uDFFF\r\t]*"`
- Identifier string pattern – `"[A-Za-z_][A-Za-z0-9_]*"`
- AWS Glue ARN string pattern – `"arn:aws:glue:.*"`
- AWS IAM ARN string pattern – `"arn:aws:iam::\d{12}:role/.*"`
- AWS KMS ARN string pattern – `"^$|arn:aws:kms:.*"`
- Version string pattern – `"^[a-zA-Z0-9-_]+$"`
- Log group string pattern – `"[\.\-_/#A-Za-z0-9]+"`
- Log-stream string pattern – `"[^:*]*"`

Exceptions

AccessDeniedException Structure

Access to a resource was denied.

Fields

- `Message` – UTF-8 string.

  A message describing the problem.

AlreadyExistsException Structure

A resource to be created or added already exists.

Fields

- `Message` – UTF-8 string.

  A message describing the problem.

ConcurrentModificationException Structure

Two processes are trying to modify a resource simultaneously.

Fields

- `Message` – UTF-8 string.

  A message describing the problem.

ConcurrentRunsExceededException Structure

Too many jobs are being run concurrently.

Fields

- `Message` – UTF-8 string.

  A message describing the problem.

CrawlerNotRunningException Structure

The specified crawler is not running.

Fields

- `Message` – UTF-8 string.

  A message describing the problem.

CrawlerRunningException Structure

The operation cannot be performed because the crawler is already running.

Fields

- `Message` – UTF-8 string.

  A message describing the problem.

CrawlerStoppingException Structure

The specified crawler is stopping.

Fields

- `Message` – UTF-8 string.

  A message describing the problem.

EntityNotFoundException Structure

A specified entity does not exist

Fields

- `Message` – UTF-8 string.

  A message describing the problem.

IdempotentParameterMismatchException Structure

The same unique identifier was associated with two different records.

Fields

- `Message` – UTF-8 string.

  A message describing the problem.

InternalServiceException Structure

An internal service error occurred.

Fields

- `Message` – UTF-8 string.

  A message describing the problem.

InvalidExecutionEngineException Structure

An unknown or invalid execution engine was specified.

Fields

- `message` – UTF-8 string.

  A message describing the problem.

InvalidInputException Structure

The input provided was not valid.

Fields

- Message – UTF-8 string.

  A message describing the problem.

InvalidTaskStatusTransitionException Structure

Proper transition from one task to the next failed.

Fields

- message – UTF-8 string.

  A message describing the problem.

JobDefinitionErrorException Structure

A job definition is not valid.

Fields

- message – UTF-8 string.

  A message describing the problem.

JobRunInTerminalStateException Structure

The terminal state of a job run signals a failure.

Fields

- message – UTF-8 string.

  A message describing the problem.

JobRunInvalidStateTransitionException Structure

A job run encountered an invalid transition from source state to target state.

Fields

- jobRunId – UTF-8 string, not less than 1 or more than 255 bytes long, matching the Single-line string pattern.

  The Id of the job run in question.

- message – UTF-8 string.

  A message describing the problem.

- sourceState – UTF-8 string (valid values: STARTING | RUNNING | STOPPING | STOPPED | SUCCEEDED | FAILED | TIMEOUT).

  The source state.

- `targetState` – UTF-8 string (valid values: `STARTING` | `RUNNING` | `STOPPING` | `STOPPED` | `SUCCEEDED` | `FAILED` | `TIMEOUT`).

  The target state.

JobRunNotInTerminalStateException Structure

A job run is not in a terminal state.

Fields

- `message` – UTF-8 string.

  A message describing the problem.

LateRunnerException Structure

A job runner is late.

Fields

- `Message` – UTF-8 string.

  A message describing the problem.

NoScheduleException Structure

There is no applicable schedule.

Fields

- `Message` – UTF-8 string.

  A message describing the problem.

OperationTimeoutException Structure

The operation timed out.

Fields

- `Message` – UTF-8 string.

  A message describing the problem.

ResourceNumberLimitExceededException Structure

A resource numerical limit was exceeded.

Fields

- `Message` – UTF-8 string.

  A message describing the problem.

SchedulerNotRunningException Structure

The specified scheduler is not running.

Fields

- `Message` – UTF-8 string.

  A message describing the problem.

SchedulerRunningException Structure

The specified scheduler is already running.

Fields

- `Message` – UTF-8 string.

  A message describing the problem.

SchedulerTransitioningException Structure

The specified scheduler is transitioning.

Fields

- `Message` – UTF-8 string.

  A message describing the problem.

UnrecognizedRunnerException Structure

The job runner was not recognized.

Fields

- `Message` – UTF-8 string.

  A message describing the problem.

ValidationException Structure

A value could not be validated.

Fields

- `Message` – UTF-8 string.

  A message describing the problem.

VersionMismatchException Structure

There was a version conflict.

Fields

- `Message` – UTF-8 string.

  A message describing the problem.

Document History for AWS Glue

The following table describes important changes to the documentation for AWS Glue.

- **Latest API version:** 2018-04-10
- **Latest documentation update:** April 10, 2018

Change	Description	Date
Support timeout of jobs.	Added information about setting a timeout threshold when a job runs.	April 10, 2018
Support Scala ETL script and trigger jobs based on additional run states.	Added information about using Scala as the ETL programming language. In addition, the trigger API now supports firing when any conditions are met (in addition to all conditions). Also, jobs can be triggered based on a "failed" or "stopped" job run (in addition to a "succeeded" job run).	January 12, 2018
Support XML data sources and new crawler configuration option.	Added information about classifying XML data sources and new crawler option for partition changes.	November 16, 2017
New transforms, support for additional Amazon RDS database engines, and development endpoint enhancements	Added information about the map and filter transforms, support for Amazon RDS Microsoft SQL Server and Amazon RDS Oracle, and new features for development endpoints.	September 29, 2017
AWS Glue initial release	This is the initial release of the AWS Glue Developer Guide.	August 14, 2017

AWS Glossary

For the latest AWS terminology, see the AWS Glossary in the *AWS General Reference.*

www.ingramcontent.com/pod-product-compliance
Lightning Source LLC
LaVergne TN
LVHW082036050326

832904LV00005B/207